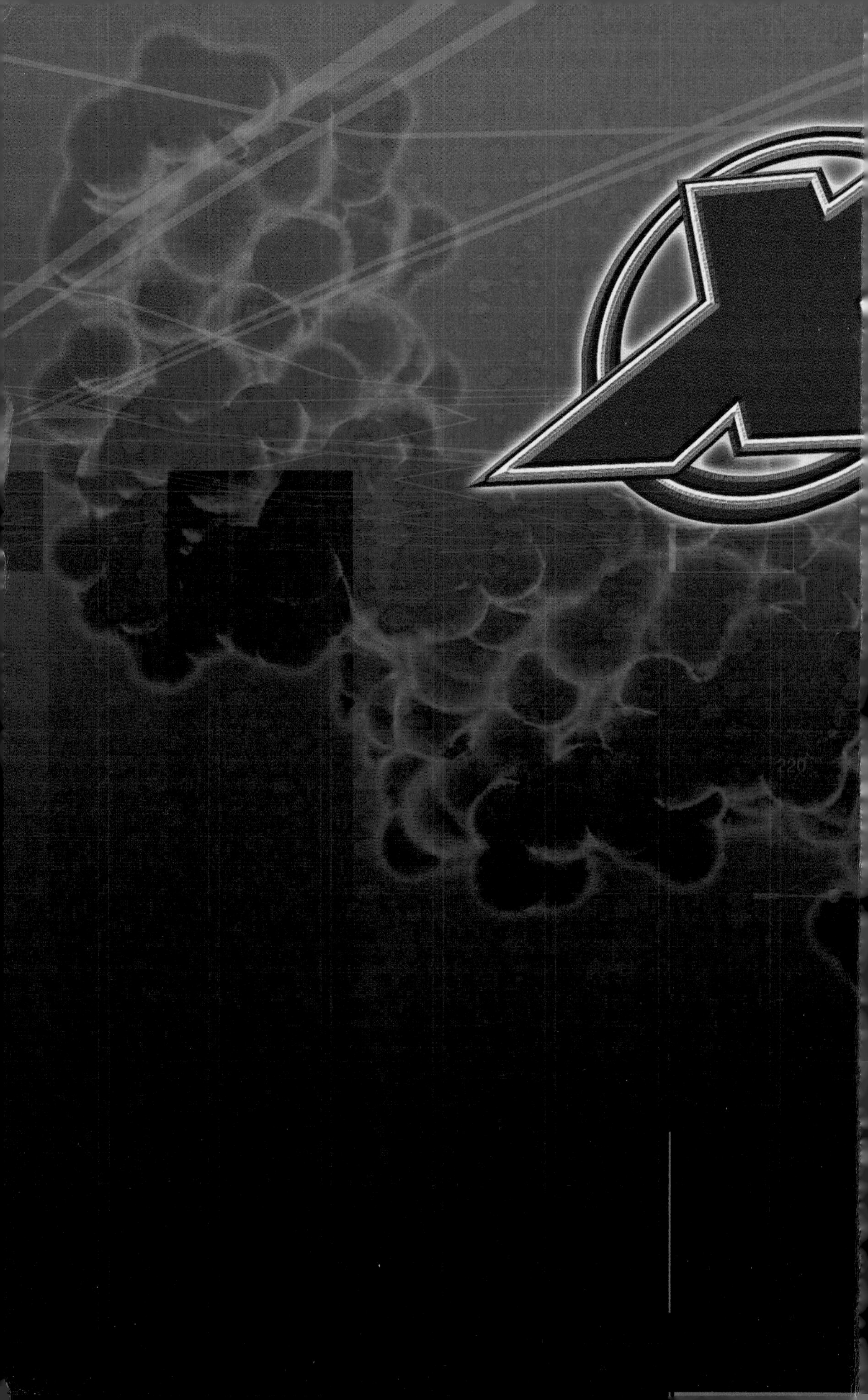

ASTONISHING X-MEN

GIFTED

writer_**JOSS WHEDON**

artist_**JOHN CASSADAY**

colorist_**LAURA MARTIN**
letterer_**CHRIS ELIOPOULOS**

cover_art_**JOHN CASSADAY**

assistant_editor_**STEPHANIE MOORE**
assistant_editor_**SEAN RYAN**
assistant_editor_**CORY SEDLMEIER**
editor_**MIKE MARTS**

collections_editor_**JEFF YOUNGQUIST**
assistant_editor_**JENNIFER GRÜNWALD**
book_designer_**JEOF VITA**
creative_director_**TOM MARVELLI**

editor_in_chief_**JOE QUESADA**
publisher_**DAN BUCKLEY**

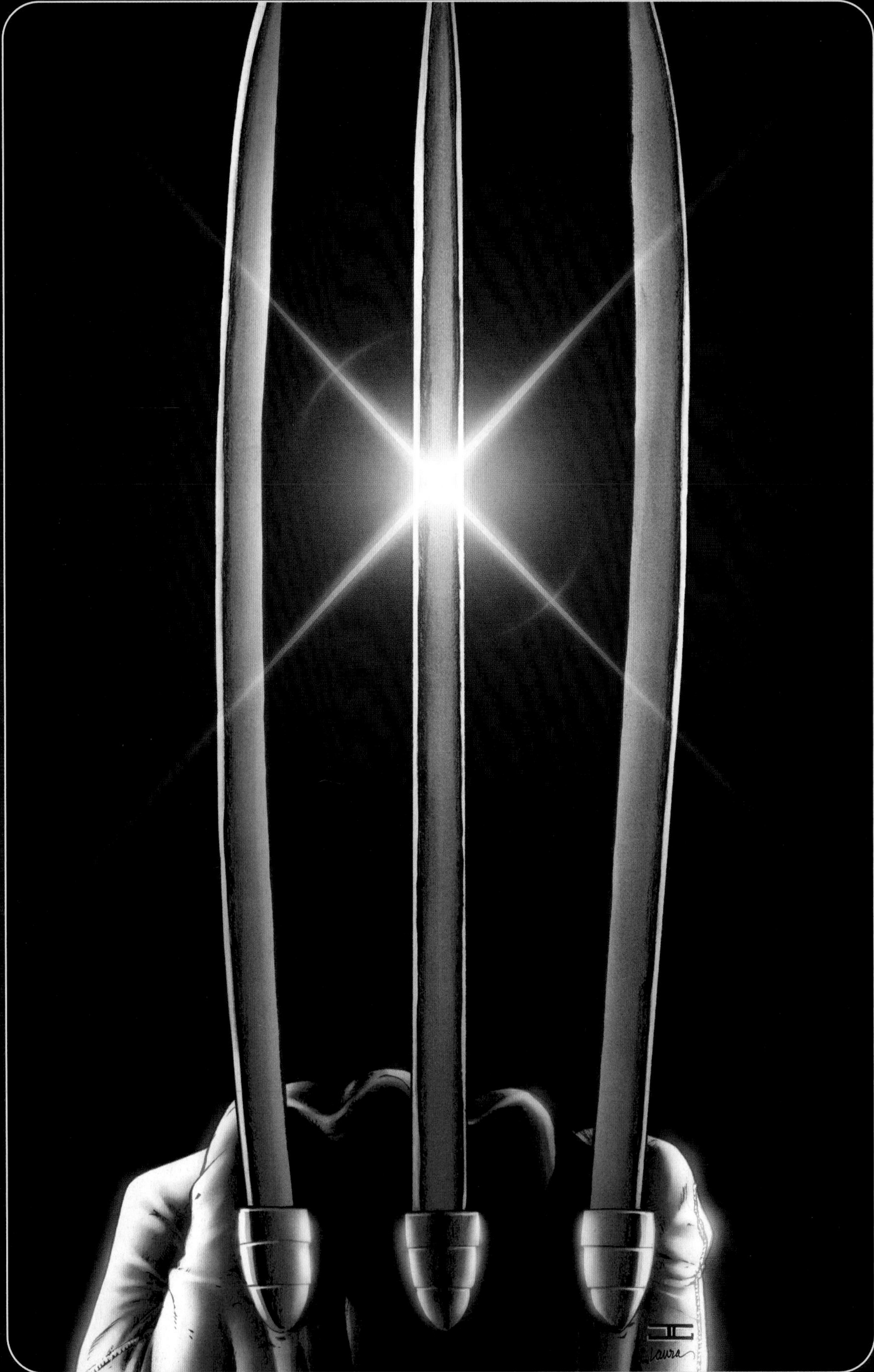

01

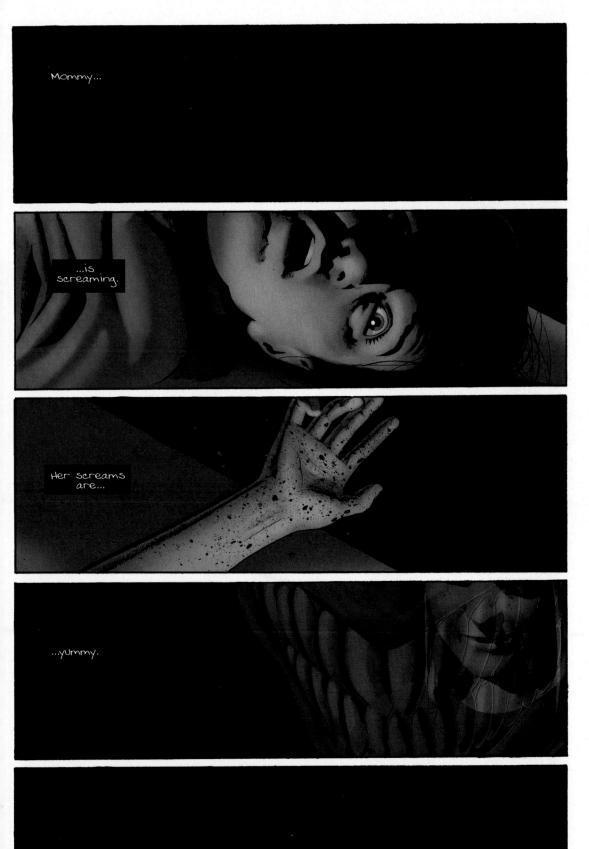

Mommy...

...is
screaming.

Her screams
are...

...yummy.

Daddy...

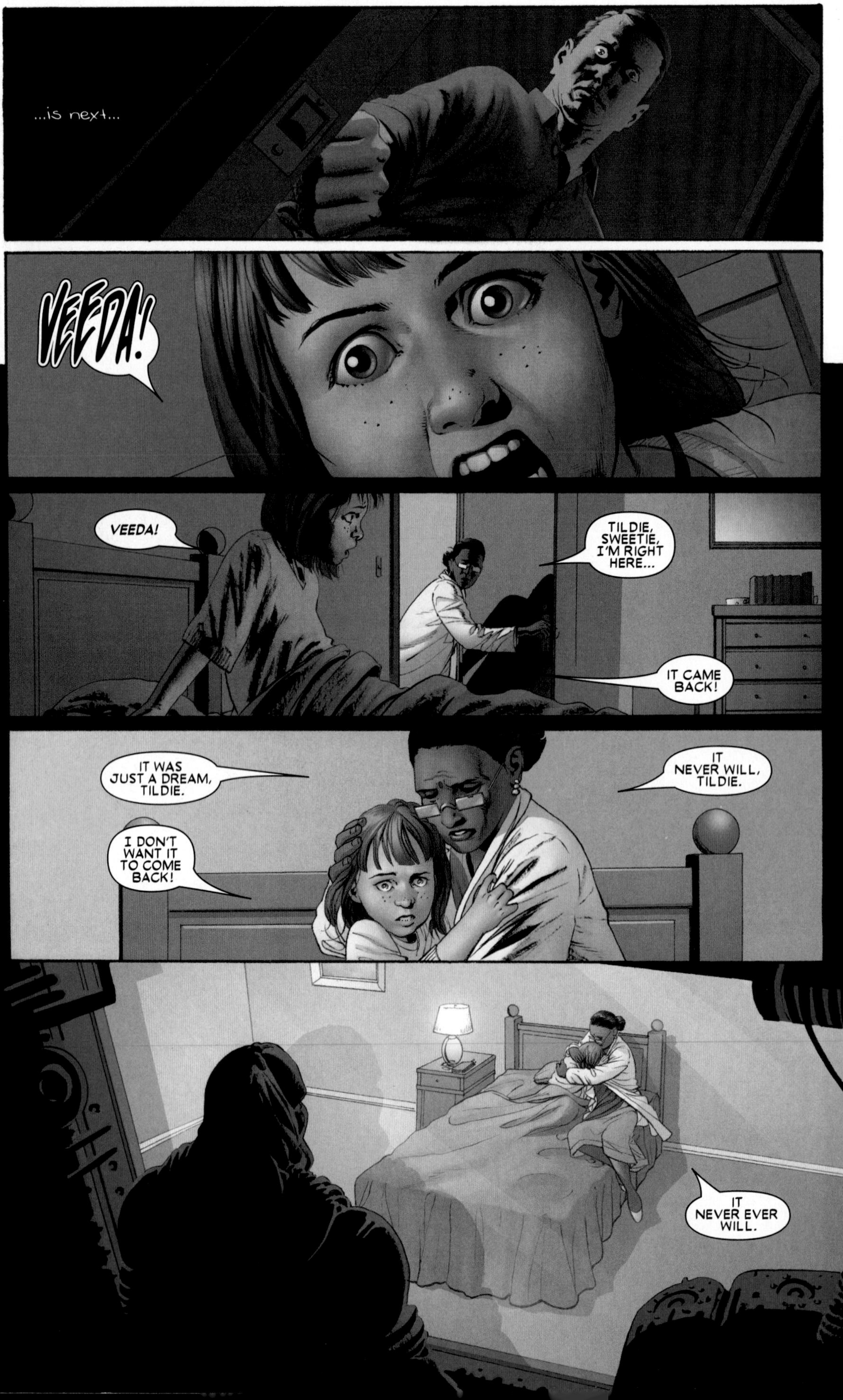
...is next...
VEEDA!
VEEDA!
TILDIE, SWEETIE, I'M RIGHT HERE...
IT CAME BACK!
IT WAS JUST A DREAM, TILDIE.
I DON'T WANT IT TO COME BACK!
IT NEVER WILL, TILDIE.
IT NEVER EVER WILL.

GIFTED

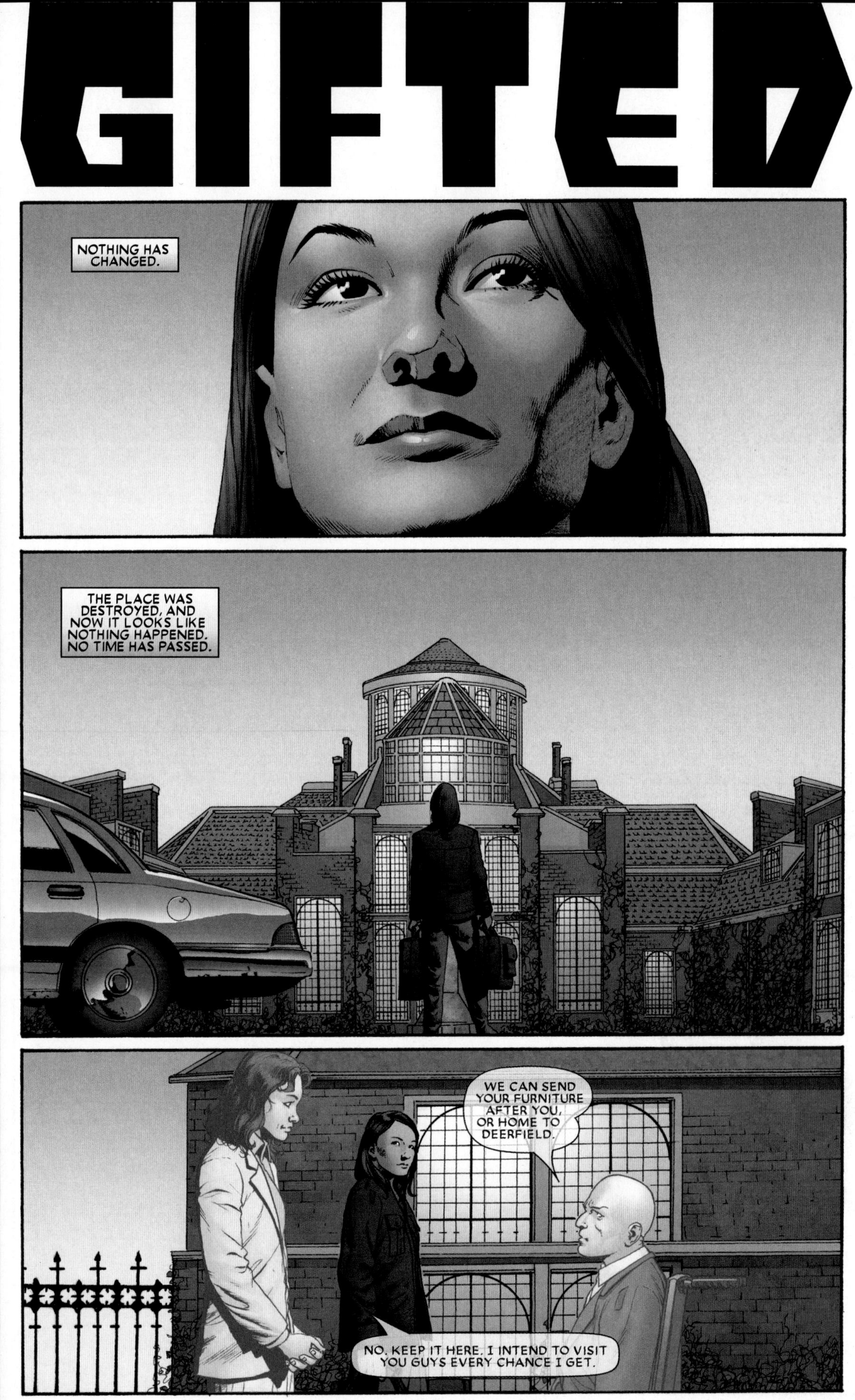
NOTHING HAS CHANGED.
THE PLACE WAS DESTROYED, AND NOW IT LOOKS LIKE NOTHING HAPPENED. NO TIME HAS PASSED.
WE CAN SEND YOUR FURNITURE AFTER YOU, OR HOME TO DEERFIELD.
NO. KEEP IT HERE. I INTEND TO VISIT YOU GUYS EVERY CHANCE I GET.

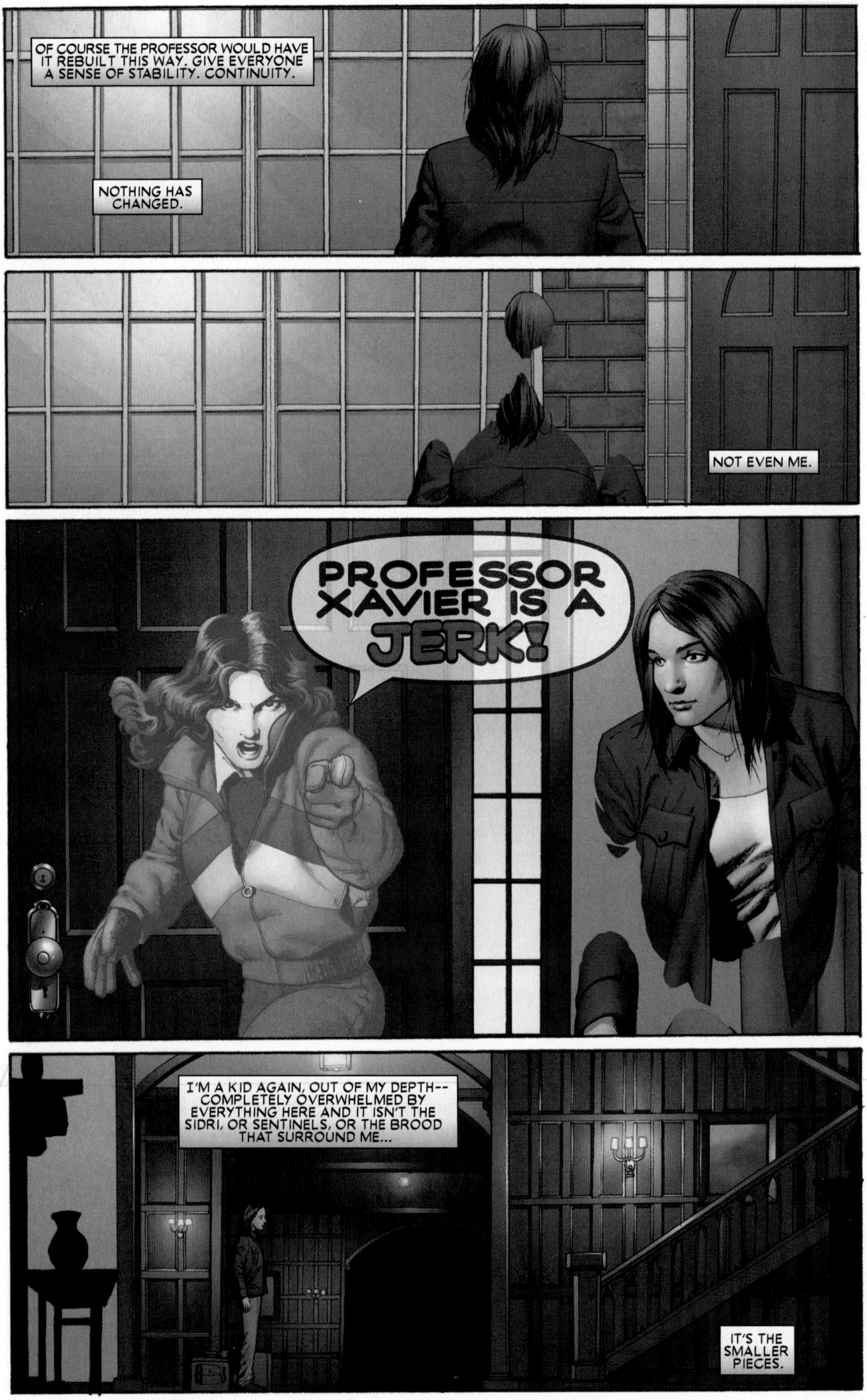
OF COURSE THE PROFESSOR WOULD HAVE IT REBUILT THIS WAY. GIVE EVERYONE A SENSE OF STABILITY. CONTINUITY.
NOTHING HAS CHANGED.
NOT EVEN ME.
PROFESSOR XAVIER IS A JERK!
I'M A KID AGAIN, OUT OF MY DEPTH-- COMPLETELY OVERWHELMED BY EVERYTHING HERE AND IT ISN'T THE SIDRI, OR SENTINELS, OR THE BROOD THAT SURROUND ME...
IT'S THE SMALLER PIECES.

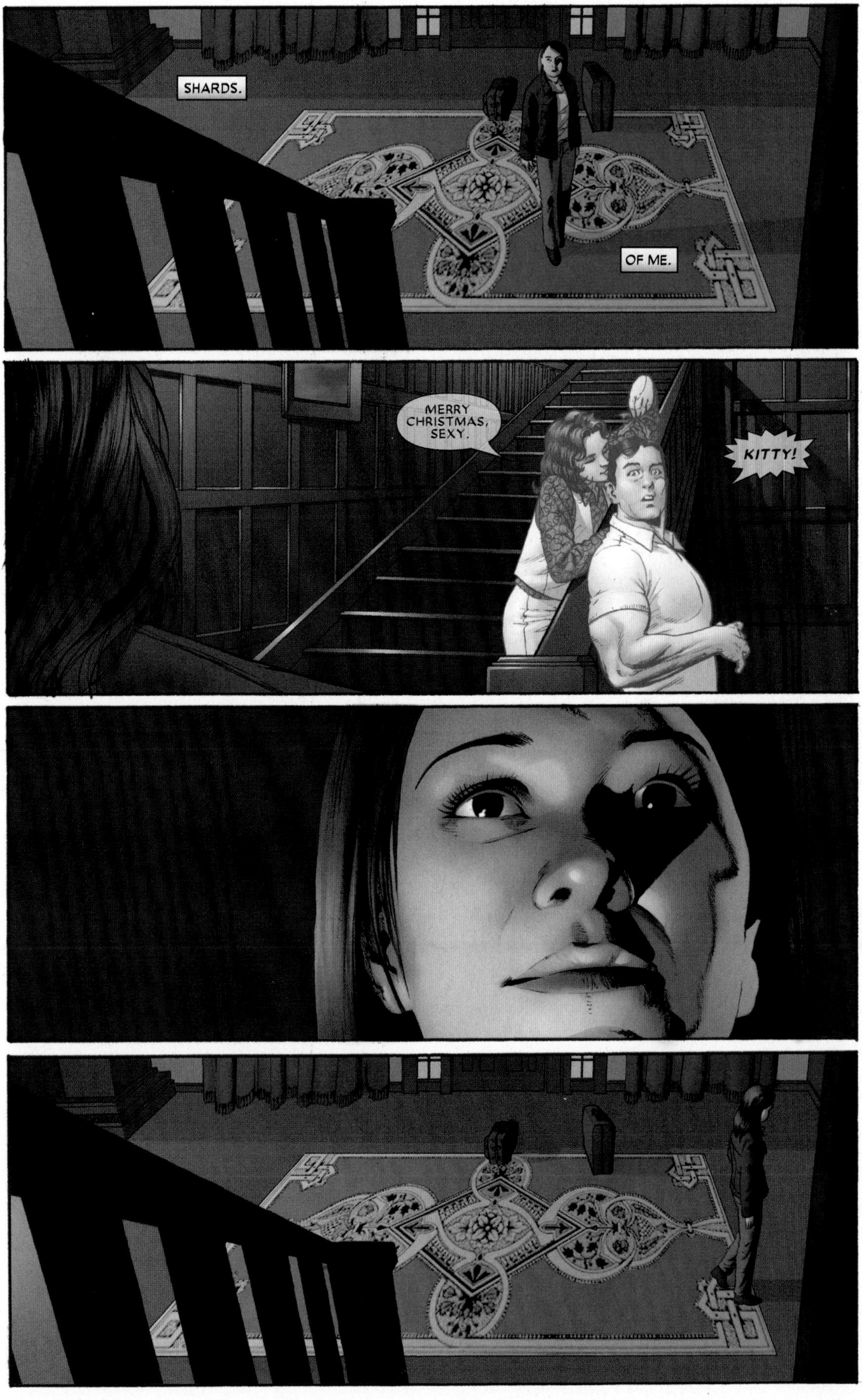
SHARDS.
OF ME.
MERRY CHRISTMAS, SEXY.
KITTY!

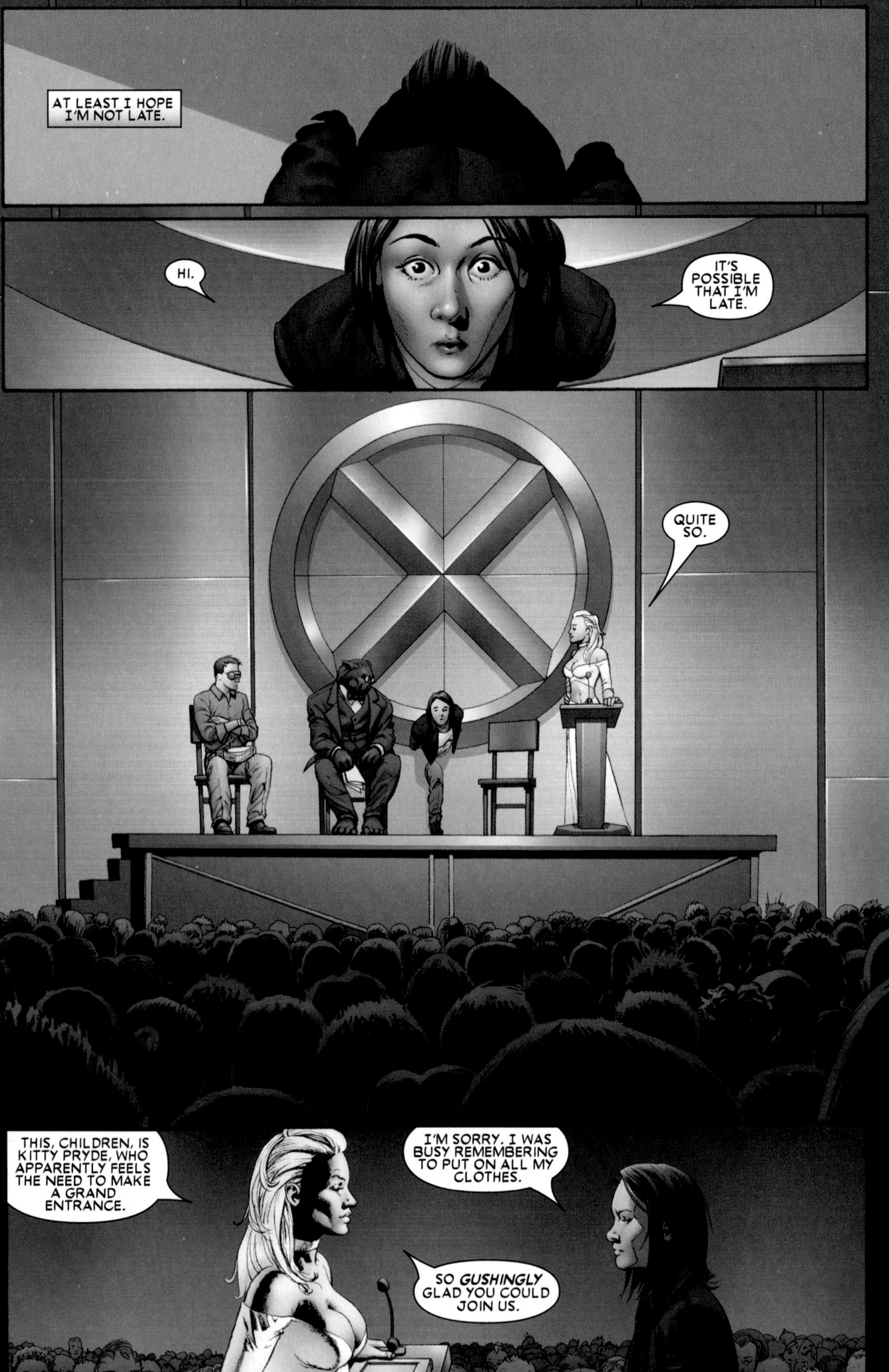
AT LEAST I HOPE I'M NOT LATE.
HI.
IT'S POSSIBLE THAT I'M LATE.
QUITE SO.
THIS, CHILDREN, IS KITTY PRYDE, WHO APPARENTLY FEELS THE NEED TO MAKE A GRAND ENTRANCE.
I'M SORRY. I WAS BUSY REMEMBERING TO PUT ON ALL MY CLOTHES.
SO *GUSHINGLY* GLAD YOU COULD JOIN US.

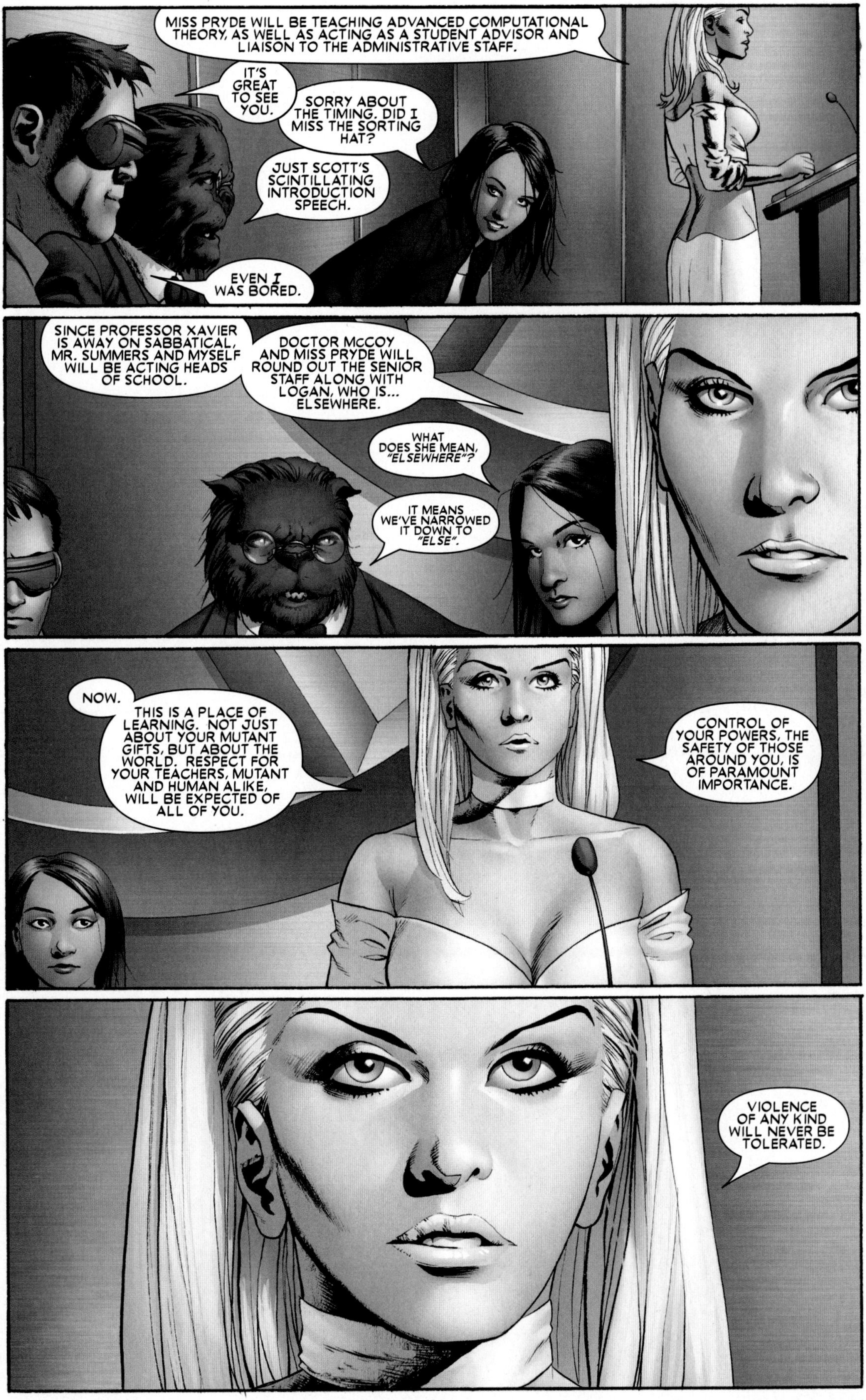
MISS PRYDE WILL BE TEACHING ADVANCED COMPUTATIONAL THEORY, AS WELL AS ACTING AS A STUDENT ADVISOR AND LIAISON TO THE ADMINISTRATIVE STAFF.
IT'S GREAT TO SEE YOU.
SORRY ABOUT THE TIMING. DID I MISS THE SORTING HAT?
JUST SCOTT'S SCINTILLATING INTRODUCTION SPEECH.
EVEN *I* WAS BORED.
SINCE PROFESSOR XAVIER IS AWAY ON SABBATICAL, MR. SUMMERS AND MYSELF WILL BE ACTING HEADS OF SCHOOL.
DOCTOR McCOY AND MISS PRYDE WILL ROUND OUT THE SENIOR STAFF ALONG WITH LOGAN, WHO IS... ELSEWHERE.
WHAT DOES SHE MEAN, *"ELSEWHERE"*?
IT MEANS WE'VE NARROWED IT DOWN TO *"ELSE"*.
NOW.
THIS IS A PLACE OF LEARNING. NOT JUST ABOUT YOUR MUTANT GIFTS, BUT ABOUT THE WORLD. RESPECT FOR YOUR TEACHERS, MUTANT AND HUMAN ALIKE, WILL BE EXPECTED OF ALL OF YOU.
CONTROL OF YOUR POWERS, THE SAFETY OF THOSE AROUND YOU, IS OF PARAMOUNT IMPORTANCE.
VIOLENCE OF ANY KIND WILL NEVER BE TOLERATED.

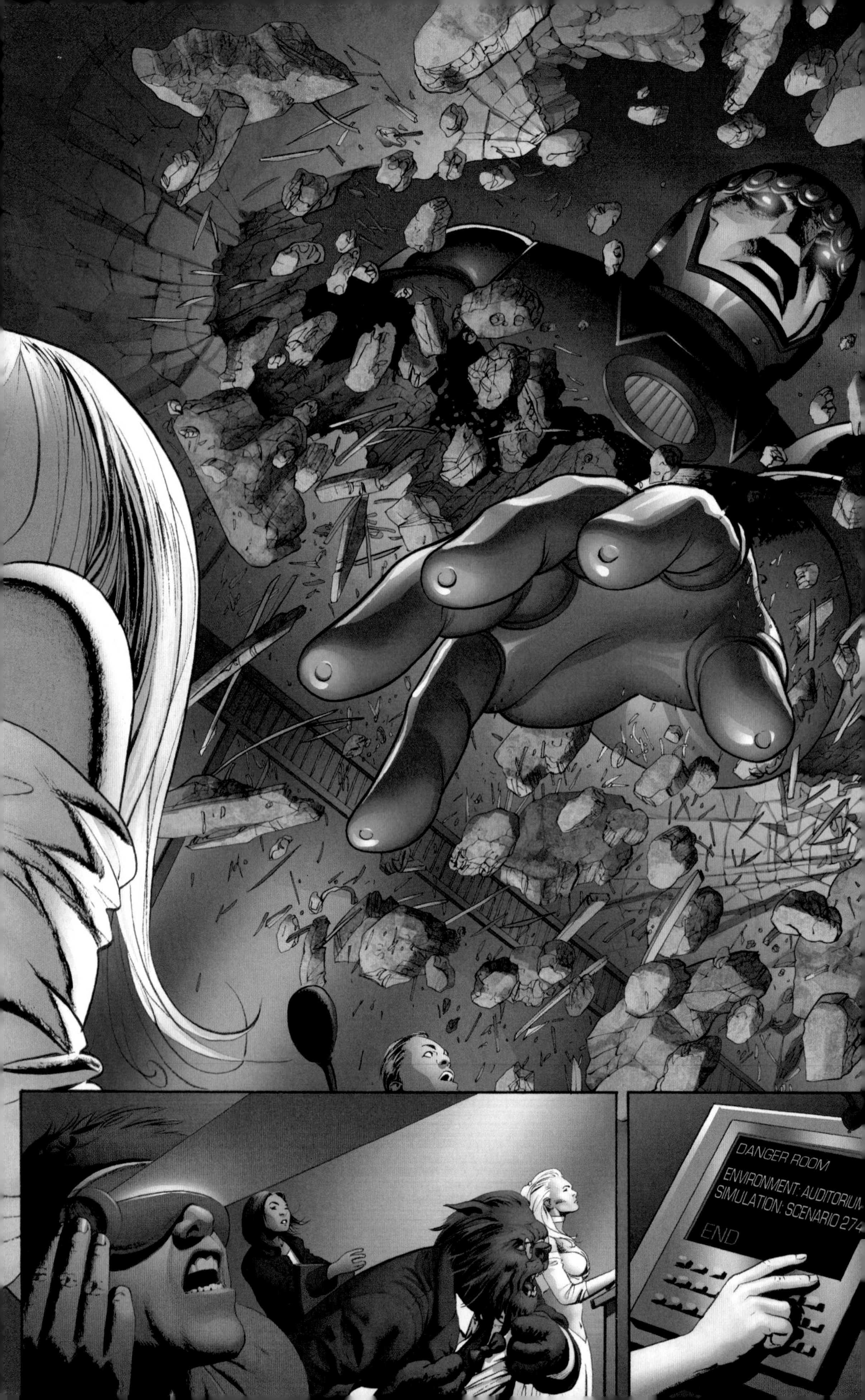
DANGER ROOM
ENVIRONMENT: AUDITORIUM
SIMULATION: SCENARIO 274
END

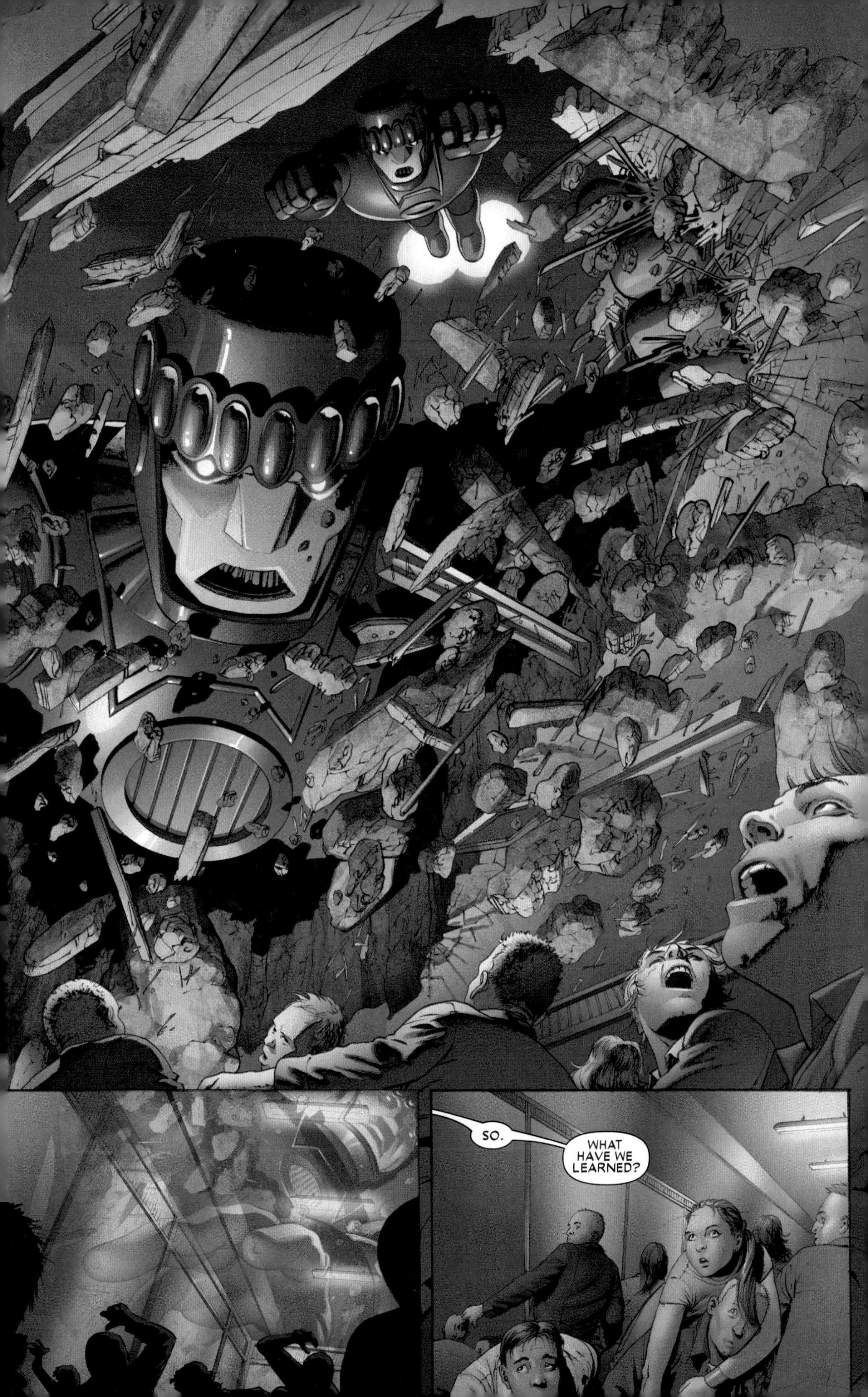
SO.
WHAT HAVE WE LEARNED?

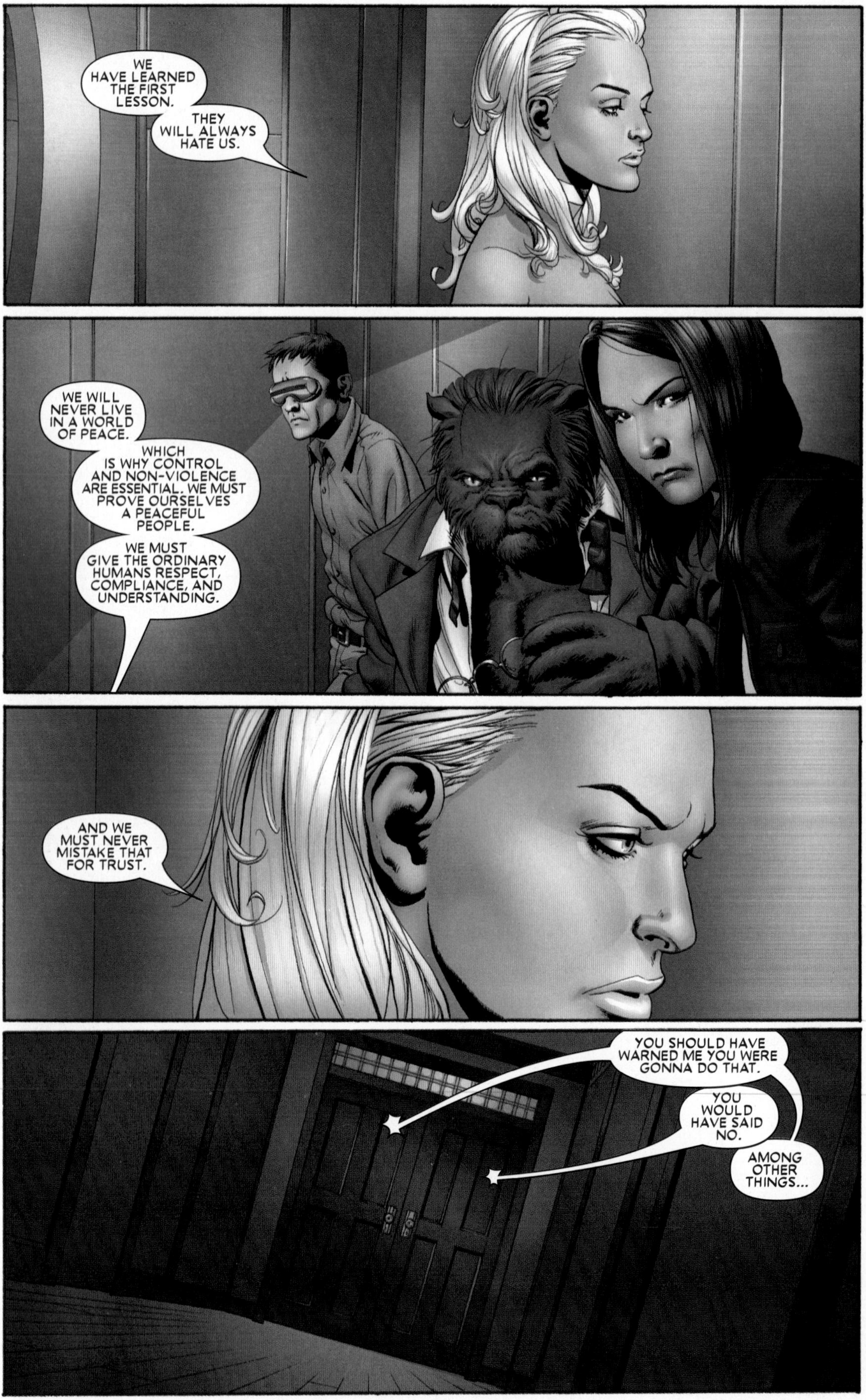
WE HAVE LEARNED THE FIRST LESSON.
THEY WILL ALWAYS HATE US.
WE WILL NEVER LIVE IN A WORLD OF PEACE.
WHICH IS WHY CONTROL AND NON-VIOLENCE ARE ESSENTIAL. WE MUST PROVE OURSELVES A PEACEFUL PEOPLE.
WE MUST GIVE THE ORDINARY HUMANS RESPECT, COMPLIANCE, AND UNDERSTANDING.
AND WE MUST NEVER MISTAKE THAT FOR TRUST.
YOU SHOULD HAVE WARNED ME YOU WERE GONNA DO THAT.
YOU WOULD HAVE SAID NO.
AMONG OTHER THINGS...

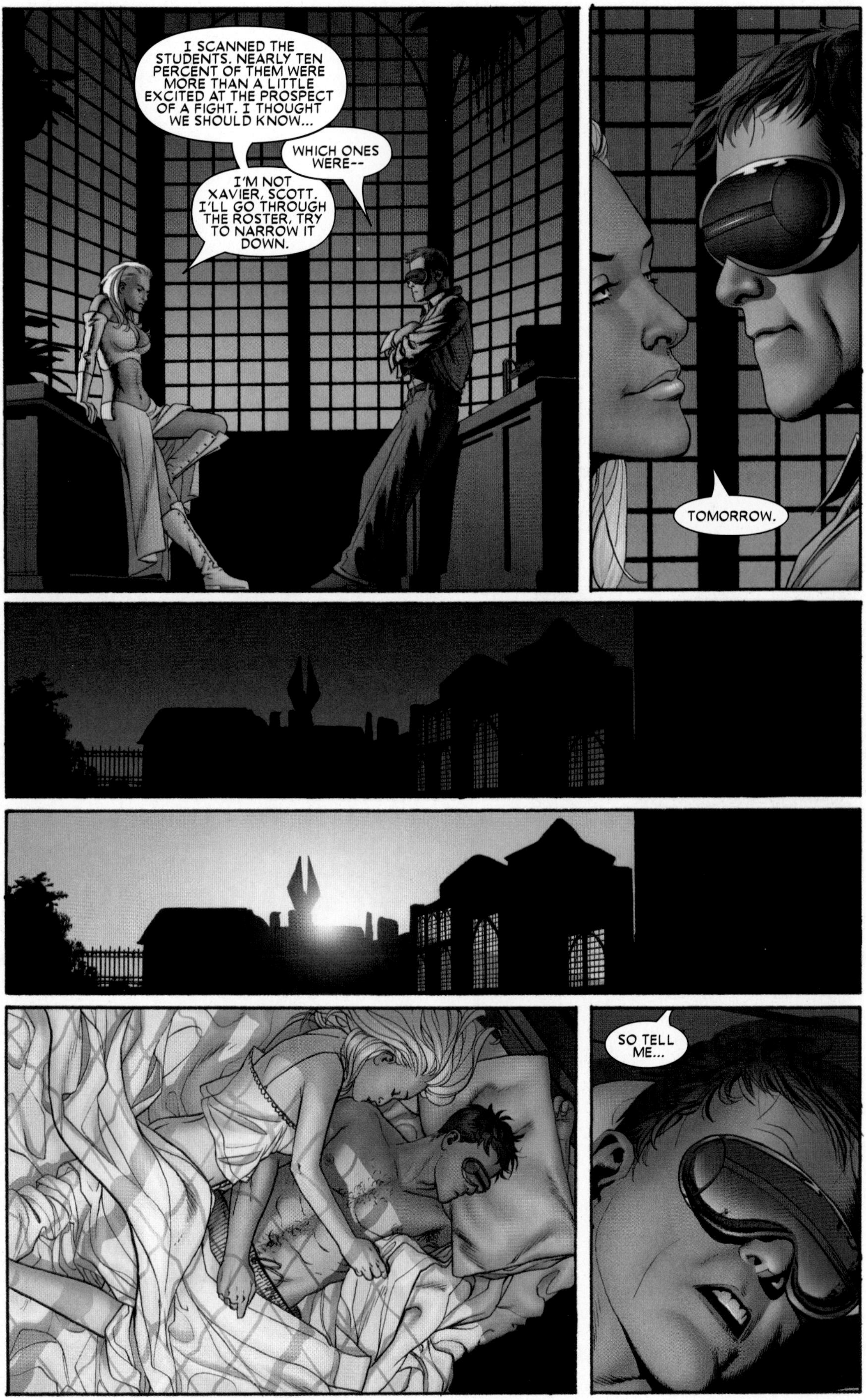
I SCANNED THE STUDENTS. NEARLY TEN PERCENT OF THEM WERE MORE THAN A LITTLE EXCITED AT THE PROSPECT OF A FIGHT. I THOUGHT WE SHOULD KNOW...
WHICH ONES WERE--
I'M NOT XAVIER, SCOTT. I'LL GO THROUGH THE ROSTER, TRY TO NARROW IT DOWN.
TOMORROW.
SO TELL ME...

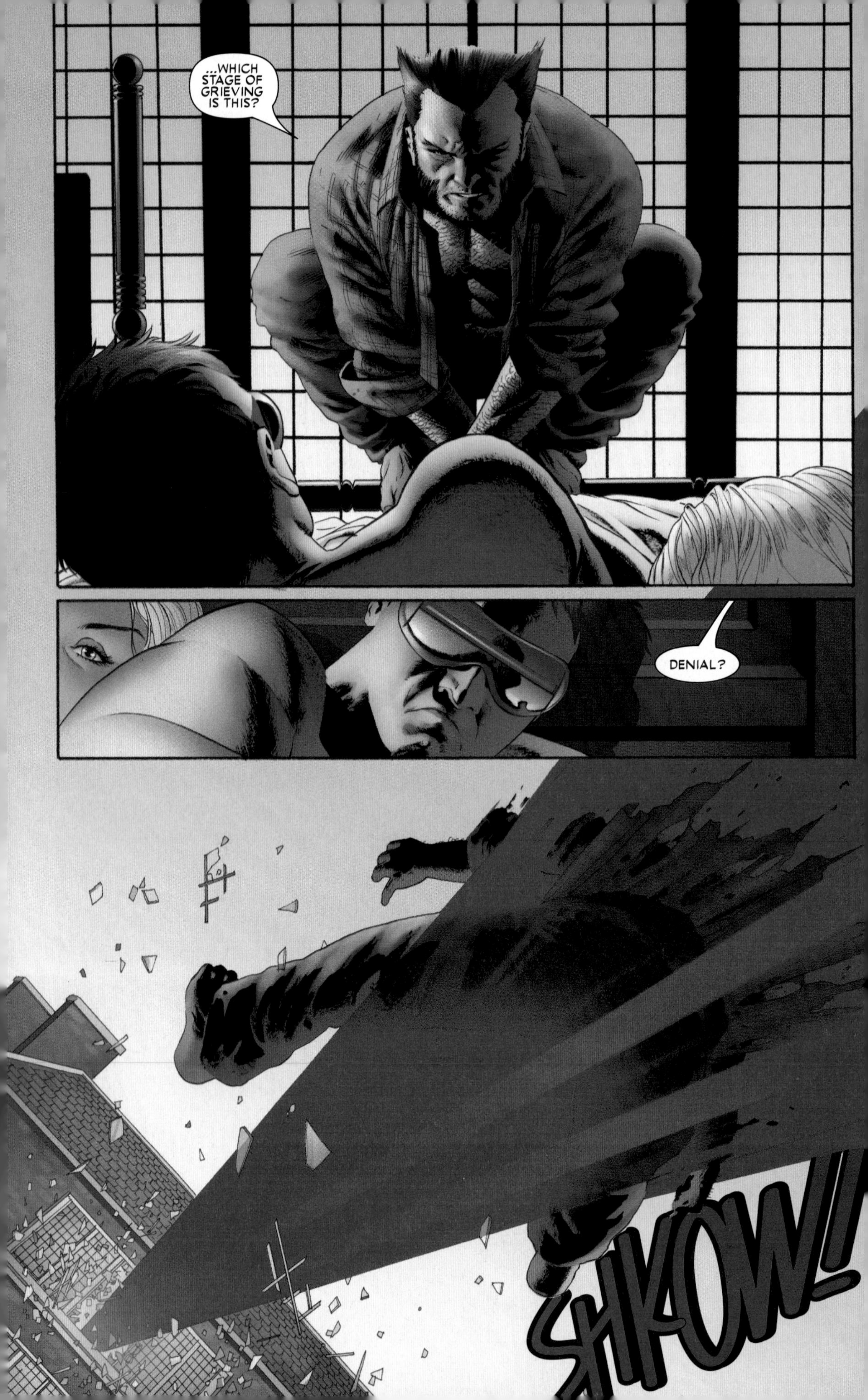
...WHICH STAGE OF GRIEVING IS THIS?
DENIAL?
SHKOW!!

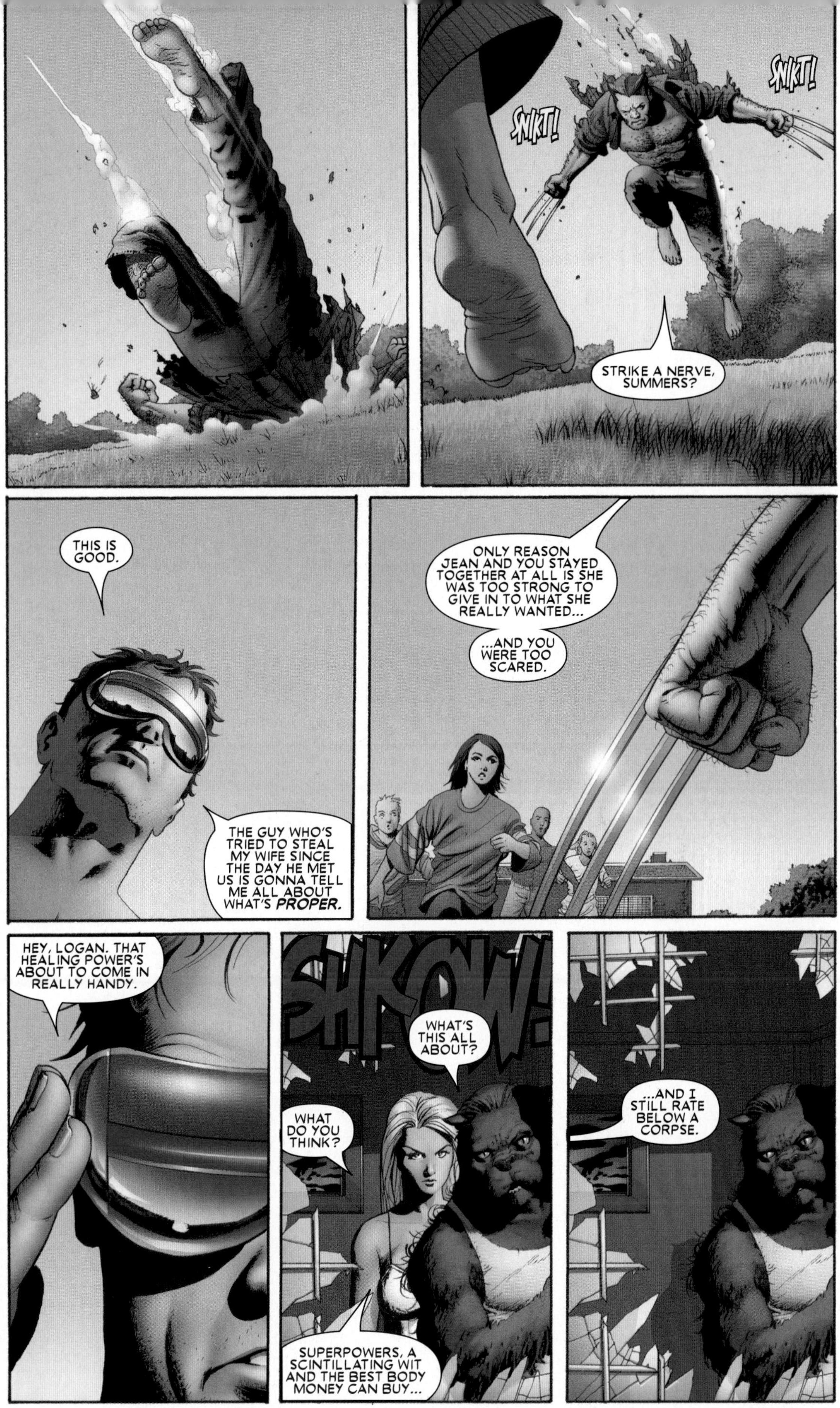
SNIKT!
SNIKT!
STRIKE A NERVE, SUMMERS?
THIS IS GOOD.
THE GUY WHO'S TRIED TO STEAL MY WIFE SINCE THE DAY HE MET US IS GONNA TELL ME ALL ABOUT WHAT'S PROPER.
ONLY REASON JEAN AND YOU STAYED TOGETHER AT ALL IS SHE WAS TOO STRONG TO GIVE IN TO WHAT SHE REALLY WANTED...
...AND YOU WERE TOO SCARED.
HEY, LOGAN. THAT HEALING POWER'S ABOUT TO COME IN REALLY HANDY.
SHKOW!
WHAT'S THIS ALL ABOUT?
WHAT DO YOU THINK?
SUPERPOWERS, A SCINTILLATING WIT AND THE BEST BODY MONEY CAN BUY...
...AND I STILL RATE BELOW A CORPSE.

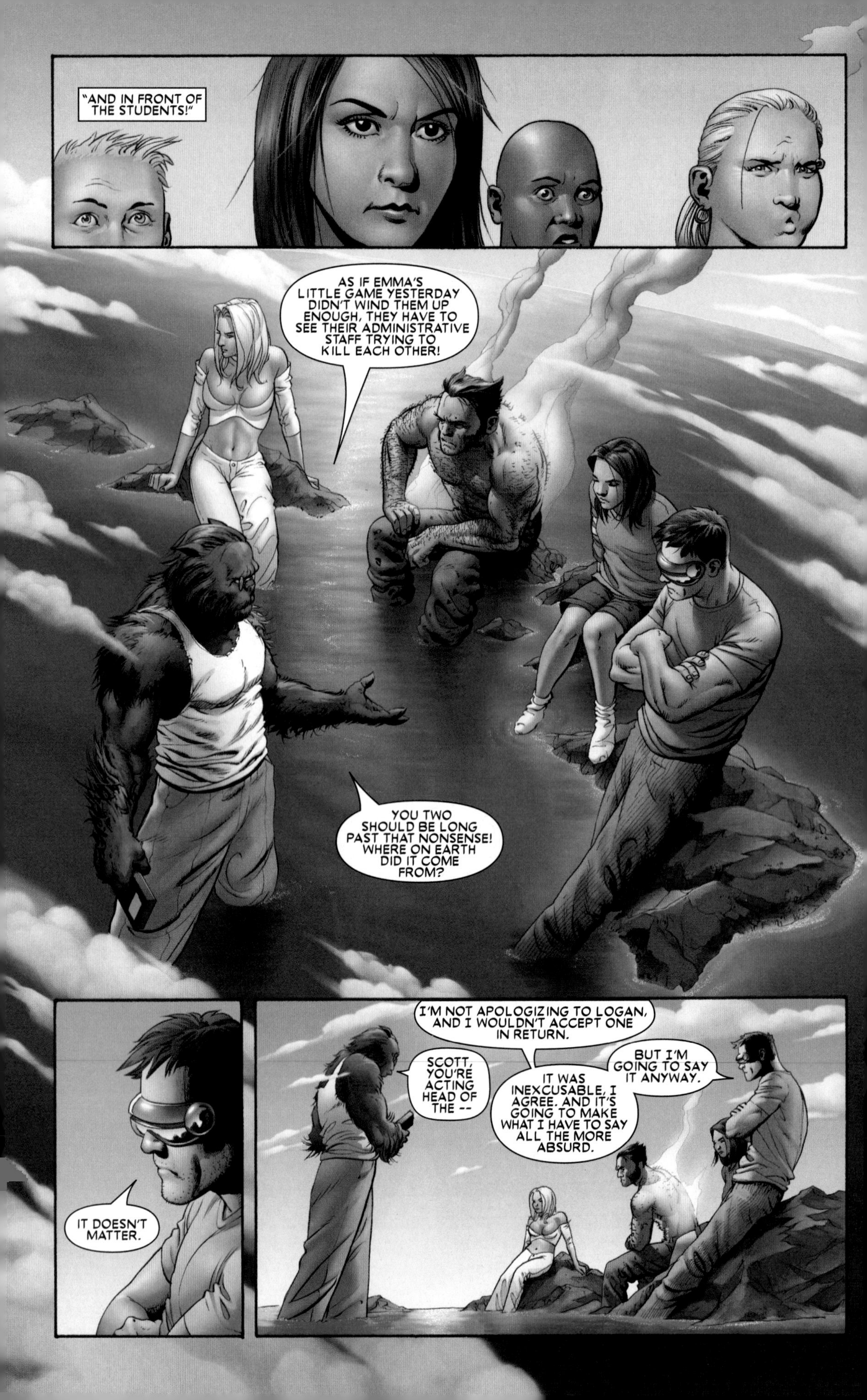
"AND IN FRONT OF THE STUDENTS!"
AS IF EMMA'S LITTLE GAME YESTERDAY DIDN'T WIND THEM UP ENOUGH, THEY HAVE TO SEE THEIR ADMINISTRATIVE STAFF TRYING TO KILL EACH OTHER!
YOU TWO SHOULD BE LONG PAST THAT NONSENSE! WHERE ON EARTH DID IT COME FROM?
IT DOESN'T MATTER.
I'M NOT APOLOGIZING TO LOGAN, AND I WOULDN'T ACCEPT ONE IN RETURN.
SCOTT, YOU'RE ACTING HEAD OF THE --
IT WAS INEXCUSABLE, I AGREE. AND IT'S GOING TO MAKE WHAT I HAVE TO SAY ALL THE MORE ABSURD.
BUT I'M GOING TO SAY IT ANYWAY.

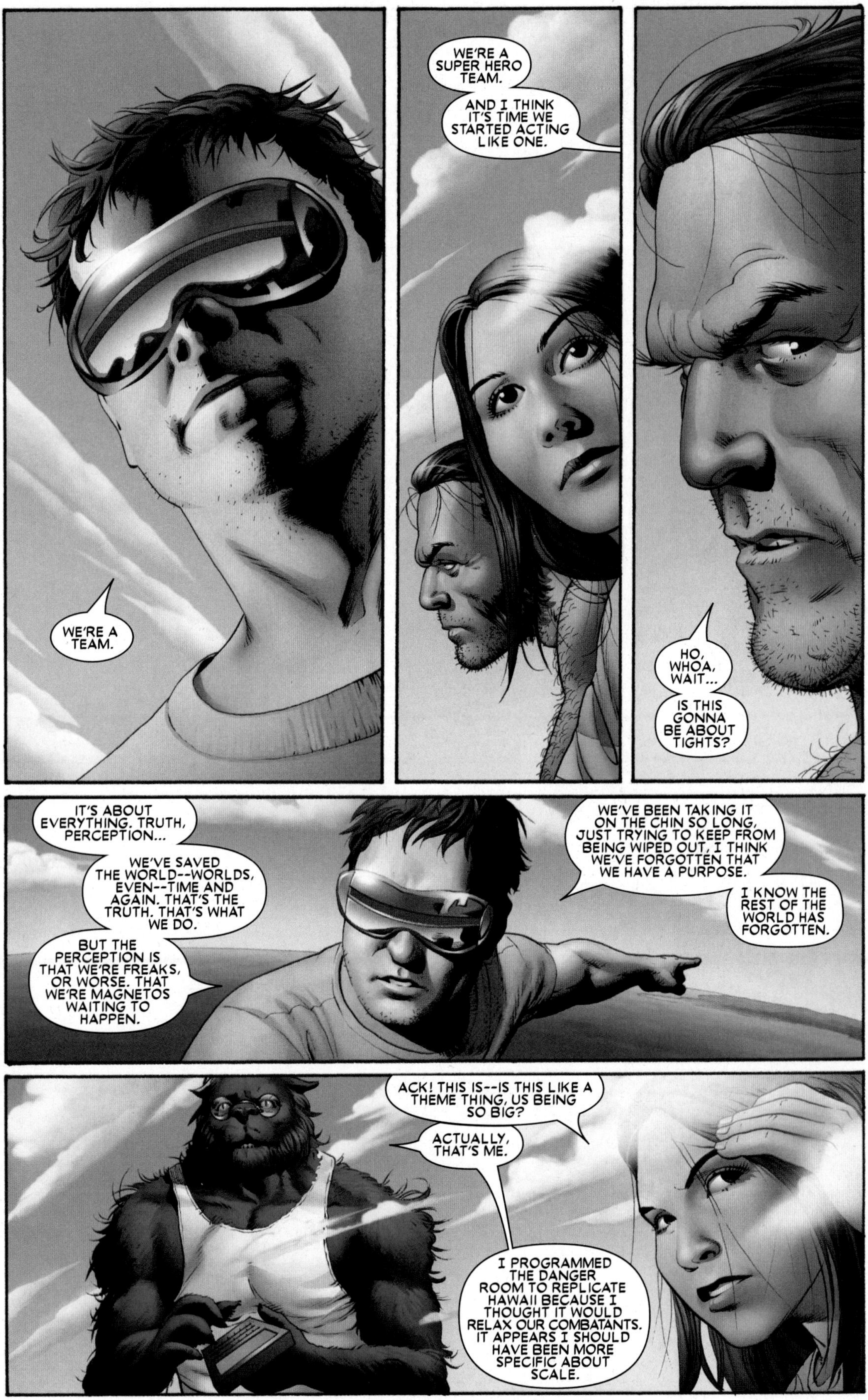
WE'RE A TEAM.
WE'RE A SUPER HERO TEAM.
AND I THINK IT'S TIME WE STARTED ACTING LIKE ONE.
HO, WHOA, WAIT...
IS THIS GONNA BE ABOUT TIGHTS?
IT'S ABOUT EVERYTHING. TRUTH, PERCEPTION...
WE'VE SAVED THE WORLD--WORLDS, EVEN--TIME AND AGAIN. THAT'S THE TRUTH. THAT'S WHAT WE DO.
BUT THE PERCEPTION IS THAT WE'RE FREAKS, OR WORSE. THAT WE'RE MAGNETOS WAITING TO HAPPEN.
WE'VE BEEN TAKING IT ON THE CHIN SO LONG, JUST TRYING TO KEEP FROM BEING WIPED OUT, I THINK WE'VE FORGOTTEN THAT WE HAVE A PURPOSE.
I KNOW THE REST OF THE WORLD HAS FORGOTTEN.
ACK! THIS IS--IS THIS LIKE A THEME THING, US BEING SO BIG?
ACTUALLY, THAT'S ME.
I PROGRAMMED THE DANGER ROOM TO REPLICATE HAWAII BECAUSE I THOUGHT IT WOULD RELAX OUR COMBATANTS. IT APPEARS I SHOULD HAVE BEEN MORE SPECIFIC ABOUT SCALE.

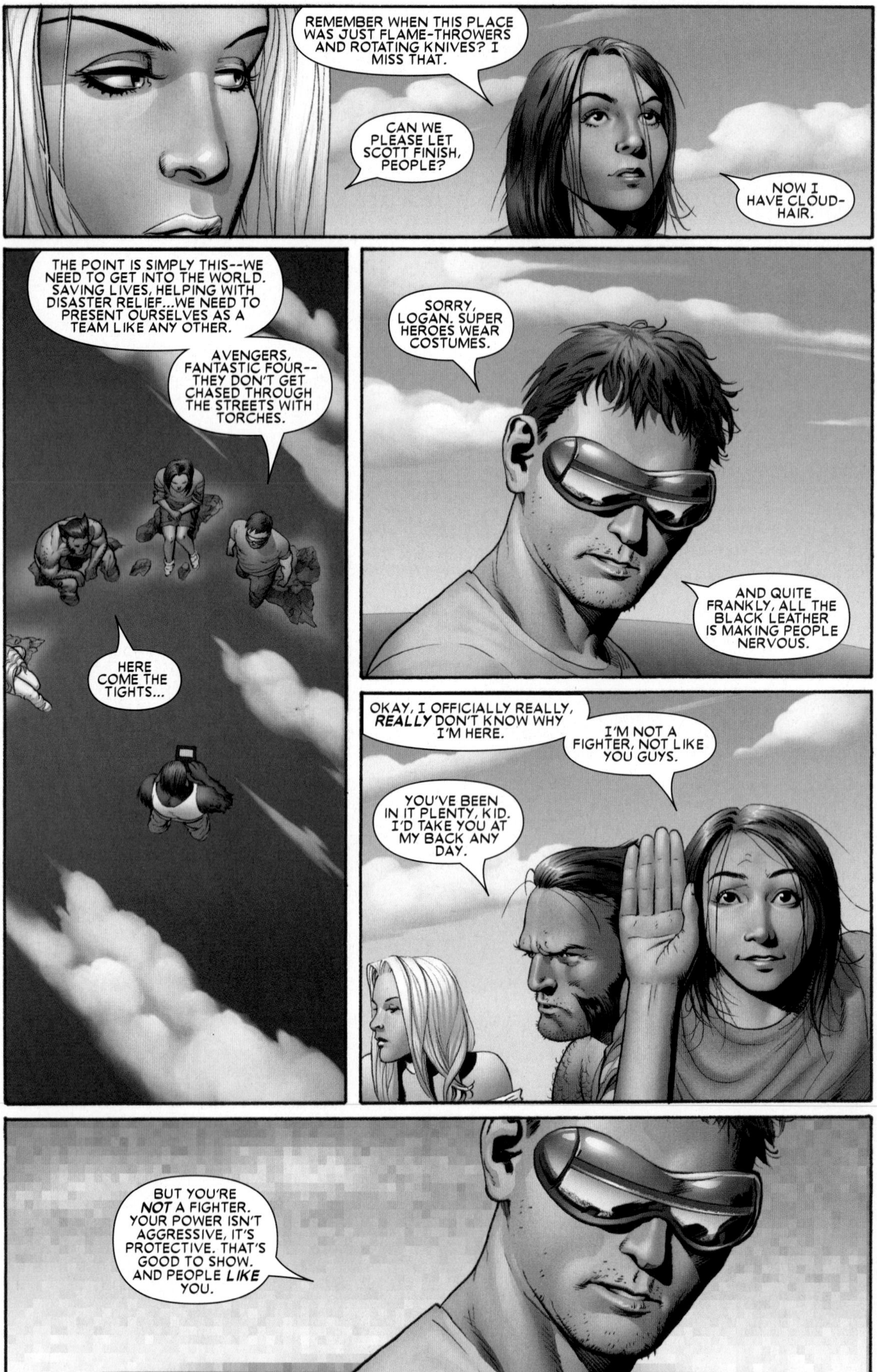
REMEMBER WHEN THIS PLACE WAS JUST FLAME-THROWERS AND ROTATING KNIVES? I MISS THAT.
CAN WE PLEASE LET SCOTT FINISH, PEOPLE?
NOW I HAVE CLOUD-HAIR.
THE POINT IS SIMPLY THIS--WE NEED TO GET INTO THE WORLD. SAVING LIVES, HELPING WITH DISASTER RELIEF...WE NEED TO PRESENT OURSELVES AS A TEAM LIKE ANY OTHER.
AVENGERS, FANTASTIC FOUR--THEY DON'T GET CHASED THROUGH THE STREETS WITH TORCHES.
HERE COME THE TIGHTS...
SORRY, LOGAN. SUPER HEROES WEAR COSTUMES.
AND QUITE FRANKLY, ALL THE BLACK LEATHER IS MAKING PEOPLE NERVOUS.
OKAY, I OFFICIALLY REALLY, REALLY DON'T KNOW WHY I'M HERE.
I'M NOT A FIGHTER, NOT LIKE YOU GUYS.
YOU'VE BEEN IN IT PLENTY, KID. I'D TAKE YOU AT MY BACK ANY DAY.
BUT YOU'RE NOT A FIGHTER. YOUR POWER ISN'T AGGRESSIVE, IT'S PROTECTIVE. THAT'S GOOD TO SHOW. AND PEOPLE LIKE YOU.

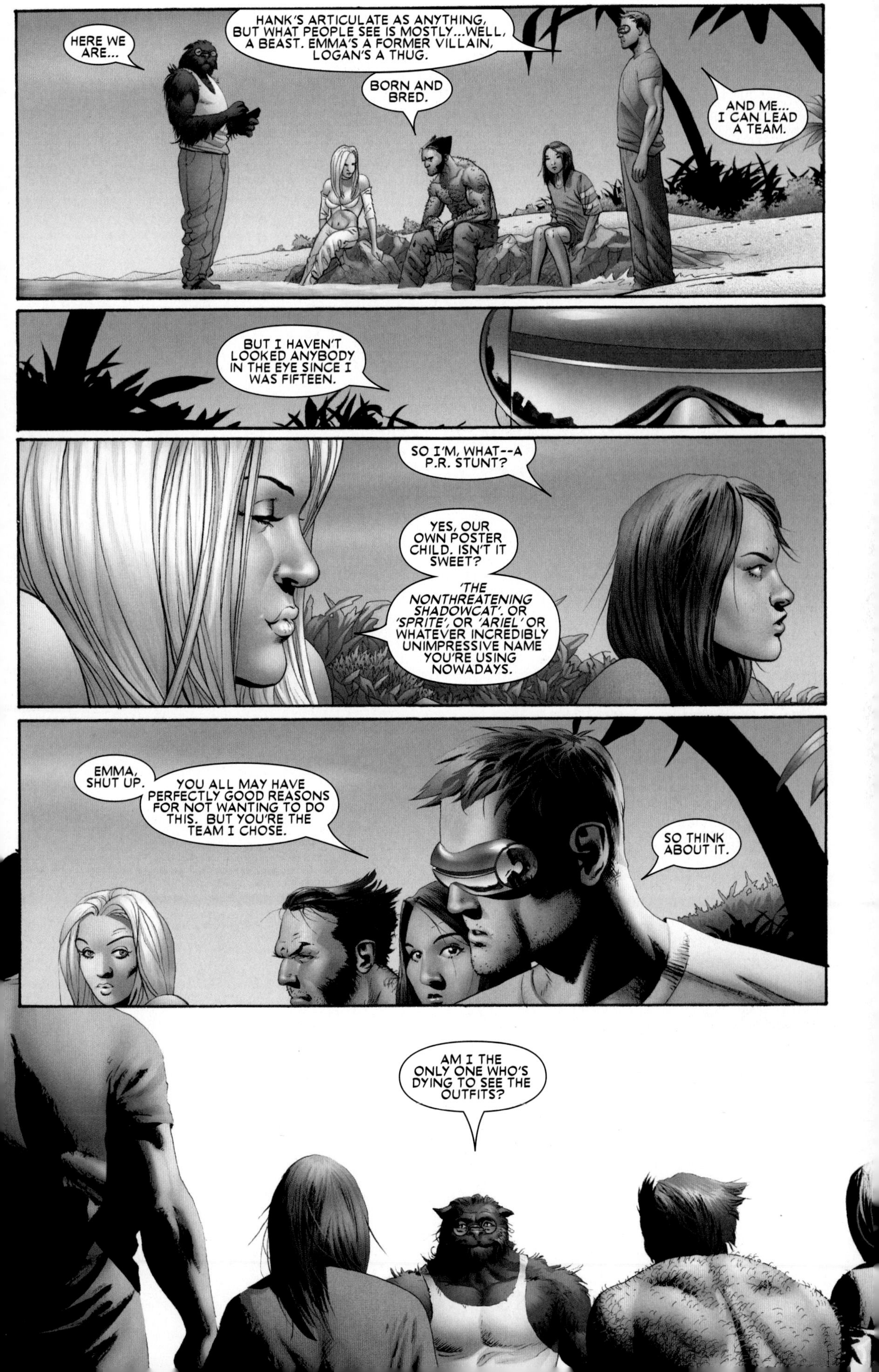

HERE WE ARE...
HANK'S ARTICULATE AS ANYTHING, BUT WHAT PEOPLE SEE IS MOSTLY...WELL, A BEAST. EMMA'S A FORMER VILLAIN, LOGAN'S A THUG.
BORN AND BRED.
AND ME... I CAN LEAD A TEAM.
BUT I HAVEN'T LOOKED ANYBODY IN THE EYE SINCE I WAS FIFTEEN.
SO I'M, WHAT--A P.R. STUNT?
YES, OUR OWN POSTER CHILD. ISN'T IT SWEET?
'THE NONTHREATENING SHADOWCAT'. OR *'SPRITE'*, OR *'ARIEL'* OR WHATEVER INCREDIBLY UNIMPRESSIVE NAME YOU'RE USING NOWADAYS.
EMMA, SHUT UP.
YOU ALL MAY HAVE PERFECTLY GOOD REASONS FOR NOT WANTING TO DO THIS. BUT YOU'RE THE TEAM I CHOSE.
SO THINK ABOUT IT.
AM I THE ONLY ONE WHO'S DYING TO SEE THE OUTFITS?

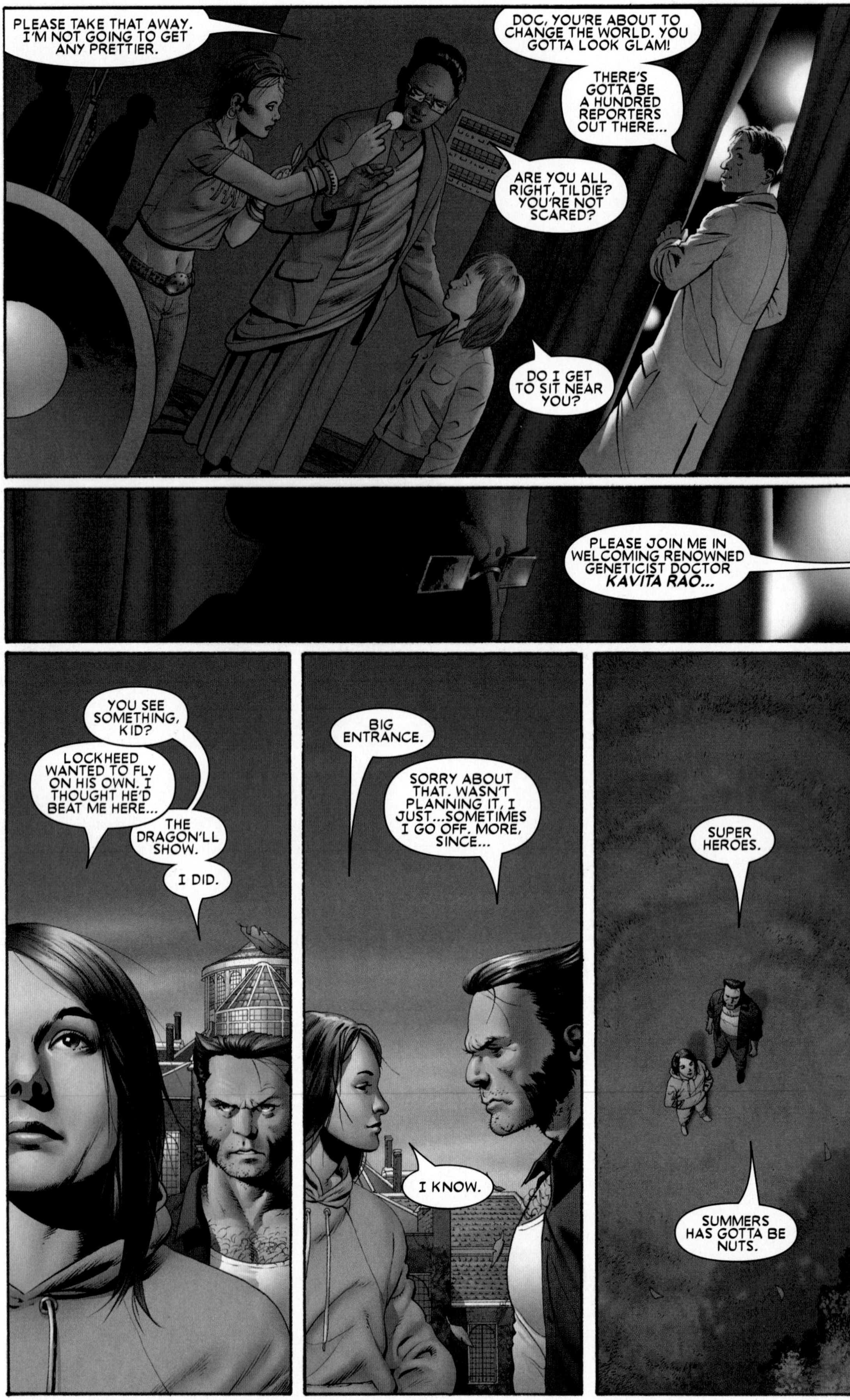
PLEASE TAKE THAT AWAY. I'M NOT GOING TO GET ANY PRETTIER.
DOC, YOU'RE ABOUT TO CHANGE THE WORLD. YOU GOTTA LOOK GLAM!
THERE'S GOTTA BE A HUNDRED REPORTERS OUT THERE...
ARE YOU ALL RIGHT, TILDIE? YOU'RE NOT SCARED?
DO I GET TO SIT NEAR YOU?
PLEASE JOIN ME IN WELCOMING RENOWNED GENETICIST DOCTOR *KAVITA RAO...*
YOU SEE SOMETHING, KID?
LOCKHEED WANTED TO FLY ON HIS OWN. I THOUGHT HE'D BEAT ME HERE...
THE DRAGON'LL SHOW.
I DID.
BIG ENTRANCE.
SORRY ABOUT THAT. WASN'T PLANNING IT, I JUST...SOMETIMES I GO OFF. MORE, SINCE...
I KNOW.
SUPER HEROES.
SUMMERS HAS GOTTA BE NUTS.

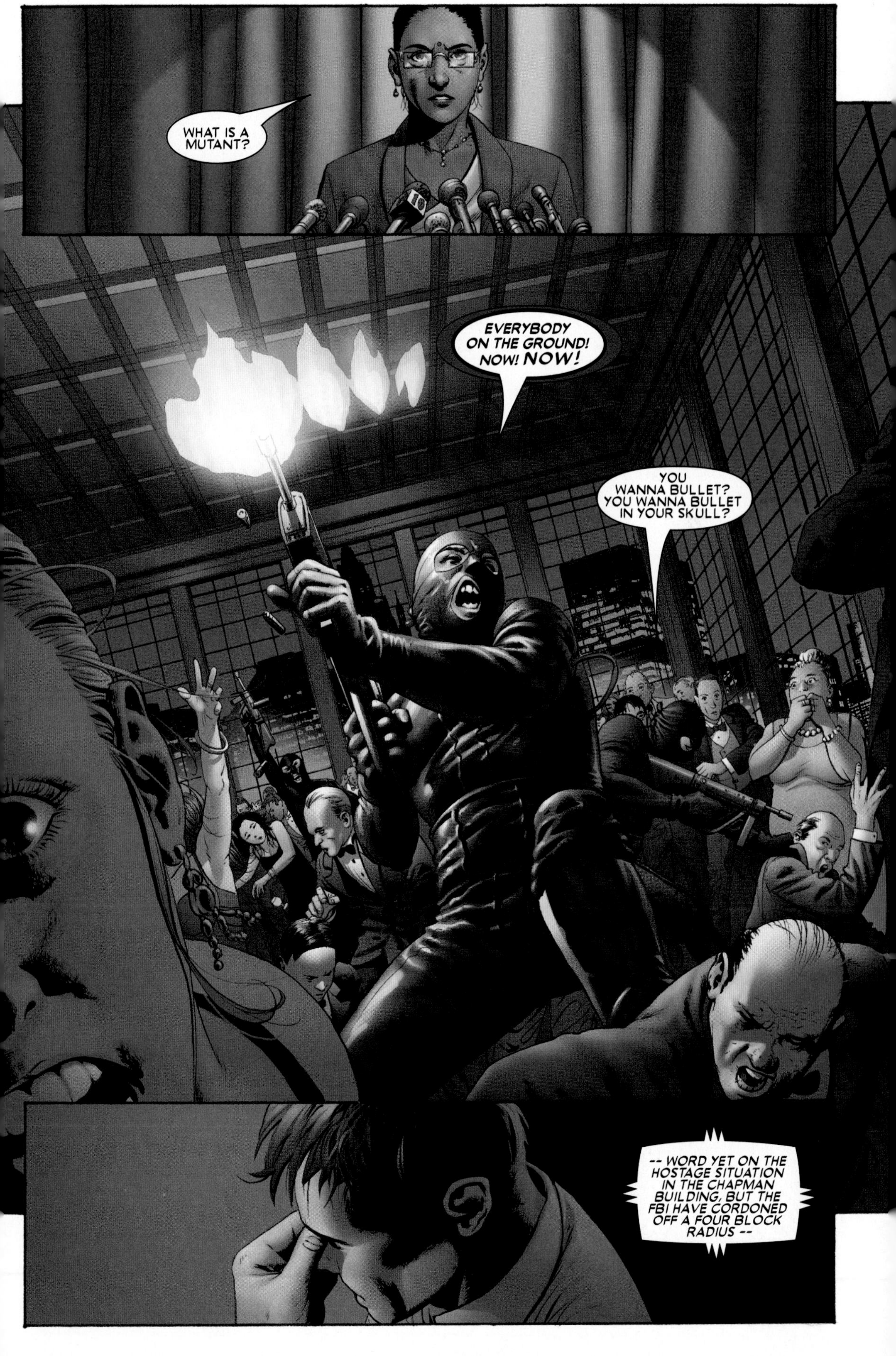
WHAT IS A MUTANT?
EVERYBODY ON THE GROUND! NOW! NOW!
YOU WANNA BULLET? YOU WANNA BULLET IN YOUR SKULL?
-- WORD YET ON THE HOSTAGE SITUATION IN THE CHAPMAN BUILDING, BUT THE FBI HAVE CORDONED OFF A FOUR BLOCK RADIUS --

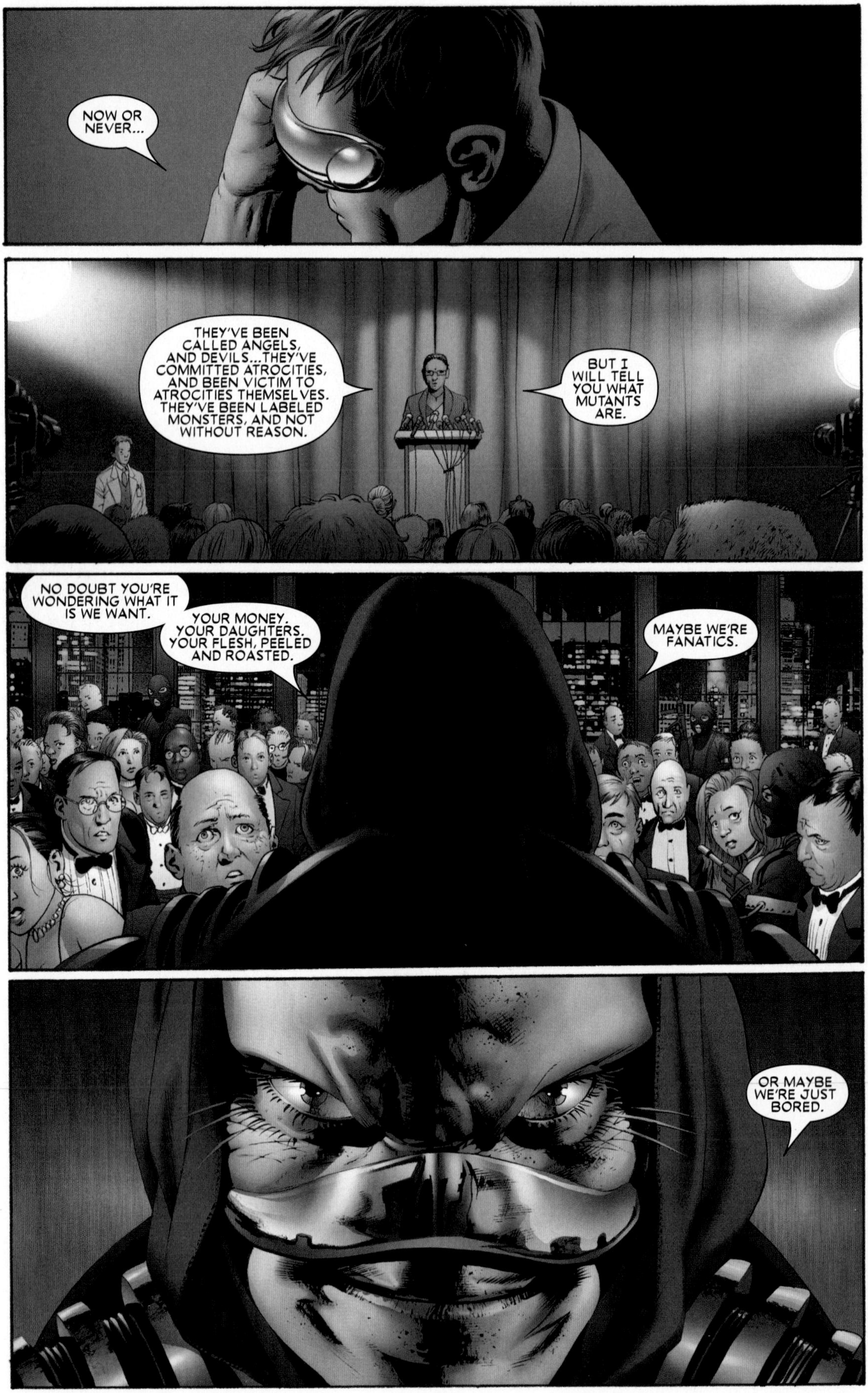
NOW OR NEVER...
THEY'VE BEEN CALLED ANGELS, AND DEVILS...THEY'VE COMMITTED ATROCITIES, AND BEEN VICTIM TO ATROCITIES THEMSELVES. THEY'VE BEEN LABELED MONSTERS, AND NOT WITHOUT REASON.
BUT I WILL TELL YOU WHAT MUTANTS ARE.
NO DOUBT YOU'RE WONDERING WHAT IT IS WE WANT.
YOUR MONEY. YOUR DAUGHTERS. YOUR FLESH, PEELED AND ROASTED.
MAYBE WE'RE FANATICS.
OR MAYBE WE'RE JUST BORED.

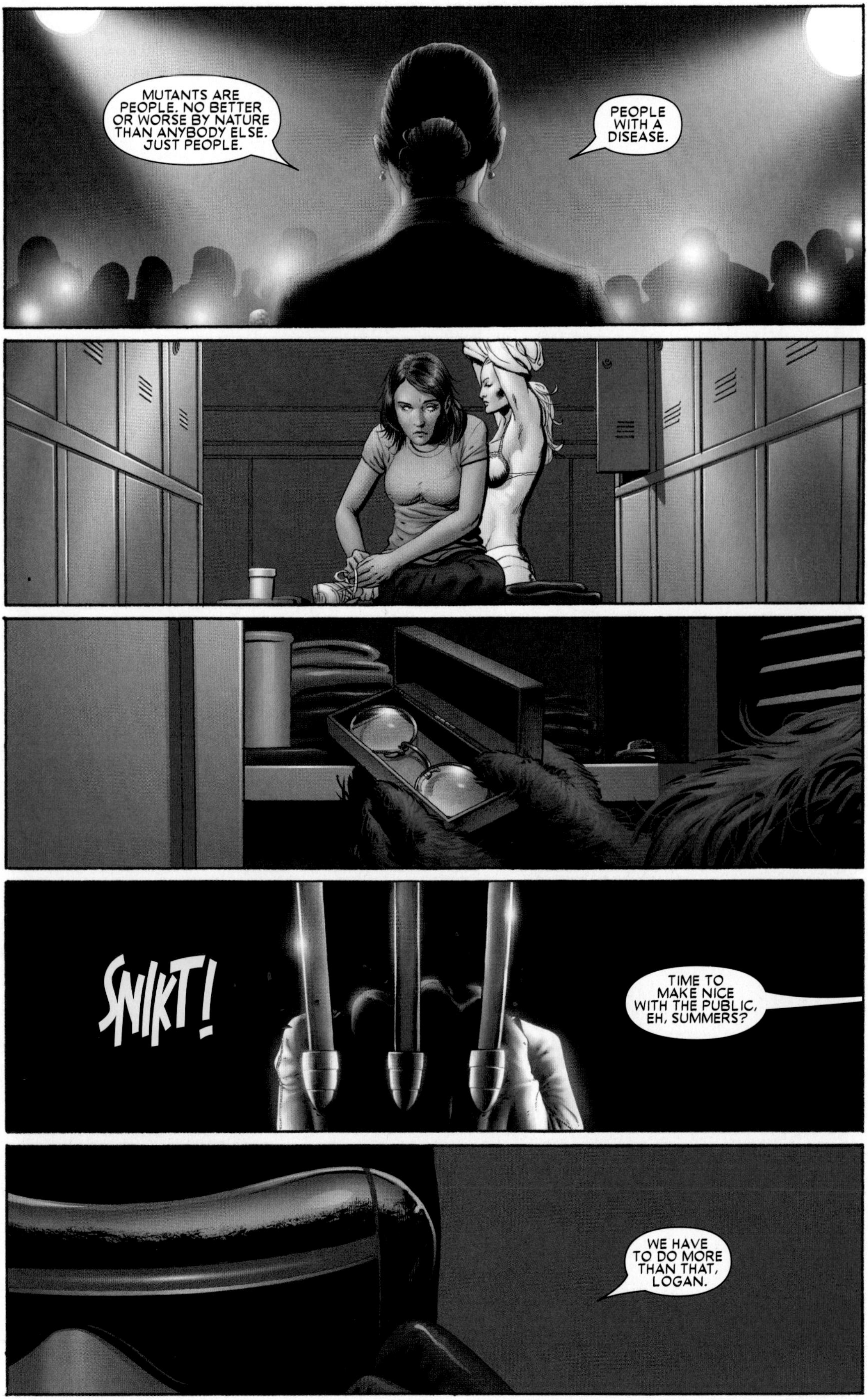
MUTANTS ARE PEOPLE. NO BETTER OR WORSE BY NATURE THAN ANYBODY ELSE. JUST PEOPLE.
PEOPLE WITH A DISEASE.
SNIKT!
TIME TO MAKE NICE WITH THE PUBLIC, EH, SUMMERS?
WE HAVE TO DO MORE THAN THAT, LOGAN.

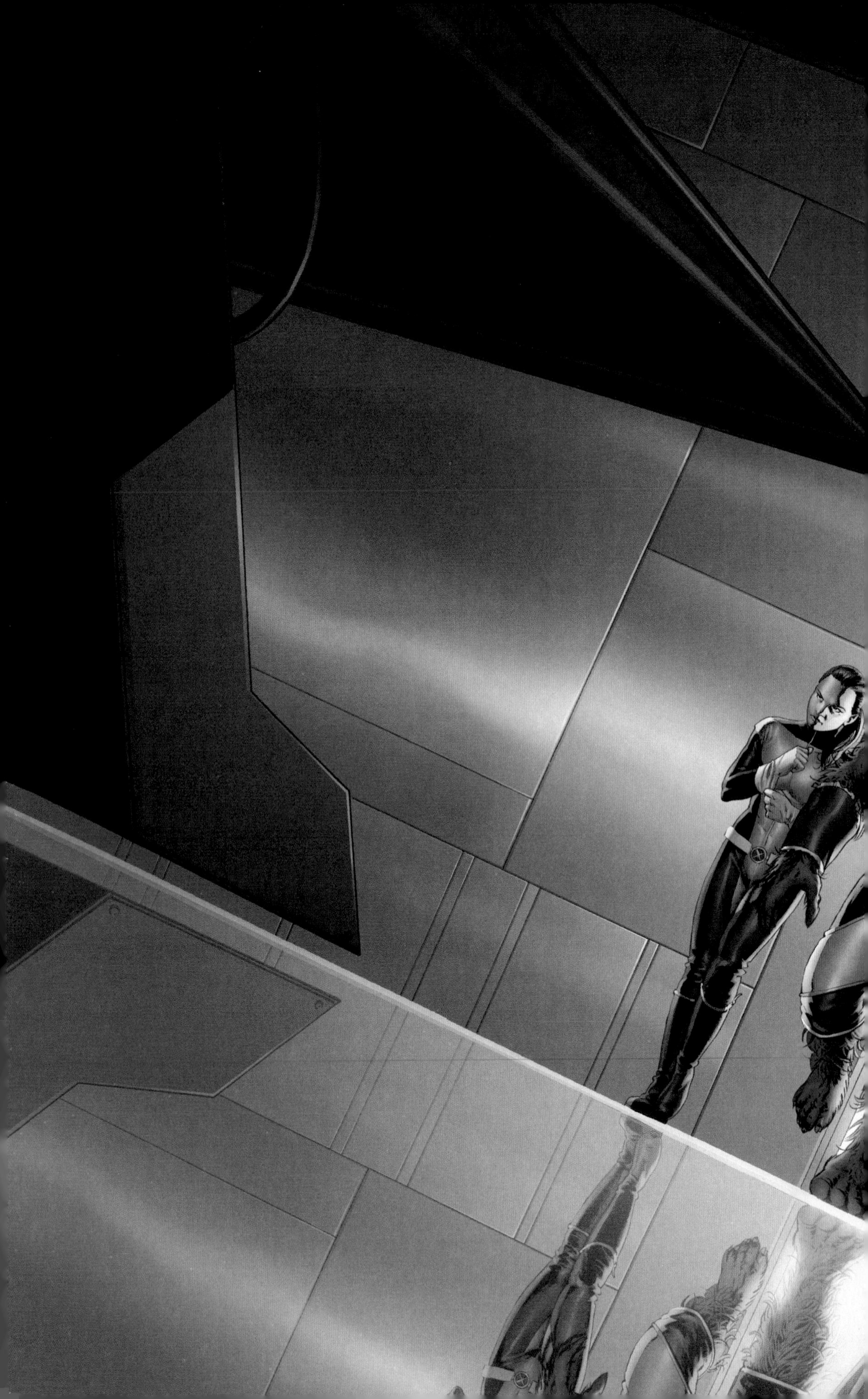

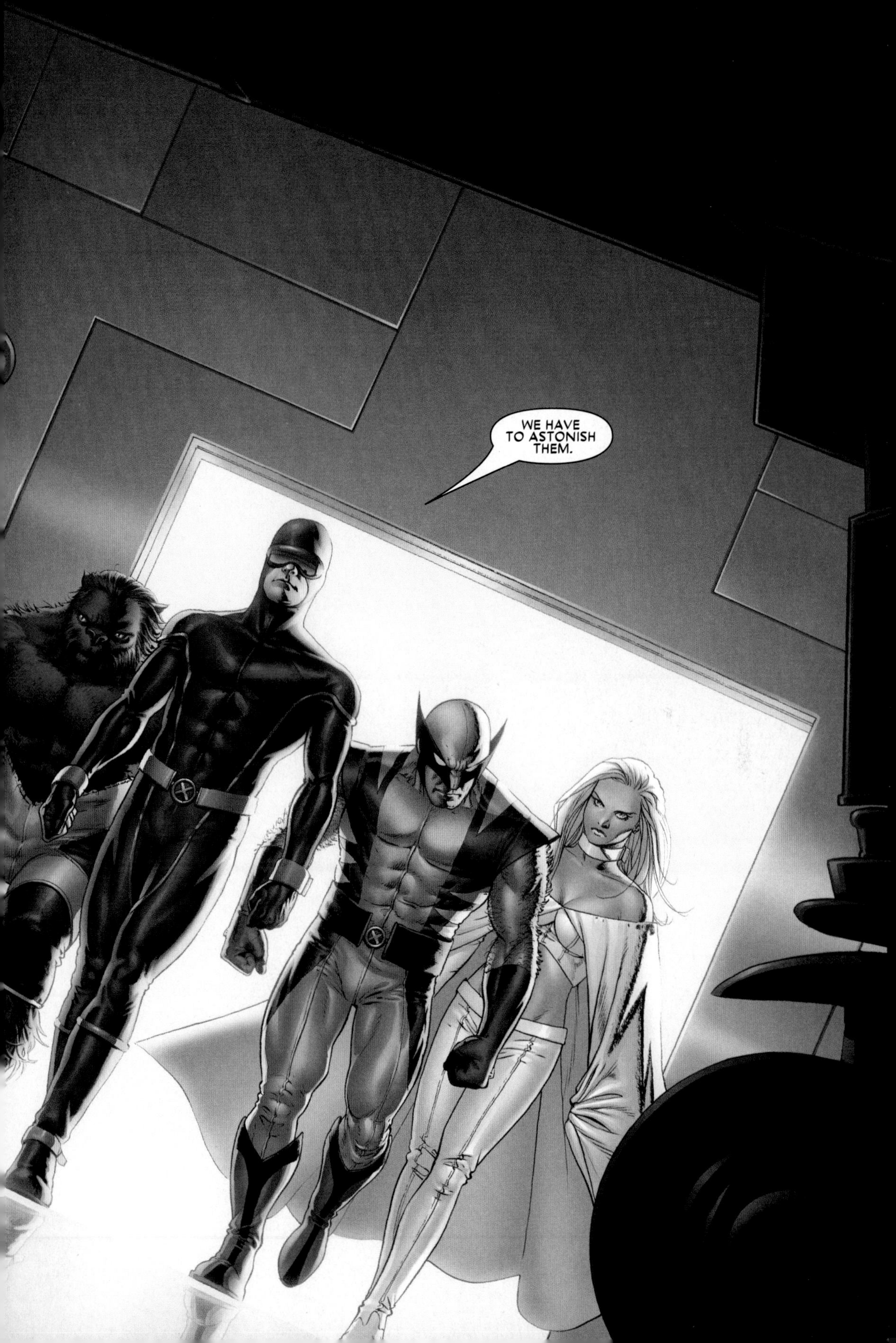
WE HAVE TO ASTONISH THEM.

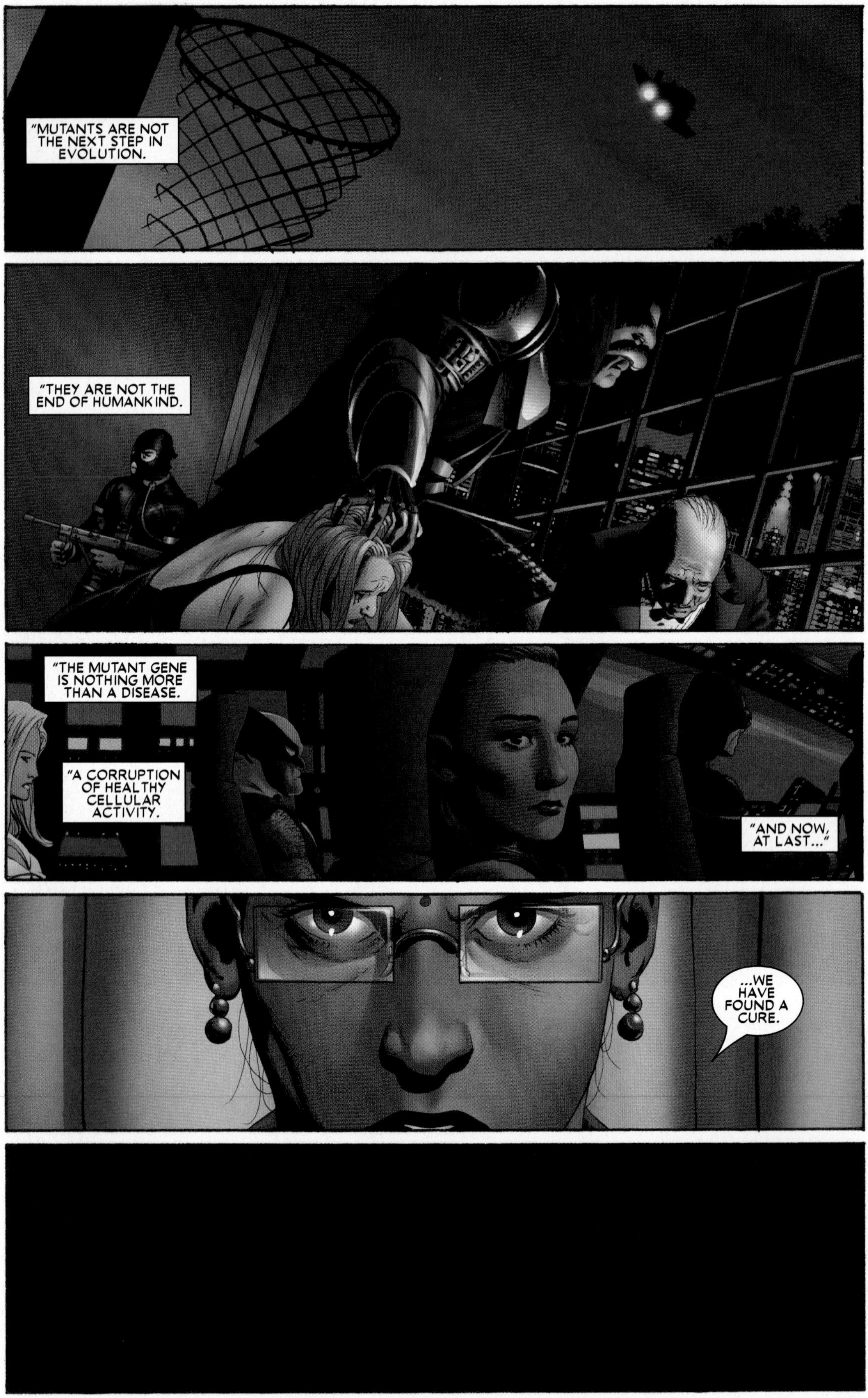
"MUTANTS ARE NOT THE NEXT STEP IN EVOLUTION.
"THEY ARE NOT THE END OF HUMANKIND.
"THE MUTANT GENE IS NOTHING MORE THAN A DISEASE.
"A CORRUPTION OF HEALTHY CELLULAR ACTIVITY.
"AND NOW, AT LAST..."
...WE HAVE FOUND A CURE.

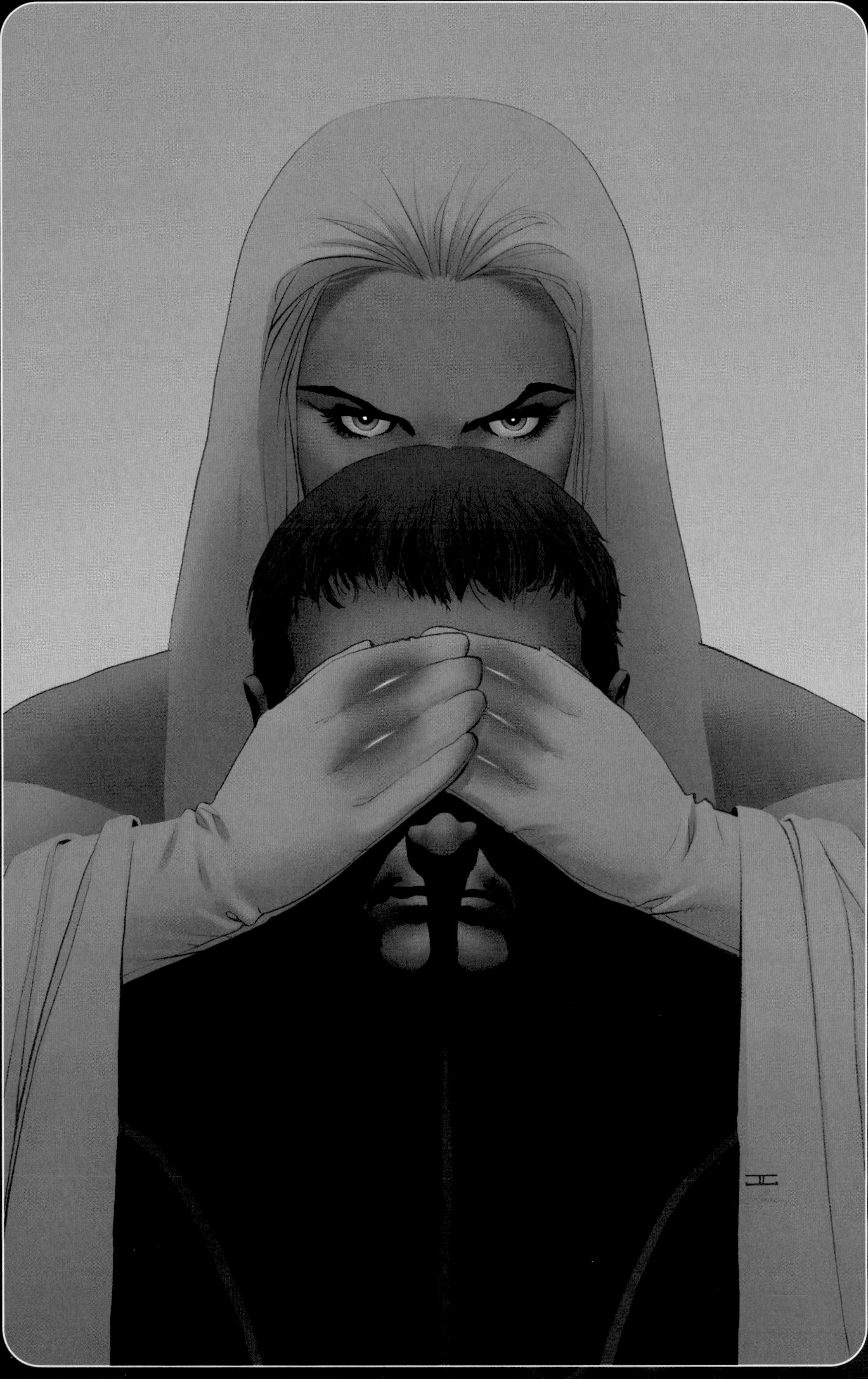

02

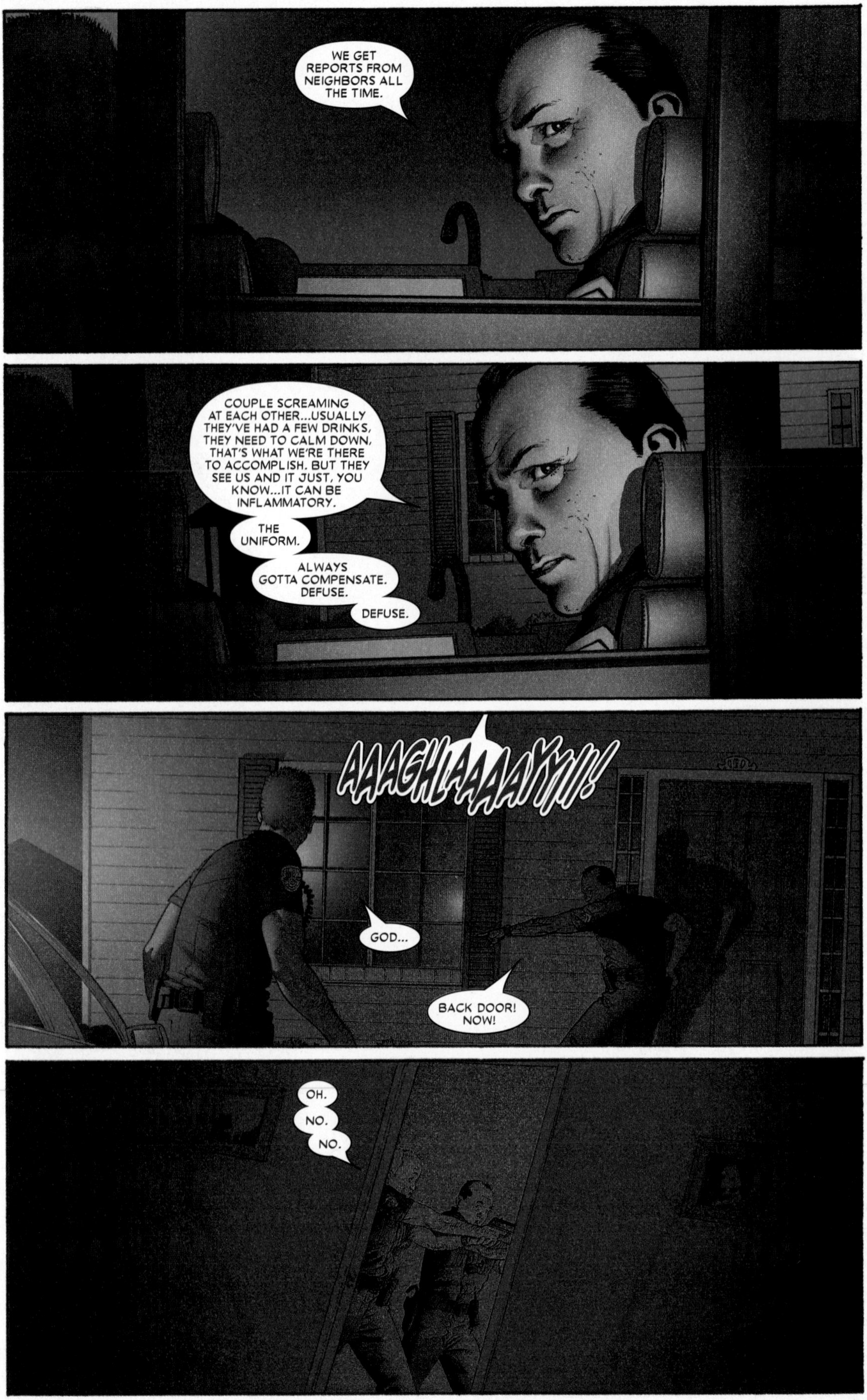
WE GET REPORTS FROM NEIGHBORS ALL THE TIME.
COUPLE SCREAMING AT EACH OTHER...USUALLY THEY'VE HAD A FEW DRINKS, THEY NEED TO CALM DOWN, THAT'S WHAT WE'RE THERE TO ACCOMPLISH. BUT THEY SEE US AND IT JUST, YOU KNOW...IT CAN BE INFLAMMATORY.
THE UNIFORM.
ALWAYS GOTTA COMPENSATE. DEFUSE.
DEFUSE.
AAAGHLAAAAAYYII!
GOD...
BACK DOOR! NOW!
OH.
NO.
NO.

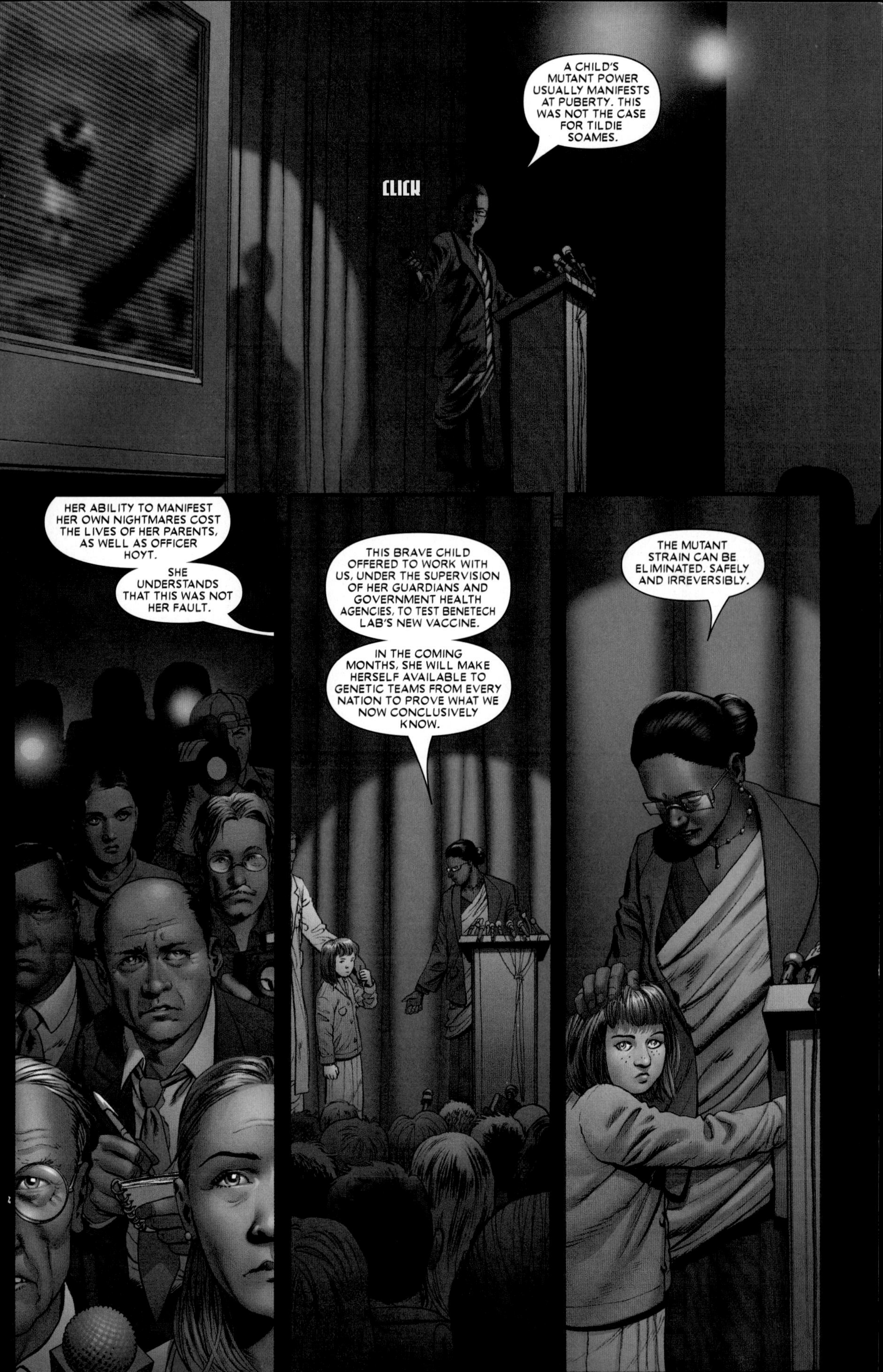
A CHILD'S MUTANT POWER USUALLY MANIFESTS AT PUBERTY. THIS WAS NOT THE CASE FOR TILDIE SOAMES.
CLICK
HER ABILITY TO MANIFEST HER OWN NIGHTMARES COST THE LIVES OF HER PARENTS, AS WELL AS OFFICER HOYT.
SHE UNDERSTANDS THAT THIS WAS NOT HER FAULT.
THIS BRAVE CHILD OFFERED TO WORK WITH US, UNDER THE SUPERVISION OF HER GUARDIANS AND GOVERNMENT HEALTH AGENCIES, TO TEST BENETECH LAB'S NEW VACCINE.
IN THE COMING MONTHS, SHE WILL MAKE HERSELF AVAILABLE TO GENETIC TEAMS FROM EVERY NATION TO PROVE WHAT WE NOW CONCLUSIVELY KNOW.
THE MUTANT STRAIN CAN BE ELIMINATED. SAFELY AND IRREVERSIBLY.

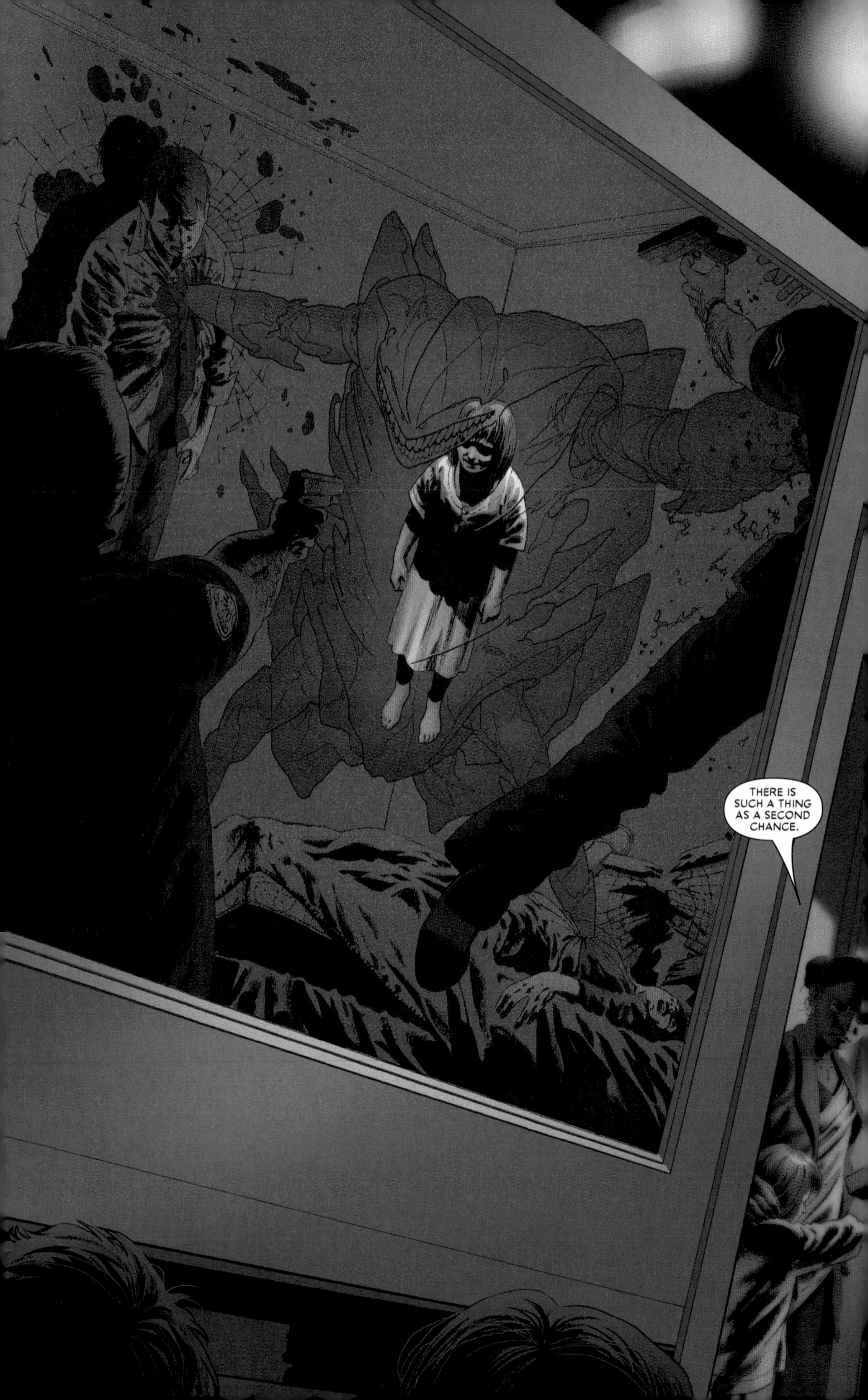
THERE IS SUCH A THING AS A SECOND CHANCE.

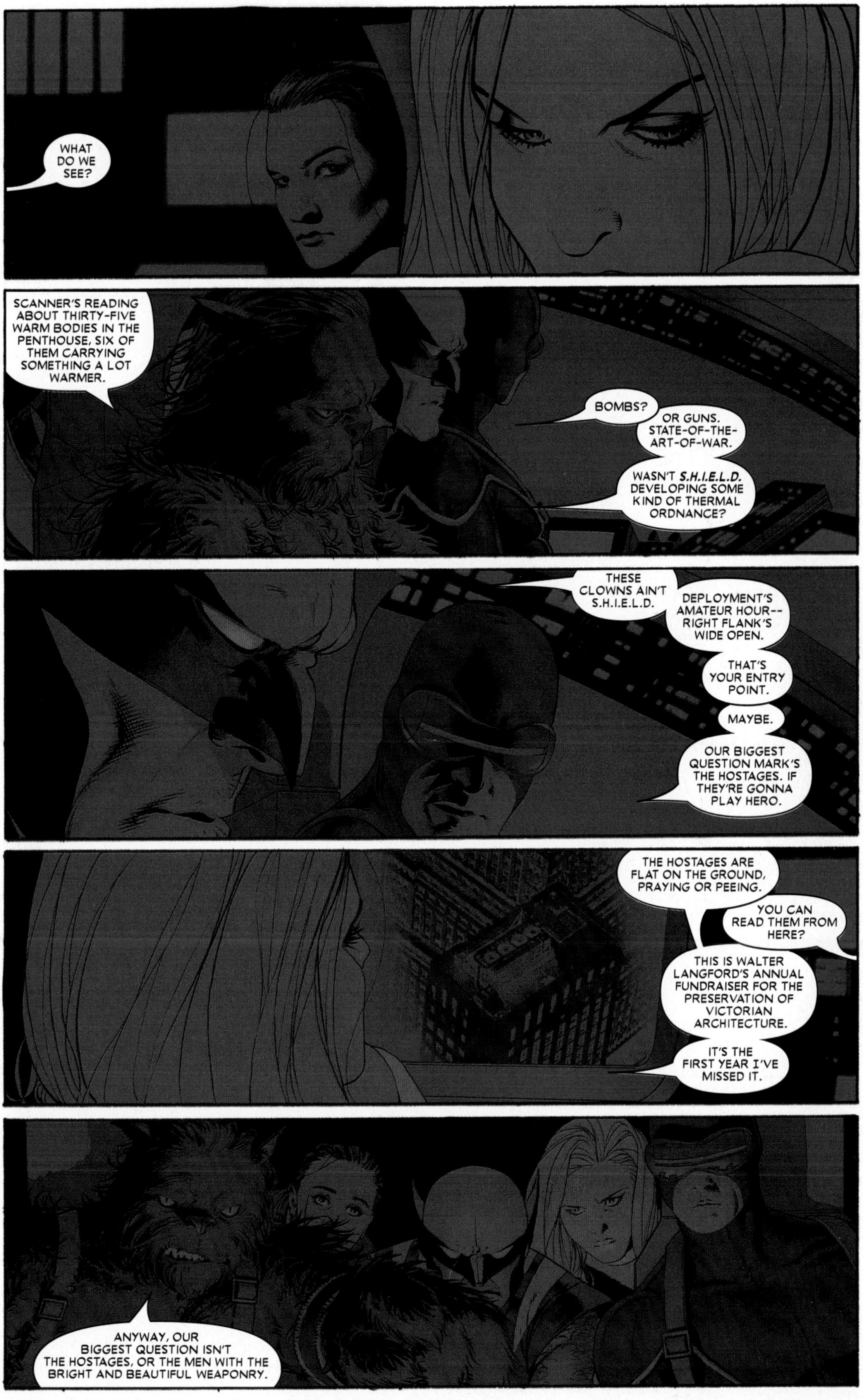
WHAT DO WE SEE?
SCANNER'S READING ABOUT THIRTY-FIVE WARM BODIES IN THE PENTHOUSE, SIX OF THEM CARRYING SOMETHING A LOT WARMER.
BOMBS?
OR GUNS. STATE-OF-THE-ART-OF-WAR.
WASN'T *S.H.I.E.L.D.* DEVELOPING SOME KIND OF THERMAL ORDNANCE?
THESE CLOWNS AIN'T S.H.I.E.L.D.
DEPLOYMENT'S AMATEUR HOUR--RIGHT FLANK'S WIDE OPEN.
THAT'S YOUR ENTRY POINT.
MAYBE.
OUR BIGGEST QUESTION MARK'S THE HOSTAGES. IF THEY'RE GONNA PLAY HERO.
THE HOSTAGES ARE FLAT ON THE GROUND, PRAYING OR PEEING.
YOU CAN READ THEM FROM HERE?
THIS IS WALTER LANGFORD'S ANNUAL FUNDRAISER FOR THE PRESERVATION OF VICTORIAN ARCHITECTURE.
IT'S THE FIRST YEAR I'VE MISSED IT.
ANYWAY, OUR BIGGEST QUESTION ISN'T THE HOSTAGES, OR THE MEN WITH THE BRIGHT AND BEAUTIFUL WEAPONRY.

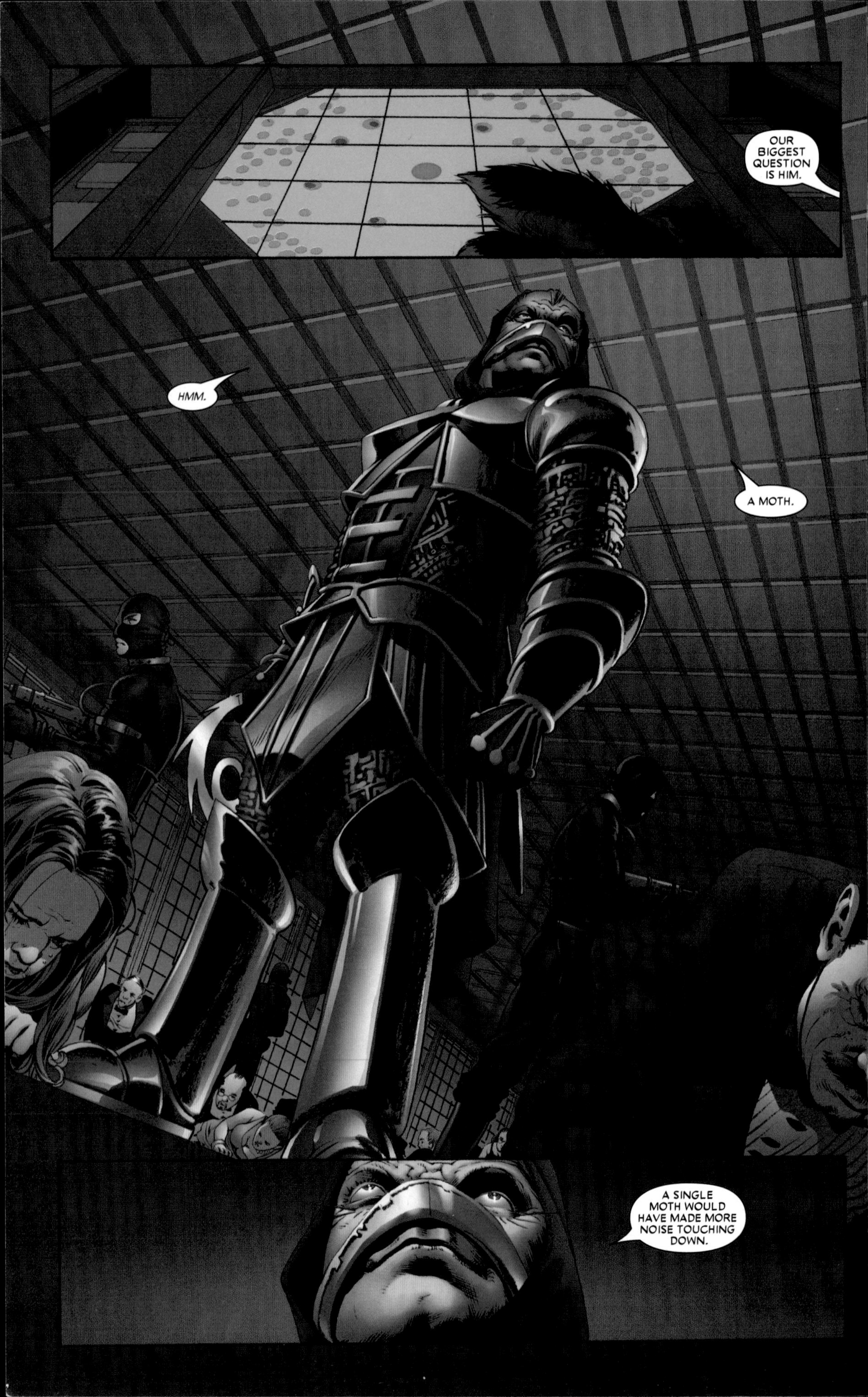
OUR BIGGEST QUESTION IS HIM.
HMM.
A MOTH.
A SINGLE MOTH WOULD HAVE MADE MORE NOISE TOUCHING DOWN.

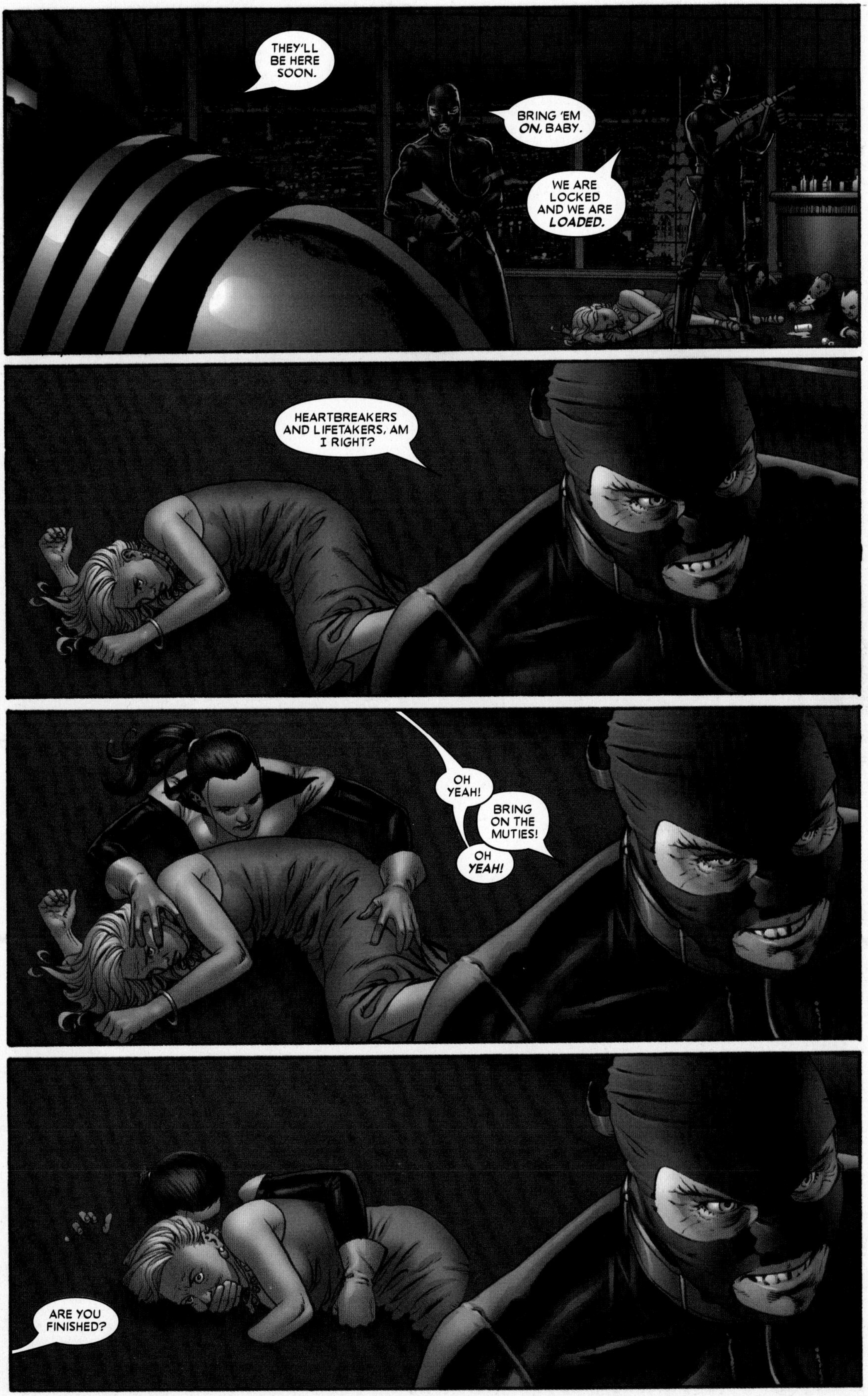
THEY'LL BE HERE SOON.
BRING 'EM *ON,* BABY.
WE ARE LOCKED AND WE ARE ***LOADED.***
HEARTBREAKERS AND LIFETAKERS, AM I RIGHT?
OH YEAH!
BRING ON THE MUTIES!
OH ***YEAH!***
ARE YOU FINISHED?

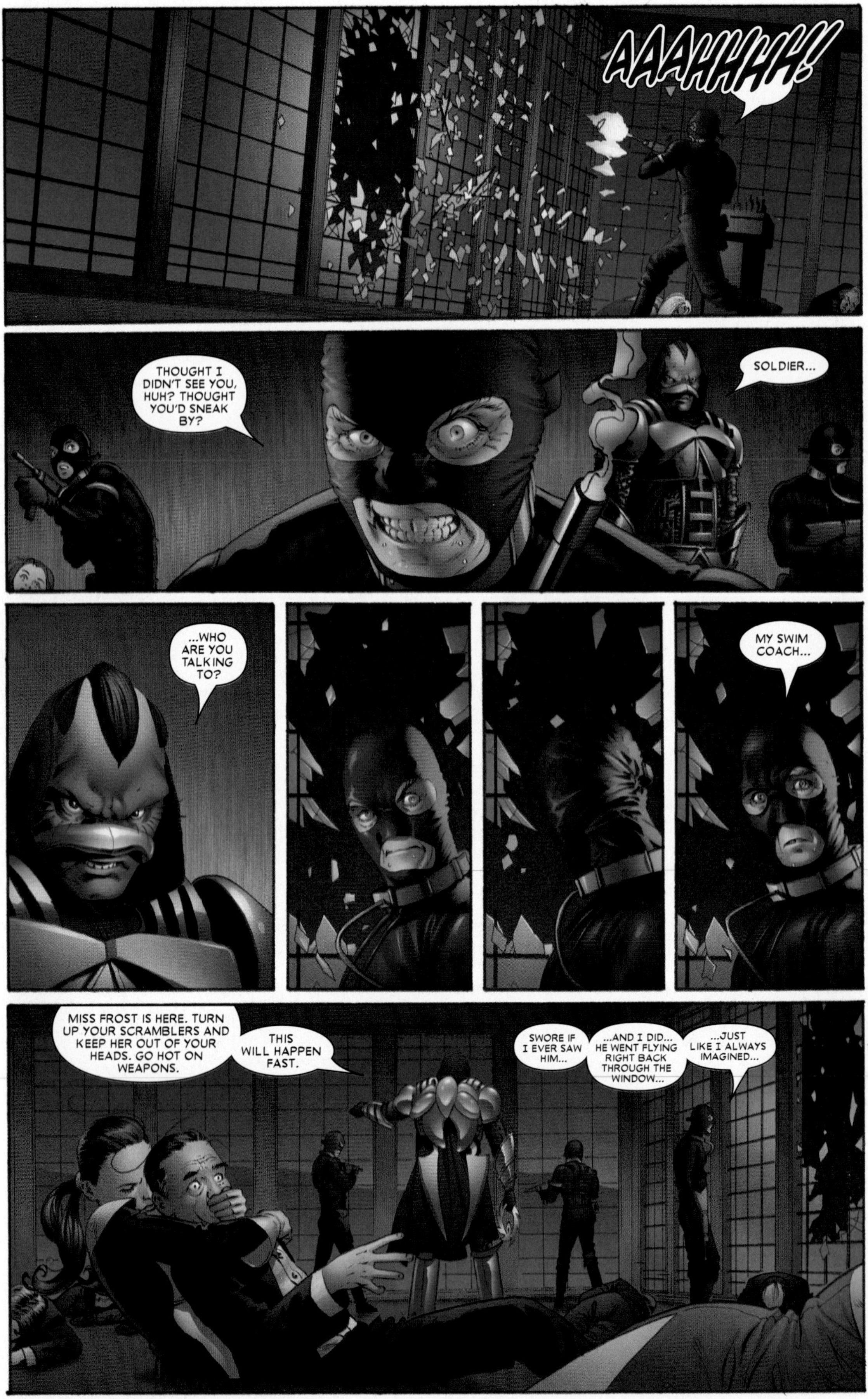
AAAHHHH!
THOUGHT I DIDN'T SEE YOU, HUH? THOUGHT YOU'D SNEAK BY?
SOLDIER...
...WHO ARE YOU TALKING TO?
MY SWIM COACH...
MISS FROST IS HERE. TURN UP YOUR SCRAMBLERS AND KEEP HER OUT OF YOUR HEADS. GO HOT ON WEAPONS.
THIS WILL HAPPEN FAST.
SWORE IF I EVER SAW HIM...
...AND I DID... HE WENT FLYING RIGHT BACK THROUGH THE WINDOW...
...JUST LIKE I ALWAYS IMAGINED...

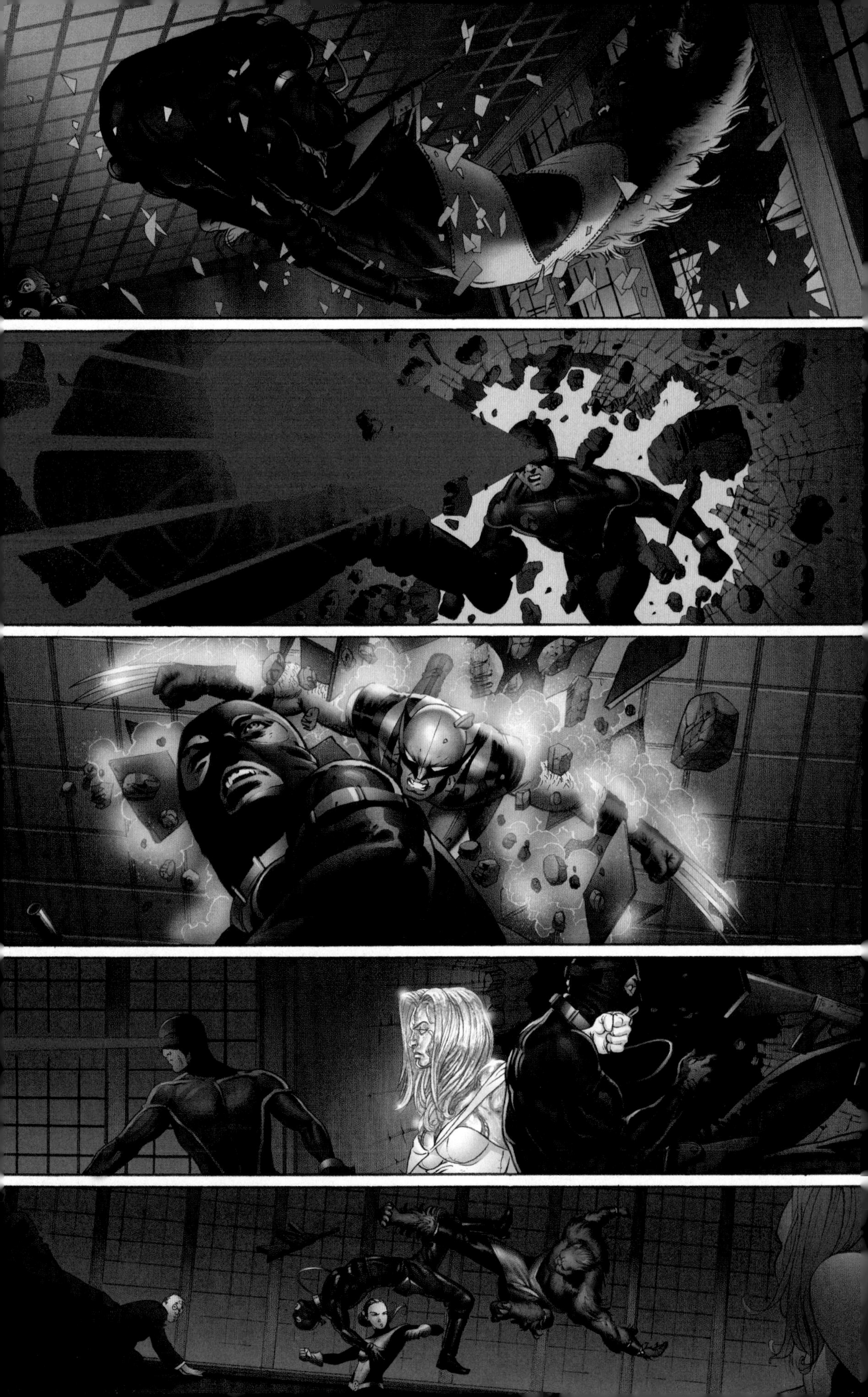

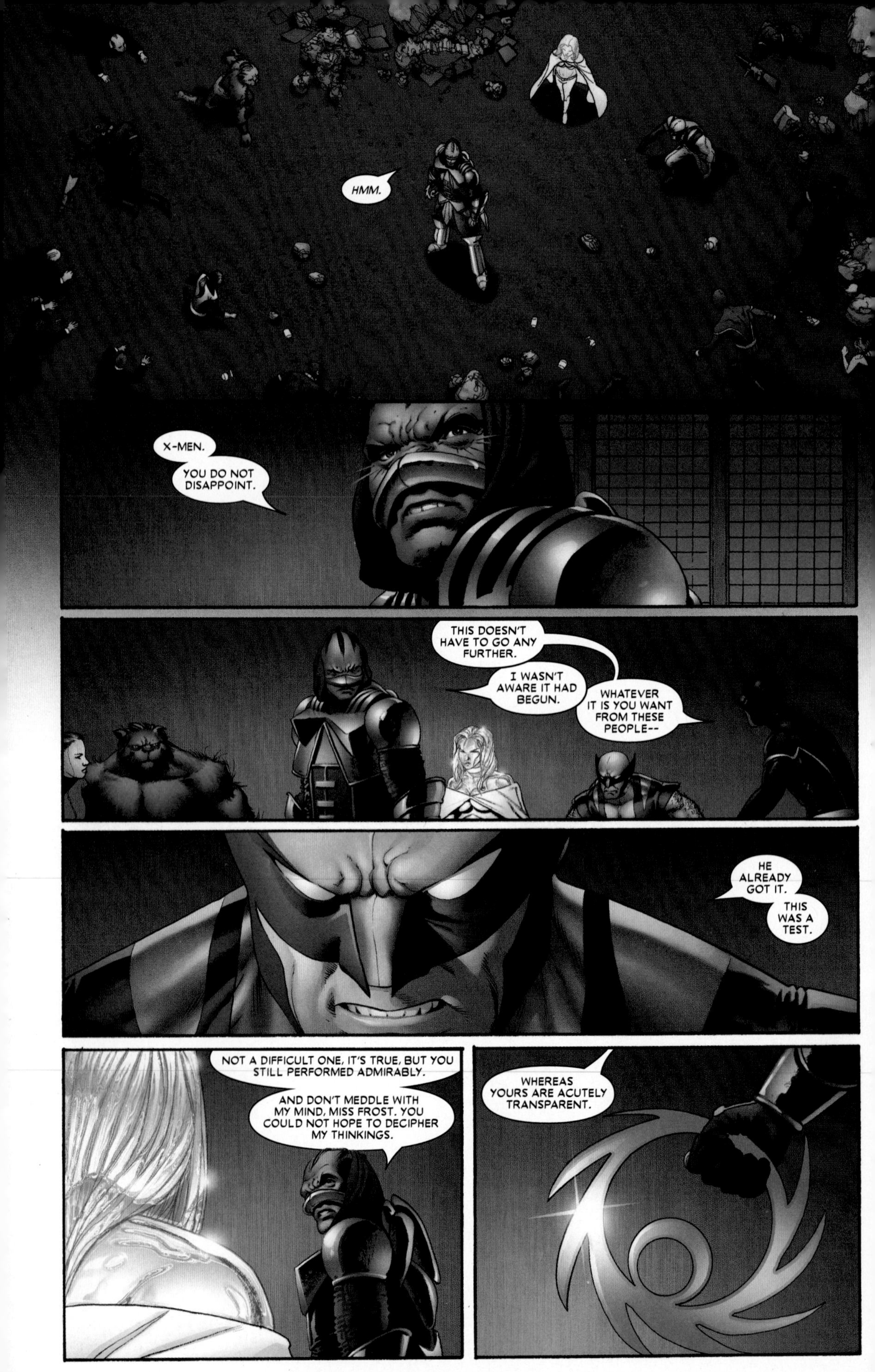
HMM.
X-MEN.
YOU DO NOT DISAPPOINT.
THIS DOESN'T HAVE TO GO ANY FURTHER.
I WASN'T AWARE IT HAD BEGUN.
WHATEVER IT IS YOU WANT FROM THESE PEOPLE--
HE ALREADY GOT IT.
THIS WAS A TEST.
NOT A DIFFICULT ONE, IT'S TRUE, BUT YOU STILL PERFORMED ADMIRABLY.
AND DON'T MEDDLE WITH MY MIND, MISS FROST. YOU COULD NOT HOPE TO DECIPHER MY THINKINGS.
WHEREAS YOURS ARE ACUTELY TRANSPARENT.

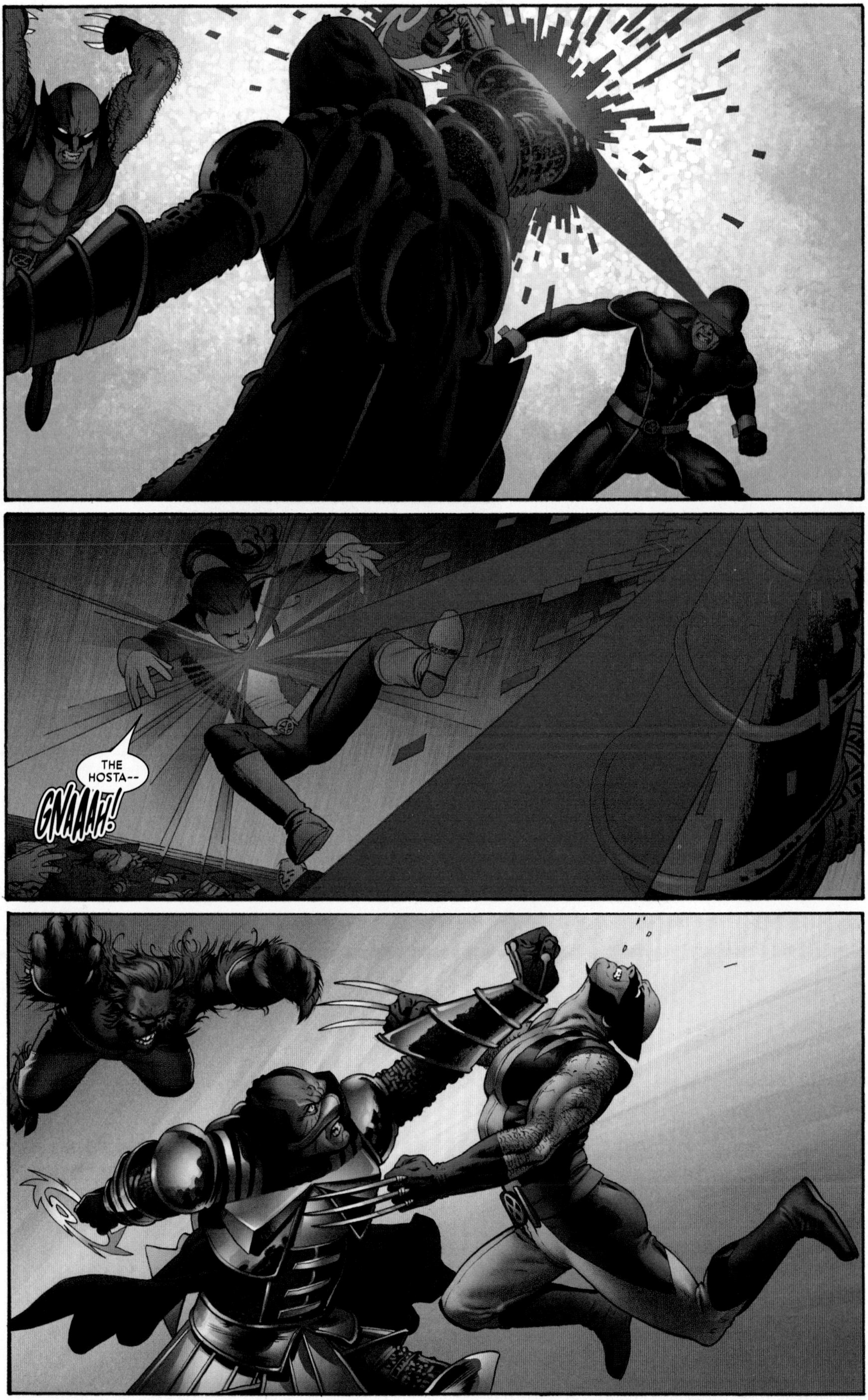
THE HOSTA--
GNAAAH!

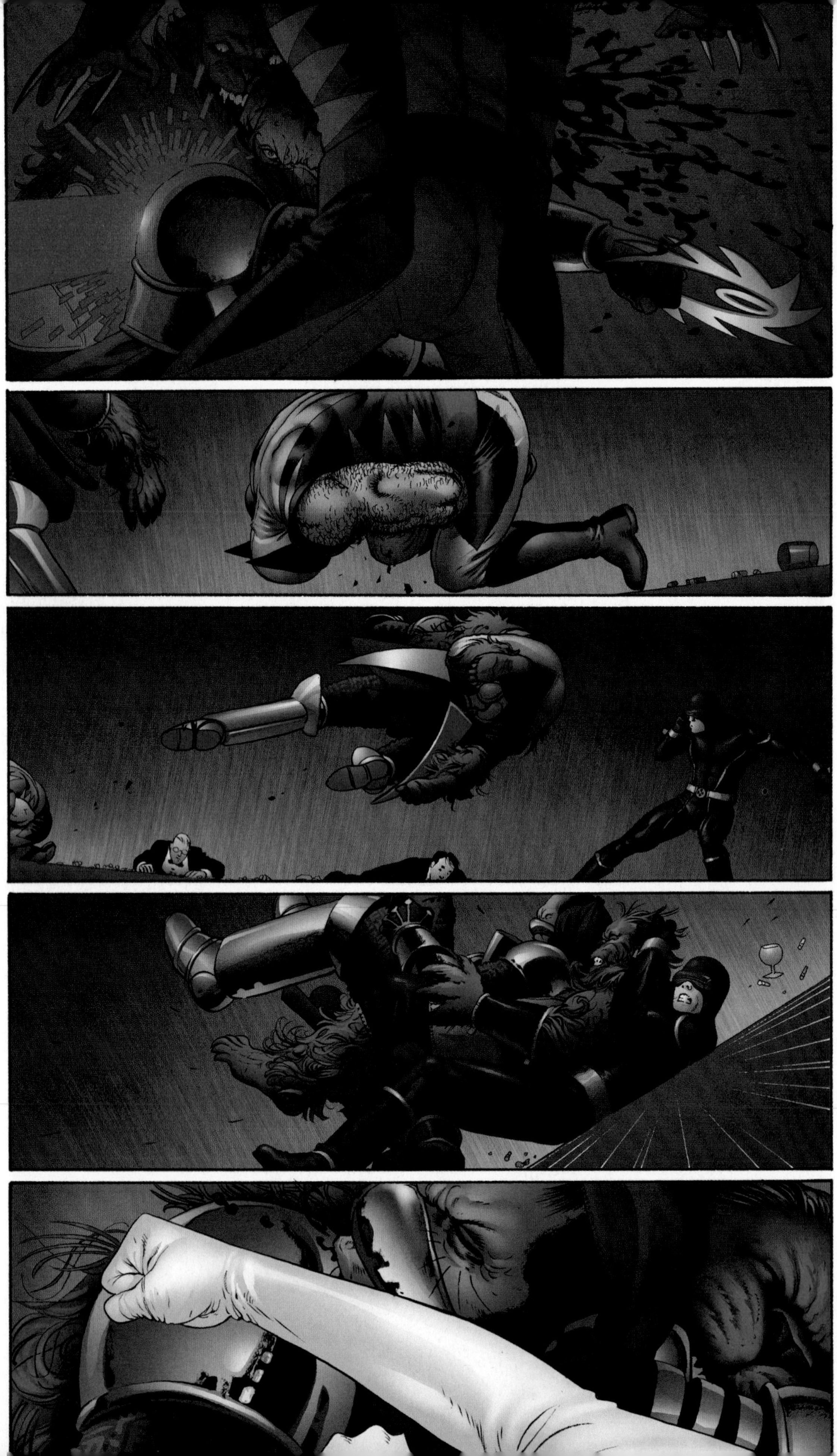

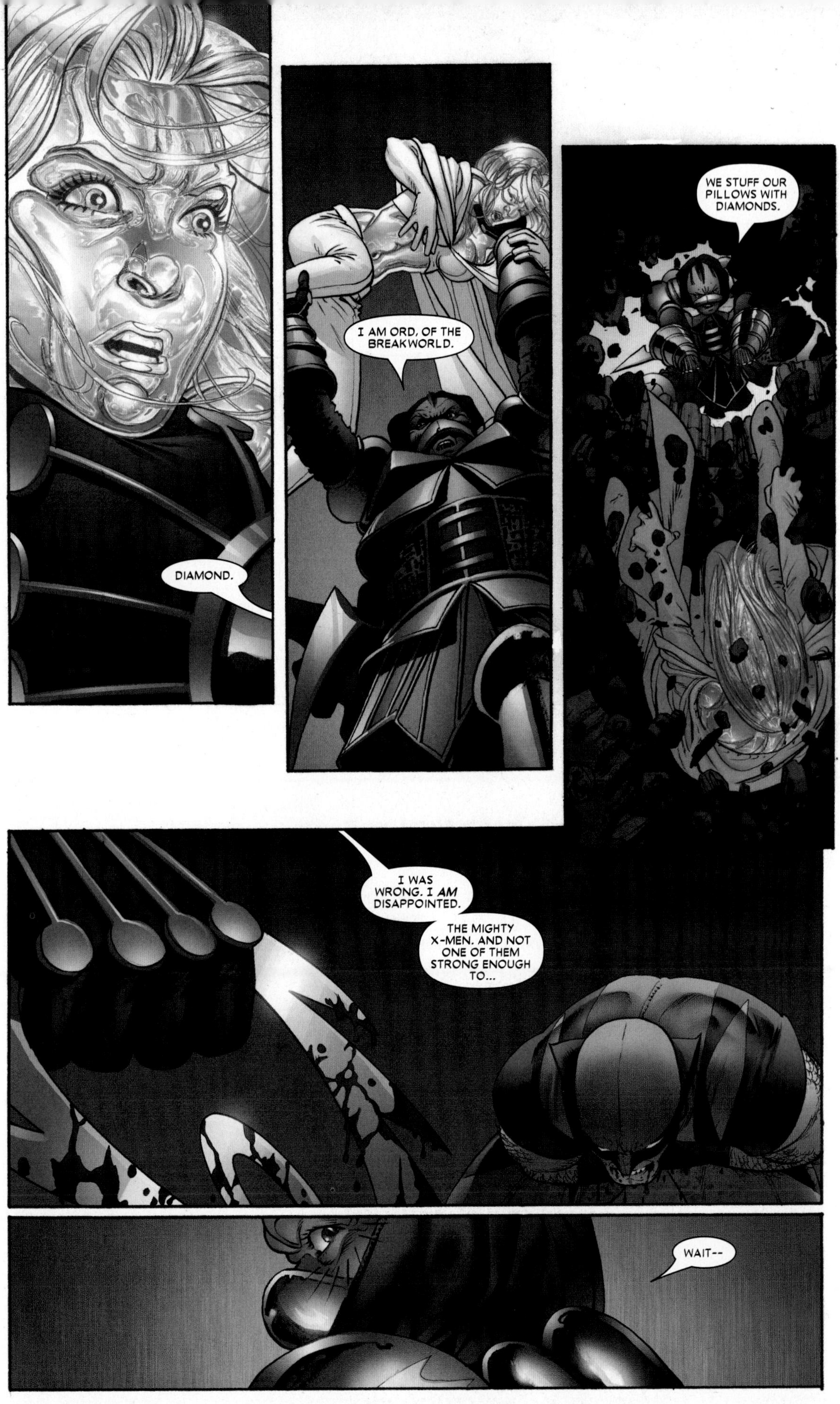
DIAMOND.
I AM ORD, OF THE BREAKWORLD.
WE STUFF OUR PILLOWS WITH DIAMONDS.
I WAS WRONG. I *AM* DISAPPOINTED.
THE MIGHTY X-MEN. AND NOT ONE OF THEM STRONG ENOUGH TO...
WAIT--

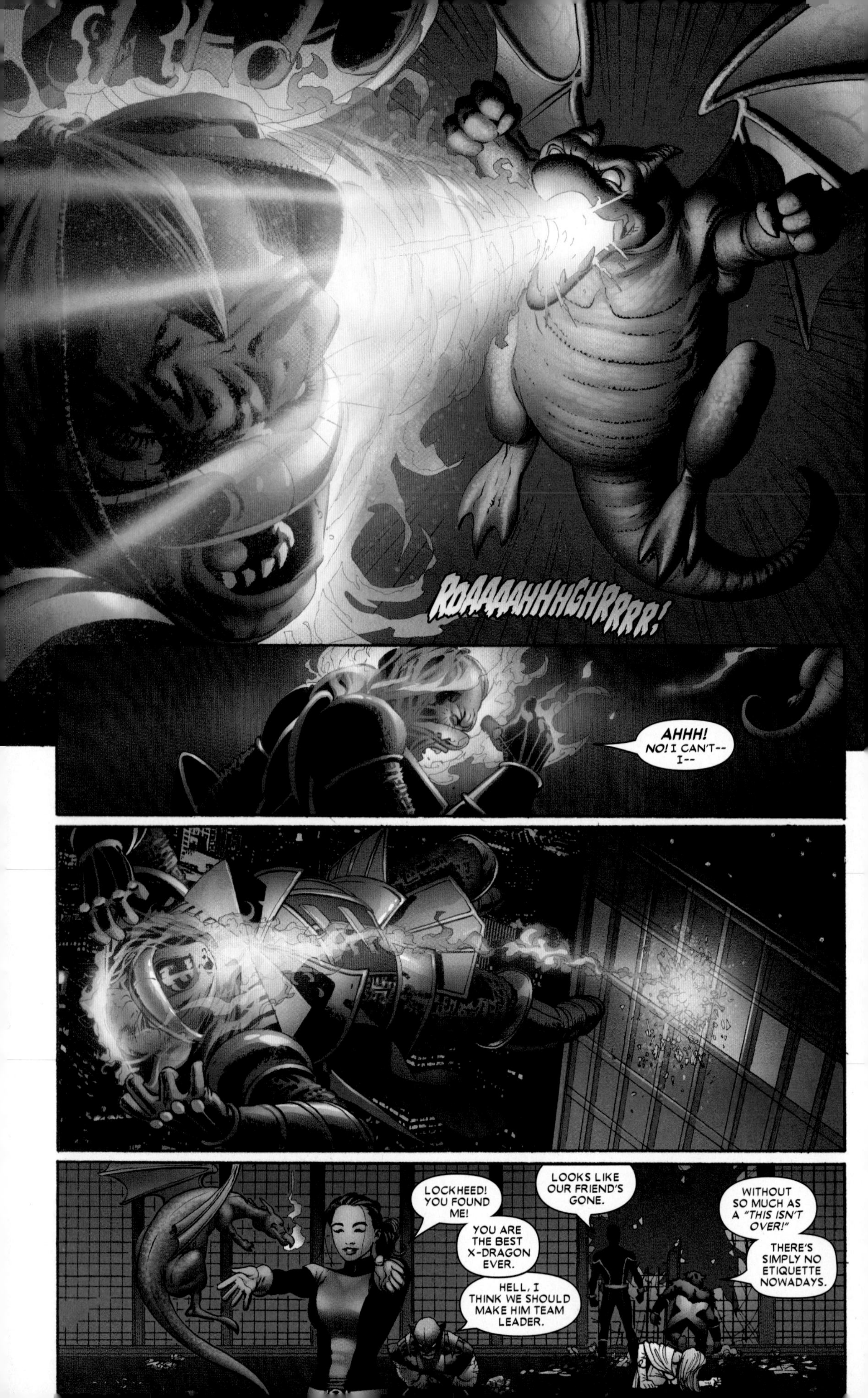
ROAAAAHHHGHRRRR!
AHHH! NO! I CAN'T-- I--
LOCKHEED! YOU FOUND ME!
YOU ARE THE BEST X-DRAGON EVER.
HELL, I THINK WE SHOULD MAKE HIM TEAM LEADER.
LOOKS LIKE OUR FRIEND'S GONE.
WITHOUT SO MUCH AS A "THIS ISN'T OVER!"
THERE'S SIMPLY NO ETIQUETTE NOWADAYS.

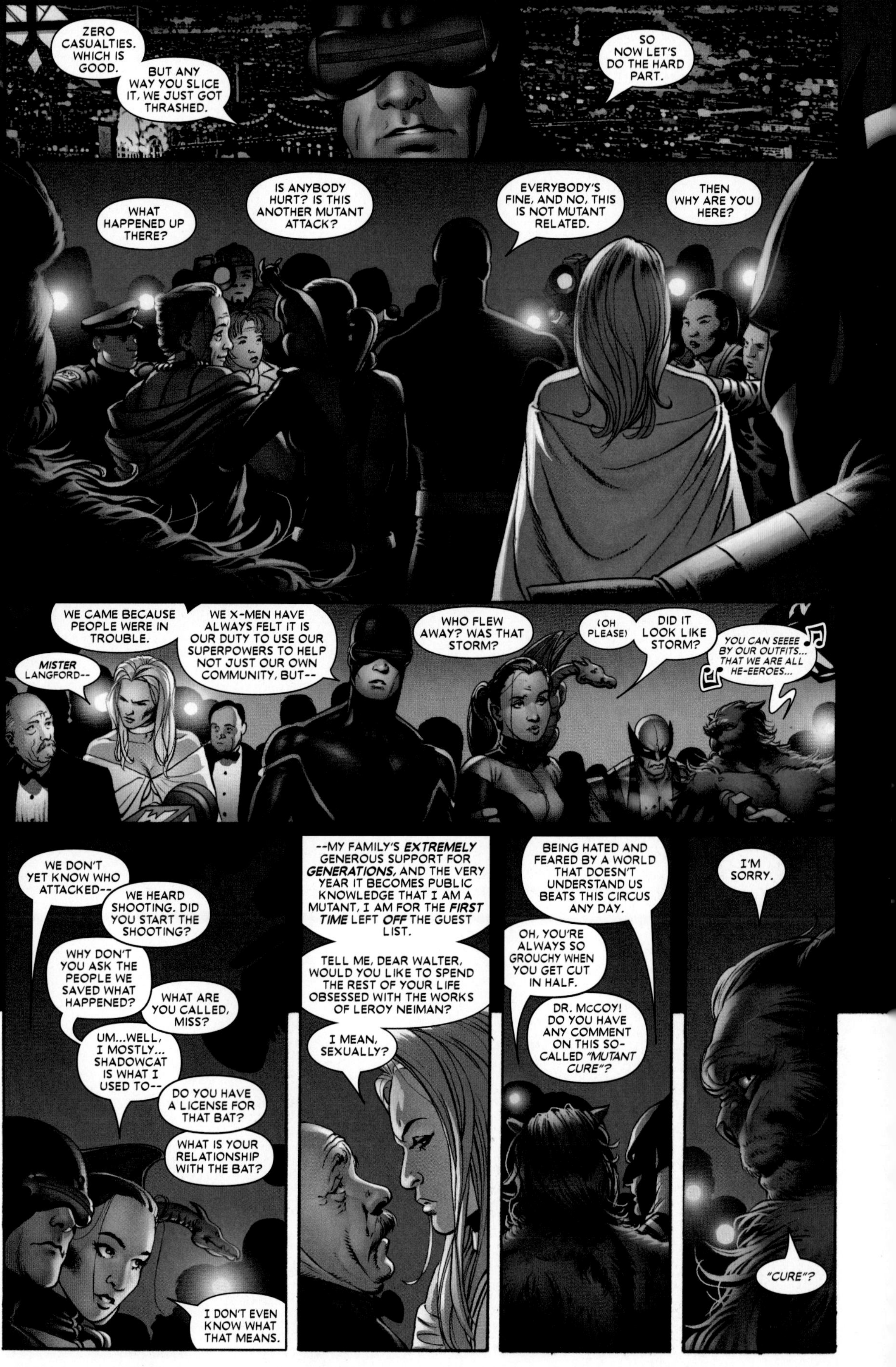
ZERO CASUALTIES. WHICH IS GOOD.
BUT ANY WAY YOU SLICE IT, WE JUST GOT THRASHED.
SO NOW LET'S DO THE HARD PART.
WHAT HAPPENED UP THERE?
IS ANYBODY HURT? IS THIS ANOTHER MUTANT ATTACK?
EVERYBODY'S FINE, AND NO, THIS IS NOT MUTANT RELATED.
THEN WHY ARE YOU HERE?
WE CAME BECAUSE PEOPLE WERE IN TROUBLE.
WE X-MEN HAVE ALWAYS FELT IT IS OUR DUTY TO USE OUR SUPERPOWERS TO HELP NOT JUST OUR OWN COMMUNITY, BUT--
MISTER LANGFORD--
WHO FLEW AWAY? WAS THAT STORM?
(OH PLEASE)
DID IT LOOK LIKE STORM?
YOU CAN SEEEE BY OUR OUTFITS... THAT WE ARE ALL HE-EEROES...
WE DON'T YET KNOW WHO ATTACKED--
WE HEARD SHOOTING. DID YOU START THE SHOOTING?
WHY DON'T YOU ASK THE PEOPLE WE SAVED WHAT HAPPENED?
WHAT ARE YOU CALLED, MISS?
UM...WELL, I MOSTLY... SHADOWCAT IS WHAT I USED TO--
DO YOU HAVE A LICENSE FOR THAT BAT?
WHAT IS YOUR RELATIONSHIP WITH THE BAT?
I DON'T EVEN KNOW WHAT THAT MEANS.
--MY FAMILY'S *EXTREMELY* GENEROUS SUPPORT FOR *GENERATIONS,* AND THE VERY YEAR IT BECOMES PUBLIC KNOWLEDGE THAT I AM A MUTANT, I AM FOR THE *FIRST TIME* LEFT *OFF* THE GUEST LIST.
TELL ME, DEAR WALTER, WOULD YOU LIKE TO SPEND THE REST OF YOUR LIFE OBSESSED WITH THE WORKS OF LEROY NEIMAN?
I MEAN, SEXUALLY?
BEING HATED AND FEARED BY A WORLD THAT DOESN'T UNDERSTAND US BEATS THIS CIRCUS ANY DAY.
OH, YOU'RE ALWAYS SO GROUCHY WHEN YOU GET CUT IN HALF.
DR. McCOY! DO YOU HAVE ANY COMMENT ON THIS SO-CALLED *"MUTANT CURE"*?
I'M SORRY.
"CURE"?

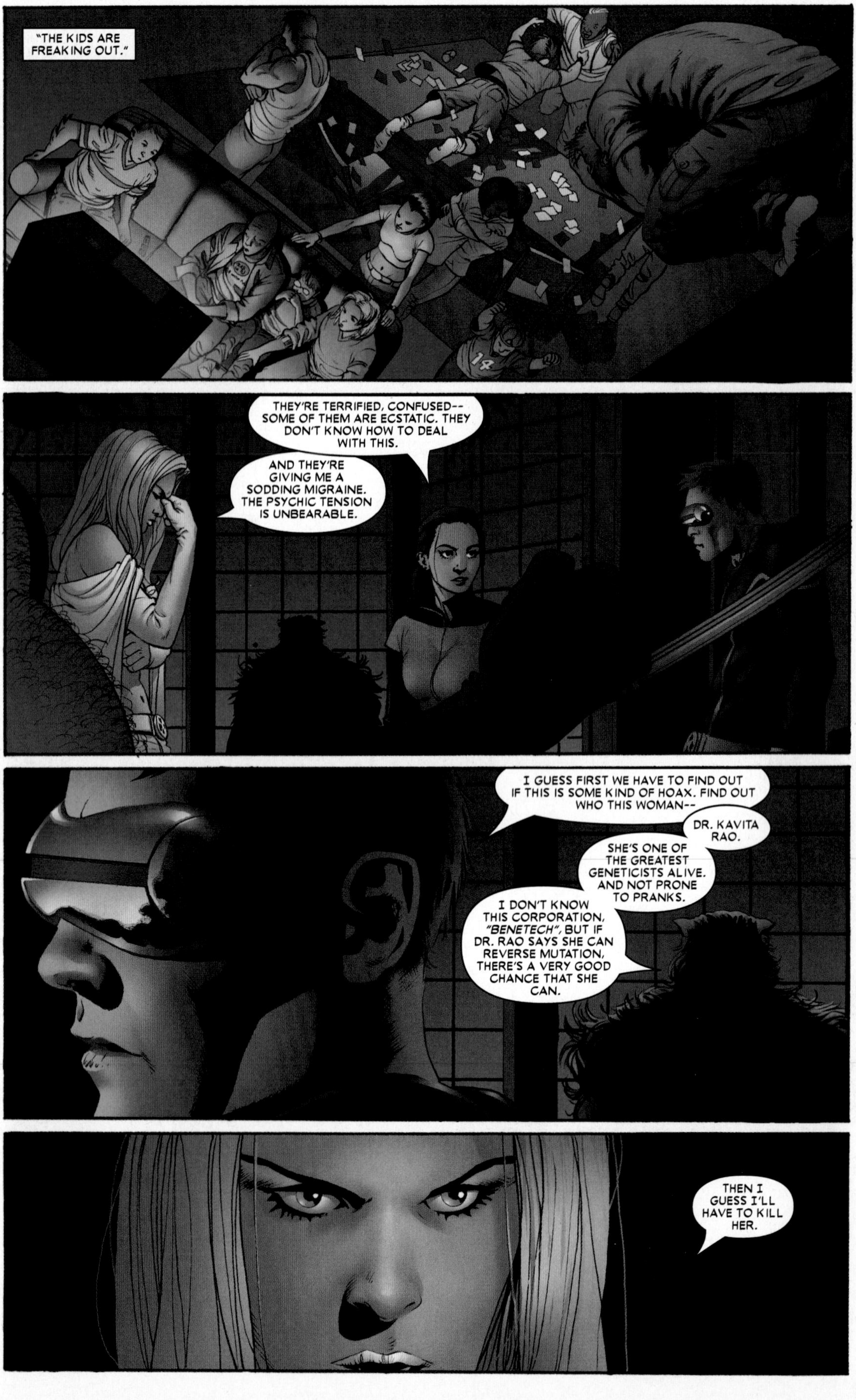
"THE KIDS ARE FREAKING OUT."
THEY'RE TERRIFIED, CONFUSED-- SOME OF THEM ARE ECSTATIC. THEY DON'T KNOW HOW TO DEAL WITH THIS.
AND THEY'RE GIVING ME A SODDING MIGRAINE. THE PSYCHIC TENSION IS UNBEARABLE.
I GUESS FIRST WE HAVE TO FIND OUT IF THIS IS SOME KIND OF HOAX. FIND OUT WHO THIS WOMAN--
DR. KAVITA RAO.
SHE'S ONE OF THE GREATEST GENETICISTS ALIVE. AND NOT PRONE TO PRANKS.
I DON'T KNOW THIS CORPORATION, *"BENETECH"*, BUT IF DR. RAO SAYS SHE CAN REVERSE MUTATION, THERE'S A VERY GOOD CHANCE THAT SHE CAN.
THEN I GUESS I'LL HAVE TO KILL HER.

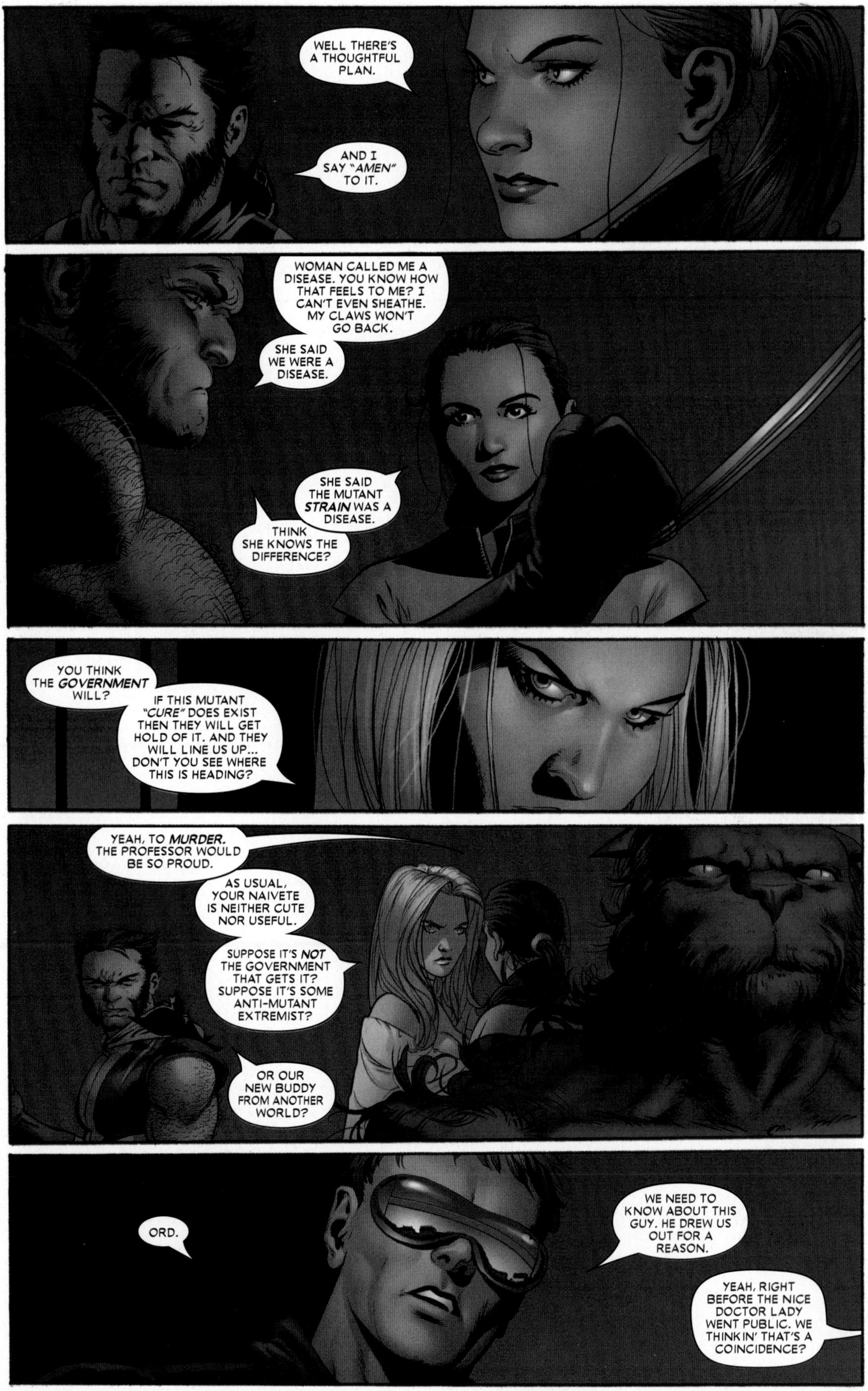
WELL THERE'S A THOUGHTFUL PLAN.
AND I SAY "AMEN" TO IT.
WOMAN CALLED ME A DISEASE. YOU KNOW HOW THAT FEELS TO ME? I CAN'T EVEN SHEATHE. MY CLAWS WON'T GO BACK.
SHE SAID WE WERE A DISEASE.
SHE SAID THE MUTANT STRAIN WAS A DISEASE.
THINK SHE KNOWS THE DIFFERENCE?
YOU THINK THE GOVERNMENT WILL?
IF THIS MUTANT "CURE" DOES EXIST THEN THEY WILL GET HOLD OF IT. AND THEY WILL LINE US UP... DON'T YOU SEE WHERE THIS IS HEADING?
YEAH, TO MURDER. THE PROFESSOR WOULD BE SO PROUD.
AS USUAL, YOUR NAIVETE IS NEITHER CUTE NOR USEFUL.
SUPPOSE IT'S NOT THE GOVERNMENT THAT GETS IT? SUPPOSE IT'S SOME ANTI-MUTANT EXTREMIST?
OR OUR NEW BUDDY FROM ANOTHER WORLD?
ORD.
WE NEED TO KNOW ABOUT THIS GUY. HE DREW US OUT FOR A REASON.
YEAH, RIGHT BEFORE THE NICE DOCTOR LADY WENT PUBLIC. WE THINKIN' THAT'S A COINCIDENCE?

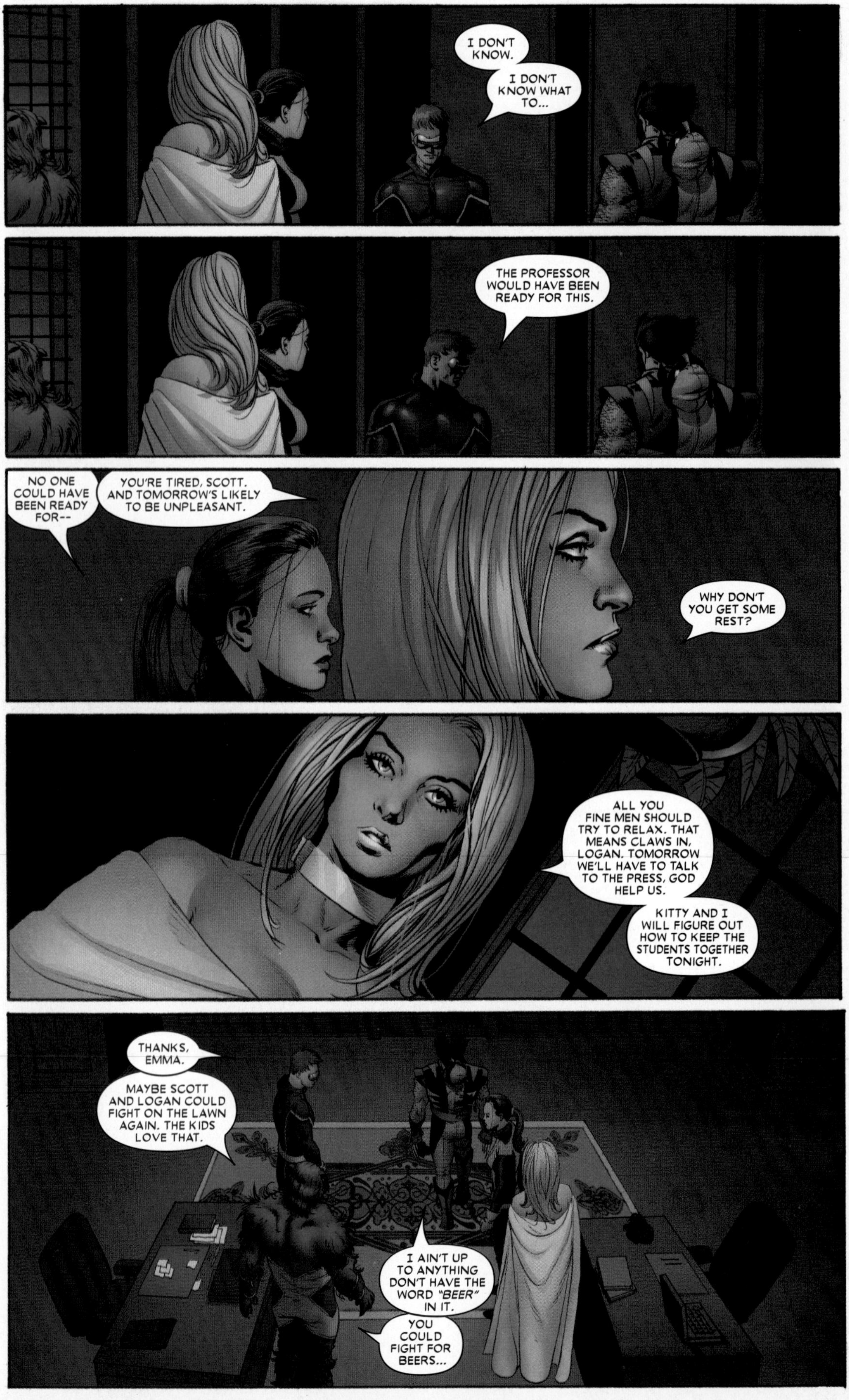
I DON'T KNOW.
I DON'T KNOW WHAT TO...
THE PROFESSOR WOULD HAVE BEEN READY FOR THIS.
NO ONE COULD HAVE BEEN READY FOR--
YOU'RE TIRED, SCOTT. AND TOMORROW'S LIKELY TO BE UNPLEASANT.
WHY DON'T YOU GET SOME REST?
ALL YOU FINE MEN SHOULD TRY TO RELAX. THAT MEANS CLAWS IN, LOGAN. TOMORROW WE'LL HAVE TO TALK TO THE PRESS, GOD HELP US.
KITTY AND I WILL FIGURE OUT HOW TO KEEP THE STUDENTS TOGETHER TONIGHT.
THANKS, EMMA.
MAYBE SCOTT AND LOGAN COULD FIGHT ON THE LAWN AGAIN. THE KIDS LOVE THAT.
I AIN'T UP TO ANYTHING DON'T HAVE THE WORD *"BEER"* IN IT.
YOU COULD FIGHT FOR BEERS...

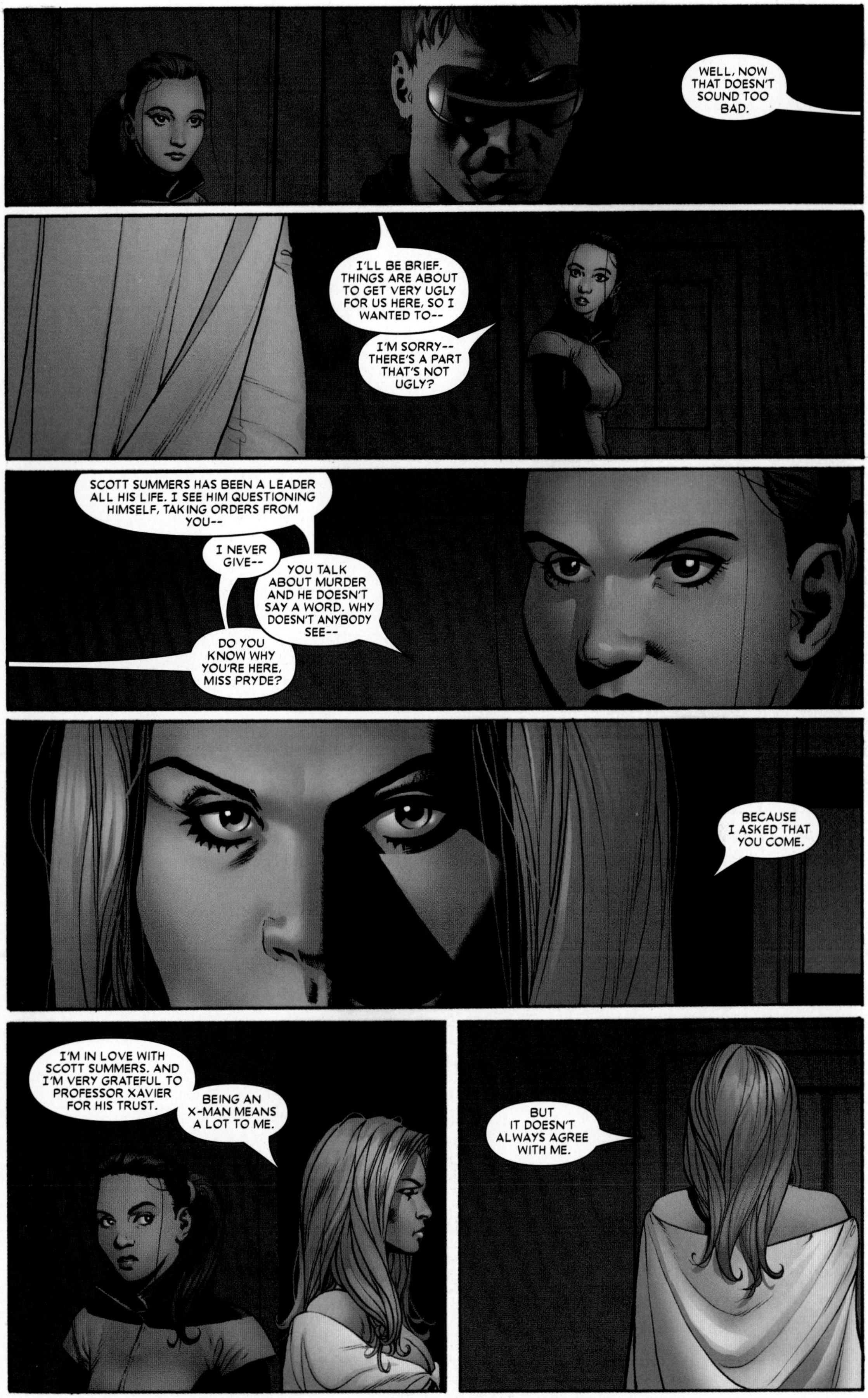
WELL, NOW THAT DOESN'T SOUND TOO BAD.
I'LL BE BRIEF. THINGS ARE ABOUT TO GET VERY UGLY FOR US HERE, SO I WANTED TO--
I'M SORRY-- THERE'S A PART THAT'S NOT UGLY?
SCOTT SUMMERS HAS BEEN A LEADER ALL HIS LIFE. I SEE HIM QUESTIONING HIMSELF, TAKING ORDERS FROM YOU--
I NEVER GIVE--
YOU TALK ABOUT MURDER AND HE DOESN'T SAY A WORD. WHY DOESN'T ANYBODY SEE--
DO YOU KNOW WHY YOU'RE HERE, MISS PRYDE?
BECAUSE I ASKED THAT YOU COME.
I'M IN LOVE WITH SCOTT SUMMERS. AND I'M VERY GRATEFUL TO PROFESSOR XAVIER FOR HIS TRUST.
BEING AN X-MAN MEANS A LOT TO ME.
BUT IT DOESN'T ALWAYS AGREE WITH ME.

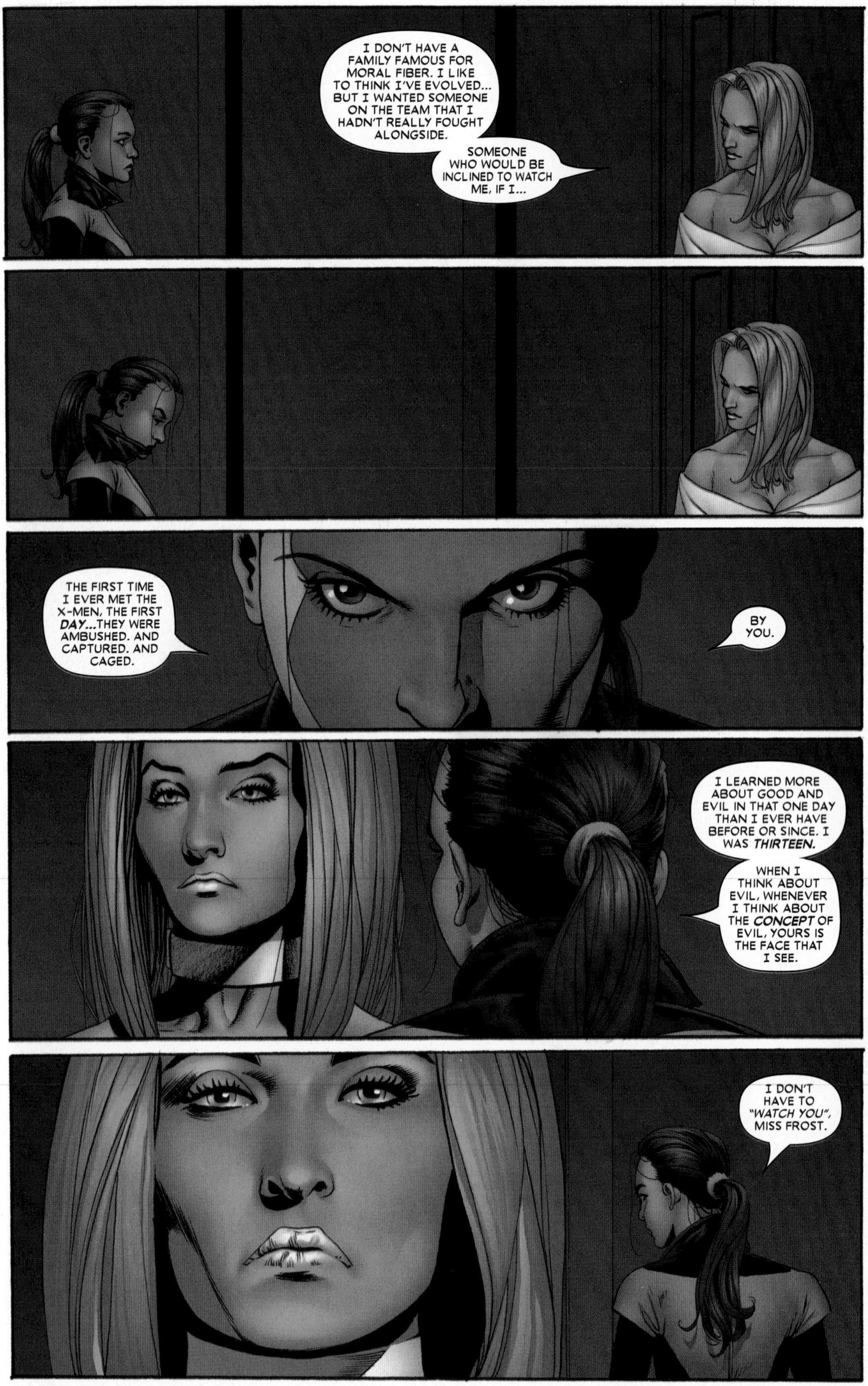
I DON'T HAVE A FAMILY FAMOUS FOR MORAL FIBER. I LIKE TO THINK I'VE EVOLVED... BUT I WANTED SOMEONE ON THE TEAM THAT I HADN'T REALLY FOUGHT ALONGSIDE.
SOMEONE WHO WOULD BE INCLINED TO WATCH ME, IF I...
THE FIRST TIME I EVER MET THE X-MEN, THE FIRST *DAY*...THEY WERE AMBUSHED. AND CAPTURED. AND CAGED.
BY YOU.
I LEARNED MORE ABOUT GOOD AND EVIL IN THAT ONE DAY THAN I EVER HAVE BEFORE OR SINCE. I WAS ***THIRTEEN.***
WHEN I THINK ABOUT EVIL, WHENEVER I THINK ABOUT THE ***CONCEPT*** OF EVIL, YOURS IS THE FACE THAT I SEE.
I DON'T HAVE TO *"WATCH YOU"*, MISS FROST.

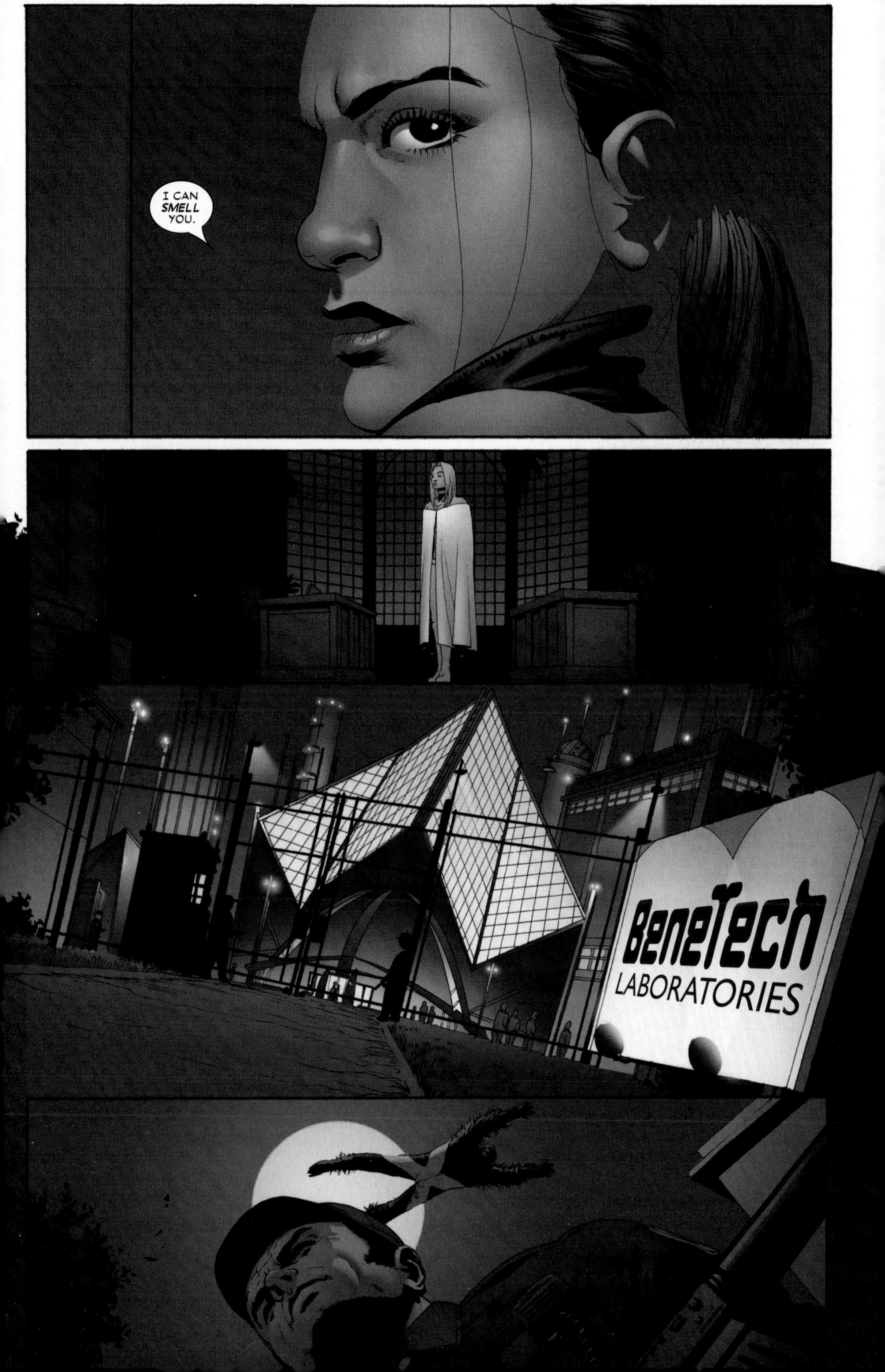
I CAN SMELL YOU.
BeneTech
LABORATORIES

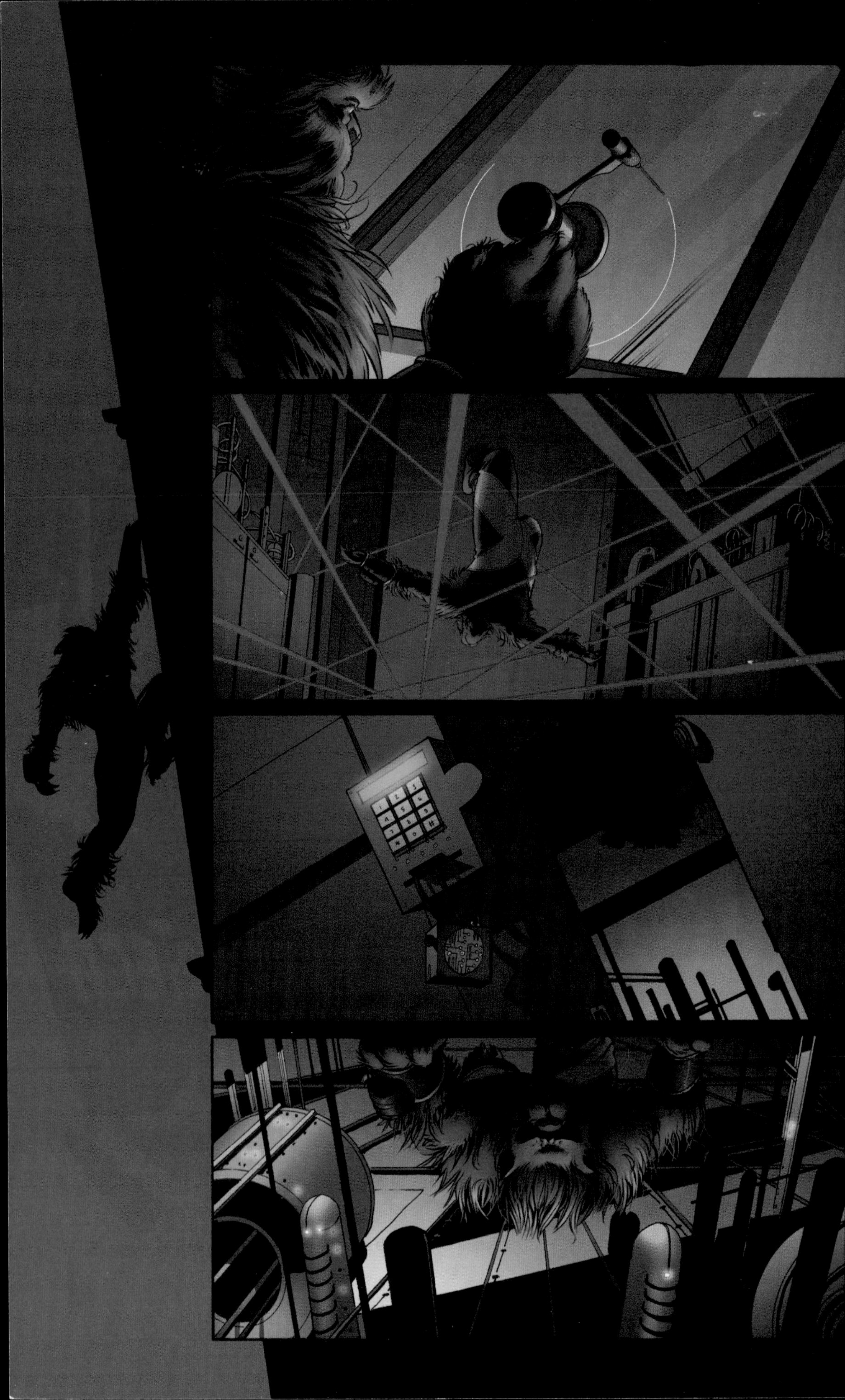

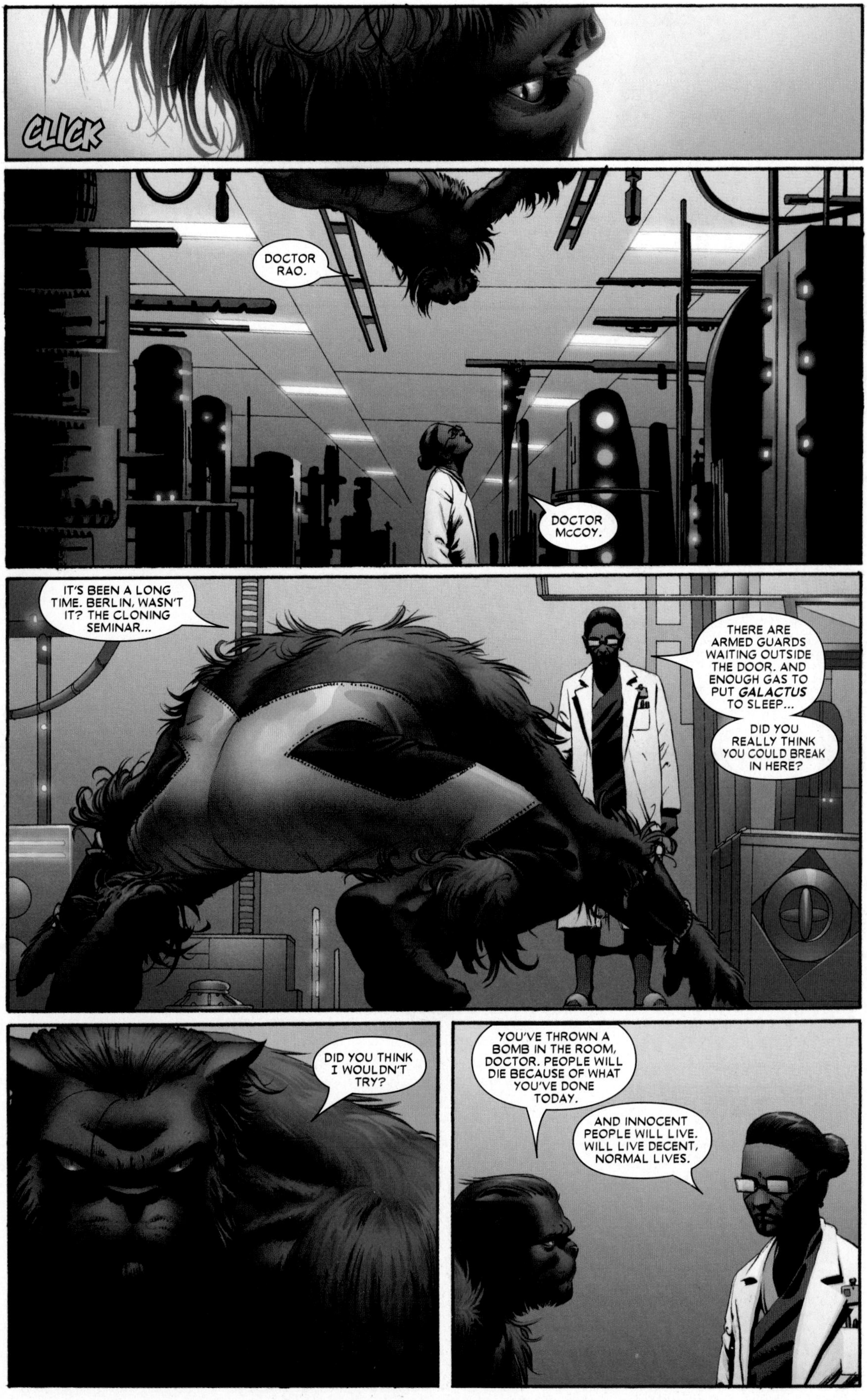
CLICK
DOCTOR RAO.
DOCTOR McCOY.
IT'S BEEN A LONG TIME. BERLIN, WASN'T IT? THE CLONING SEMINAR...
THERE ARE ARMED GUARDS WAITING OUTSIDE THE DOOR. AND ENOUGH GAS TO PUT *GALACTUS* TO SLEEP...
DID YOU REALLY THINK YOU COULD BREAK IN HERE?
DID YOU THINK I WOULDN'T TRY?
YOU'VE THROWN A BOMB IN THE ROOM, DOCTOR. PEOPLE WILL DIE BECAUSE OF WHAT YOU'VE DONE TODAY.
AND INNOCENT PEOPLE WILL LIVE. WILL LIVE DECENT, NORMAL LIVES.

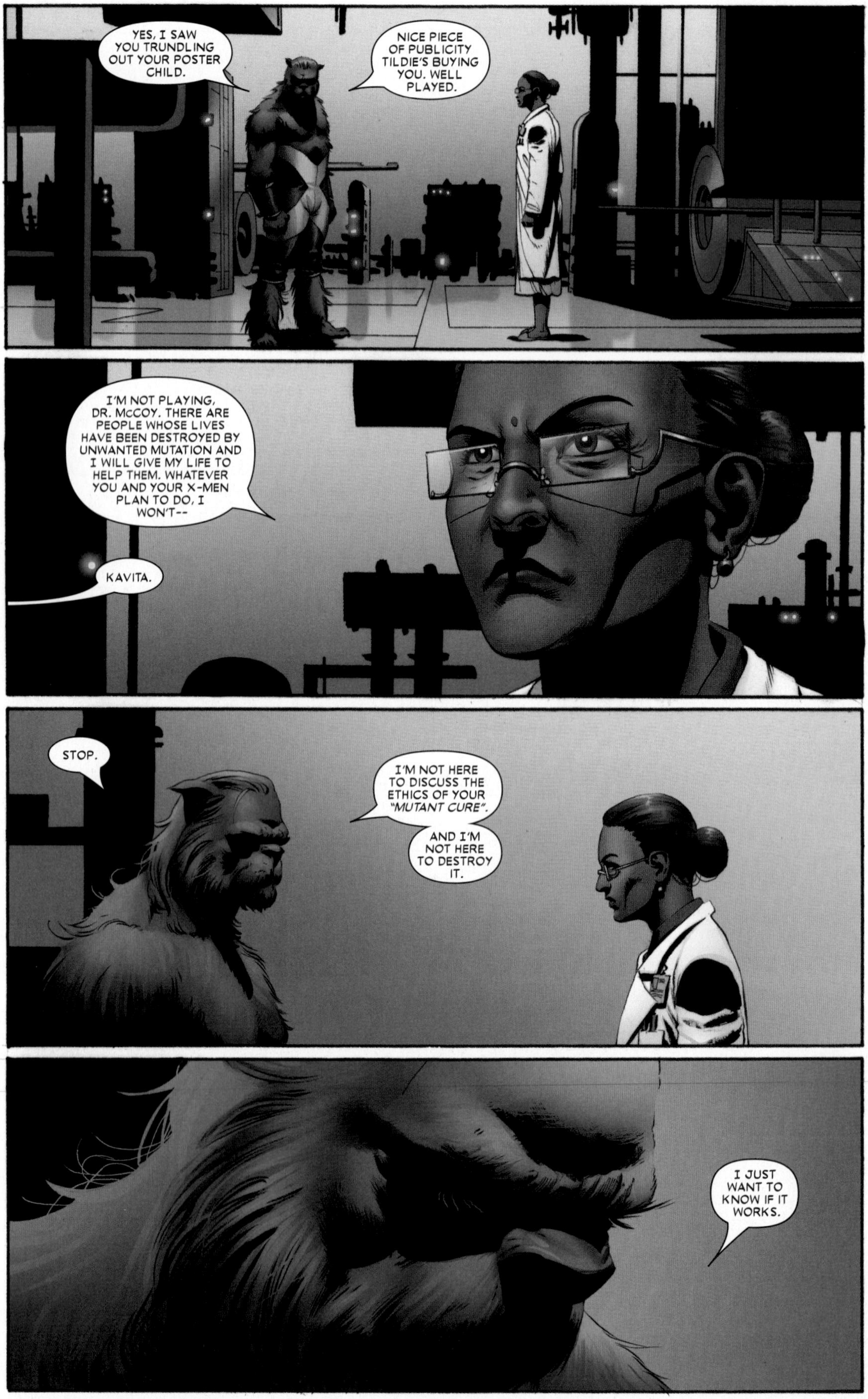
YES, I SAW YOU TRUNDLING OUT YOUR POSTER CHILD.
NICE PIECE OF PUBLICITY TILDIE'S BUYING YOU. WELL PLAYED.
I'M NOT PLAYING, DR. McCOY. THERE ARE PEOPLE WHOSE LIVES HAVE BEEN DESTROYED BY UNWANTED MUTATION AND I WILL GIVE MY LIFE TO HELP THEM. WHATEVER YOU AND YOUR X-MEN PLAN TO DO, I WON'T--
KAVITA.
STOP.
I'M NOT HERE TO DISCUSS THE ETHICS OF YOUR *"MUTANT CURE"*.
AND I'M NOT HERE TO DESTROY IT.
I JUST WANT TO KNOW IF IT WORKS.

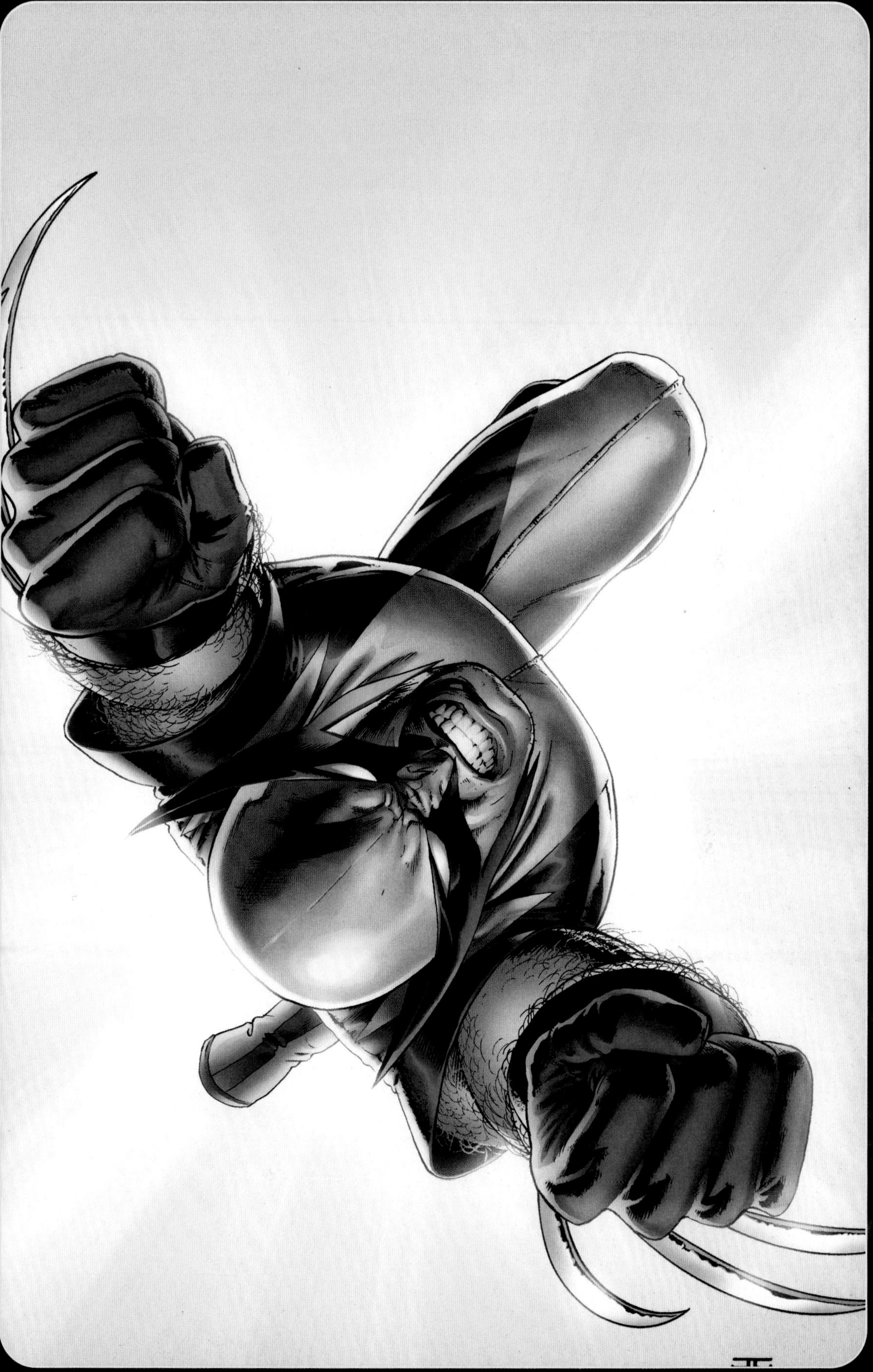

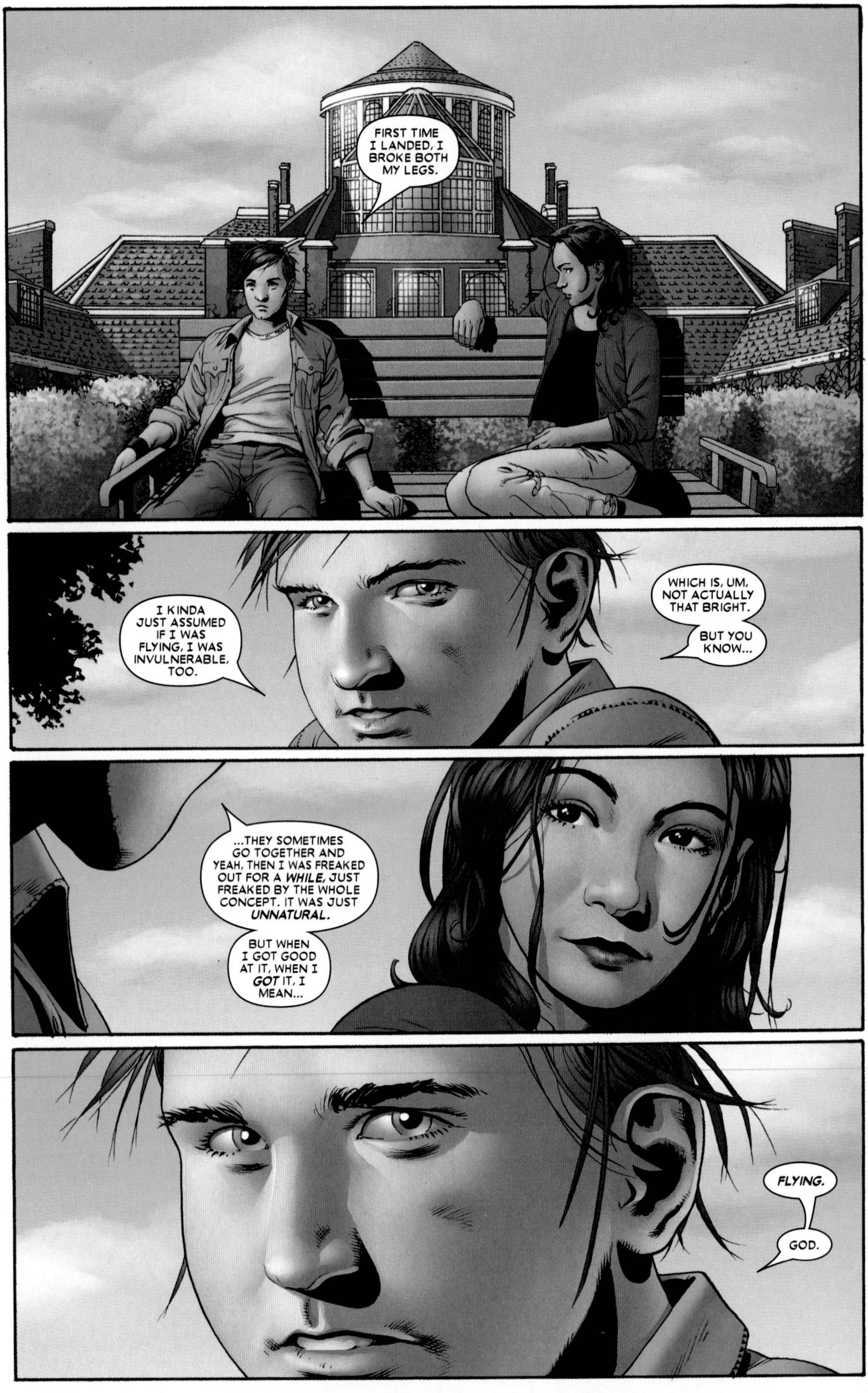
FIRST TIME I LANDED, I BROKE BOTH MY LEGS.
I KINDA JUST ASSUMED IF I WAS FLYING, I WAS INVULNERABLE, TOO.
WHICH IS, UM, NOT ACTUALLY THAT BRIGHT.
BUT YOU KNOW...
...THEY SOMETIMES GO TOGETHER AND YEAH, THEN I WAS FREAKED OUT FOR A *WHILE,* JUST FREAKED BY THE WHOLE CONCEPT. IT WAS JUST ***UNNATURAL.***
BUT WHEN I GOT GOOD AT IT, WHEN I ***GOT*** IT, I MEAN...
FLYING.
GOD.

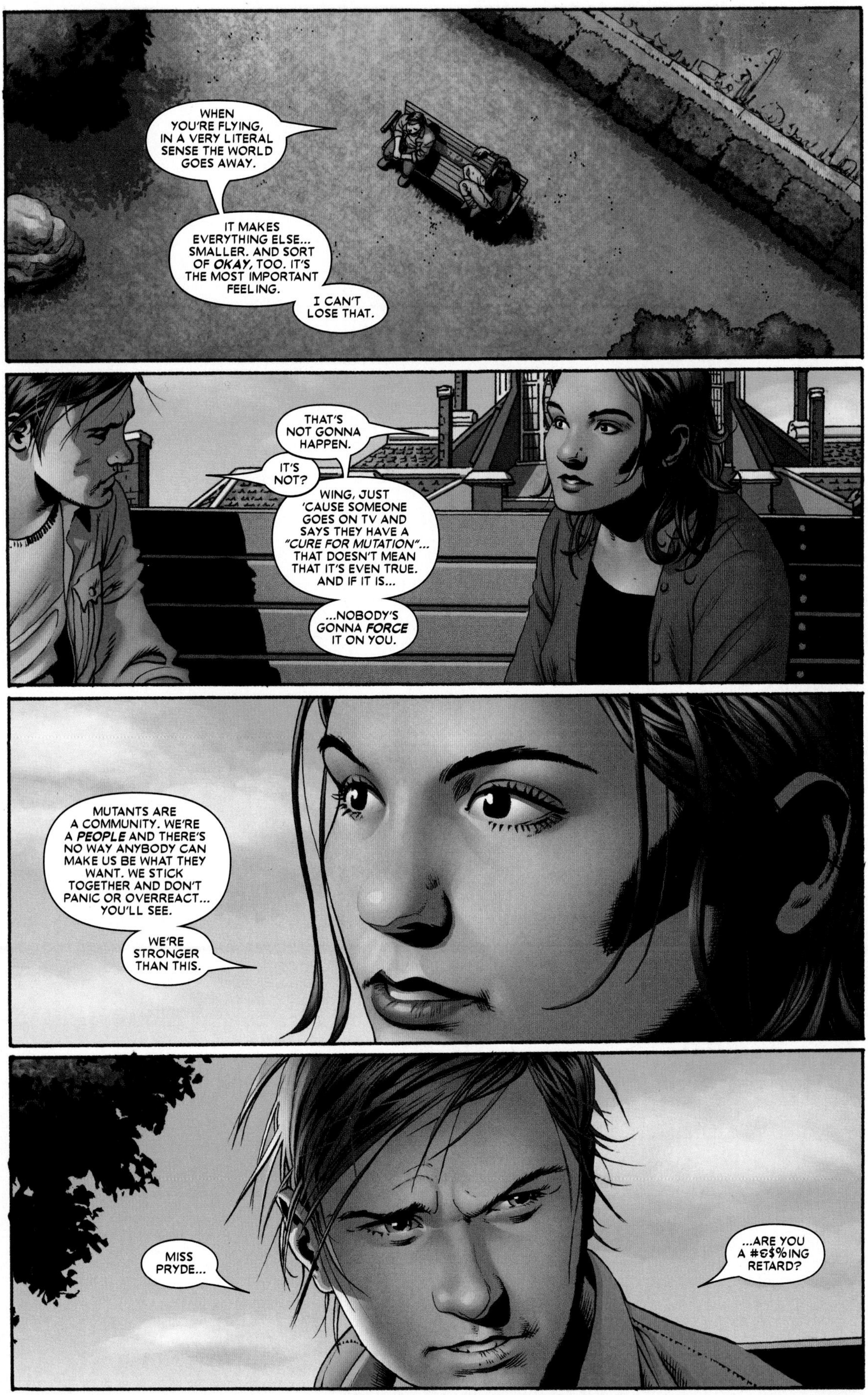
WHEN YOU'RE FLYING, IN A VERY LITERAL SENSE THE WORLD GOES AWAY.
IT MAKES EVERYTHING ELSE... SMALLER. AND SORT OF *OKAY,* TOO. IT'S THE MOST IMPORTANT FEELING.
I CAN'T LOSE THAT.
THAT'S NOT GONNA HAPPEN.
IT'S NOT?
WING, JUST 'CAUSE SOMEONE GOES ON TV AND SAYS THEY HAVE A *"CURE FOR MUTATION"*... THAT DOESN'T MEAN THAT IT'S EVEN TRUE. AND IF IT IS...
...NOBODY'S GONNA *FORCE* IT ON YOU.
MUTANTS ARE A COMMUNITY. WE'RE A *PEOPLE* AND THERE'S NO WAY ANYBODY CAN MAKE US BE WHAT THEY WANT. WE STICK TOGETHER AND DON'T PANIC OR OVERREACT... YOU'LL SEE.
WE'RE STRONGER THAN THIS.
MISS PRYDE...
...ARE YOU A #&$%ING RETARD?

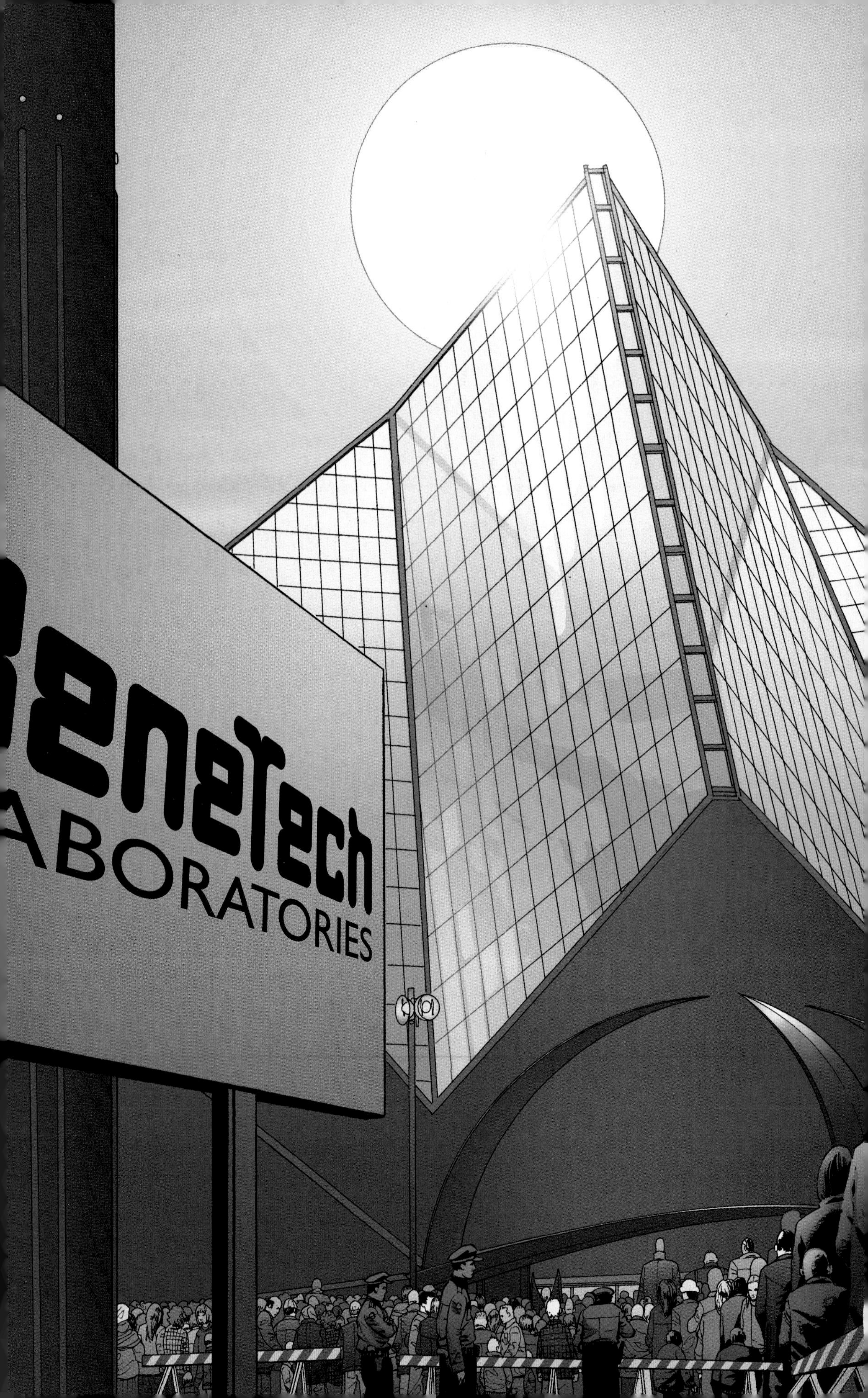
enetech
ABORATORIES

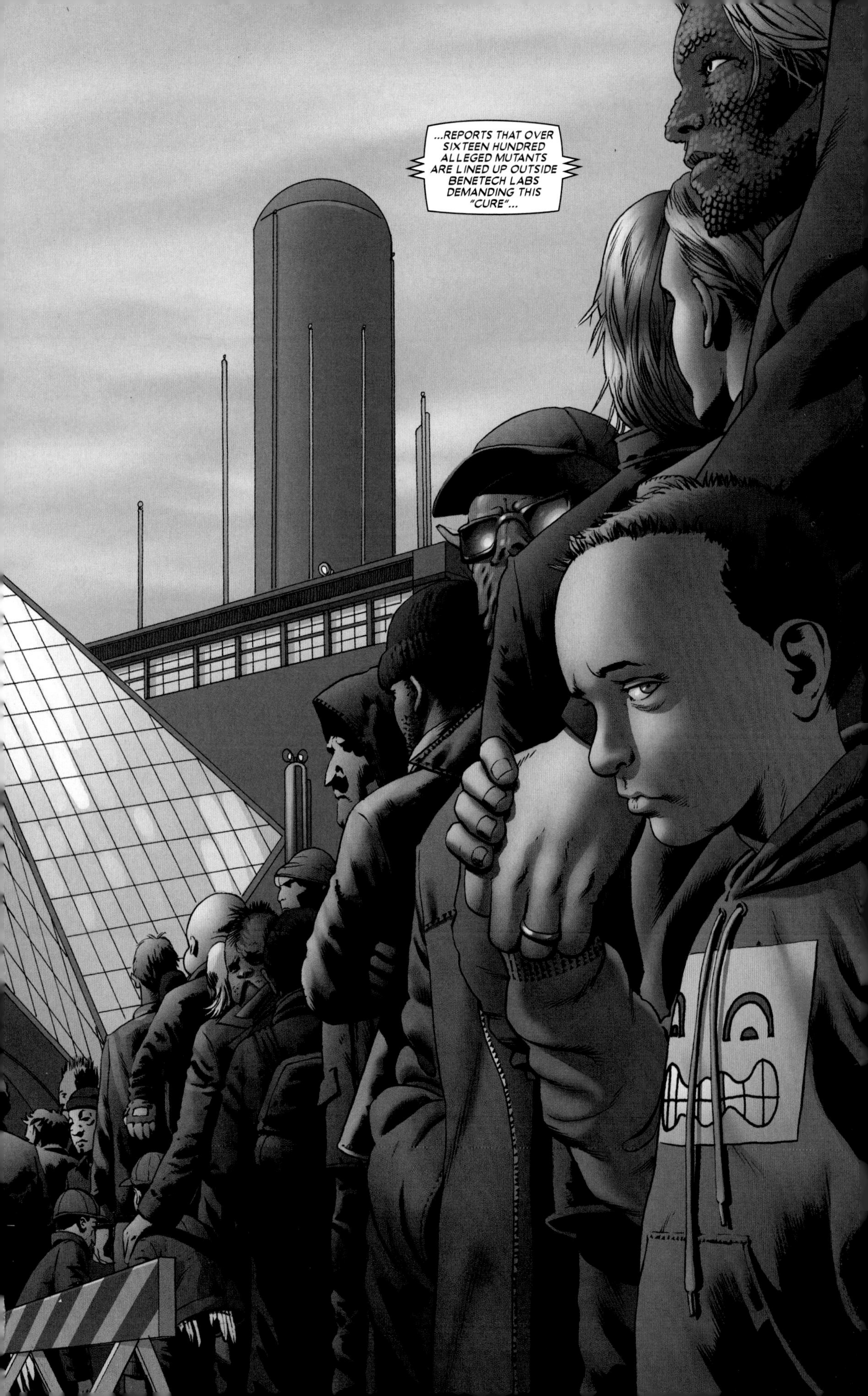
...REPORTS THAT OVER SIXTEEN HUNDRED ALLEGED MUTANTS ARE LINED UP OUTSIDE BENETECH LABS DEMANDING THIS "CURE"...

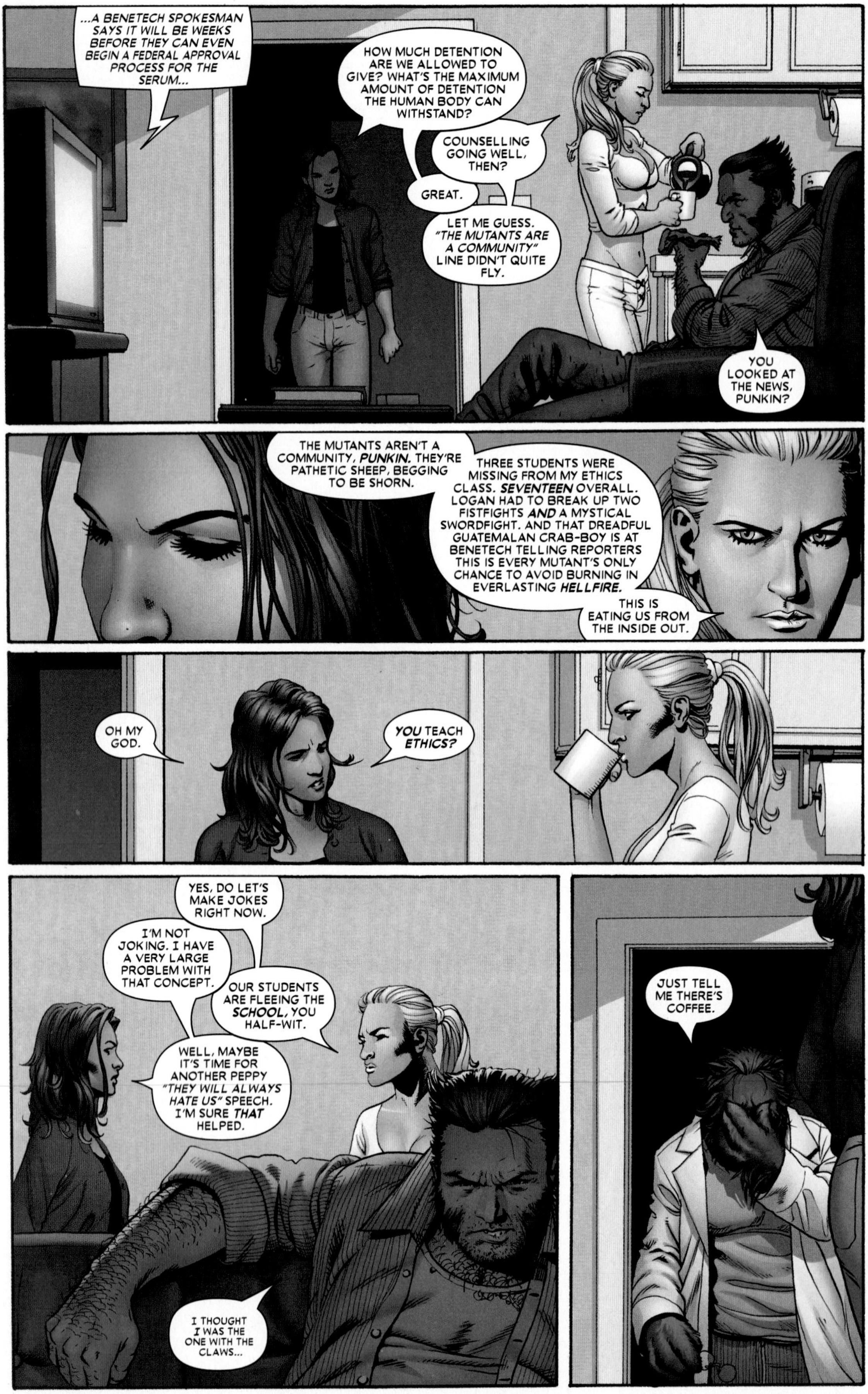
...A BENETECH SPOKESMAN SAYS IT WILL BE WEEKS BEFORE THEY CAN EVEN BEGIN A FEDERAL APPROVAL PROCESS FOR THE SERUM...
HOW MUCH DETENTION ARE WE ALLOWED TO GIVE? WHAT'S THE MAXIMUM AMOUNT OF DETENTION THE HUMAN BODY CAN WITHSTAND?
COUNSELLING GOING WELL, THEN?
GREAT.
LET ME GUESS. "THE MUTANTS ARE A COMMUNITY" LINE DIDN'T QUITE FLY.
YOU LOOKED AT THE NEWS, PUNKIN?
THE MUTANTS AREN'T A COMMUNITY, PUNKIN. THEY'RE PATHETIC SHEEP, BEGGING TO BE SHORN.
THREE STUDENTS WERE MISSING FROM MY ETHICS CLASS. SEVENTEEN OVERALL. LOGAN HAD TO BREAK UP TWO FISTFIGHTS AND A MYSTICAL SWORDFIGHT. AND THAT DREADFUL GUATEMALAN CRAB-BOY IS AT BENETECH TELLING REPORTERS THIS IS EVERY MUTANT'S ONLY CHANCE TO AVOID BURNING IN EVERLASTING HELLFIRE.
THIS IS EATING US FROM THE INSIDE OUT.
OH MY GOD.
YOU TEACH ETHICS?
YES, DO LET'S MAKE JOKES RIGHT NOW.
I'M NOT JOKING. I HAVE A VERY LARGE PROBLEM WITH THAT CONCEPT.
OUR STUDENTS ARE FLEEING THE SCHOOL, YOU HALF-WIT.
WELL, MAYBE IT'S TIME FOR ANOTHER PEPPY "THEY WILL ALWAYS HATE US" SPEECH. I'M SURE THAT HELPED.
I THOUGHT I WAS THE ONE WITH THE CLAWS...
JUST TELL ME THERE'S COFFEE.

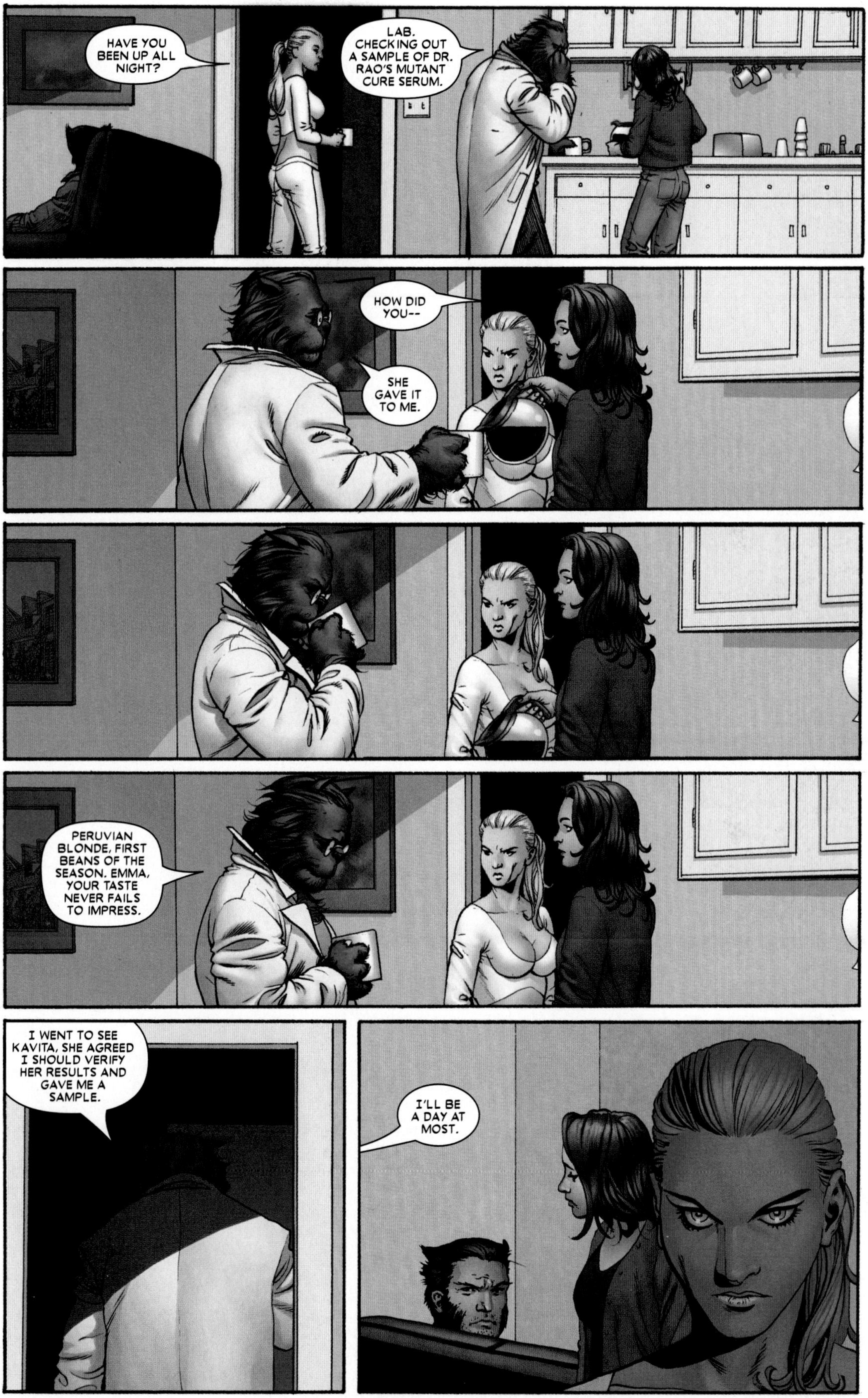

HAVE YOU BEEN UP ALL NIGHT?
LAB. CHECKING OUT A SAMPLE OF DR. RAO'S MUTANT CURE SERUM.
HOW DID YOU--
SHE GAVE IT TO ME.
PERUVIAN BLONDE, FIRST BEANS OF THE SEASON. EMMA, YOUR TASTE NEVER FAILS TO IMPRESS.
I WENT TO SEE KAVITA, SHE AGREED I SHOULD VERIFY HER RESULTS AND GAVE ME A SAMPLE.
I'LL BE A DAY AT MOST.

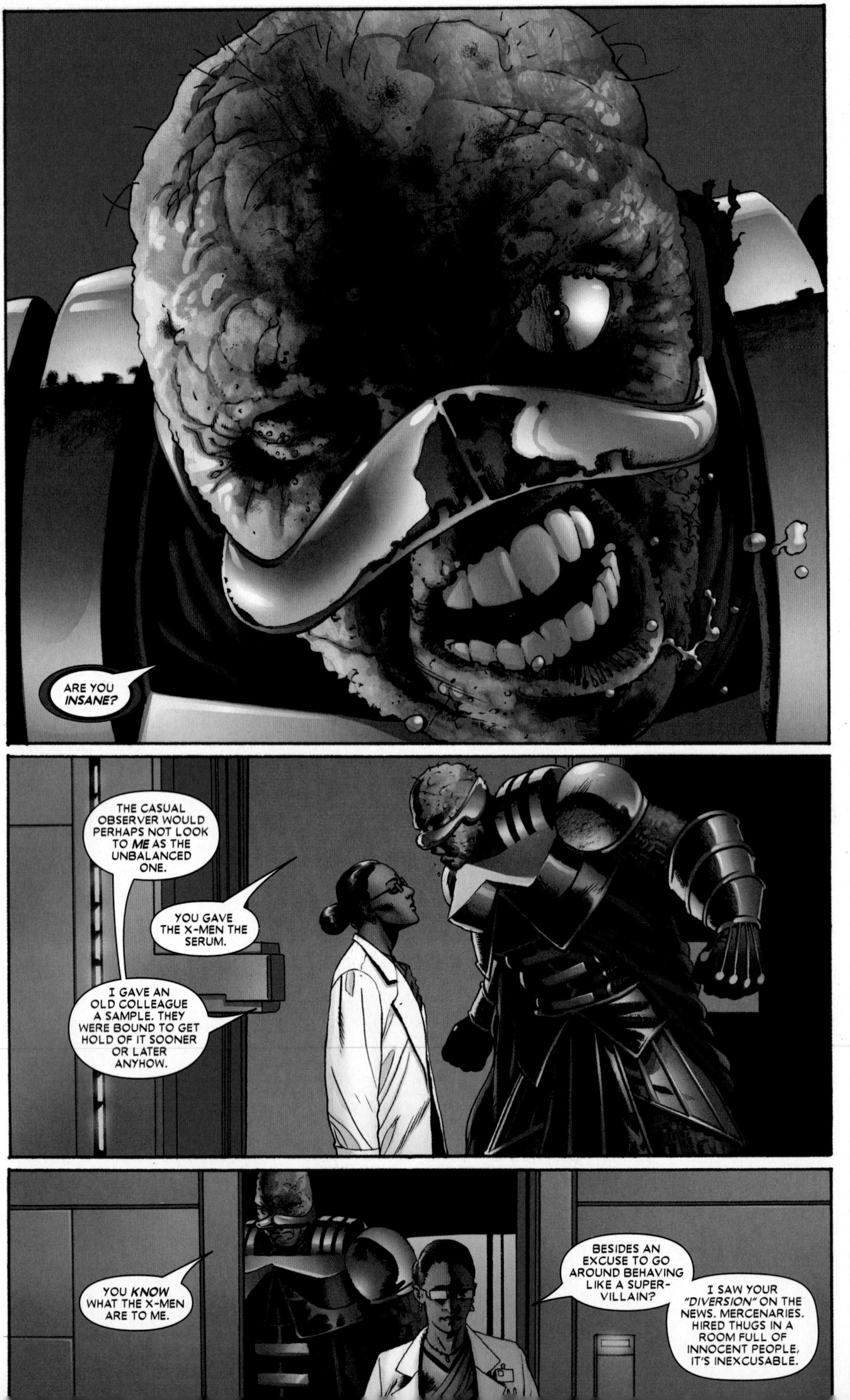
ARE YOU INSANE?
THE CASUAL OBSERVER WOULD PERHAPS NOT LOOK TO ME AS THE UNBALANCED ONE.
YOU GAVE THE X-MEN THE SERUM.
I GAVE AN OLD COLLEAGUE A SAMPLE. THEY WERE BOUND TO GET HOLD OF IT SOONER OR LATER ANYHOW.
YOU KNOW WHAT THE X-MEN ARE TO ME.
BESIDES AN EXCUSE TO GO AROUND BEHAVING LIKE A SUPER-VILLAIN?
I SAW YOUR "DIVERSION" ON THE NEWS. MERCENARIES. HIRED THUGS IN A ROOM FULL OF INNOCENT PEOPLE, IT'S INEXCUSABLE.

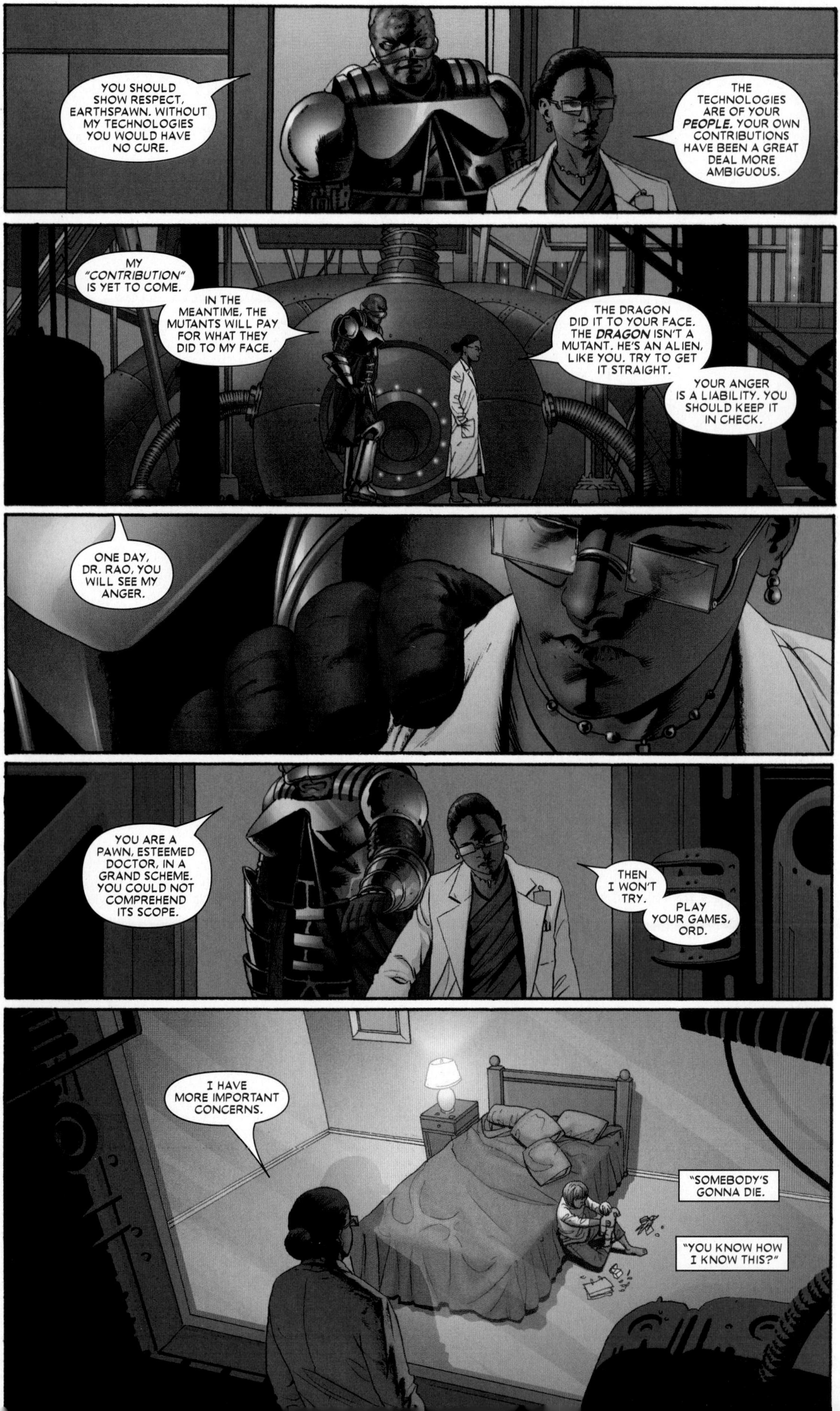
YOU SHOULD SHOW RESPECT, EARTHSPAWN. WITHOUT MY TECHNOLOGIES YOU WOULD HAVE NO CURE.
THE TECHNOLOGIES ARE OF YOUR PEOPLE. YOUR OWN CONTRIBUTIONS HAVE BEEN A GREAT DEAL MORE AMBIGUOUS.
MY "CONTRIBUTION" IS YET TO COME.
IN THE MEANTIME, THE MUTANTS WILL PAY FOR WHAT THEY DID TO MY FACE.
THE DRAGON DID IT TO YOUR FACE. THE DRAGON ISN'T A MUTANT. HE'S AN ALIEN, LIKE YOU. TRY TO GET IT STRAIGHT.
YOUR ANGER IS A LIABILITY. YOU SHOULD KEEP IT IN CHECK.
ONE DAY, DR. RAO, YOU WILL SEE MY ANGER.
YOU ARE A PAWN, ESTEEMED DOCTOR, IN A GRAND SCHEME. YOU COULD NOT COMPREHEND ITS SCOPE.
THEN I WON'T TRY.
PLAY YOUR GAMES, ORD.
I HAVE MORE IMPORTANT CONCERNS.
"SOMEBODY'S GONNA DIE.
"YOU KNOW HOW I KNOW THIS?"

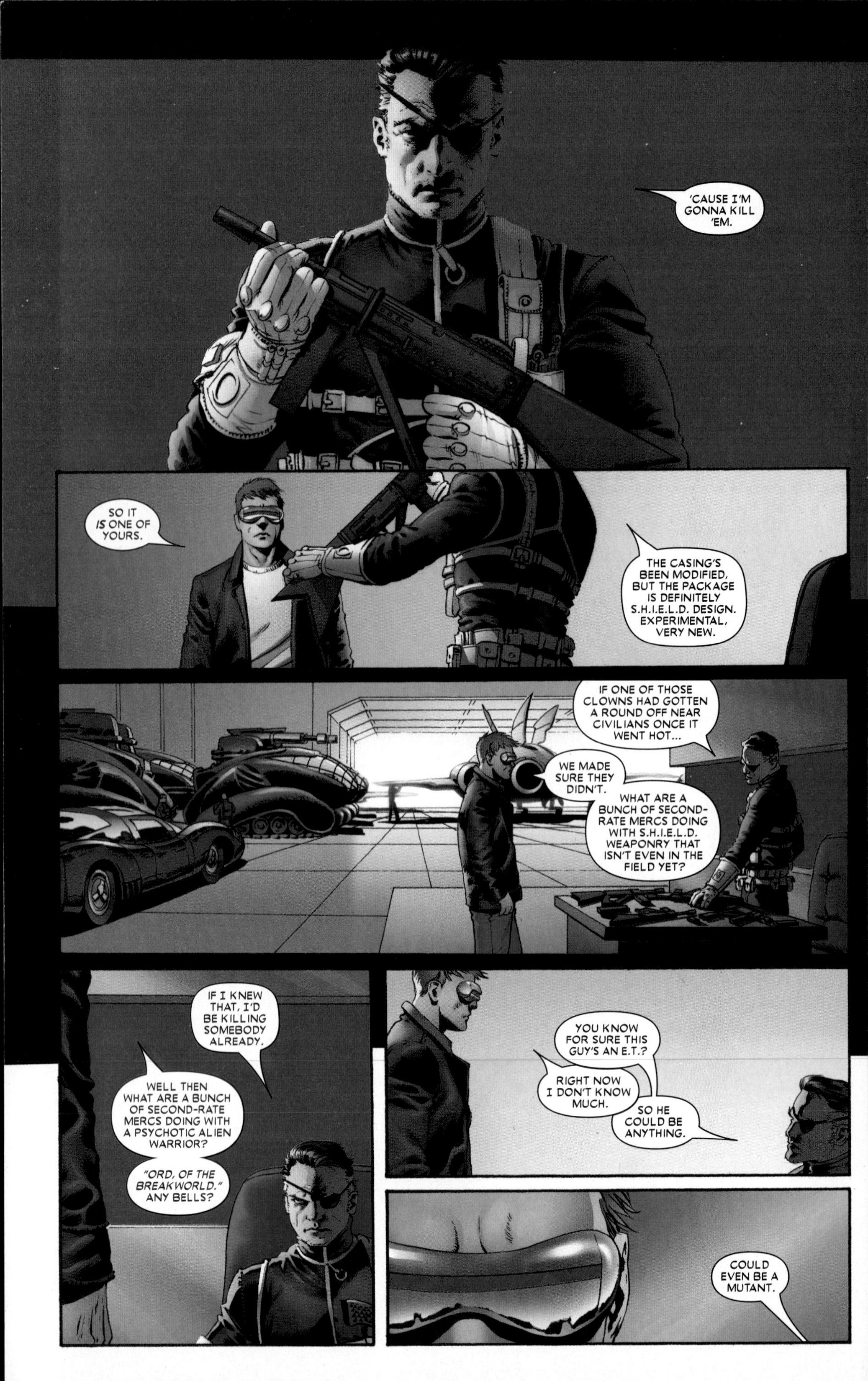
'CAUSE I'M GONNA KILL 'EM.
SO IT *IS* ONE OF YOURS.
THE CASING'S BEEN MODIFIED, BUT THE PACKAGE IS DEFINITELY S.H.I.E.L.D. DESIGN. EXPERIMENTAL, VERY NEW.
IF ONE OF THOSE CLOWNS HAD GOTTEN A ROUND OFF NEAR CIVILIANS ONCE IT WENT HOT...
WE MADE SURE THEY DIDN'T.
WHAT ARE A BUNCH OF SECOND-RATE MERCS DOING WITH S.H.I.E.L.D. WEAPONRY THAT ISN'T EVEN IN THE FIELD YET?
IF I KNEW THAT, I'D BE KILLING SOMEBODY ALREADY.
WELL THEN WHAT ARE A BUNCH OF SECOND-RATE MERCS DOING WITH A PSYCHOTIC ALIEN WARRIOR?
"ORD, OF THE *BREAKWORLD*." ANY BELLS?
YOU KNOW FOR SURE THIS GUY'S AN E.T.?
RIGHT NOW I DON'T KNOW MUCH.
SO HE COULD BE ANYTHING.
COULD EVEN BE A MUTANT.

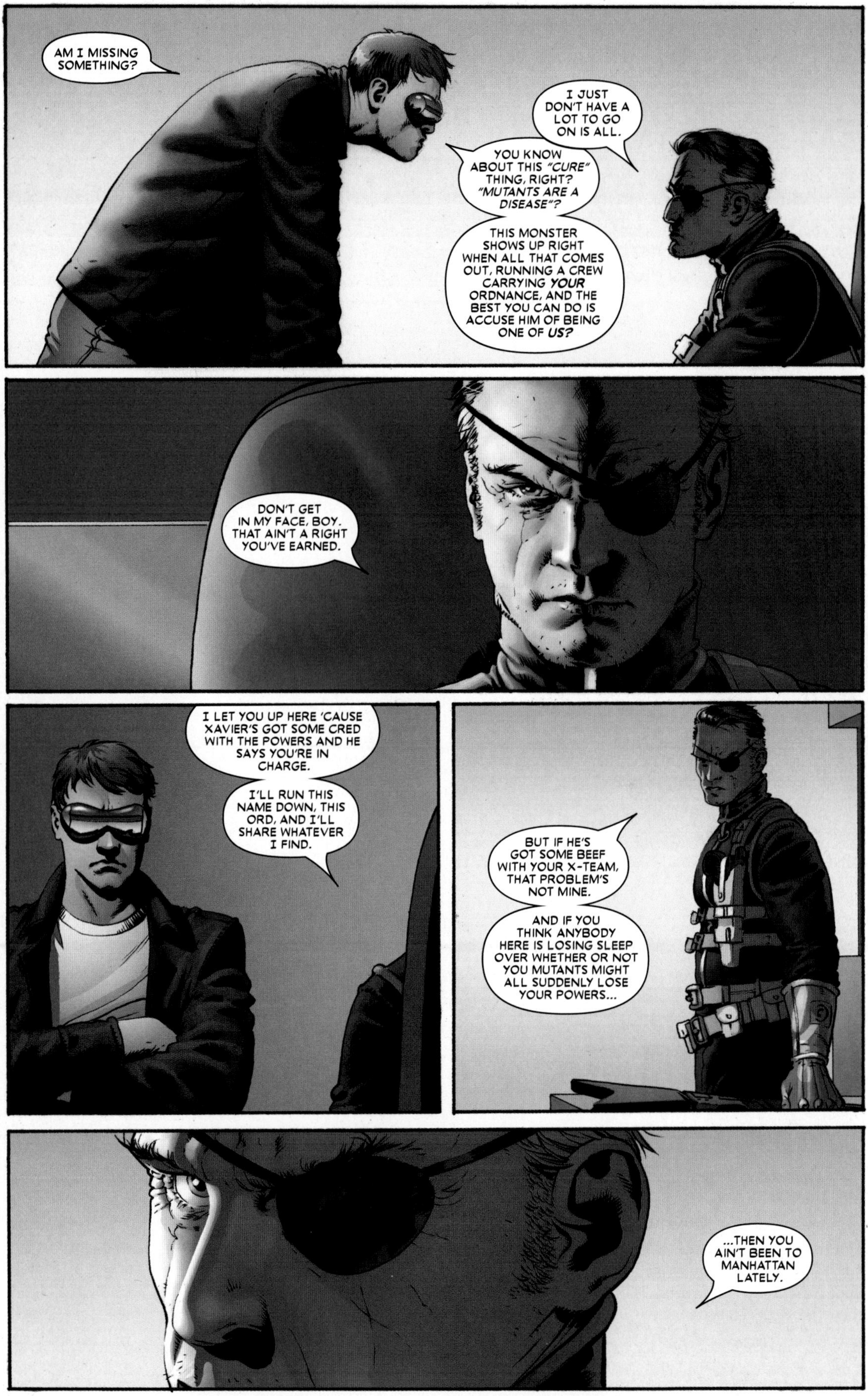
AM I MISSING SOMETHING?
I JUST DON'T HAVE A LOT TO GO ON IS ALL.
YOU KNOW ABOUT THIS "CURE" THING, RIGHT? "MUTANTS ARE A DISEASE"?
THIS MONSTER SHOWS UP RIGHT WHEN ALL THAT COMES OUT, RUNNING A CREW CARRYING YOUR ORDNANCE, AND THE BEST YOU CAN DO IS ACCUSE HIM OF BEING ONE OF US?
DON'T GET IN MY FACE, BOY. THAT AIN'T A RIGHT YOU'VE EARNED.
I LET YOU UP HERE 'CAUSE XAVIER'S GOT SOME CRED WITH THE POWERS AND HE SAYS YOU'RE IN CHARGE.
I'LL RUN THIS NAME DOWN, THIS ORD, AND I'LL SHARE WHATEVER I FIND.
BUT IF HE'S GOT SOME BEEF WITH YOUR X-TEAM, THAT PROBLEM'S NOT MINE.
AND IF YOU THINK ANYBODY HERE IS LOSING SLEEP OVER WHETHER OR NOT YOU MUTANTS MIGHT ALL SUDDENLY LOSE YOUR POWERS...
...THEN YOU AIN'T BEEN TO MANHATTAN LATELY.

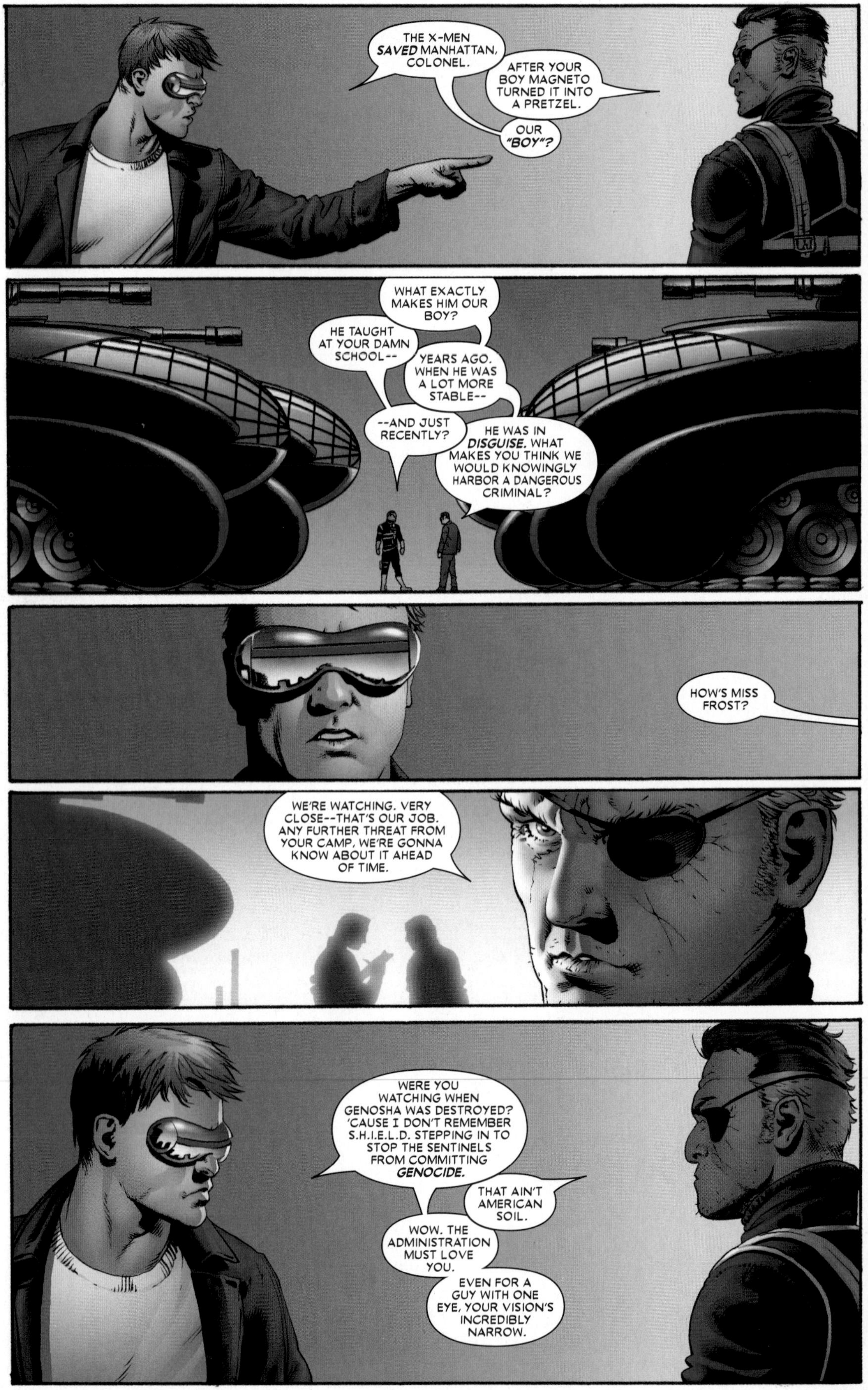
THE X-MEN SAVED MANHATTAN, COLONEL.
AFTER YOUR BOY MAGNETO TURNED IT INTO A PRETZEL.
OUR "BOY"?
WHAT EXACTLY MAKES HIM OUR BOY?
HE TAUGHT AT YOUR DAMN SCHOOL--
YEARS AGO. WHEN HE WAS A LOT MORE STABLE--
--AND JUST RECENTLY?
HE WAS IN DISGUISE. WHAT MAKES YOU THINK WE WOULD KNOWINGLY HARBOR A DANGEROUS CRIMINAL?
HOW'S MISS FROST?
WE'RE WATCHING. VERY CLOSE--THAT'S OUR JOB. ANY FURTHER THREAT FROM YOUR CAMP, WE'RE GONNA KNOW ABOUT IT AHEAD OF TIME.
WERE YOU WATCHING WHEN GENOSHA WAS DESTROYED? 'CAUSE I DON'T REMEMBER S.H.I.E.L.D. STEPPING IN TO STOP THE SENTINELS FROM COMMITTING GENOCIDE.
THAT AIN'T AMERICAN SOIL.
WOW. THE ADMINISTRATION MUST LOVE YOU.
EVEN FOR A GUY WITH ONE EYE, YOUR VISION'S INCREDIBLY NARROW.

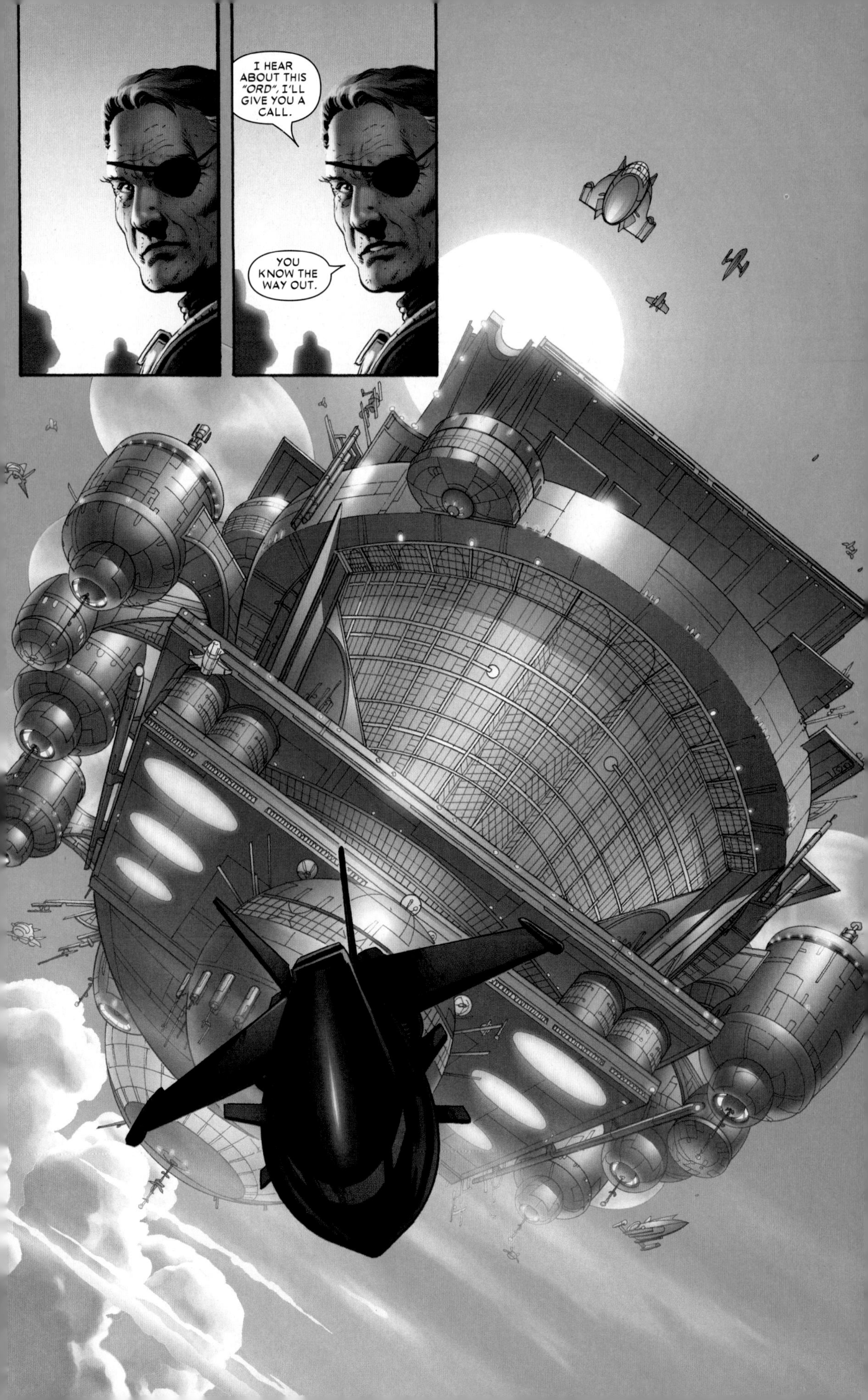
I HEAR ABOUT THIS "ORD", I'LL GIVE YOU A CALL.
YOU KNOW THE WAY OUT.

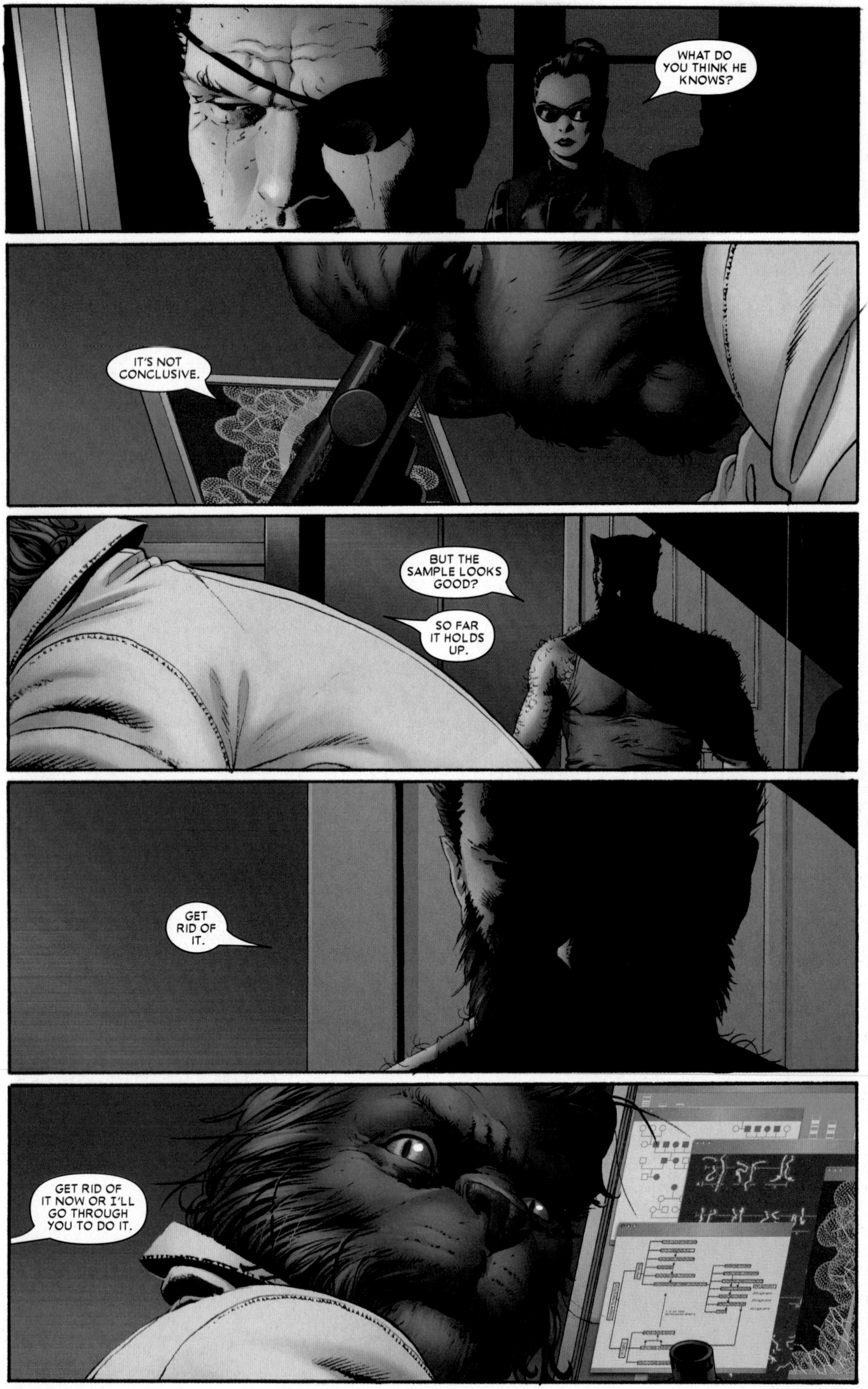
WHAT DO YOU THINK HE KNOWS?
IT'S NOT CONCLUSIVE.
BUT THE SAMPLE LOOKS GOOD?
SO FAR IT HOLDS UP.
GET RID OF IT.
GET RID OF IT NOW OR I'LL GO THROUGH YOU TO DO IT.

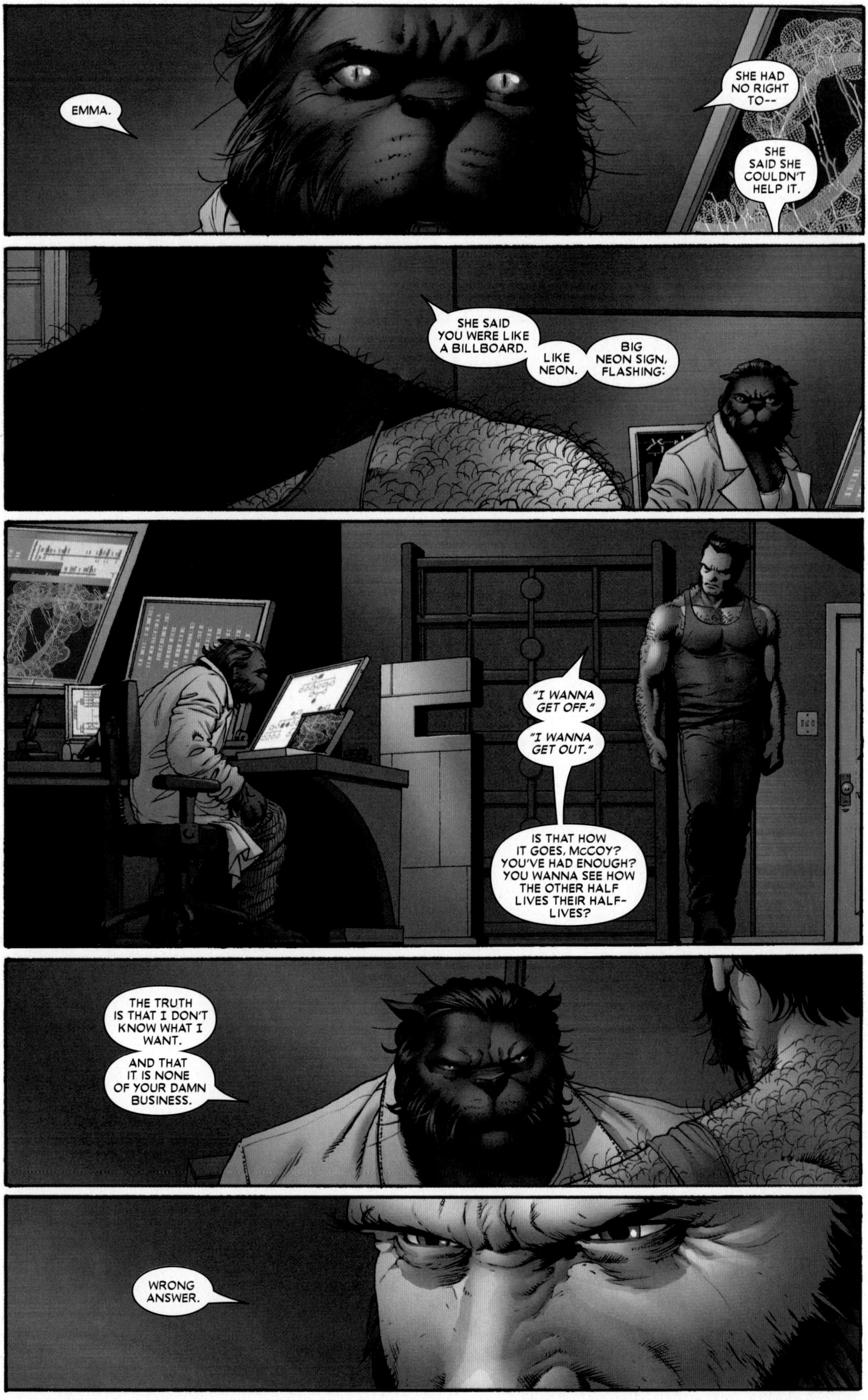
EMMA.
SHE HAD NO RIGHT TO--
SHE SAID SHE COULDN'T HELP IT.
SHE SAID YOU WERE LIKE A BILLBOARD.
LIKE NEON.
BIG NEON SIGN, FLASHING:
"I WANNA GET OFF."
"I WANNA GET OUT."
IS THAT HOW IT GOES, McCOY? YOU'VE HAD ENOUGH? YOU WANNA SEE HOW THE OTHER HALF LIVES THEIR HALF-LIVES?
THE TRUTH IS THAT I DON'T KNOW WHAT I WANT.
AND THAT IT IS NONE OF YOUR DAMN BUSINESS.
WRONG ANSWER.

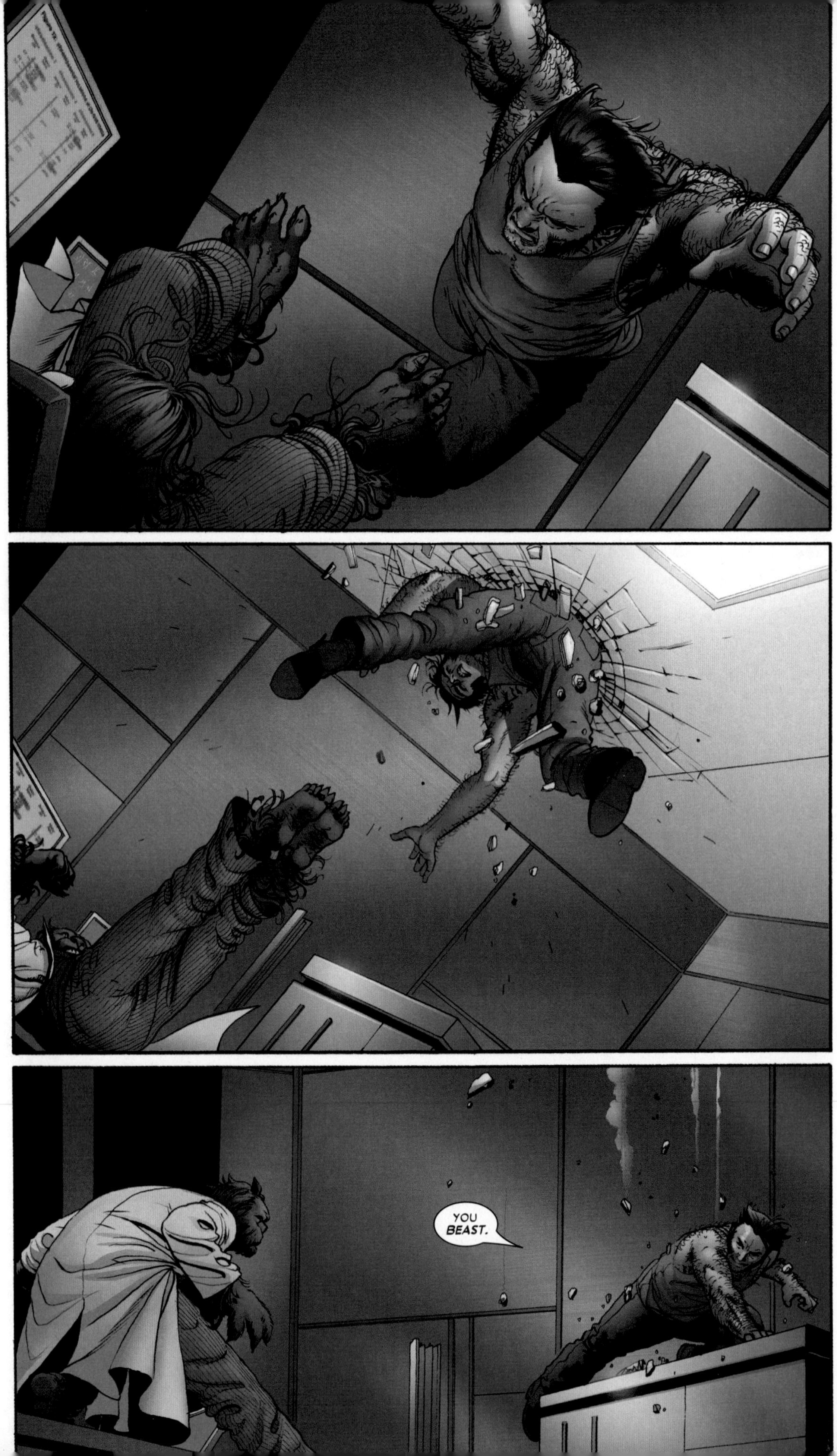
YOU *BEAST.*

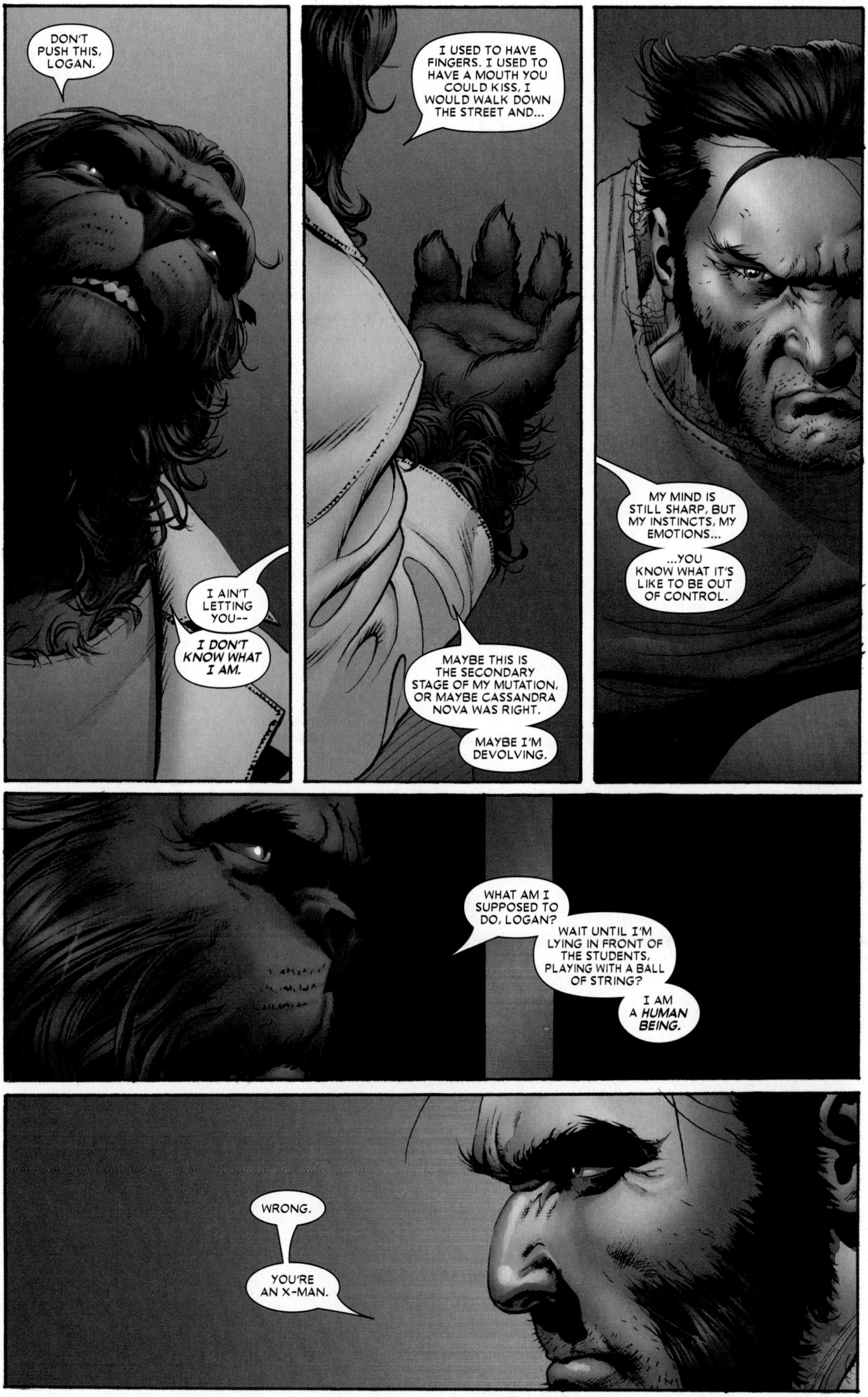
DON'T PUSH THIS, LOGAN.
I AIN'T LETTING YOU--
I DON'T KNOW WHAT I AM.
I USED TO HAVE FINGERS. I USED TO HAVE A MOUTH YOU COULD KISS, I WOULD WALK DOWN THE STREET AND...
MAYBE THIS IS THE SECONDARY STAGE OF MY MUTATION, OR MAYBE CASSANDRA NOVA WAS RIGHT.
MAYBE I'M DEVOLVING.
MY MIND IS STILL SHARP, BUT MY INSTINCTS, MY EMOTIONS...
...YOU KNOW WHAT IT'S LIKE TO BE OUT OF CONTROL.
WHAT AM I SUPPOSED TO DO, LOGAN?
WAIT UNTIL I'M LYING IN FRONT OF THE STUDENTS, PLAYING WITH A BALL OF STRING?
I AM A HUMAN BEING.
WRONG.
YOU'RE AN X-MAN.

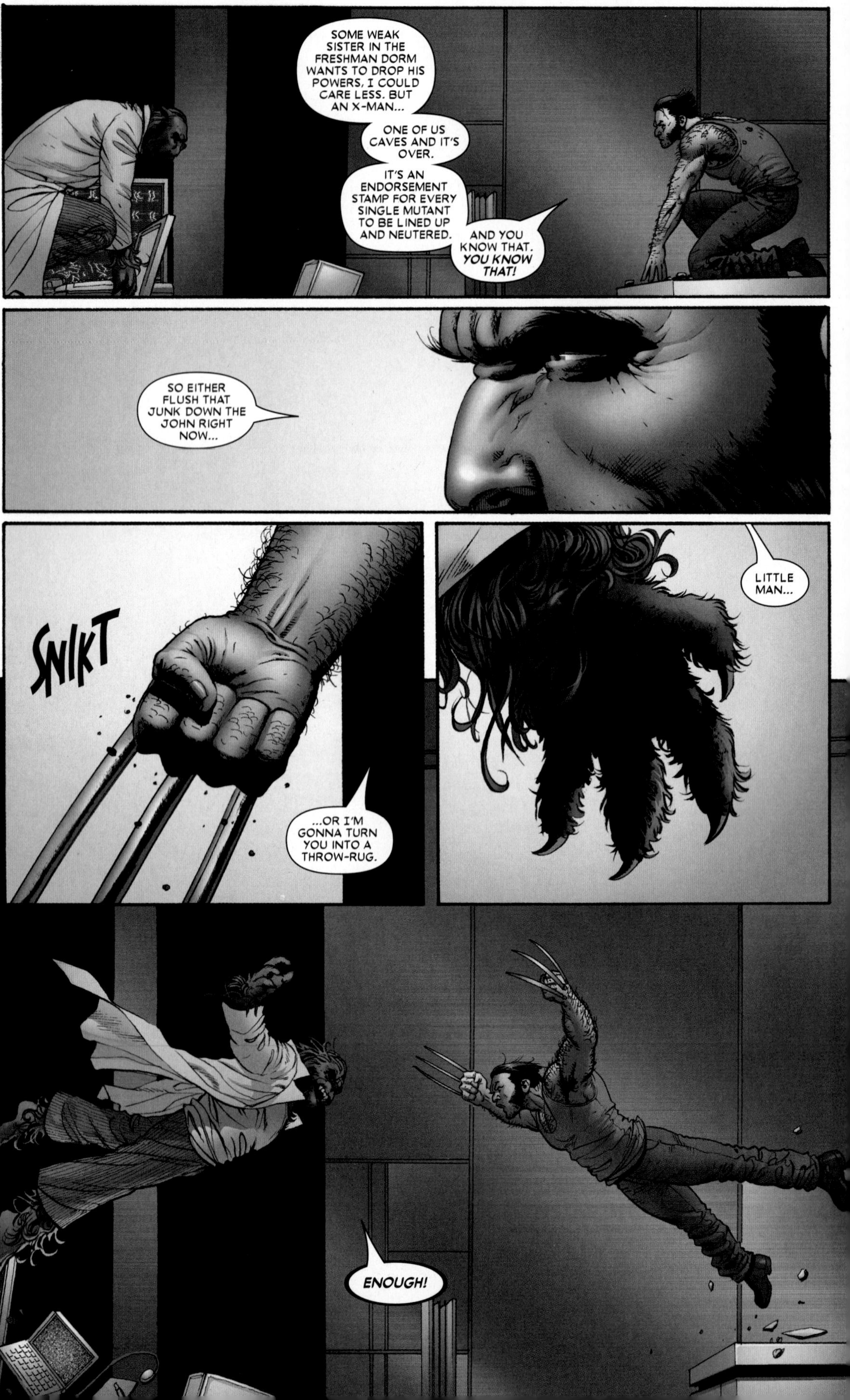
SOME WEAK SISTER IN THE FRESHMAN DORM WANTS TO DROP HIS POWERS, I COULD CARE LESS. BUT AN X-MAN...
ONE OF US CAVES AND IT'S OVER.
IT'S AN ENDORSEMENT STAMP FOR EVERY SINGLE MUTANT TO BE LINED UP AND NEUTERED.
AND YOU KNOW THAT. *YOU KNOW THAT!*
SO EITHER FLUSH THAT JUNK DOWN THE JOHN RIGHT NOW...
SNIKT
...OR I'M GONNA TURN YOU INTO A THROW-RUG.
LITTLE MAN...
ENOUGH!

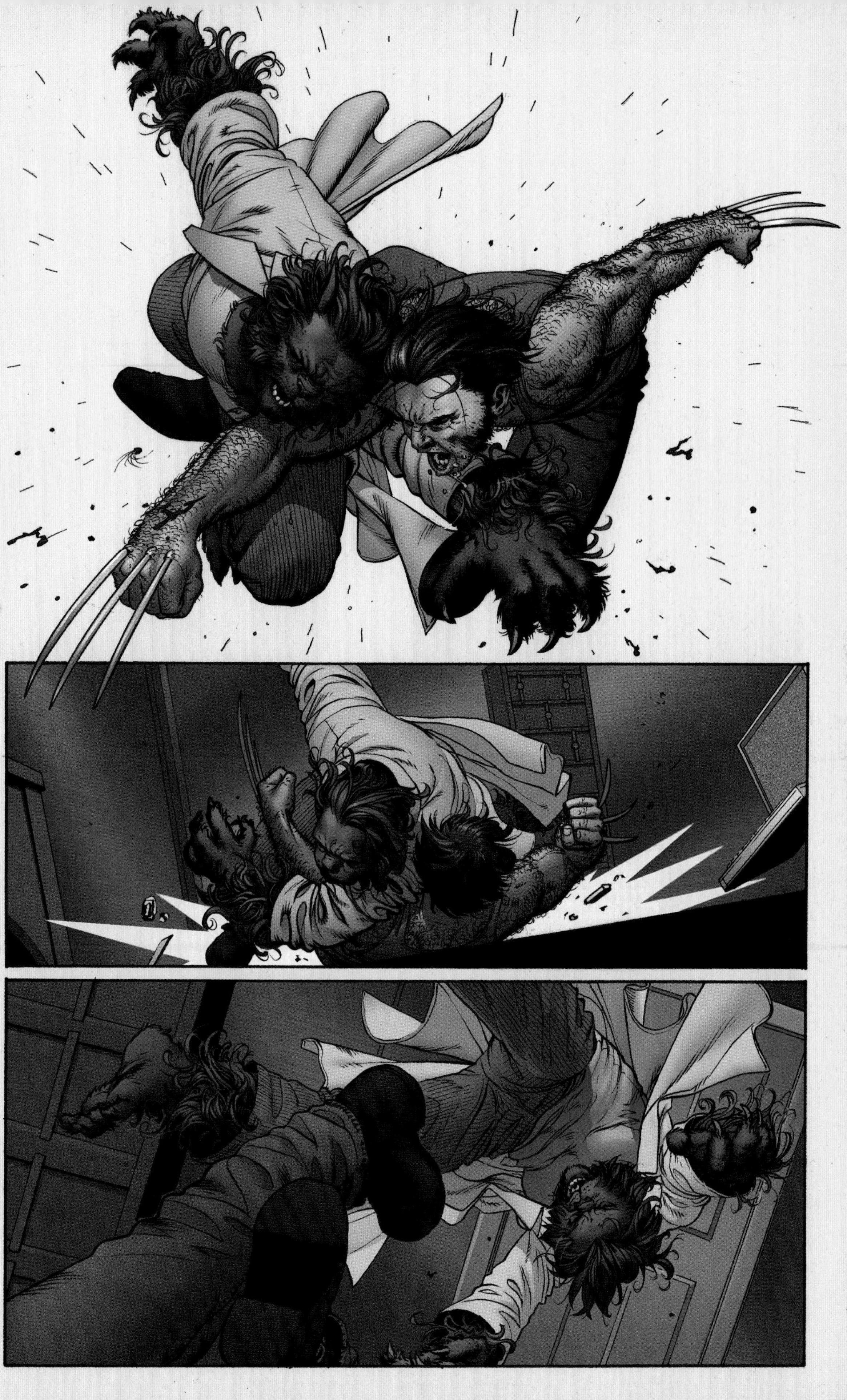

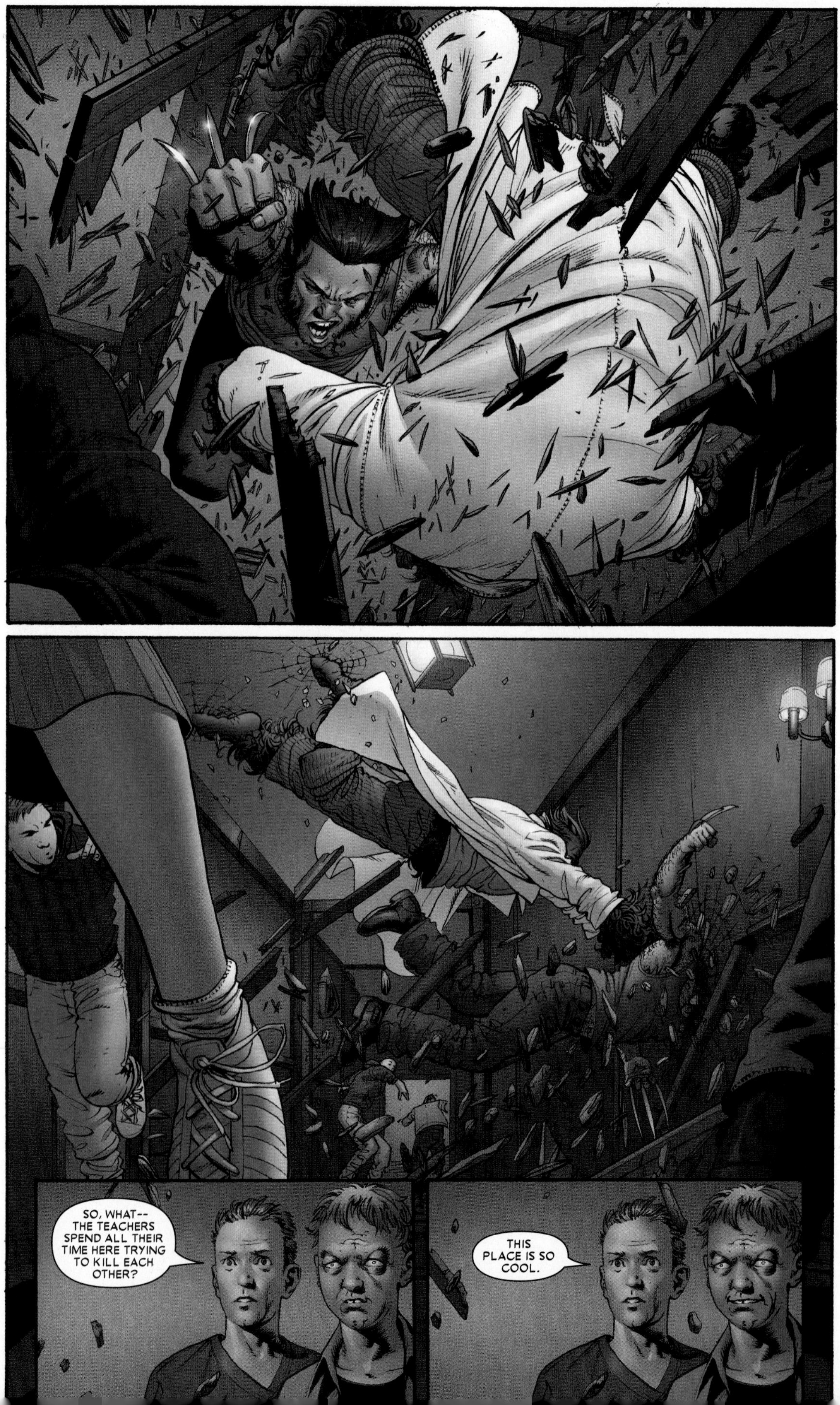
SO, WHAT-- THE TEACHERS SPEND ALL THEIR TIME HERE TRYING TO KILL EACH OTHER?
THIS PLACE IS SO COOL.

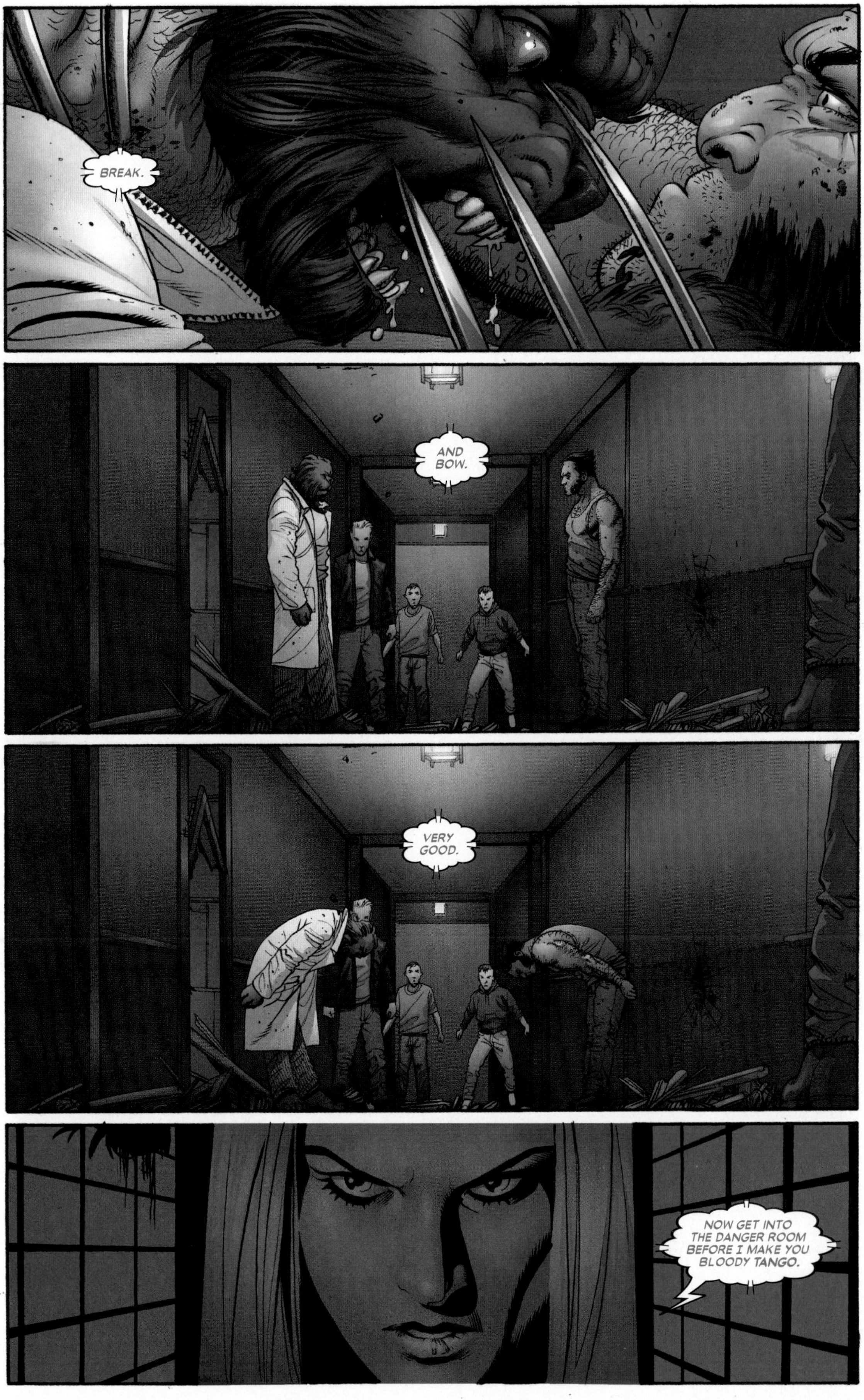
BREAK.
AND BOW.
VERY GOOD.
NOW GET INTO THE DANGER ROOM BEFORE I MAKE YOU BLOODY TANGO.

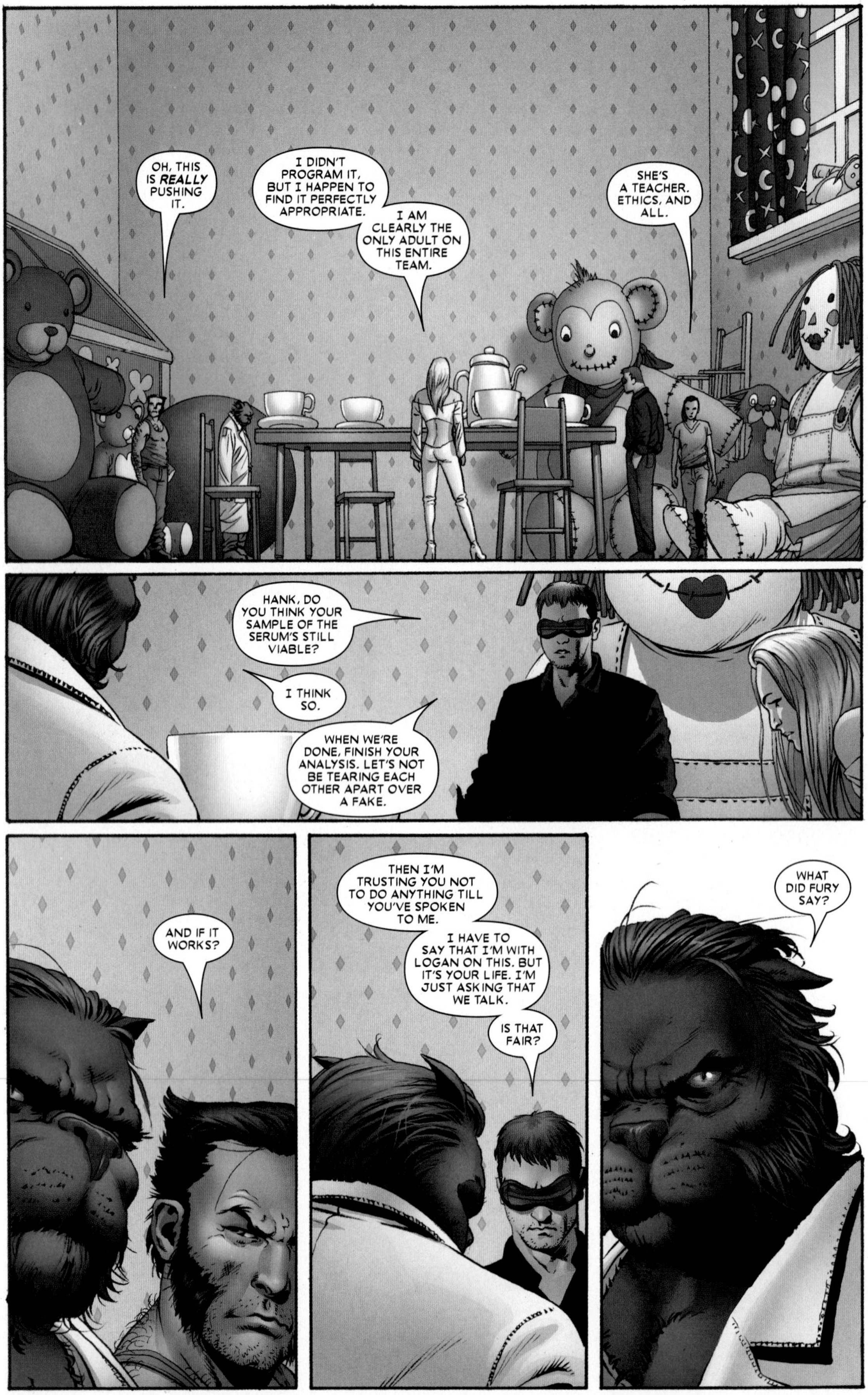
OH, THIS IS *REALLY* PUSHING IT.
I DIDN'T PROGRAM IT, BUT I HAPPEN TO FIND IT PERFECTLY APPROPRIATE.
I AM CLEARLY THE ONLY ADULT ON THIS ENTIRE TEAM.
SHE'S A TEACHER. ETHICS, AND ALL.
HANK, DO YOU THINK YOUR SAMPLE OF THE SERUM'S STILL VIABLE?
I THINK SO.
WHEN WE'RE DONE, FINISH YOUR ANALYSIS. LET'S NOT BE TEARING EACH OTHER APART OVER A FAKE.
AND IF IT WORKS?
THEN I'M TRUSTING YOU NOT TO DO ANYTHING TILL YOU'VE SPOKEN TO ME.
I HAVE TO SAY THAT I'M WITH LOGAN ON THIS. BUT IT'S YOUR LIFE. I'M JUST ASKING THAT WE TALK.
IS THAT FAIR?
WHAT DID FURY SAY?

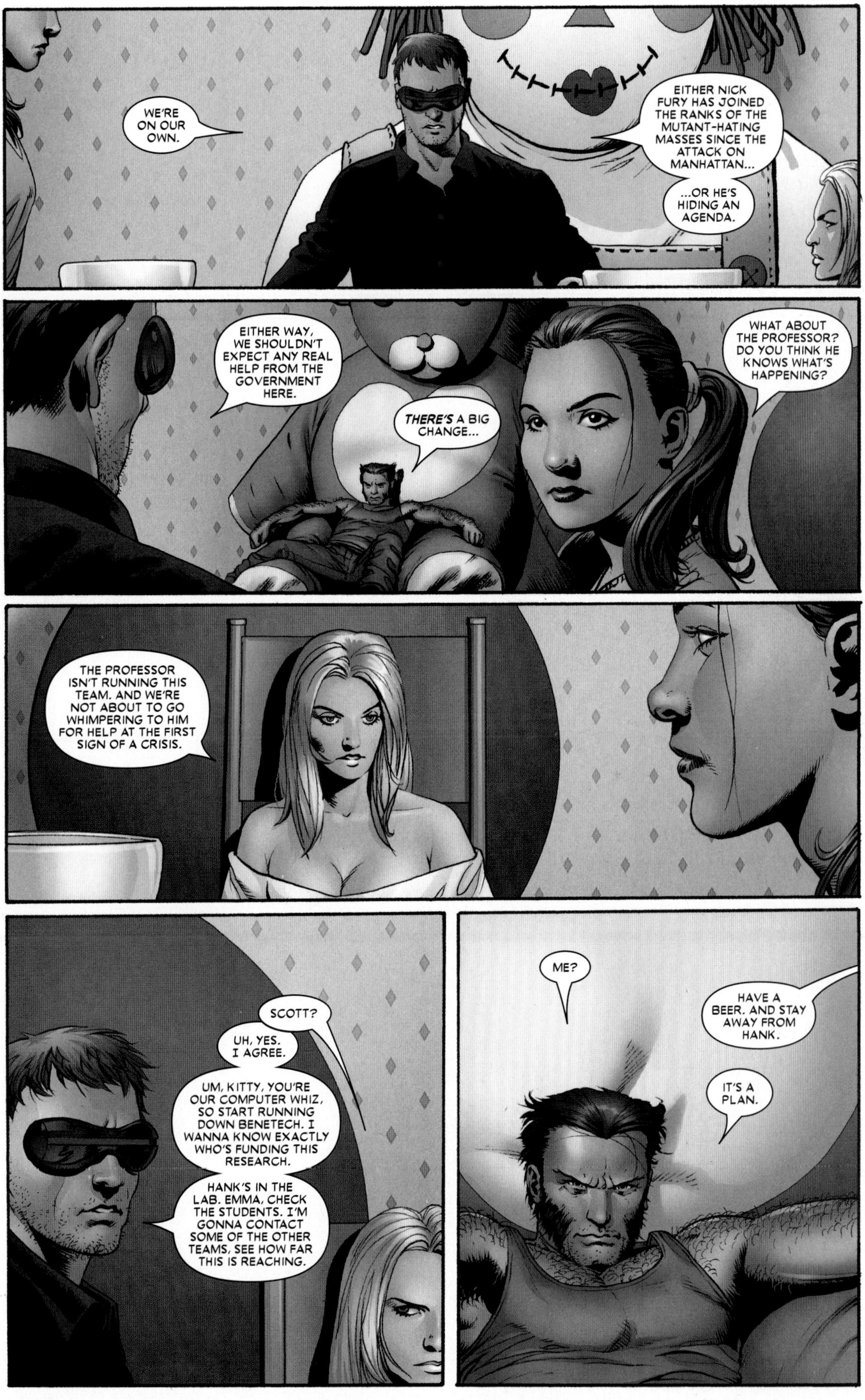
WE'RE ON OUR OWN.
EITHER NICK FURY HAS JOINED THE RANKS OF THE MUTANT-HATING MASSES SINCE THE ATTACK ON MANHATTAN...
...OR HE'S HIDING AN AGENDA.
EITHER WAY, WE SHOULDN'T EXPECT ANY REAL HELP FROM THE GOVERNMENT HERE.
THERE'S A BIG CHANGE...
WHAT ABOUT THE PROFESSOR? DO YOU THINK HE KNOWS WHAT'S HAPPENING?
THE PROFESSOR ISN'T RUNNING THIS TEAM. AND WE'RE NOT ABOUT TO GO WHIMPERING TO HIM FOR HELP AT THE FIRST SIGN OF A CRISIS.
SCOTT?
UH, YES. I AGREE.
UM, KITTY, YOU'RE OUR COMPUTER WHIZ, SO START RUNNING DOWN BENETECH. I WANNA KNOW EXACTLY WHO'S FUNDING THIS RESEARCH.
HANK'S IN THE LAB. EMMA, CHECK THE STUDENTS. I'M GONNA CONTACT SOME OF THE OTHER TEAMS, SEE HOW FAR THIS IS REACHING.
ME?
HAVE A BEER. AND STAY AWAY FROM HANK.
IT'S A PLAN.

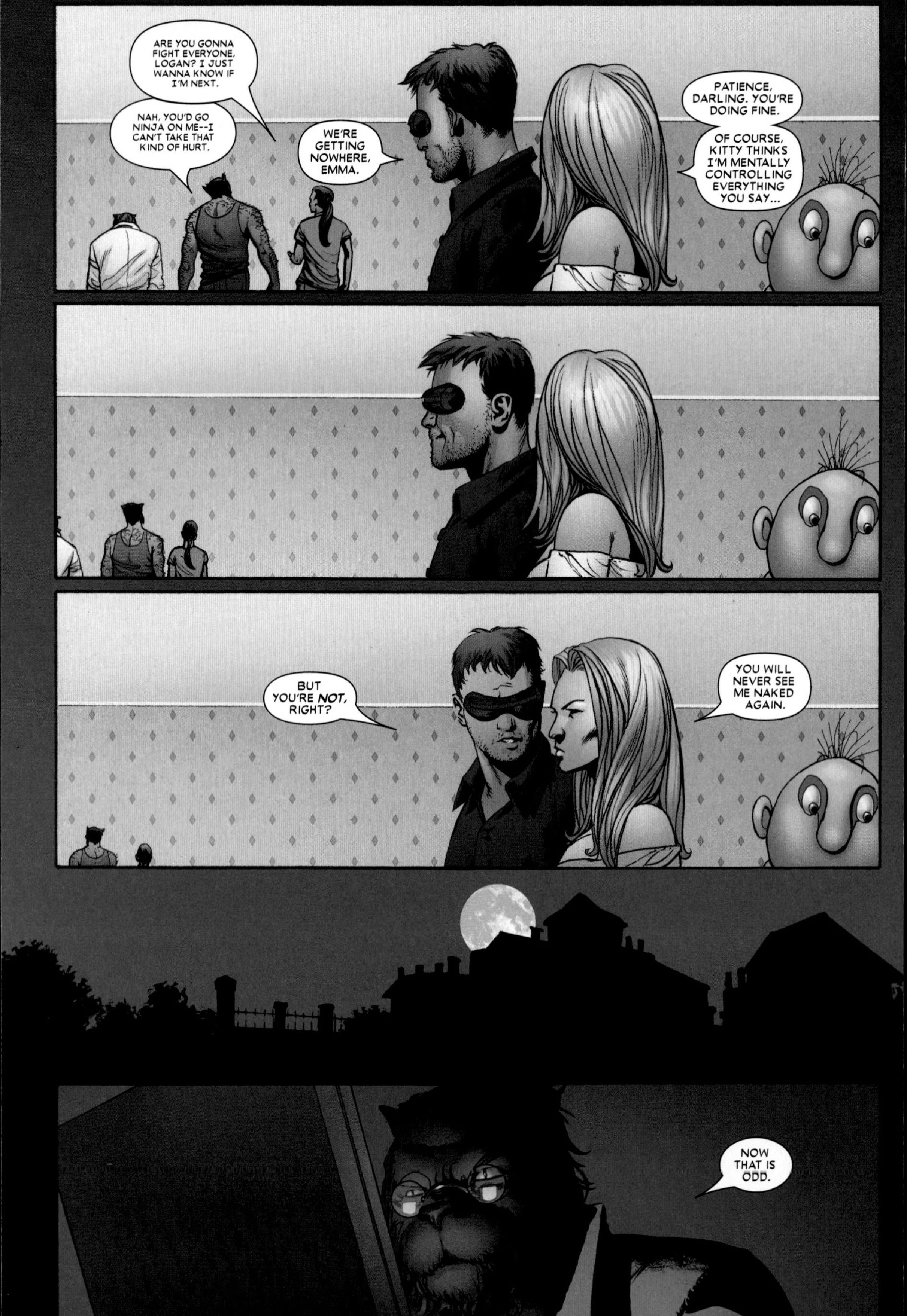
ARE YOU GONNA FIGHT EVERYONE, LOGAN? I JUST WANNA KNOW IF I'M NEXT.
NAH, YOU'D GO NINJA ON ME--I CAN'T TAKE THAT KIND OF HURT.
WE'RE GETTING NOWHERE, EMMA.
PATIENCE, DARLING. YOU'RE DOING FINE.
OF COURSE, KITTY THINKS I'M MENTALLY CONTROLLING EVERYTHING YOU SAY...
BUT YOU'RE NOT, RIGHT?
YOU WILL NEVER SEE ME NAKED AGAIN.
NOW THAT IS ODD.

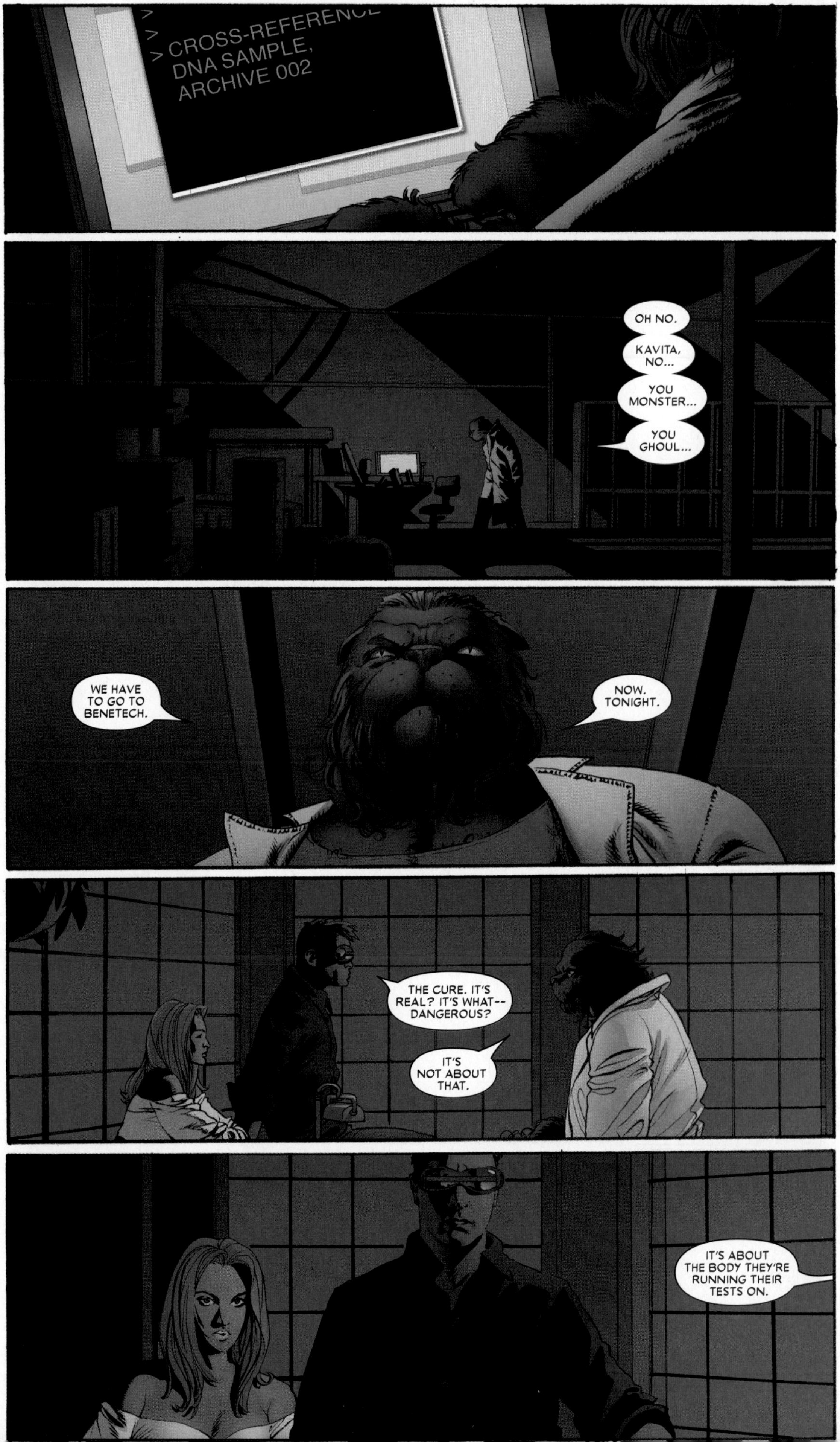
>
>
> CROSS-REFERENCE
DNA SAMPLE,
ARCHIVE 002
OH NO.
KAVITA, NO...
YOU MONSTER...
YOU GHOUL...
WE HAVE TO GO TO BENETECH.
NOW. TONIGHT.
THE CURE. IT'S REAL? IT'S WHAT-- DANGEROUS?
IT'S NOT ABOUT THAT.
IT'S ABOUT THE BODY THEY'RE RUNNING THEIR TESTS ON.

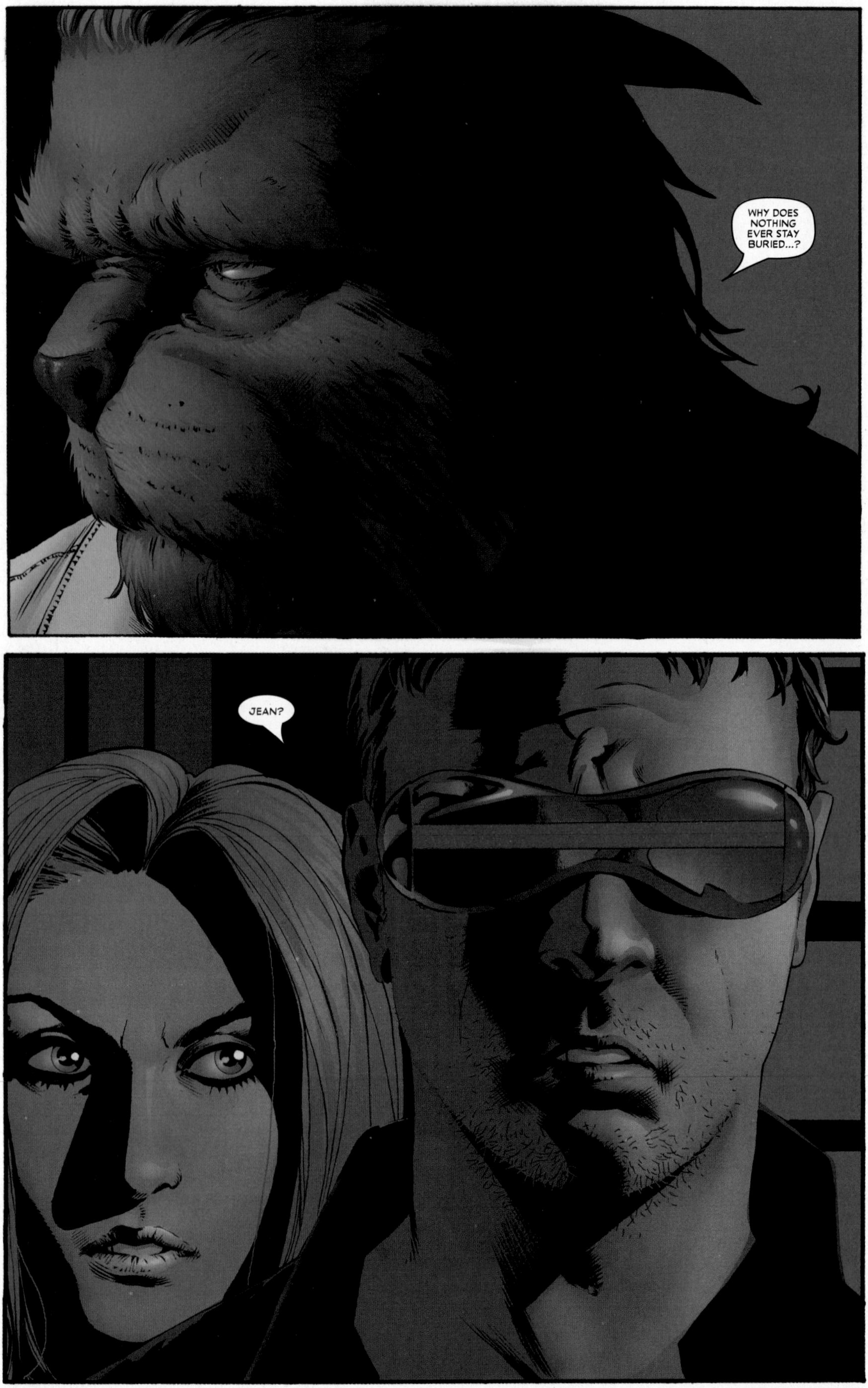
WHY DOES NOTHING EVER STAY BURIED...?
JEAN?

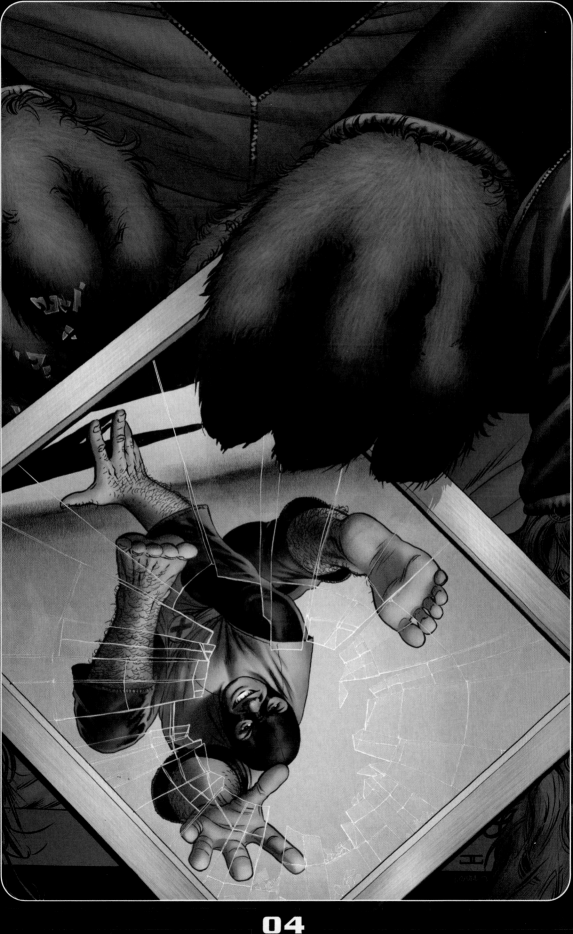

04

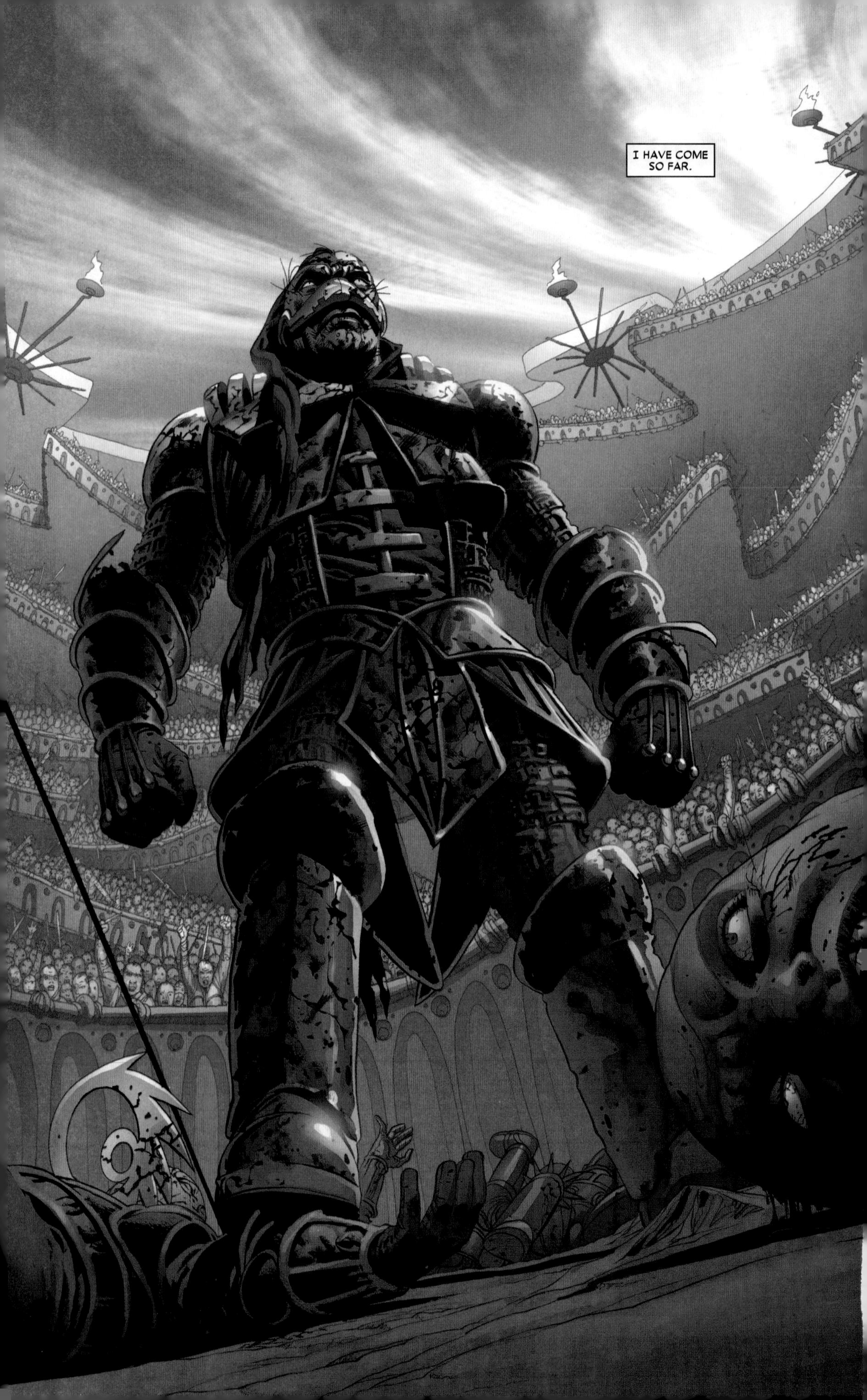
I HAVE COME SO FAR.

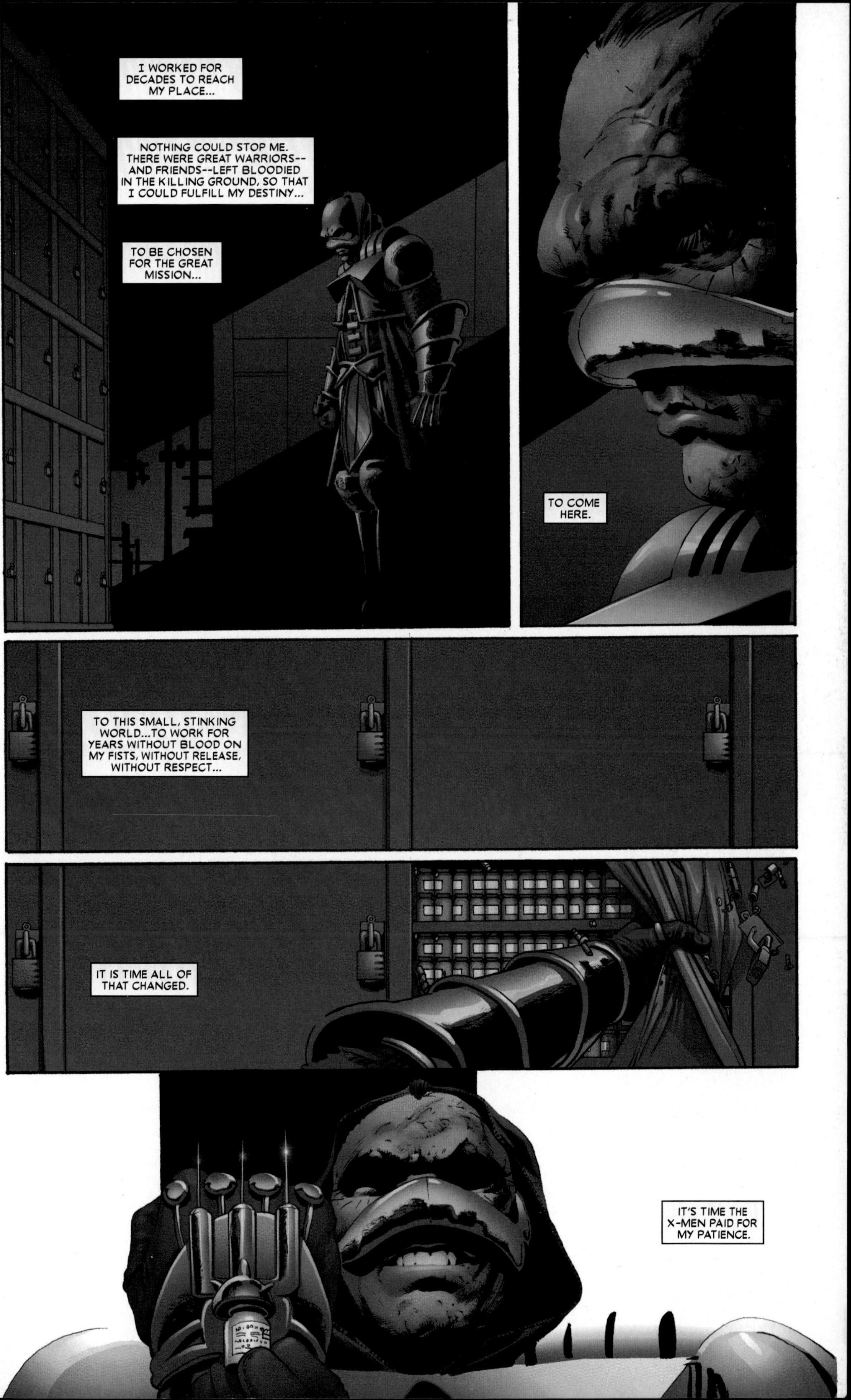
I WORKED FOR DECADES TO REACH MY PLACE...
NOTHING COULD STOP ME. THERE WERE GREAT WARRIORS--AND FRIENDS--LEFT BLOODIED IN THE KILLING GROUND, SO THAT I COULD FULFILL MY DESTINY...
TO BE CHOSEN FOR THE GREAT MISSION...
TO COME HERE.
TO THIS SMALL, STINKING WORLD...TO WORK FOR YEARS WITHOUT BLOOD ON MY FISTS, WITHOUT RELEASE, WITHOUT RESPECT...
IT IS TIME ALL OF THAT CHANGED.
IT'S TIME THE X-MEN PAID FOR MY PATIENCE.

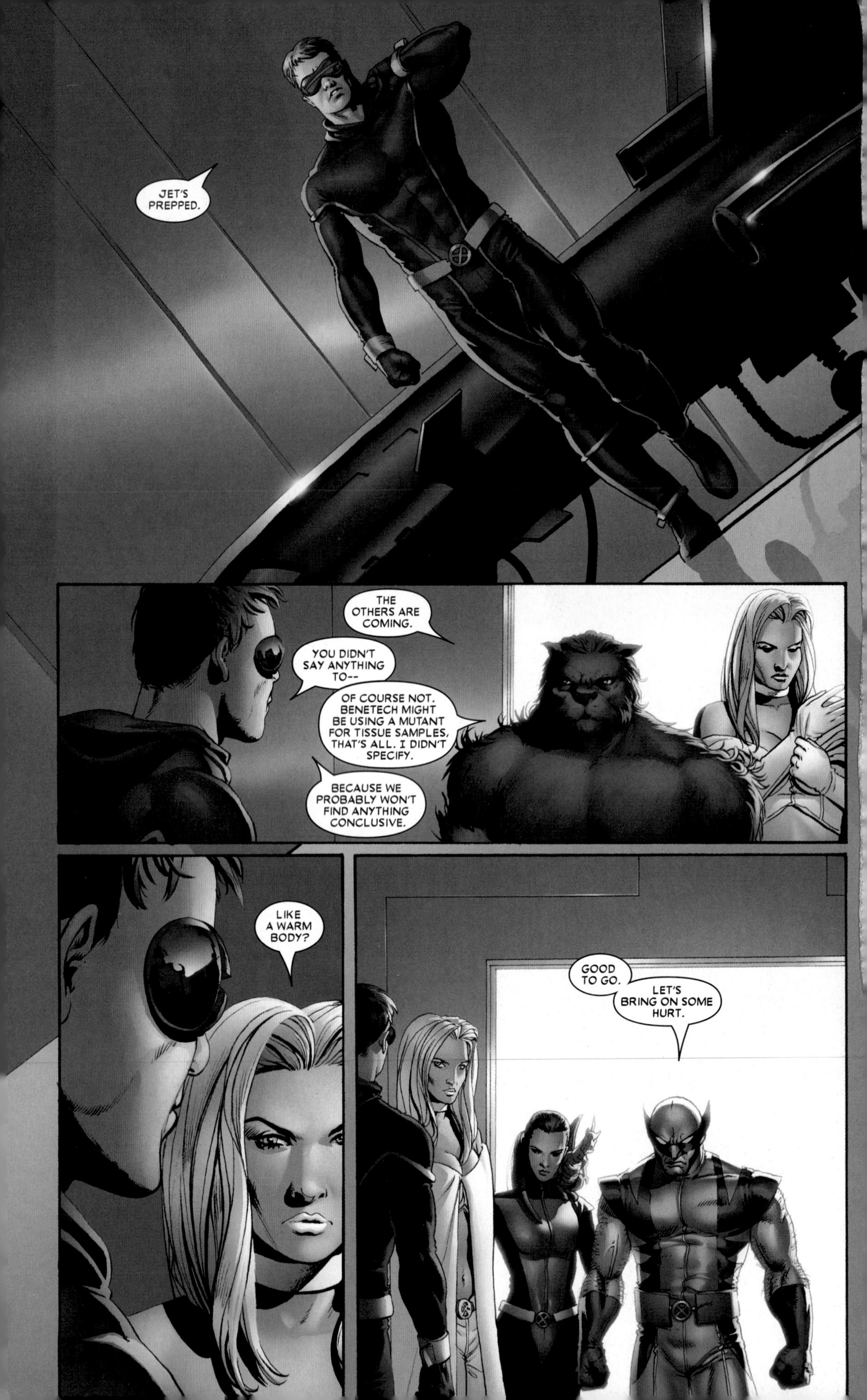
JET'S PREPPED.
THE OTHERS ARE COMING.
YOU DIDN'T SAY ANYTHING TO--
OF COURSE NOT. BENETECH MIGHT BE USING A MUTANT FOR TISSUE SAMPLES, THAT'S ALL. I DIDN'T SPECIFY.
BECAUSE WE PROBABLY WON'T FIND ANYTHING CONCLUSIVE.
LIKE A WARM BODY?
GOOD TO GO.
LET'S BRING ON SOME HURT.

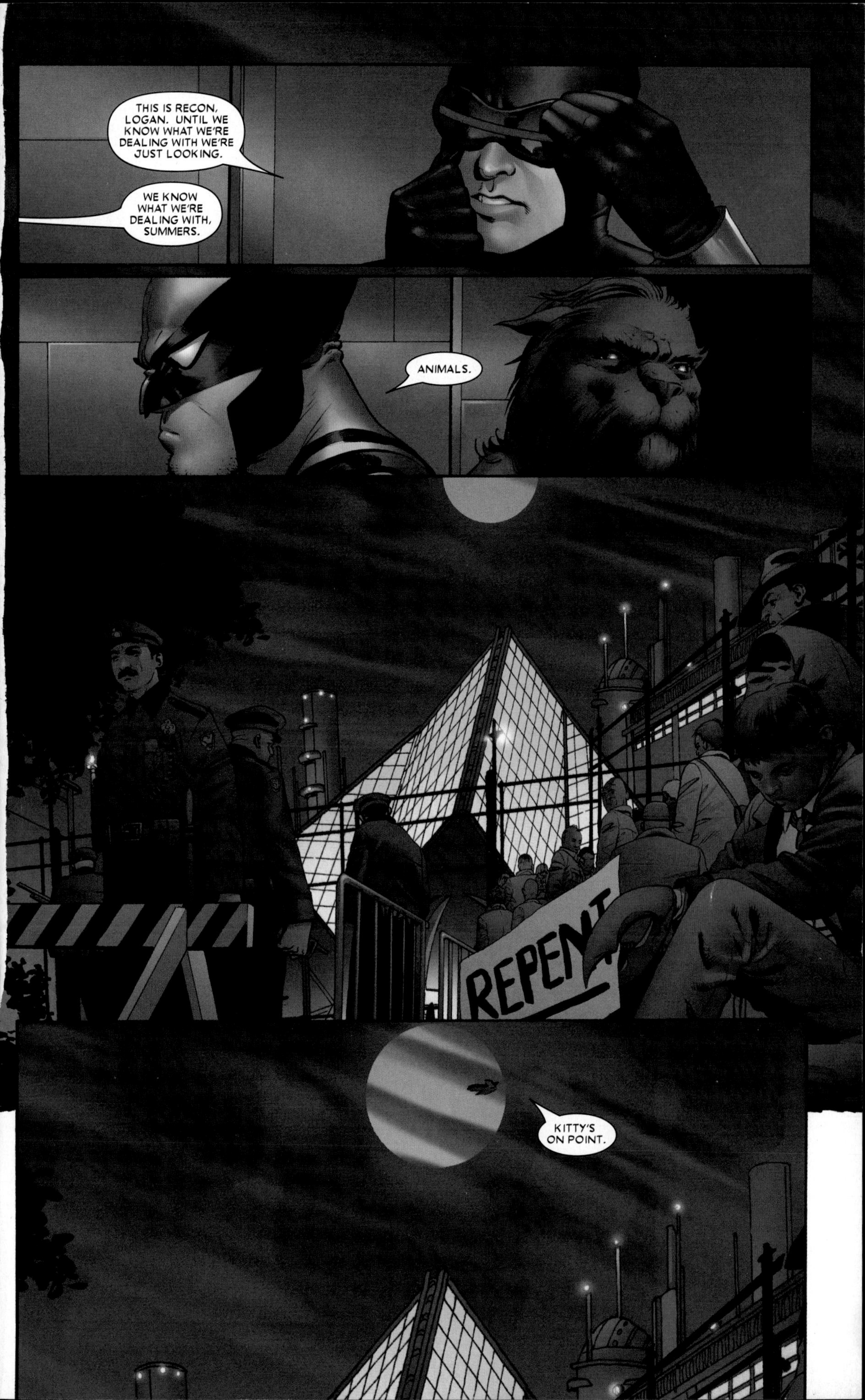
THIS IS RECON, LOGAN. UNTIL WE KNOW WHAT WE'RE DEALING WITH WE'RE JUST LOOKING.
WE KNOW WHAT WE'RE DEALING WITH, SUMMERS.
ANIMALS.
REPENT
KITTY'S ON POINT.

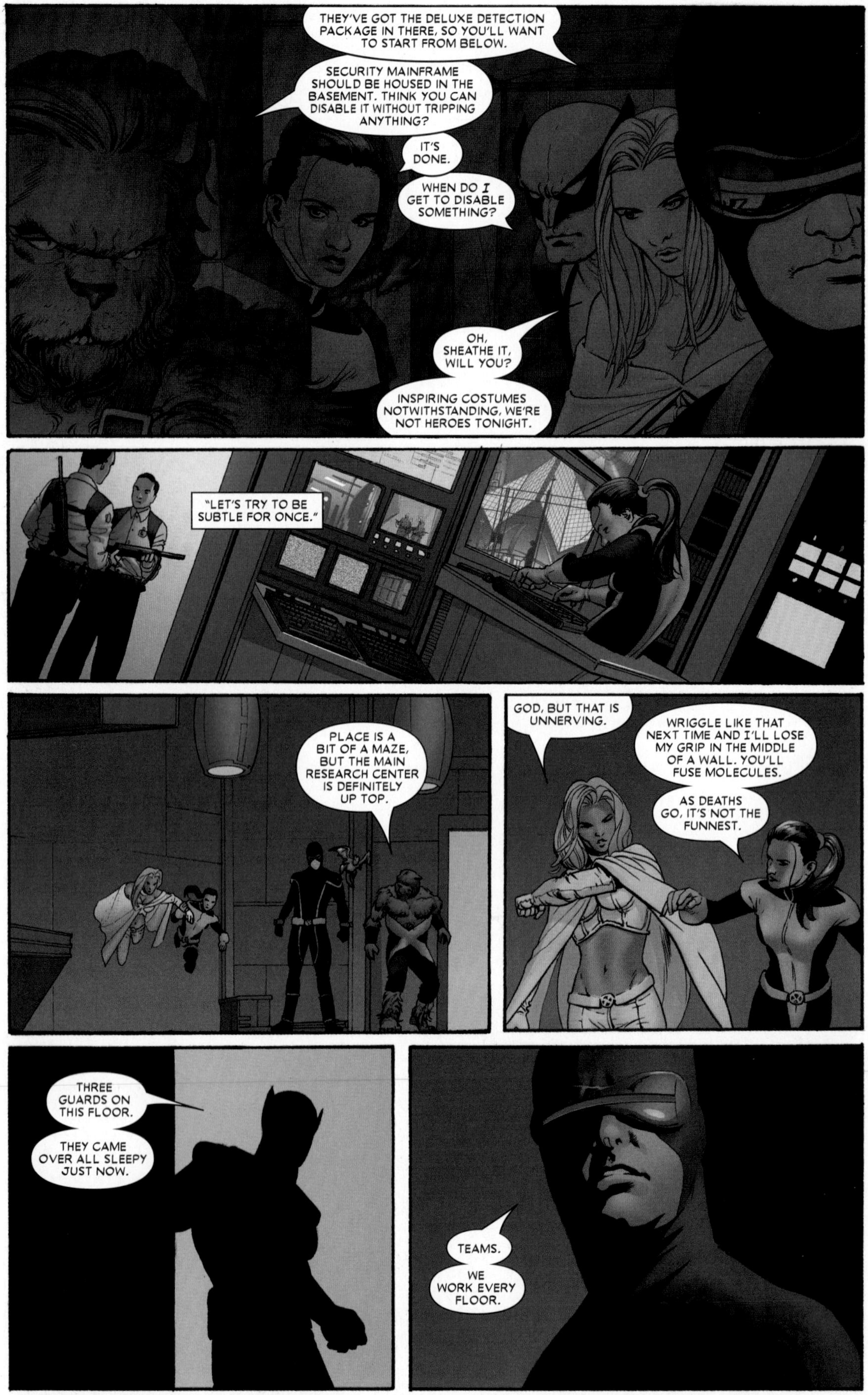
THEY'VE GOT THE DELUXE DETECTION PACKAGE IN THERE, SO YOU'LL WANT TO START FROM BELOW.
SECURITY MAINFRAME SHOULD BE HOUSED IN THE BASEMENT. THINK YOU CAN DISABLE IT WITHOUT TRIPPING ANYTHING?
IT'S DONE.
WHEN DO *I* GET TO DISABLE SOMETHING?
OH, SHEATHE IT, WILL YOU?
INSPIRING COSTUMES NOTWITHSTANDING, WE'RE NOT HEROES TONIGHT.
"LET'S TRY TO BE SUBTLE FOR ONCE."
PLACE IS A BIT OF A MAZE, BUT THE MAIN RESEARCH CENTER IS DEFINITELY UP TOP.
GOD, BUT THAT IS UNNERVING.
WRIGGLE LIKE THAT NEXT TIME AND I'LL LOSE MY GRIP IN THE MIDDLE OF A WALL. YOU'LL FUSE MOLECULES.
AS DEATHS GO, IT'S NOT THE FUNNEST.
THREE GUARDS ON THIS FLOOR.
THEY CAME OVER ALL SLEEPY JUST NOW.
TEAMS.
WE WORK EVERY FLOOR.

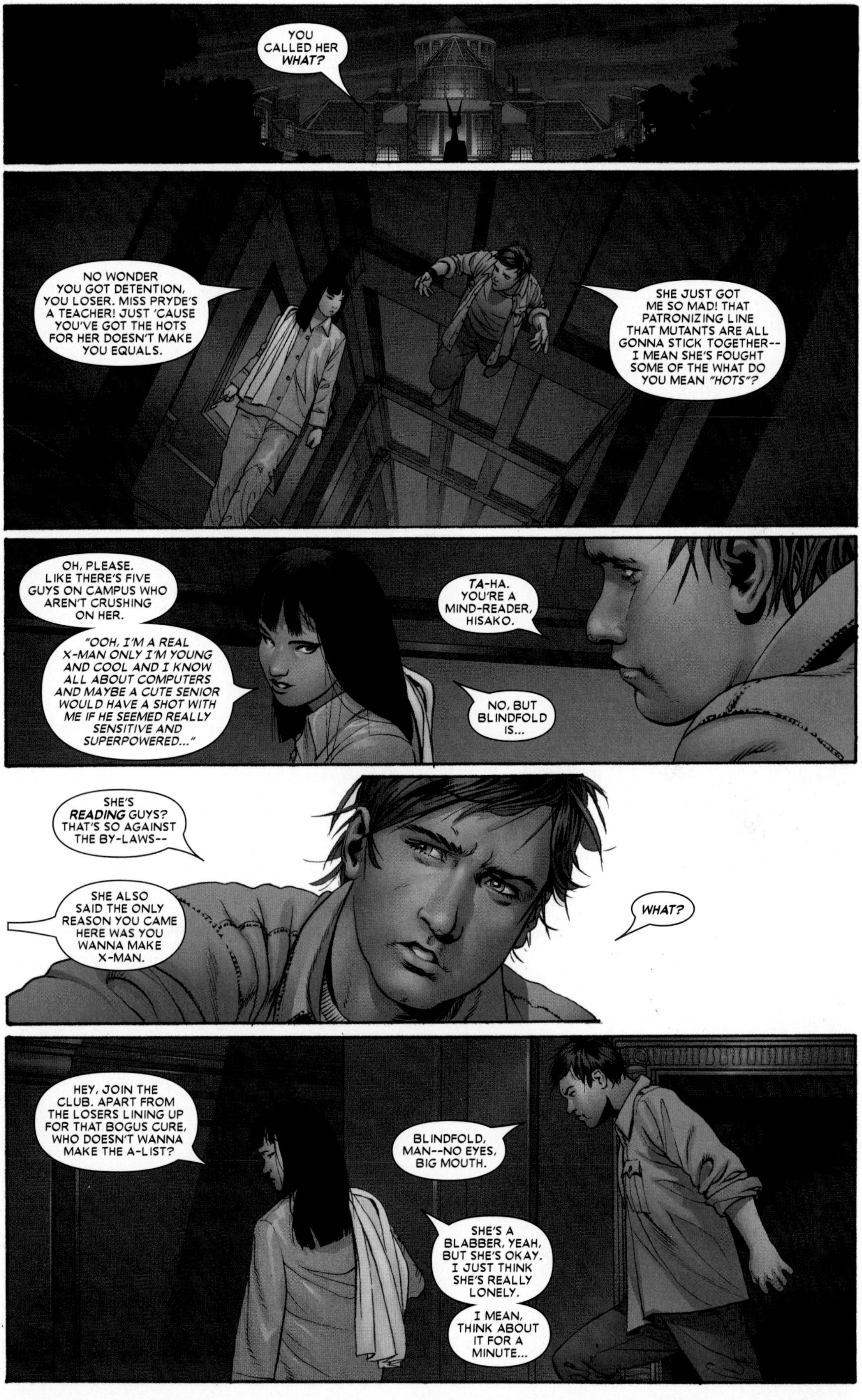
YOU CALLED HER WHAT?
NO WONDER YOU GOT DETENTION, YOU LOSER. MISS PRYDE'S A TEACHER! JUST 'CAUSE YOU'VE GOT THE HOTS FOR HER DOESN'T MAKE YOU EQUALS.
SHE JUST GOT ME SO MAD! THAT PATRONIZING LINE THAT MUTANTS ARE ALL GONNA STICK TOGETHER-- I MEAN SHE'S FOUGHT SOME OF THE WHAT DO YOU MEAN "HOTS"?
OH, PLEASE. LIKE THERE'S FIVE GUYS ON CAMPUS WHO AREN'T CRUSHING ON HER.
"OOH, I'M A REAL X-MAN ONLY I'M YOUNG AND COOL AND I KNOW ALL ABOUT COMPUTERS AND MAYBE A CUTE SENIOR WOULD HAVE A SHOT WITH ME IF HE SEEMED REALLY SENSITIVE AND SUPERPOWERED..."
TA-HA. YOU'RE A MIND-READER, HISAKO.
NO, BUT BLINDFOLD IS...
SHE'S READING GUYS? THAT'S SO AGAINST THE BY-LAWS--
SHE ALSO SAID THE ONLY REASON YOU CAME HERE WAS YOU WANNA MAKE X-MAN.
WHAT?
HEY, JOIN THE CLUB. APART FROM THE LOSERS LINING UP FOR THAT BOGUS CURE, WHO DOESN'T WANNA MAKE THE A-LIST?
BLINDFOLD, MAN--NO EYES, BIG MOUTH.
SHE'S A BLABBER, YEAH, BUT SHE'S OKAY. I JUST THINK SHE'S REALLY LONELY.
I MEAN, THINK ABOUT IT FOR A MINUTE...

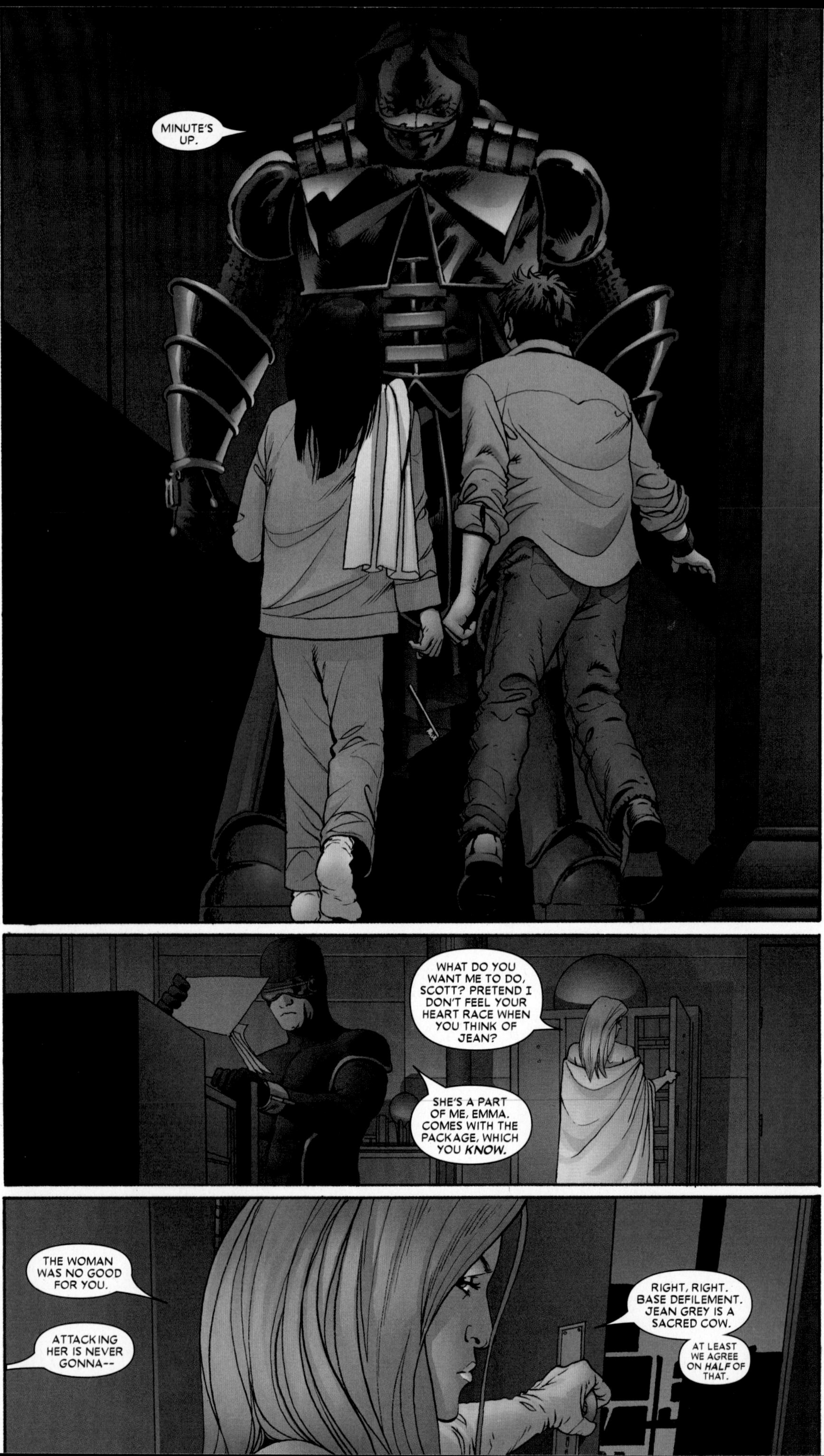
MINUTE'S UP.
WHAT DO YOU WANT ME TO DO, SCOTT? PRETEND I DON'T FEEL YOUR HEART RACE WHEN YOU THINK OF JEAN?
SHE'S A PART OF ME, EMMA. COMES WITH THE PACKAGE, WHICH YOU KNOW.
THE WOMAN WAS NO GOOD FOR YOU.
ATTACKING HER IS NEVER GONNA--
RIGHT, RIGHT. BASE DEFILEMENT. JEAN GREY IS A SACRED COW.
AT LEAST WE AGREE ON HALF OF THAT.

OKAY, THIS IS WEIRD.

IT'S METAL, LOCKHEED, AND I CAN'T FIND THE END.

THERE'S NO SUB-BASEMENT-- IT JUST GOES DOWN.

YOU STAY HERE AND DON'T EAT ANYONE.

I'M GONNA CHECK IT OUT.

"HOPE."

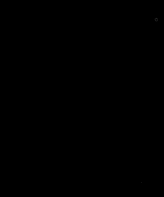

THAT'S WHAT THEY'RE CALLING THE CURE NOW. "HOPE." IT WAS ON THE NEWS.

CATCHY, EH?

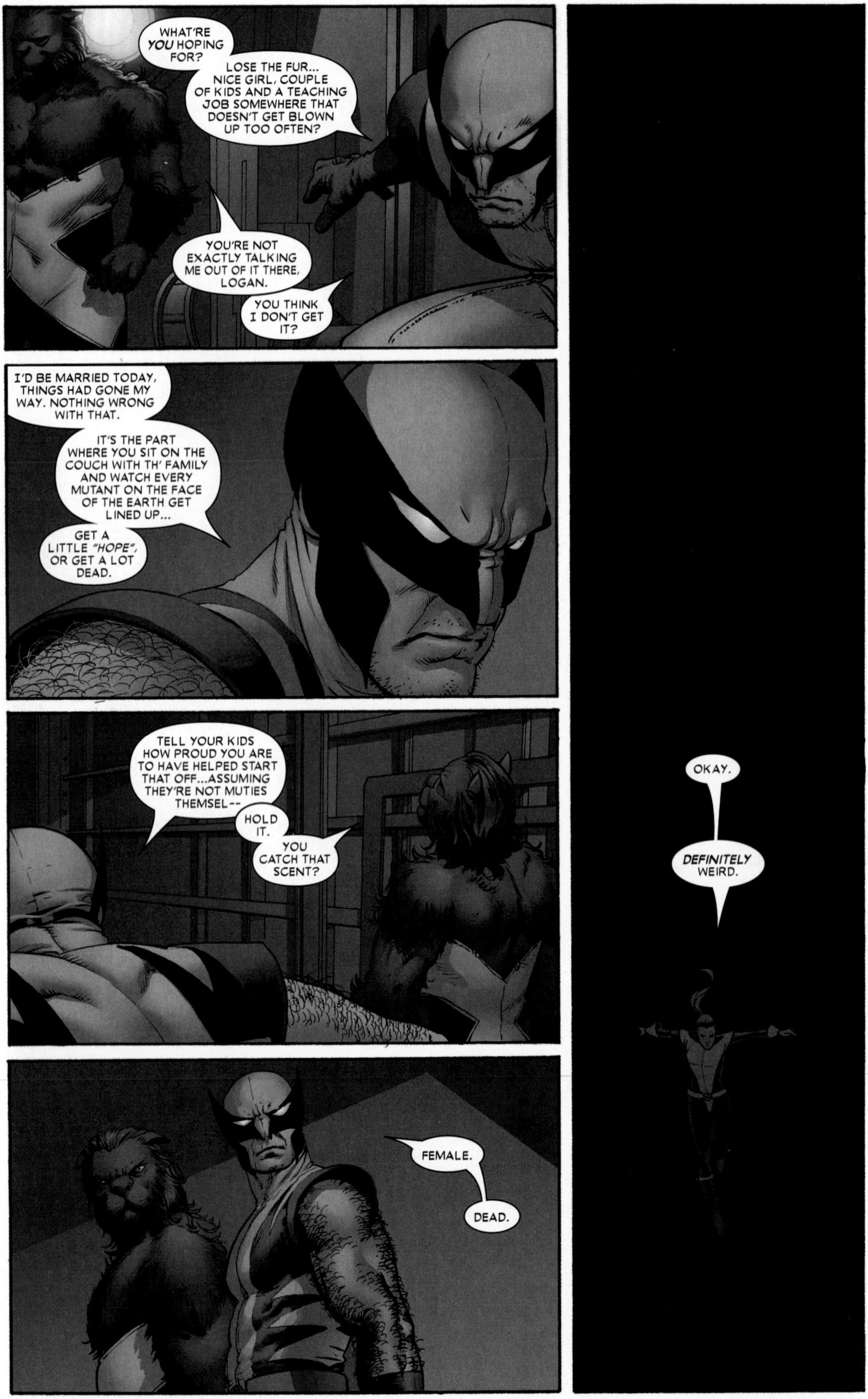
WHAT'RE *YOU* HOPING FOR?
LOSE THE FUR... NICE GIRL, COUPLE OF KIDS AND A TEACHING JOB SOMEWHERE THAT DOESN'T GET BLOWN UP TOO OFTEN?
YOU'RE NOT EXACTLY TALKING ME OUT OF IT THERE, LOGAN.
YOU THINK I DON'T GET IT?
I'D BE MARRIED TODAY, THINGS HAD GONE MY WAY. NOTHING WRONG WITH THAT.
IT'S THE PART WHERE YOU SIT ON THE COUCH WITH TH' FAMILY AND WATCH EVERY MUTANT ON THE FACE OF THE EARTH GET LINED UP...
GET A LITTLE *"HOPE"*, OR GET A LOT DEAD.
TELL YOUR KIDS HOW PROUD YOU ARE TO HAVE HELPED START THAT OFF...ASSUMING THEY'RE NOT MUTIES THEMSEL--
HOLD IT.
YOU CATCH THAT SCENT?
FEMALE.
DEAD.
OKAY.
DEFINITELY WEIRD.

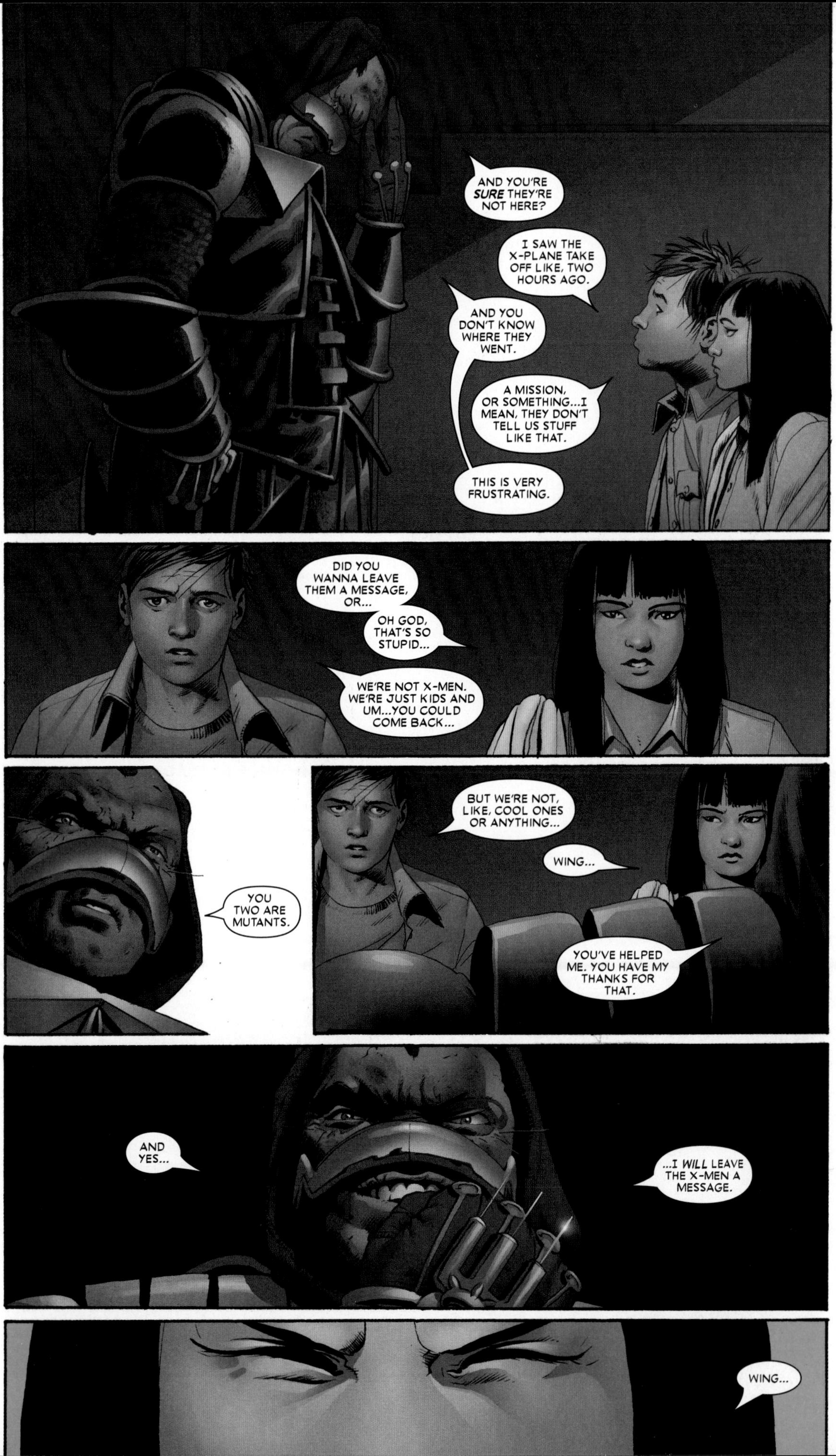
AND YOU'RE *SURE* THEY'RE NOT HERE?
I SAW THE X-PLANE TAKE OFF LIKE, TWO HOURS AGO.
AND YOU DON'T KNOW WHERE THEY WENT.
A MISSION, OR SOMETHING...I MEAN, THEY DON'T TELL US STUFF LIKE THAT.
THIS IS VERY FRUSTRATING.
DID YOU WANNA LEAVE THEM A MESSAGE, OR...
OH GOD, THAT'S SO STUPID...
WE'RE NOT X-MEN. WE'RE JUST KIDS AND UM...YOU COULD COME BACK...
YOU TWO ARE MUTANTS.
BUT WE'RE NOT, LIKE, COOL ONES OR ANYTHING...
WING...
YOU'VE HELPED ME. YOU HAVE MY THANKS FOR THAT.
AND YES...
...I *WILL* LEAVE THE X-MEN A MESSAGE.
WING...

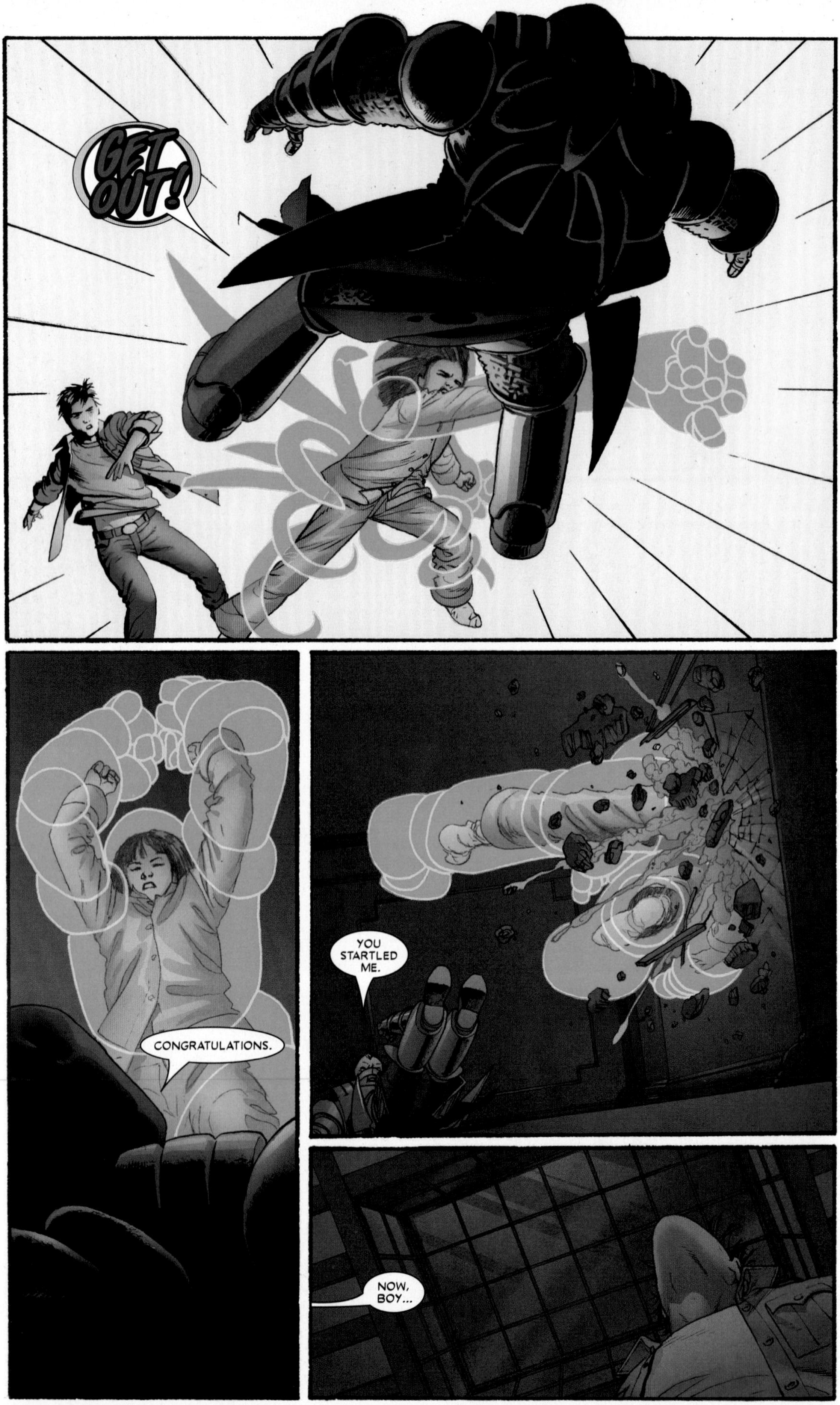
GET OUT!
CONGRATULATIONS.
YOU STARTLED ME.
NOW, BOY...

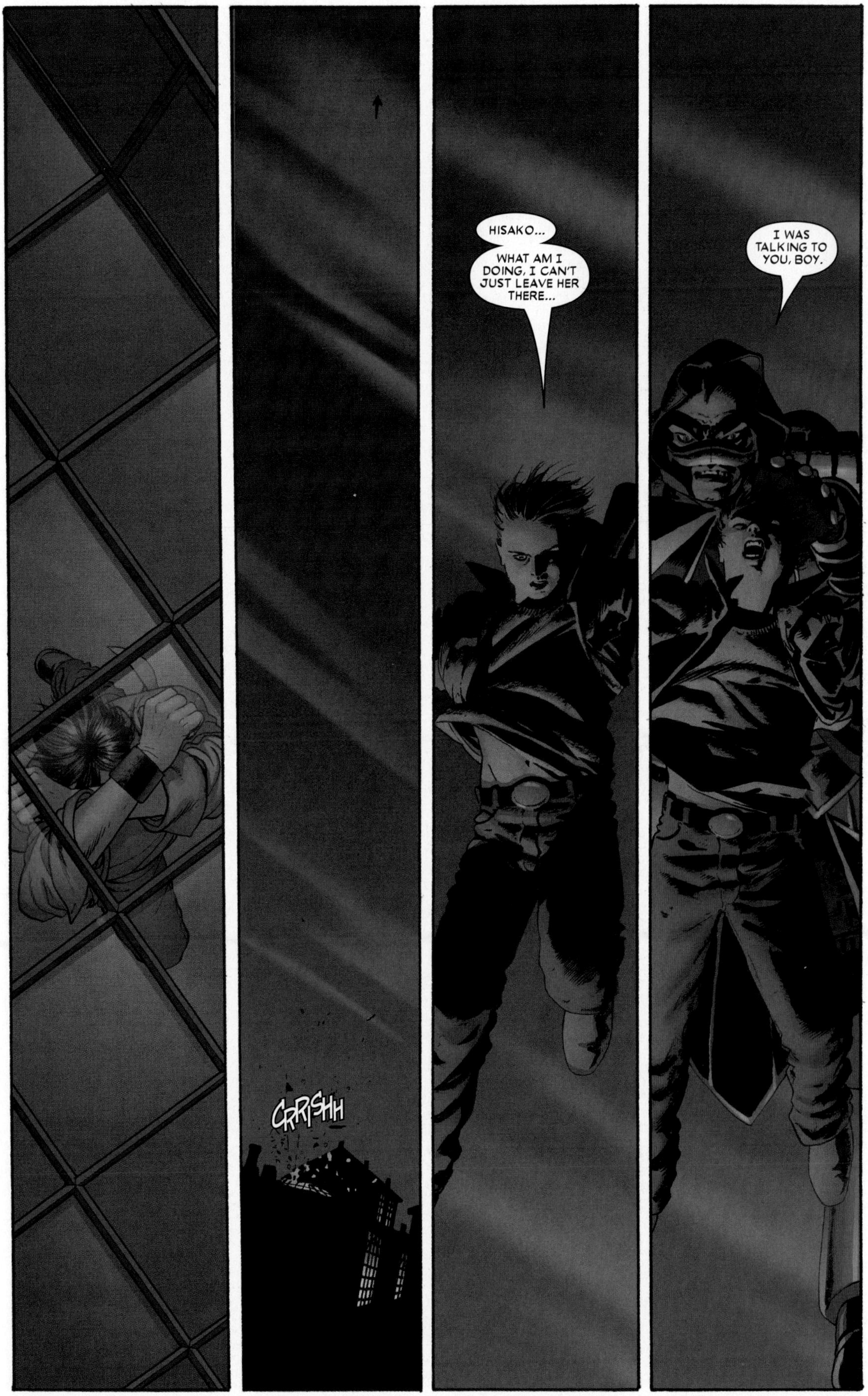
CRRISHH
HISAKO...
WHAT AM I DOING, I CAN'T JUST LEAVE HER THERE...
I WAS TALKING TO YOU, BOY.

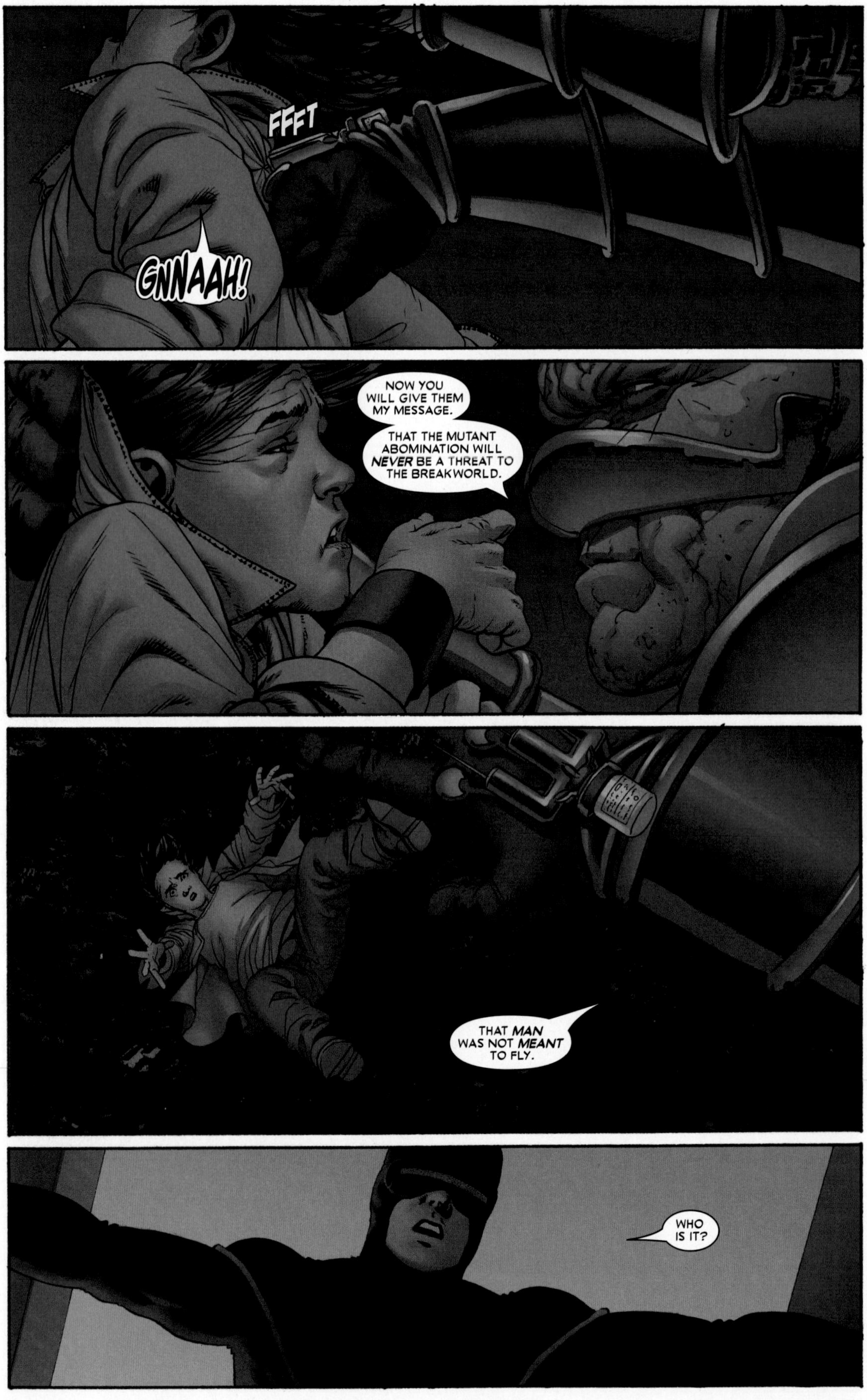
FFFT
GNNAAH!
NOW YOU WILL GIVE THEM MY MESSAGE.
THAT THE MUTANT ABOMINATION WILL *NEVER* BE A THREAT TO THE BREAKWORLD.
THAT *MAN* WAS NOT *MEANT* TO FLY.
WHO IS IT?

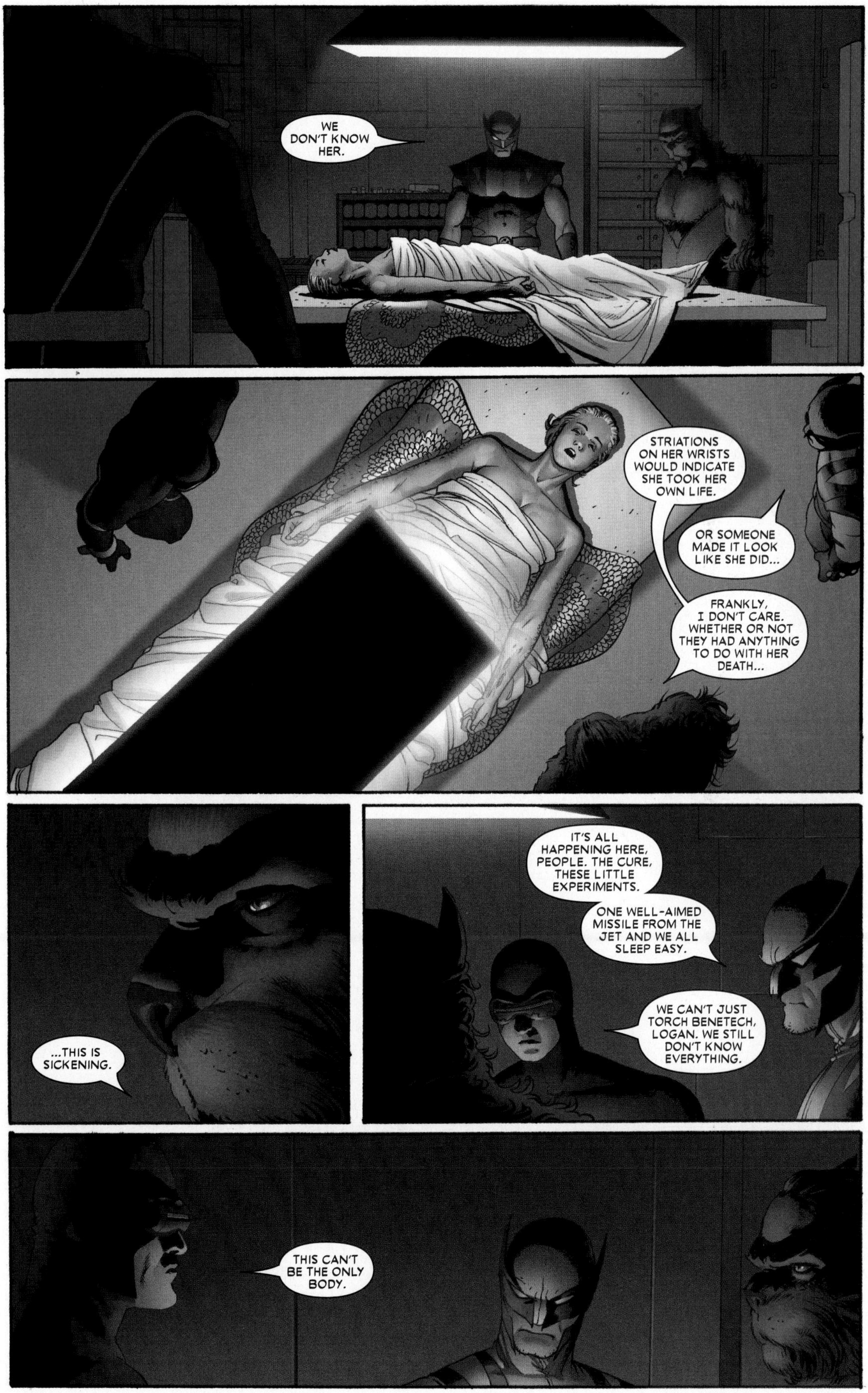
WE DON'T KNOW HER.
STRIATIONS ON HER WRISTS WOULD INDICATE SHE TOOK HER OWN LIFE.
OR SOMEONE MADE IT LOOK LIKE SHE DID...
FRANKLY, I DON'T CARE. WHETHER OR NOT THEY HAD ANYTHING TO DO WITH HER DEATH...
...THIS IS SICKENING.
IT'S ALL HAPPENING HERE, PEOPLE. THE CURE, THESE LITTLE EXPERIMENTS.
ONE WELL-AIMED MISSILE FROM THE JET AND WE ALL SLEEP EASY.
WE CAN'T JUST TORCH BENETECH, LOGAN. WE STILL DON'T KNOW EVERYTHING.
THIS CAN'T BE THE ONLY BODY.

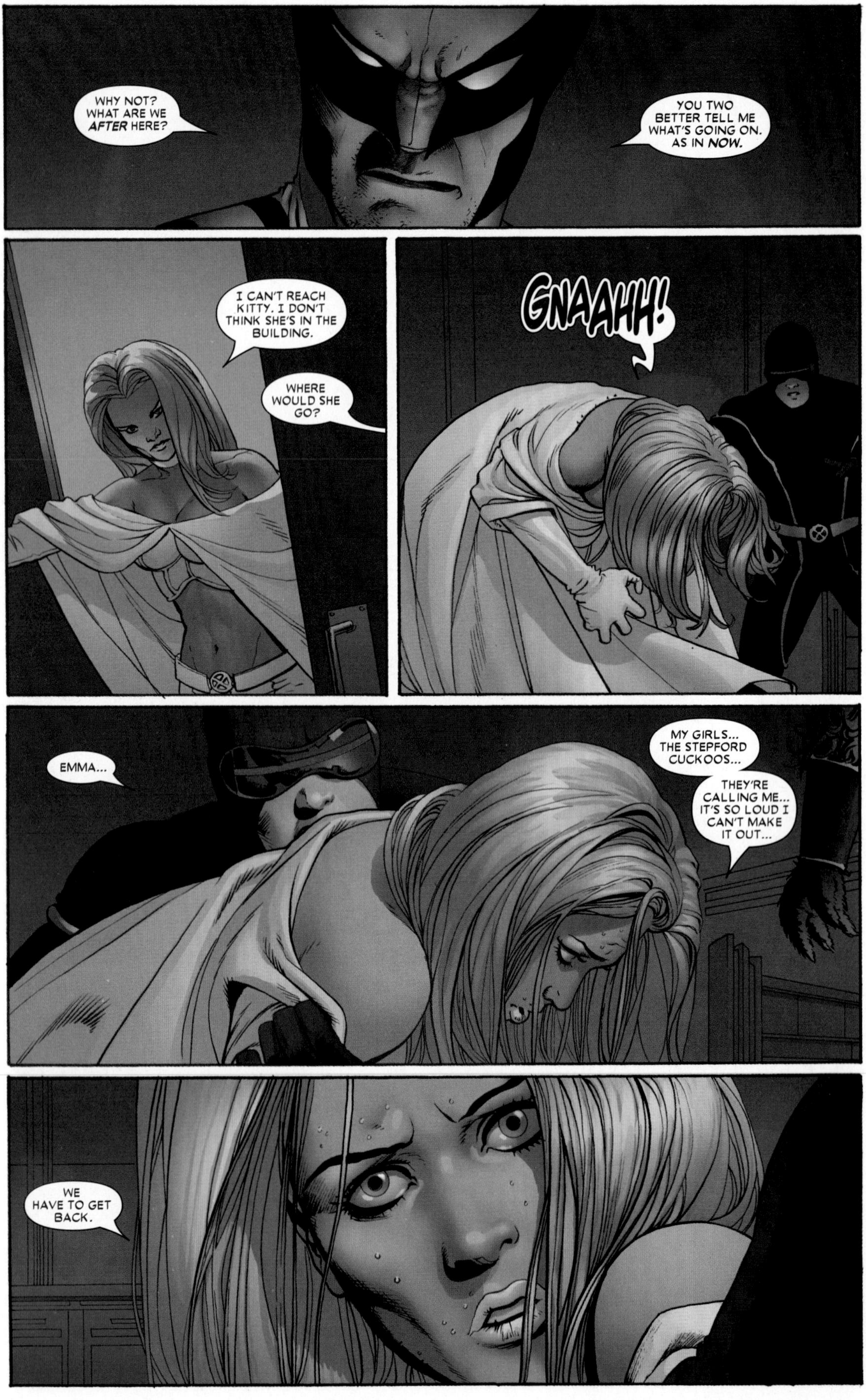
WHY NOT? WHAT ARE WE AFTER HERE?
YOU TWO BETTER TELL ME WHAT'S GOING ON. AS IN NOW.
I CAN'T REACH KITTY. I DON'T THINK SHE'S IN THE BUILDING.
WHERE WOULD SHE GO?
GNAAHH!
EMMA...
MY GIRLS... THE STEPFORD CUCKOOS...
THEY'RE CALLING ME... IT'S SO LOUD I CAN'T MAKE IT OUT...
WE HAVE TO GET BACK.

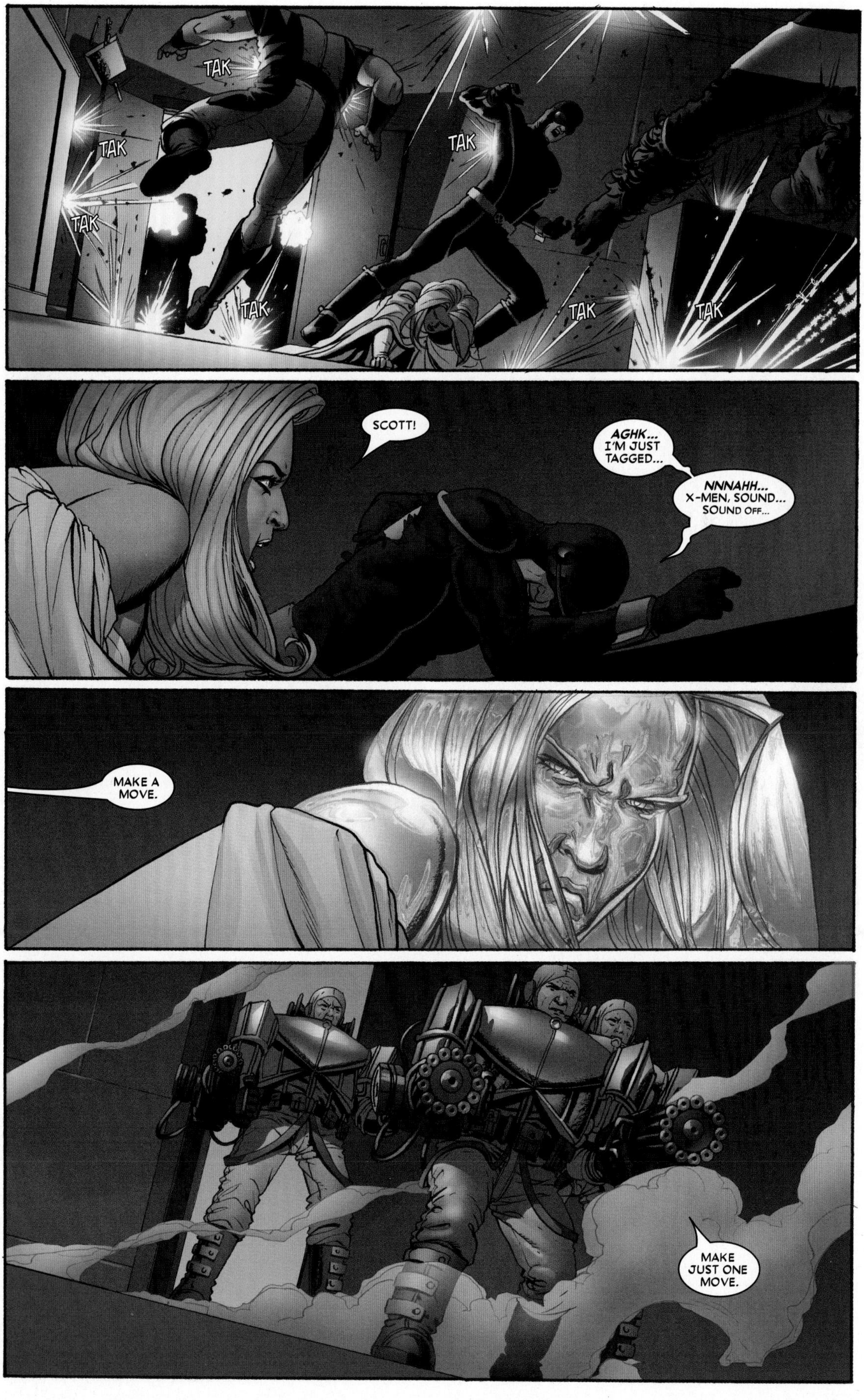
TAK
TAK
TAK
TAK
TAK
TAK
TAK
SCOTT!
AGHK... I'M JUST TAGGED...
NNNAHH... X-MEN, SOUND... SOUND OFF...
MAKE A MOVE.
MAKE JUST ONE MOVE.

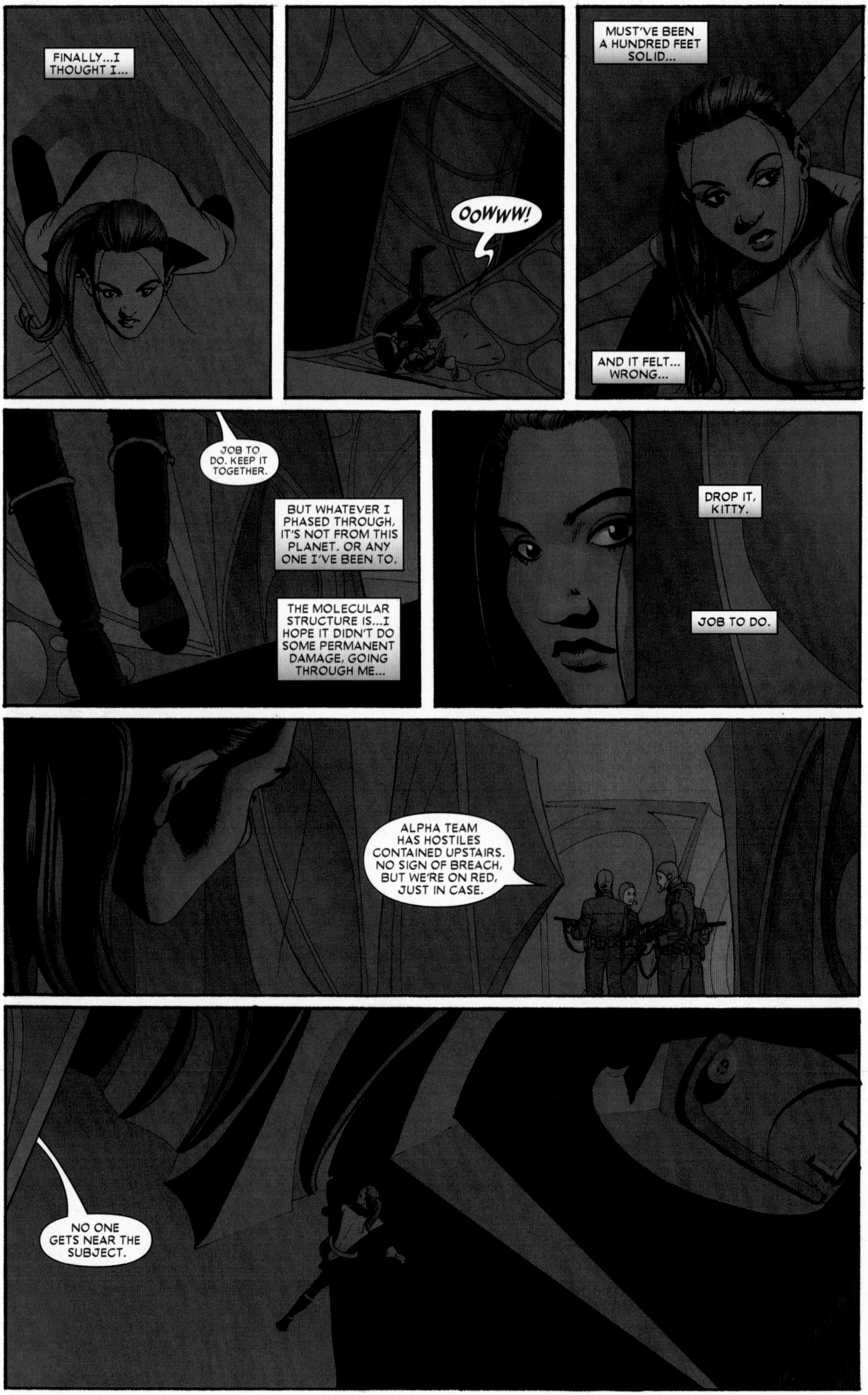
FINALLY...I THOUGHT I...
OOWWW!
MUST'VE BEEN A HUNDRED FEET SOLID...
AND IT FELT... WRONG...
JOB TO DO. KEEP IT TOGETHER.
BUT WHATEVER I PHASED THROUGH, IT'S NOT FROM THIS PLANET. OR ANY ONE I'VE BEEN TO.
THE MOLECULAR STRUCTURE IS...I HOPE IT DIDN'T DO SOME PERMANENT DAMAGE, GOING THROUGH ME...
DROP IT, KITTY.
JOB TO DO.
ALPHA TEAM HAS HOSTILES CONTAINED UPSTAIRS. NO SIGN OF BREACH, BUT WE'RE ON RED, JUST IN CASE.
NO ONE GETS NEAR THE SUBJECT.

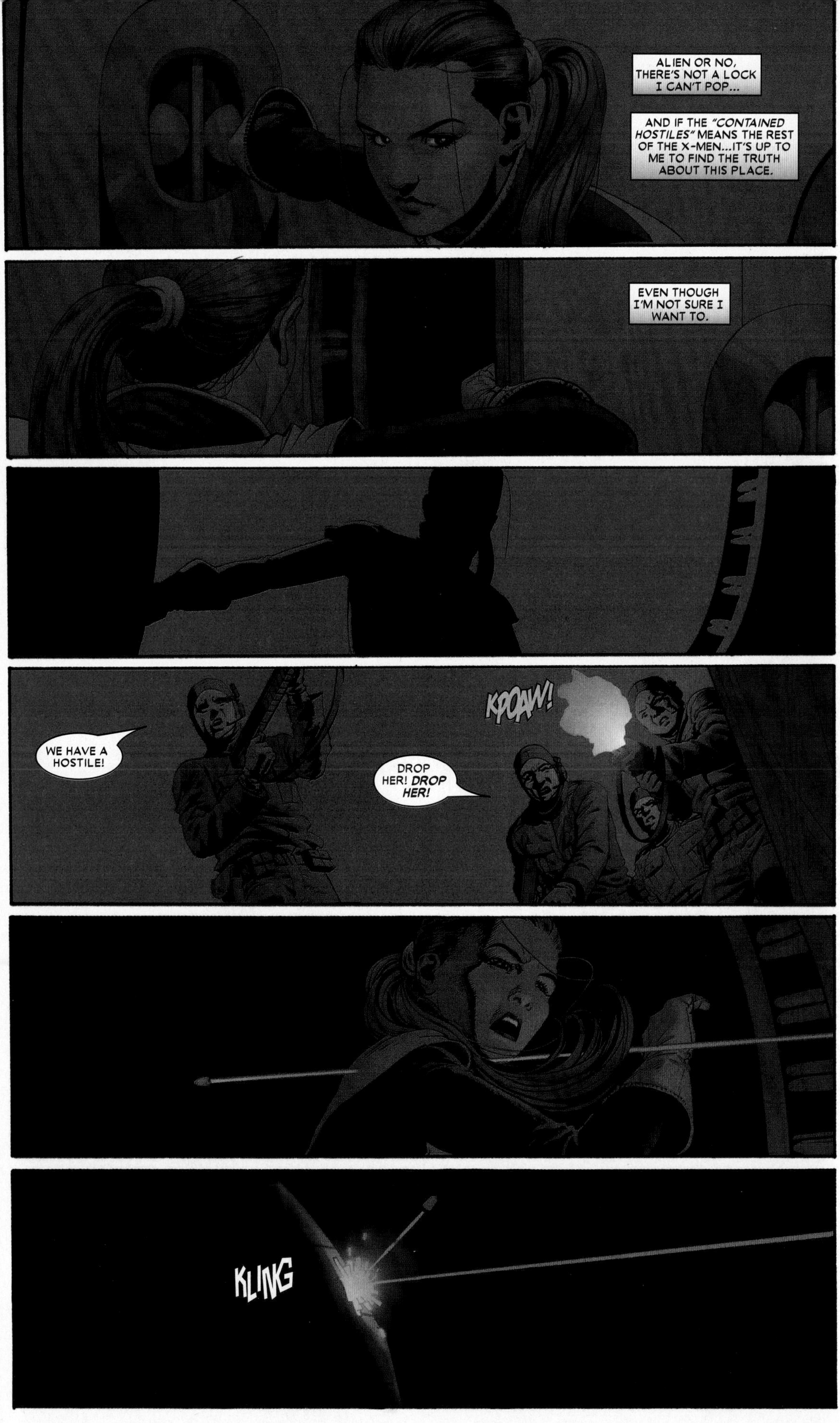
ALIEN OR NO, THERE'S NOT A LOCK I CAN'T POP...
AND IF THE *"CONTAINED HOSTILES"* MEANS THE REST OF THE X-MEN...IT'S UP TO ME TO FIND THE TRUTH ABOUT THIS PLACE.
EVEN THOUGH I'M NOT SURE I WANT TO.
KPOAW!
WE HAVE A HOSTILE!
DROP HER! *DROP HER!*
KLING

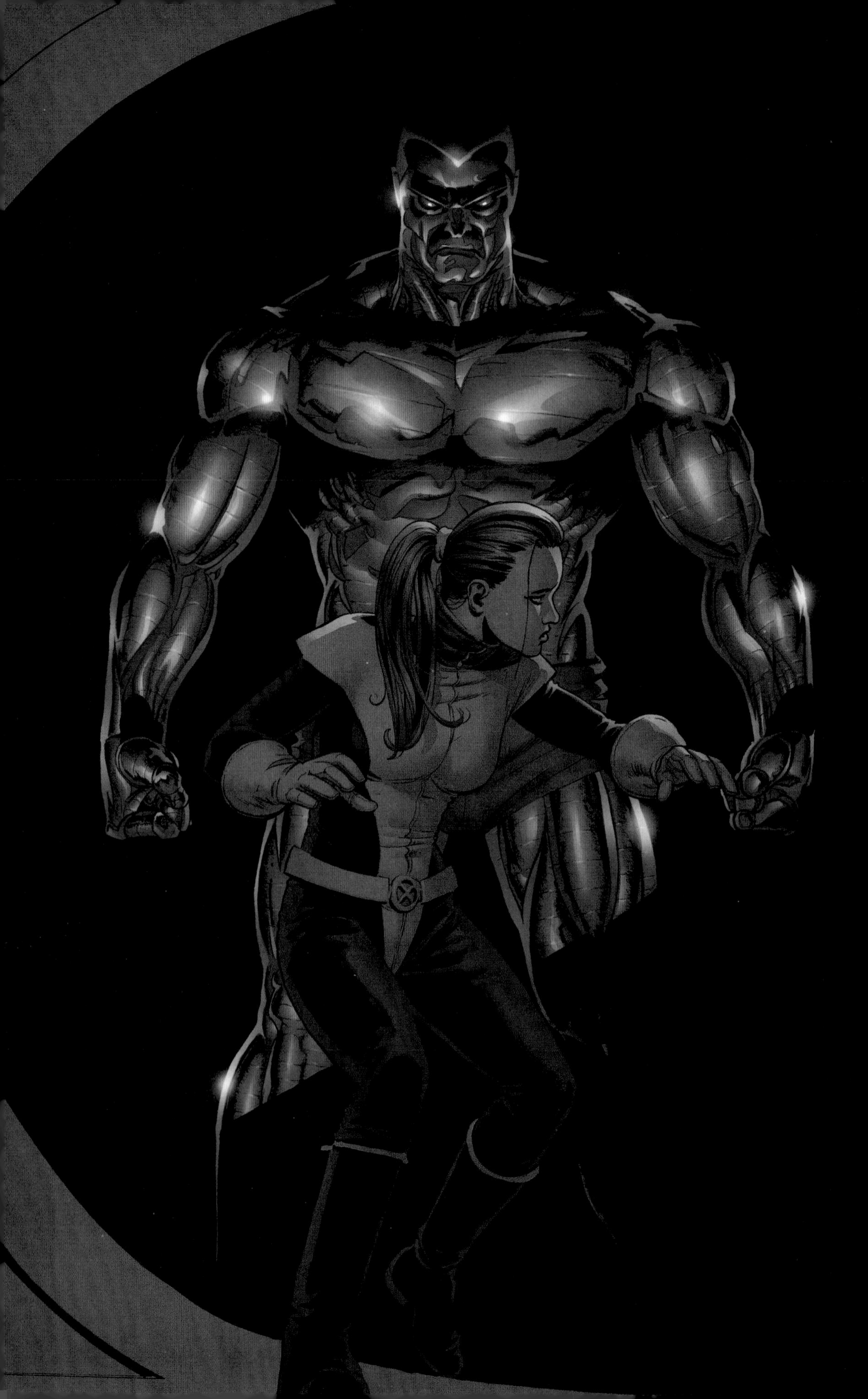

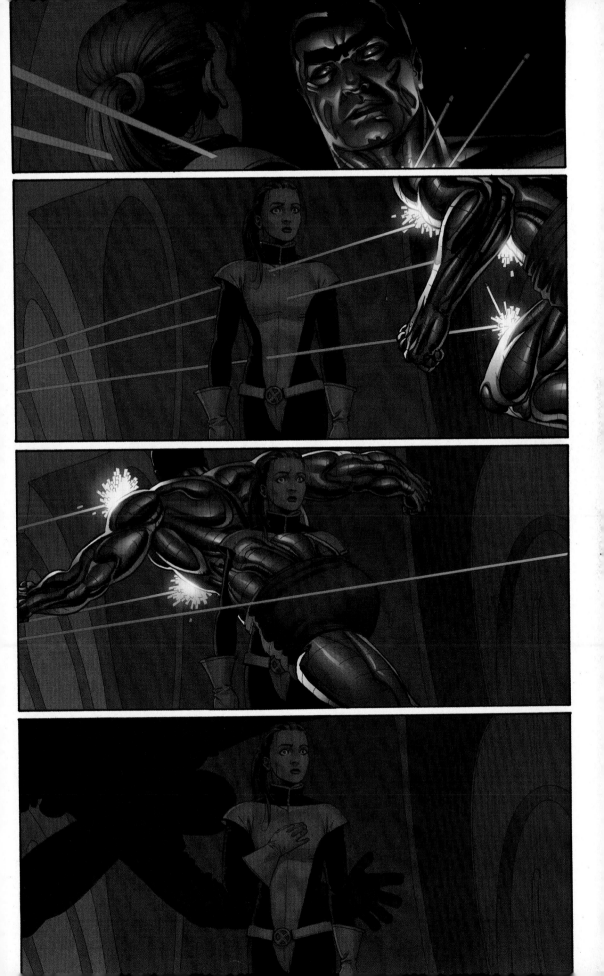

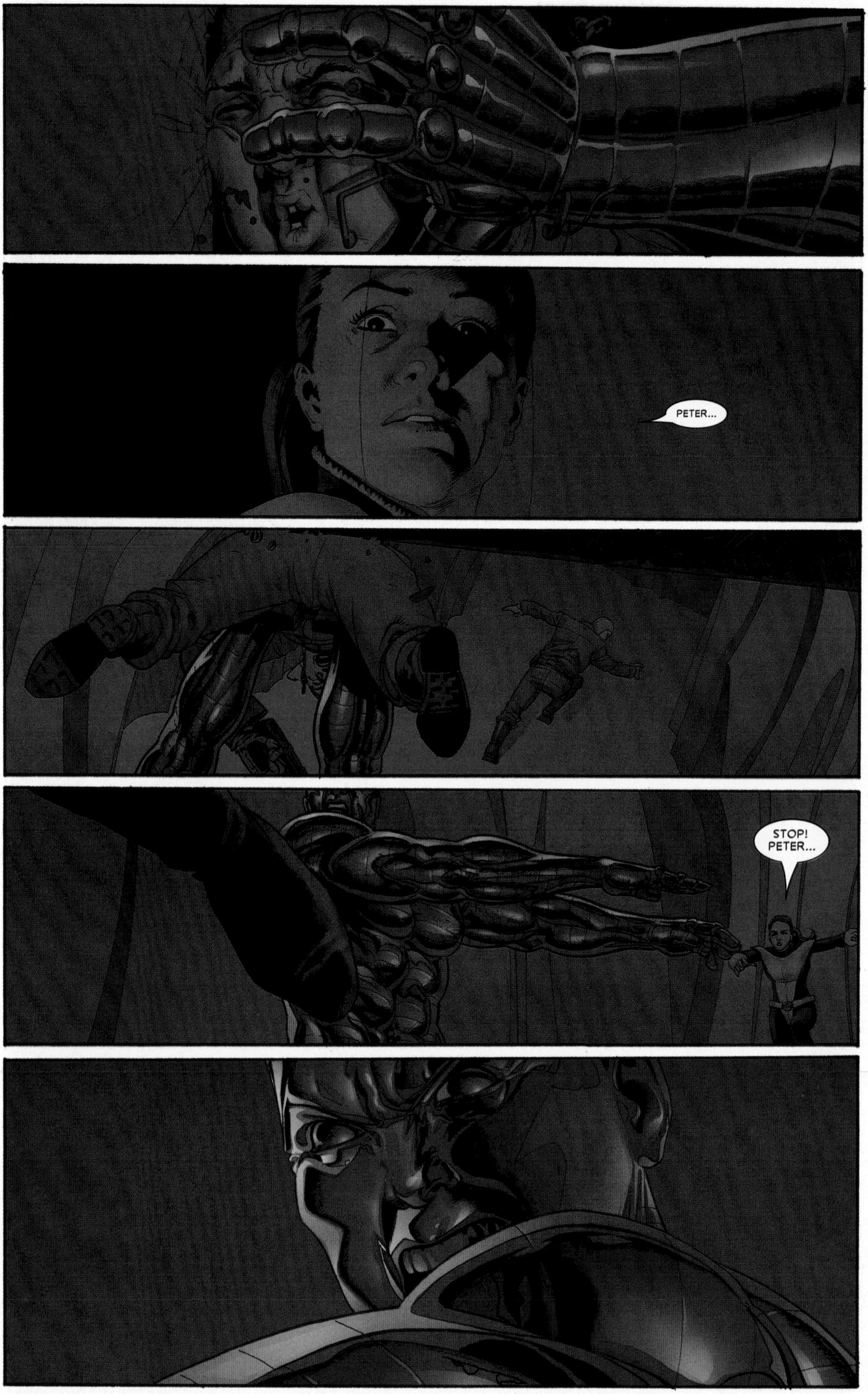
PETER...
STOP! PETER...

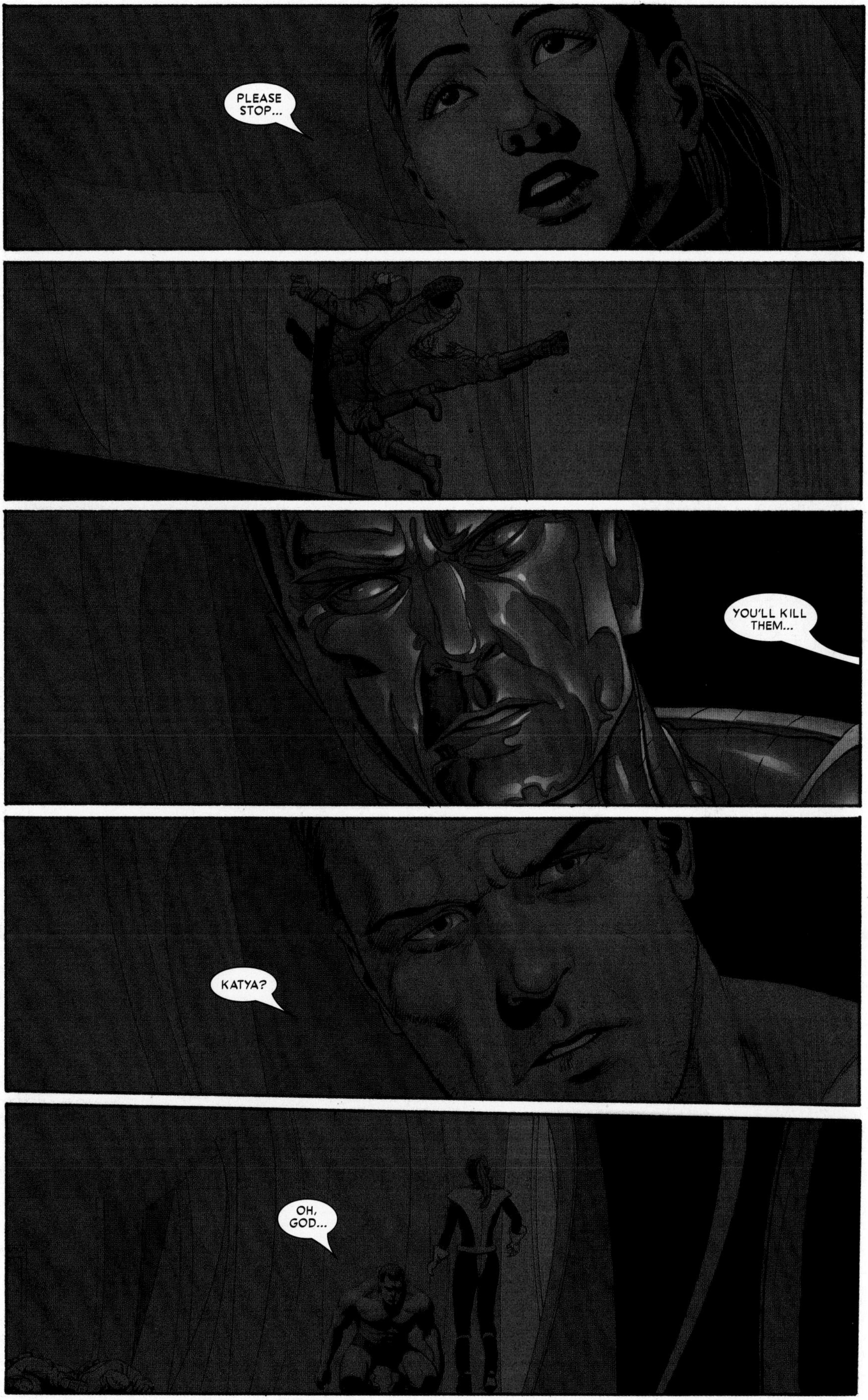
PLEASE STOP...
YOU'LL KILL THEM...
KATYA?
OH, GOD...

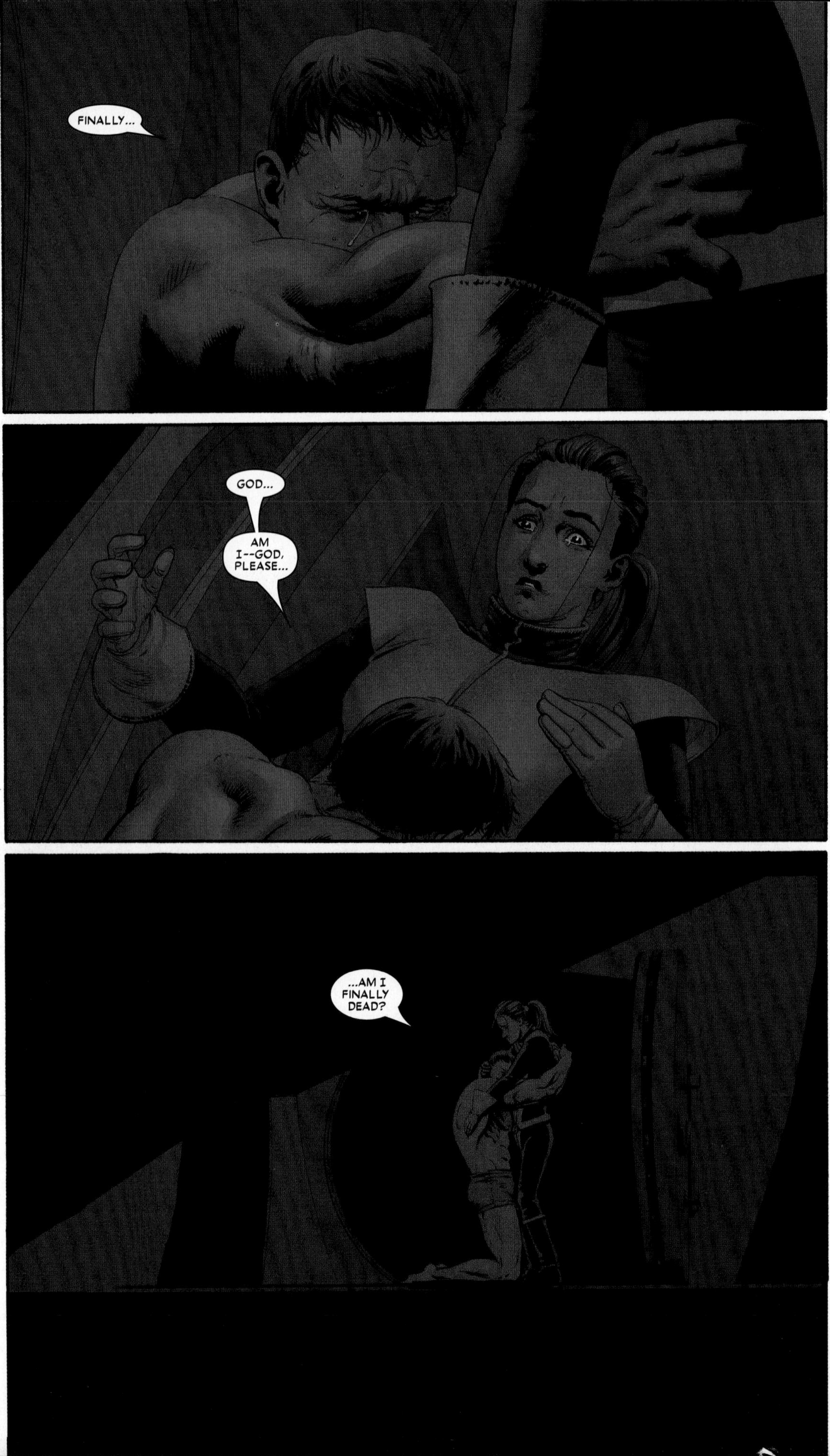
FINALLY...
GOD...
AM I--GOD, PLEASE...
...AM I FINALLY DEAD?

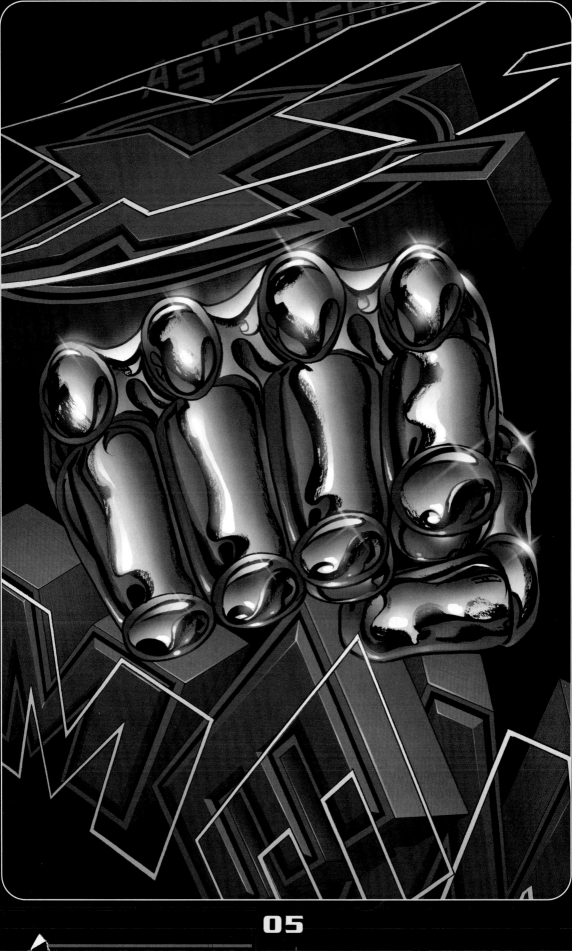

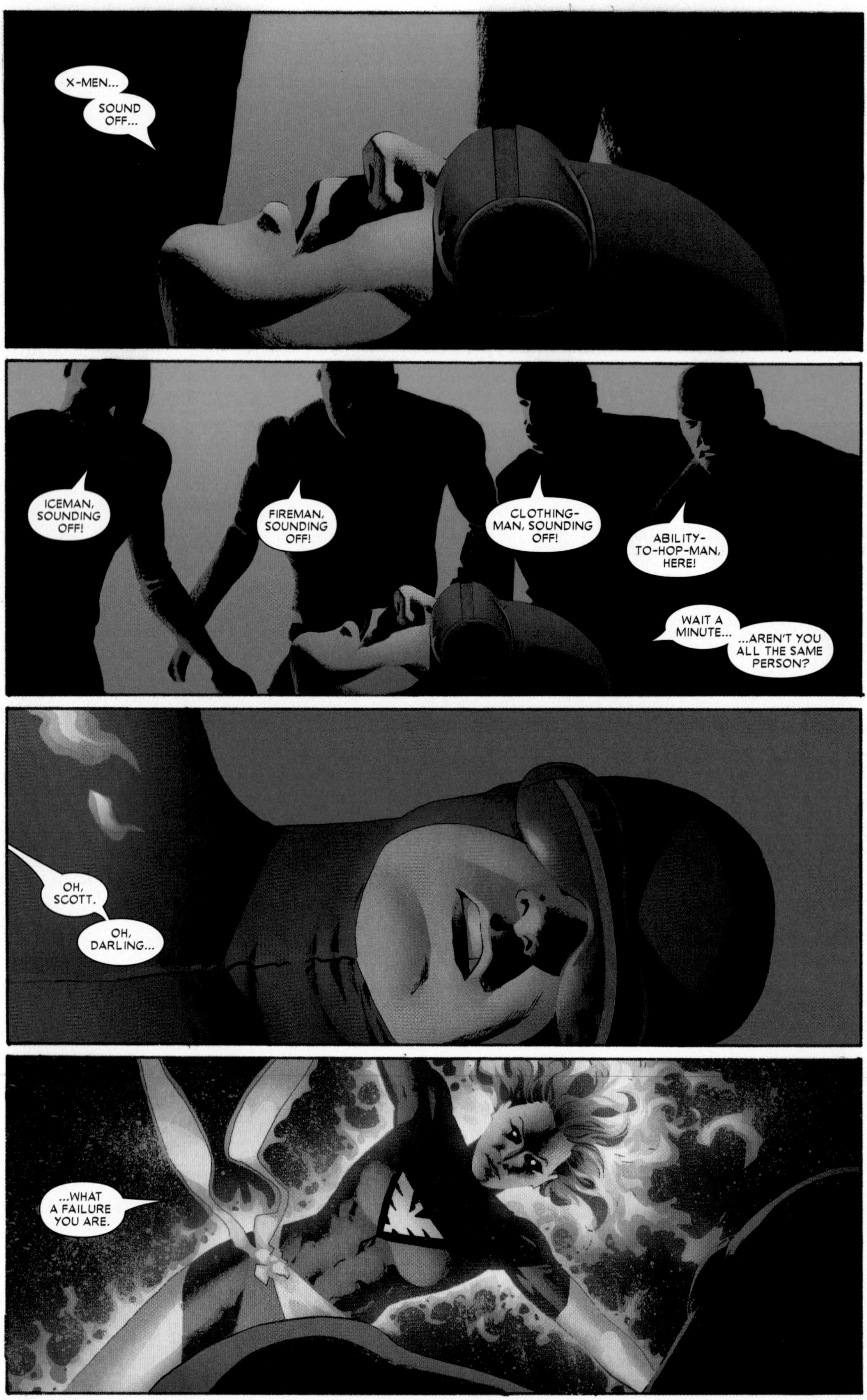
X-MEN...
SOUND OFF...
ICEMAN, SOUNDING OFF!
FIREMAN, SOUNDING OFF!
CLOTHING-MAN, SOUNDING OFF!
ABILITY-TO-HOP-MAN, HERE!
WAIT A MINUTE...
...AREN'T YOU ALL THE SAME PERSON?
OH, SCOTT.
OH, DARLING...
...WHAT A FAILURE YOU ARE.

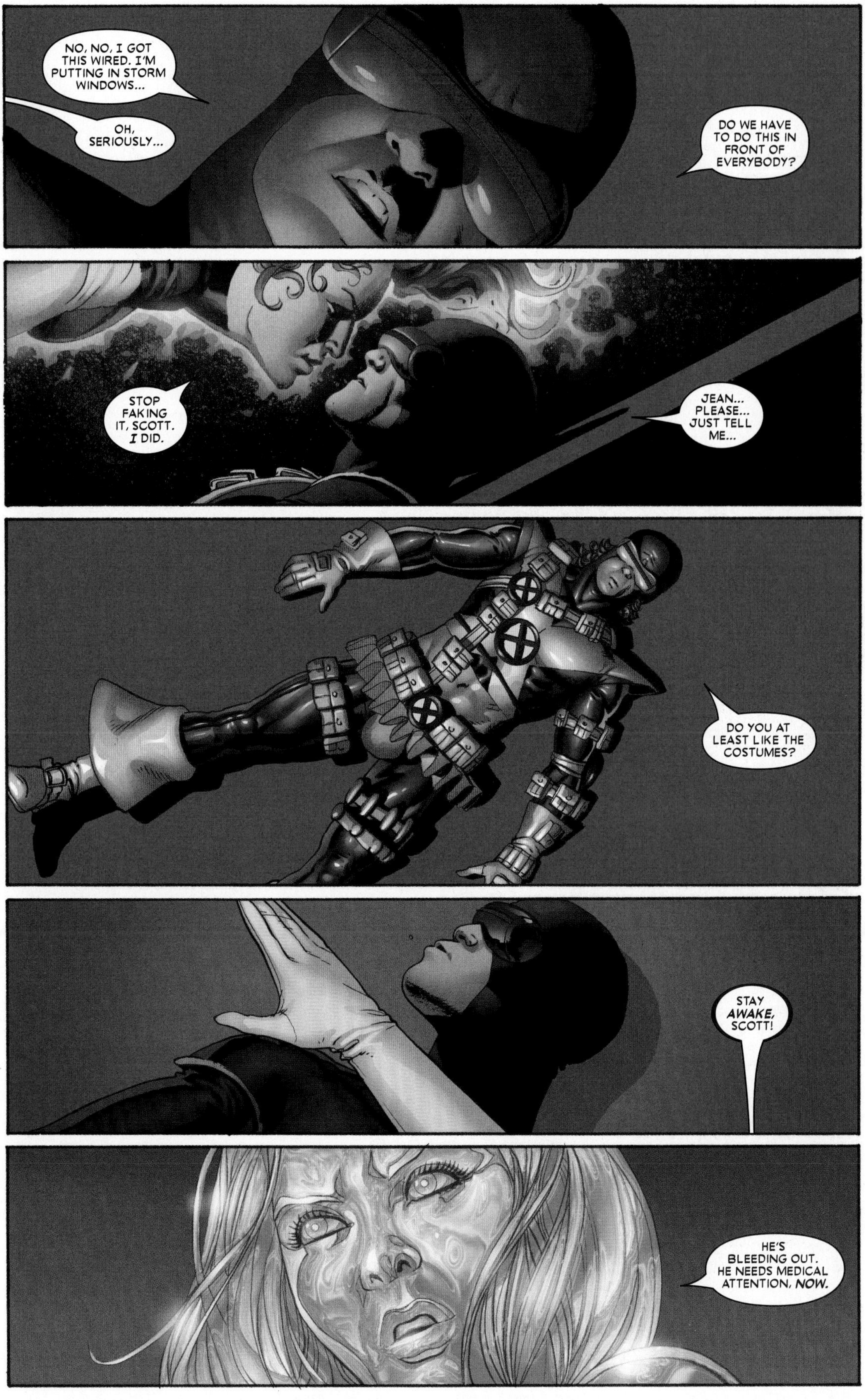
NO, NO, I GOT THIS WIRED. I'M PUTTING IN STORM WINDOWS...
OH, SERIOUSLY...
DO WE HAVE TO DO THIS IN FRONT OF EVERYBODY?
STOP FAKING IT, SCOTT. *I* DID.
JEAN... PLEASE... JUST TELL ME...
DO YOU AT LEAST LIKE THE COSTUMES?
STAY *AWAKE,* SCOTT!
HE'S BLEEDING OUT. HE NEEDS MEDICAL ATTENTION, *NOW.*

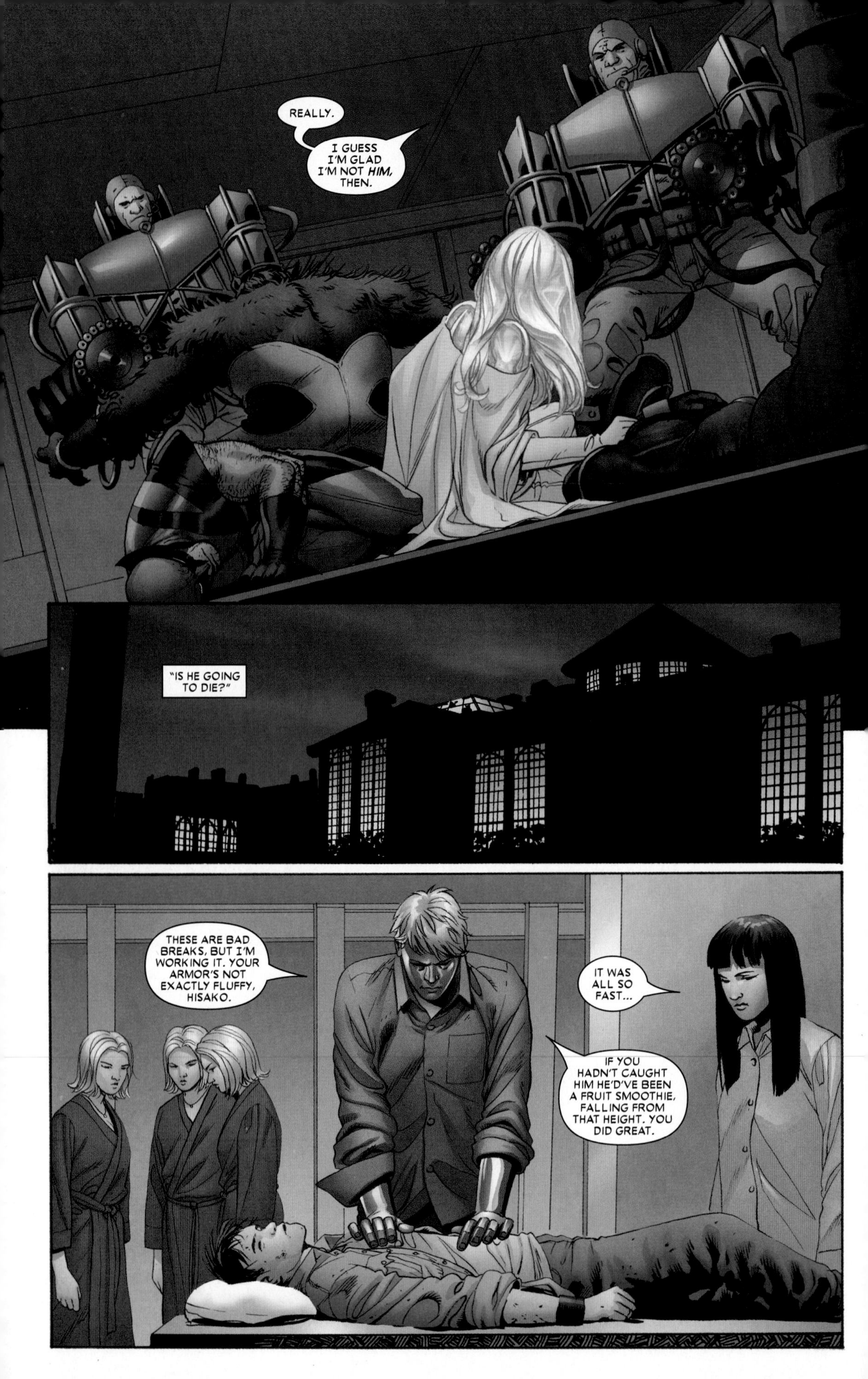
REALLY.
I GUESS I'M GLAD I'M NOT *HIM,* THEN.
"IS HE GOING TO DIE?"
THESE ARE BAD BREAKS, BUT I'M WORKING IT. YOUR ARMOR'S NOT EXACTLY FLUFFY, HISAKO.
IT WAS ALL SO FAST...
IF YOU HADN'T CAUGHT HIM HE'D'VE BEEN A FRUIT SMOOTHIE, FALLING FROM THAT HEIGHT. YOU DID GREAT.

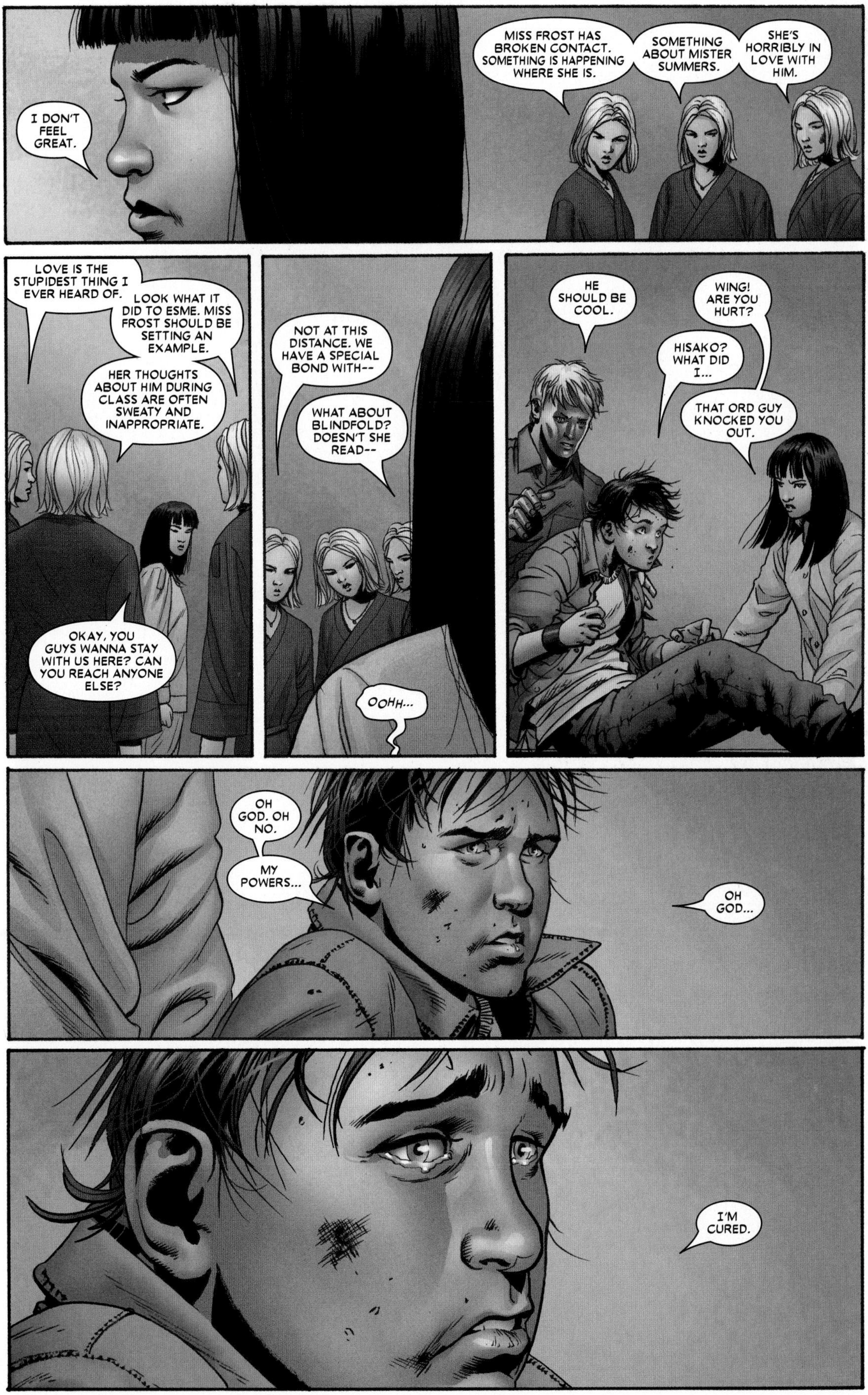
I DON'T FEEL GREAT.
MISS FROST HAS BROKEN CONTACT. SOMETHING IS HAPPENING WHERE SHE IS.
SOMETHING ABOUT MISTER SUMMERS.
SHE'S HORRIBLY IN LOVE WITH HIM.
LOVE IS THE STUPIDEST THING I EVER HEARD OF.
LOOK WHAT IT DID TO ESME. MISS FROST SHOULD BE SETTING AN EXAMPLE.
HER THOUGHTS ABOUT HIM DURING CLASS ARE OFTEN SWEATY AND INAPPROPRIATE.
OKAY, YOU GUYS WANNA STAY WITH US HERE? CAN YOU REACH ANYONE ELSE?
NOT AT THIS DISTANCE. WE HAVE A SPECIAL BOND WITH--
WHAT ABOUT BLINDFOLD? DOESN'T SHE READ--
OOHH...
HE SHOULD BE COOL.
WING! ARE YOU HURT?
HISAKO? WHAT DID I...
THAT ORD GUY KNOCKED YOU OUT.
OH GOD. OH NO.
MY POWERS...
OH GOD...
I'M CURED.

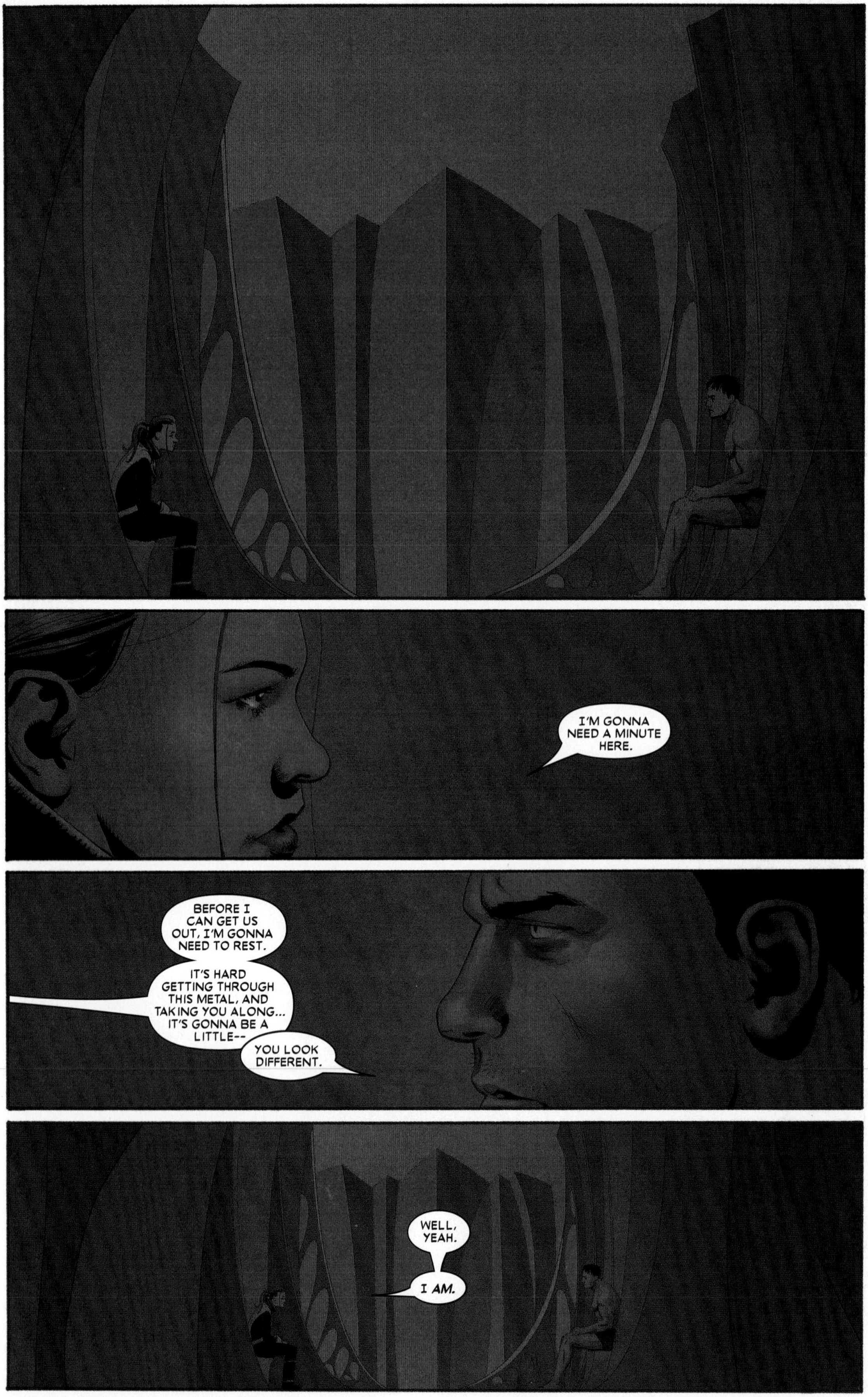
I'M GONNA NEED A MINUTE HERE.
BEFORE I CAN GET US OUT, I'M GONNA NEED TO REST.
IT'S HARD GETTING THROUGH THIS METAL, AND TAKING YOU ALONG... IT'S GONNA BE A LITTLE--
YOU LOOK DIFFERENT.
WELL, YEAH.
I AM.

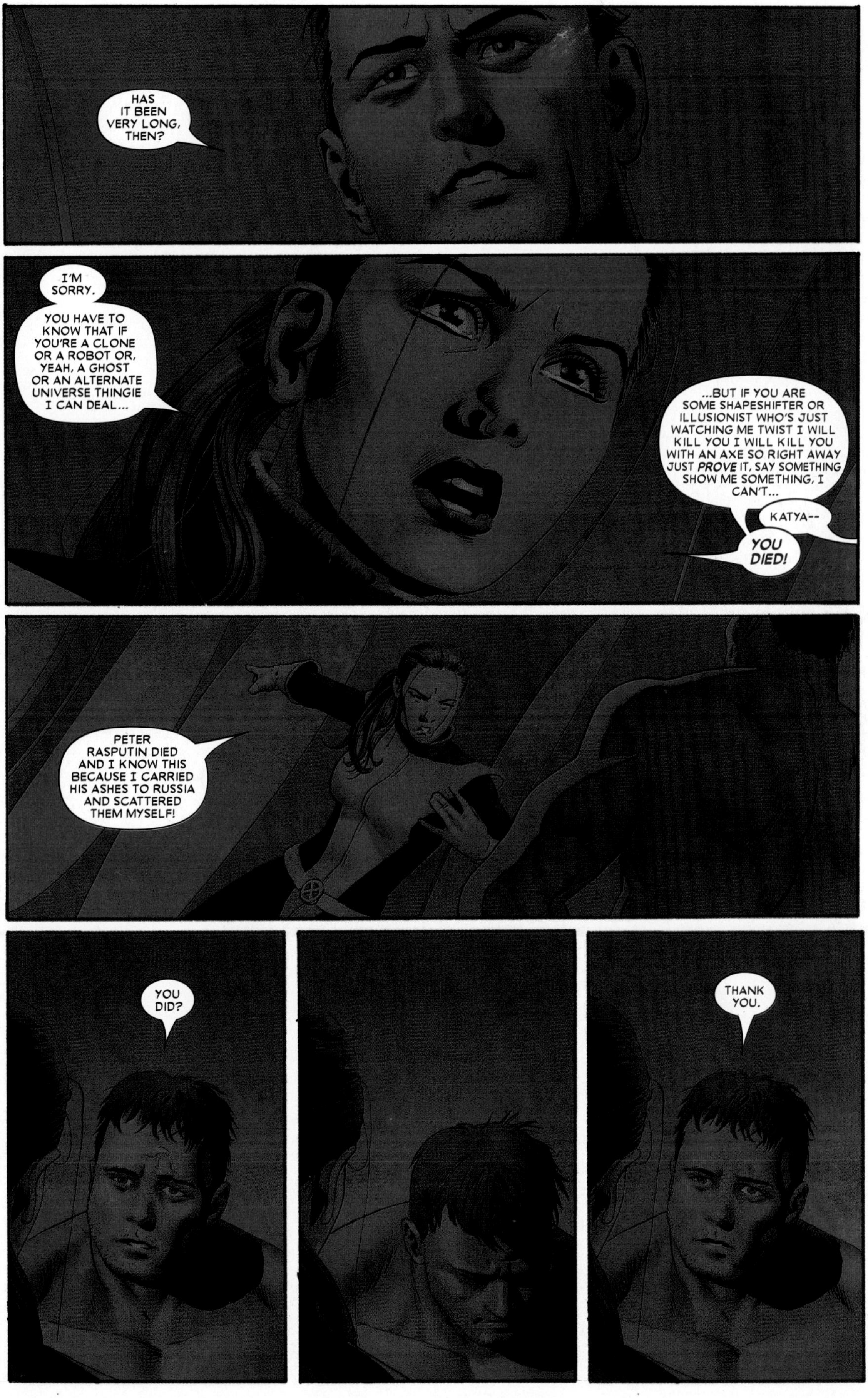
HAS IT BEEN VERY LONG, THEN?
I'M SORRY.
YOU HAVE TO KNOW THAT IF YOU'RE A CLONE OR A ROBOT OR, YEAH, A GHOST OR AN ALTERNATE UNIVERSE THINGIE I CAN DEAL...
...BUT IF YOU ARE SOME SHAPESHIFTER OR ILLUSIONIST WHO'S JUST WATCHING ME TWIST I WILL KILL YOU I WILL KILL YOU WITH AN AXE SO RIGHT AWAY JUST *PROVE* IT, SAY SOMETHING SHOW ME SOMETHING, I CAN'T...
KATYA--
YOU DIED!
PETER RASPUTIN DIED AND I KNOW THIS BECAUSE I CARRIED HIS ASHES TO RUSSIA AND SCATTERED THEM MYSELF!
YOU DID?
THANK YOU.

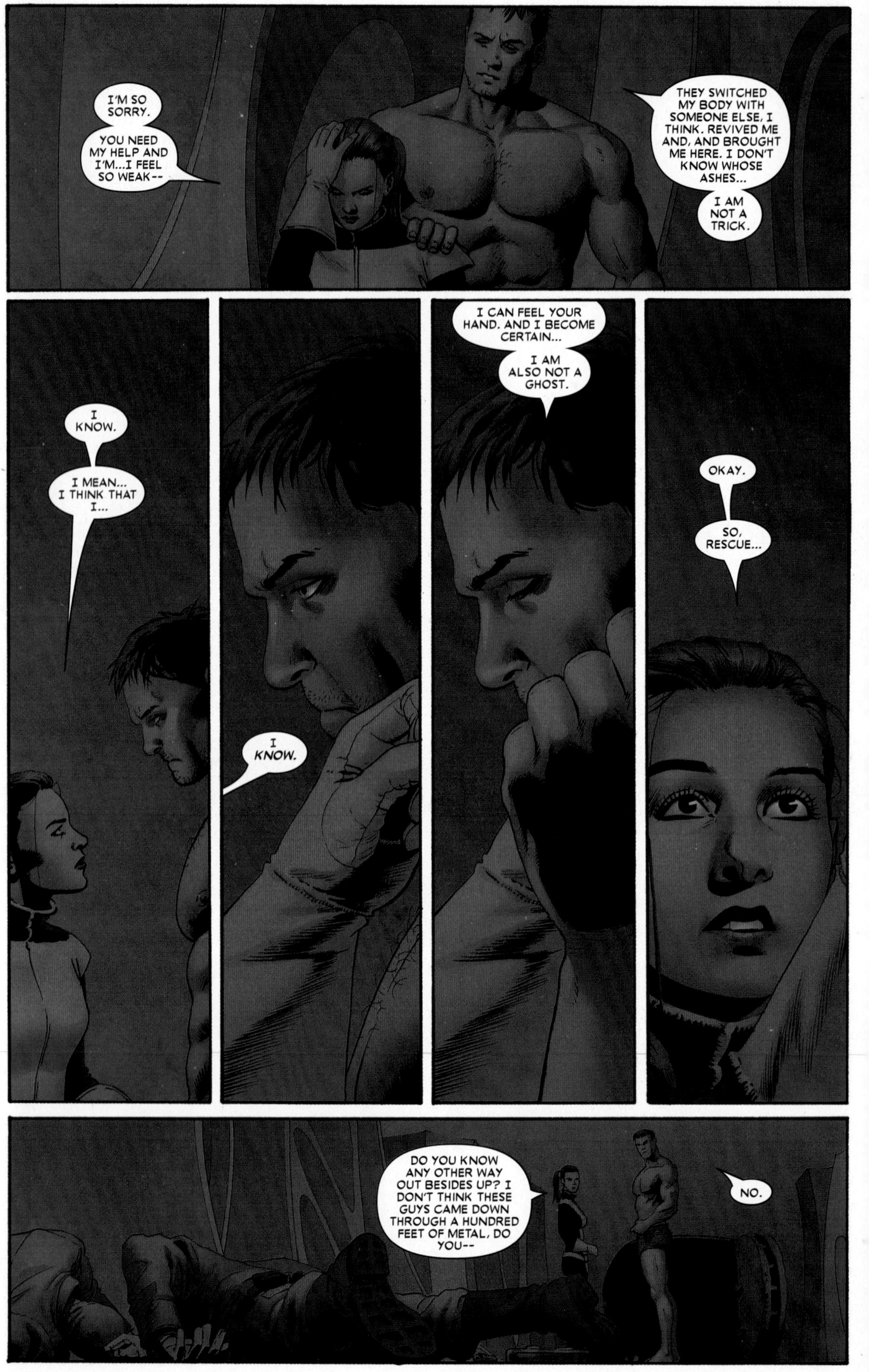

I'M SO SORRY.
YOU NEED MY HELP AND I'M...I FEEL SO WEAK--
THEY SWITCHED MY BODY WITH SOMEONE ELSE, I THINK. REVIVED ME AND, AND BROUGHT ME HERE. I DON'T KNOW WHOSE ASHES...
I AM NOT A TRICK.
I KNOW.
I MEAN... I THINK THAT I...
I KNOW.
I CAN FEEL YOUR HAND. AND I BECOME CERTAIN...
I AM ALSO NOT A GHOST.
OKAY.
SO, RESCUE...
DO YOU KNOW ANY OTHER WAY OUT BESIDES UP? I DON'T THINK THESE GUYS CAME DOWN THROUGH A HUNDRED FEET OF METAL, DO YOU--
NO.

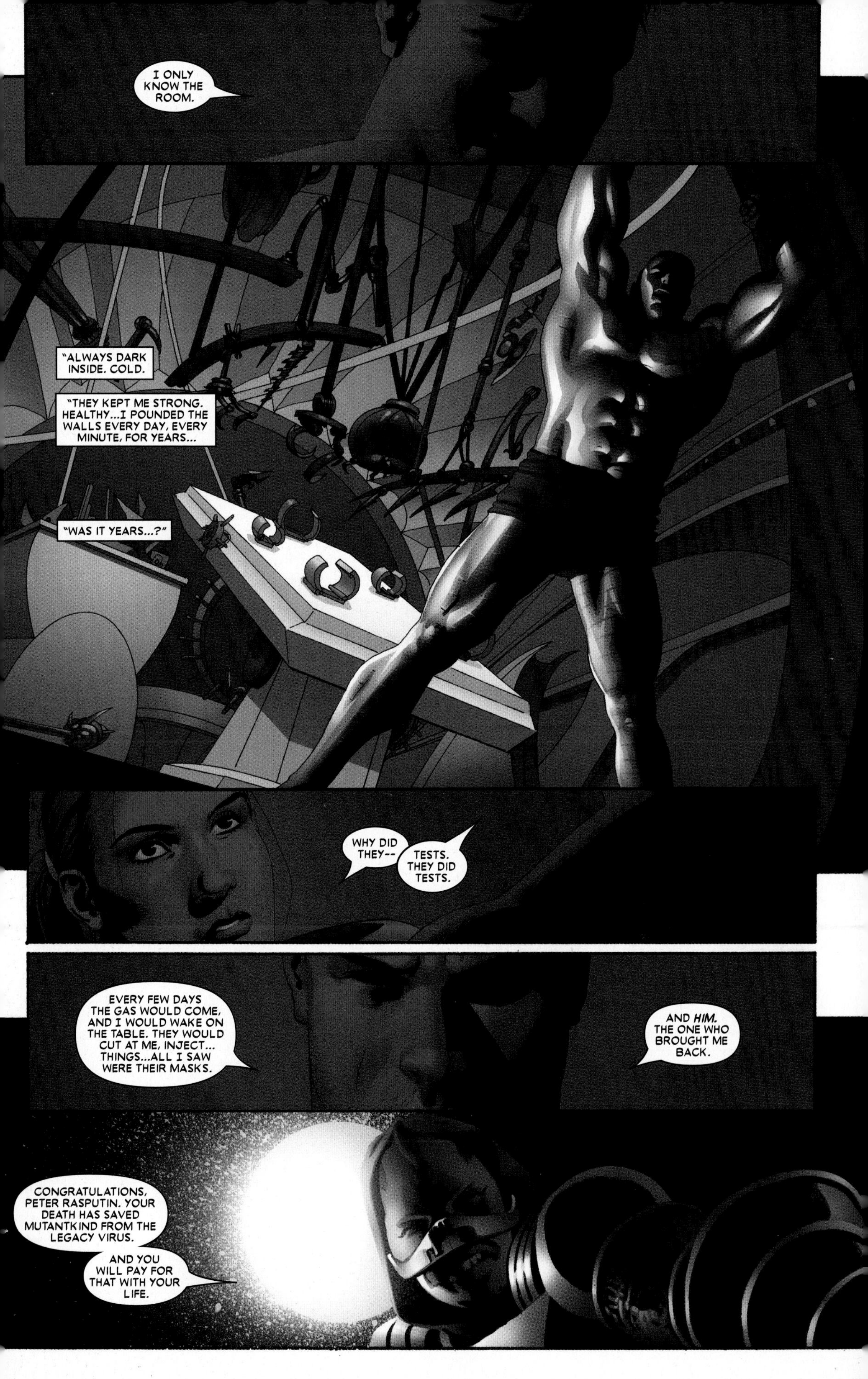
I ONLY KNOW THE ROOM.
"ALWAYS DARK INSIDE. COLD.
"THEY KEPT ME STRONG. HEALTHY...I POUNDED THE WALLS EVERY DAY, EVERY MINUTE, FOR YEARS...
"WAS IT YEARS...?"
WHY DID THEY--
TESTS. THEY DID TESTS.
EVERY FEW DAYS THE GAS WOULD COME, AND I WOULD WAKE ON THE TABLE. THEY WOULD CUT AT ME, INJECT... THINGS...ALL I SAW WERE THEIR MASKS.
AND *HIM.* THE ONE WHO BROUGHT ME BACK.
CONGRATULATIONS, PETER RASPUTIN. YOUR DEATH HAS SAVED MUTANTKIND FROM THE LEGACY VIRUS.
AND YOU WILL PAY FOR THAT WITH YOUR LIFE.

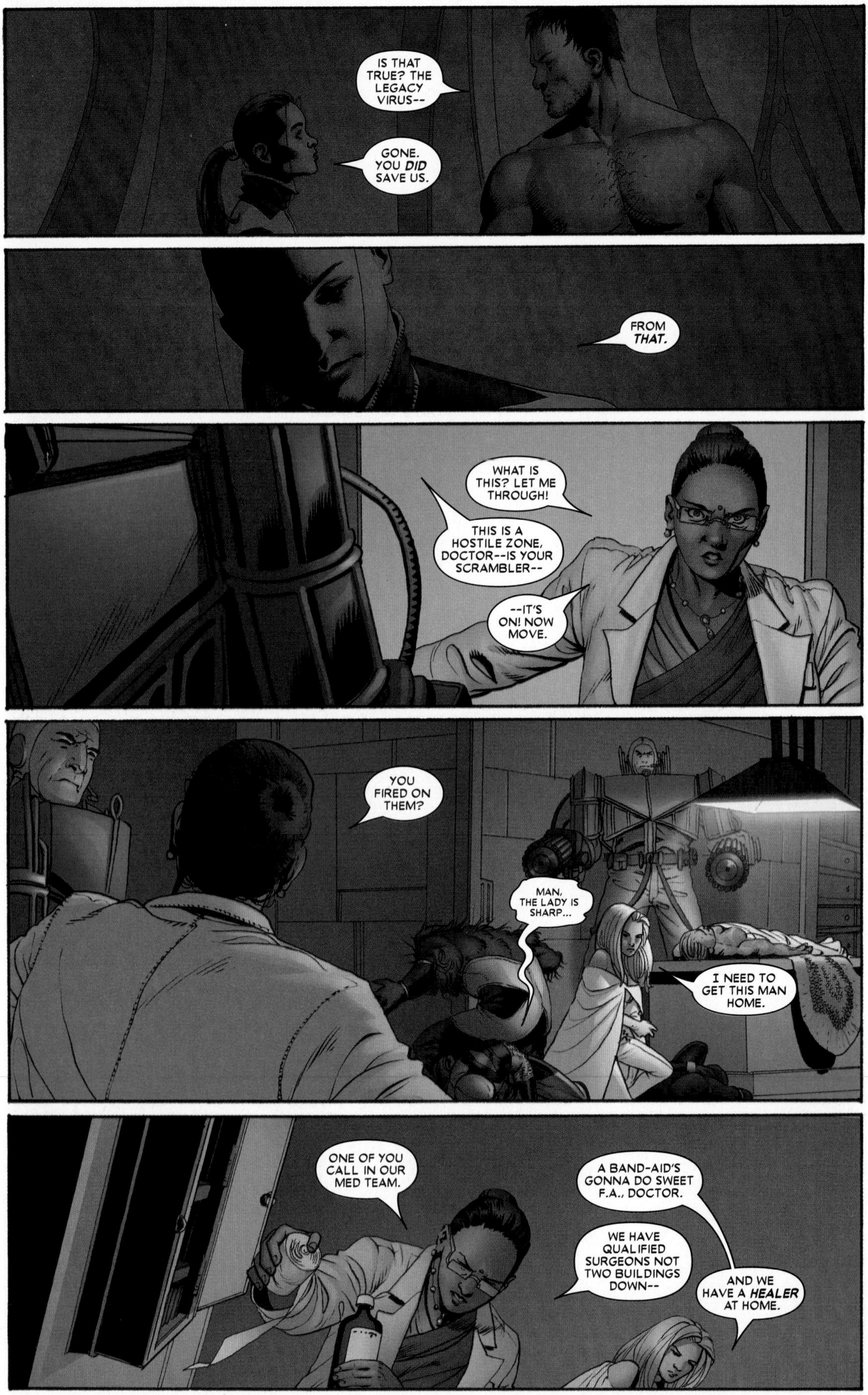
IS THAT TRUE? THE LEGACY VIRUS--
GONE. YOU *DID* SAVE US.
FROM *THAT.*
WHAT IS THIS? LET ME THROUGH!
THIS IS A HOSTILE ZONE, DOCTOR--IS YOUR SCRAMBLER--
--IT'S ON! NOW MOVE.
YOU FIRED ON THEM?
MAN, THE LADY IS SHARP...
I NEED TO GET THIS MAN HOME.
ONE OF YOU CALL IN OUR MED TEAM.
A BAND-AID'S GONNA DO SWEET F.A., DOCTOR.
WE HAVE QUALIFIED SURGEONS NOT TWO BUILDINGS DOWN--
AND WE HAVE A *HEALER* AT HOME.

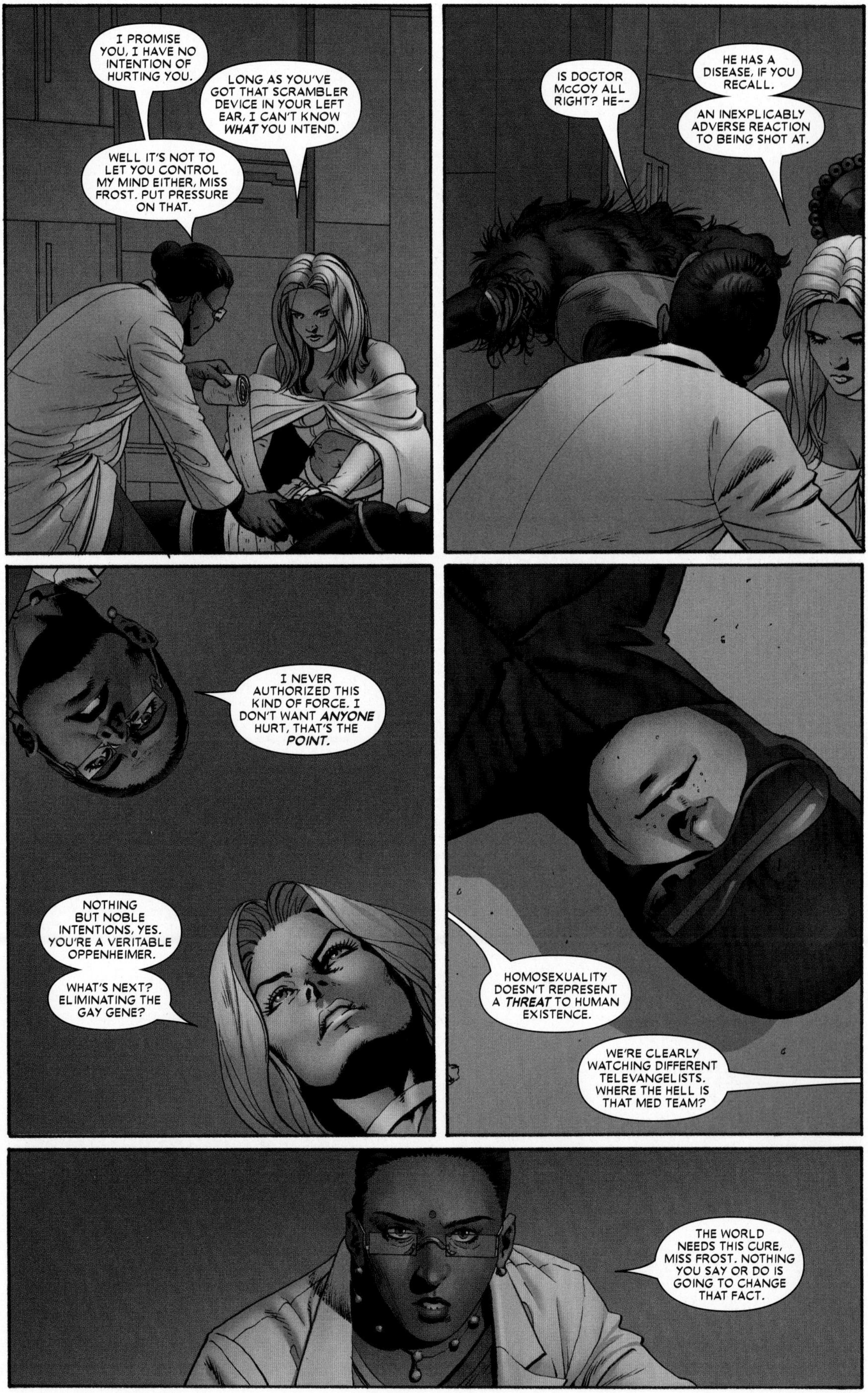
I PROMISE YOU, I HAVE NO INTENTION OF HURTING YOU.
LONG AS YOU'VE GOT THAT SCRAMBLER DEVICE IN YOUR LEFT EAR, I CAN'T KNOW *WHAT* YOU INTEND.
WELL IT'S NOT TO LET YOU CONTROL MY MIND EITHER, MISS FROST. PUT PRESSURE ON THAT.
IS DOCTOR McCOY ALL RIGHT? HE--
HE HAS A DISEASE, IF YOU RECALL.
AN INEXPLICABLY ADVERSE REACTION TO BEING SHOT AT.
I NEVER AUTHORIZED THIS KIND OF FORCE. I DON'T WANT *ANYONE* HURT, THAT'S THE *POINT.*
NOTHING BUT NOBLE INTENTIONS, YES. YOU'RE A VERITABLE OPPENHEIMER.
WHAT'S NEXT? ELIMINATING THE GAY GENE?
HOMOSEXUALITY DOESN'T REPRESENT A *THREAT* TO HUMAN EXISTENCE.
WE'RE CLEARLY WATCHING DIFFERENT TELEVANGELISTS. WHERE THE HELL IS THAT MED TEAM?
THE WORLD NEEDS THIS CURE, MISS FROST. NOTHING YOU SAY OR DO IS GOING TO CHANGE THAT FACT.

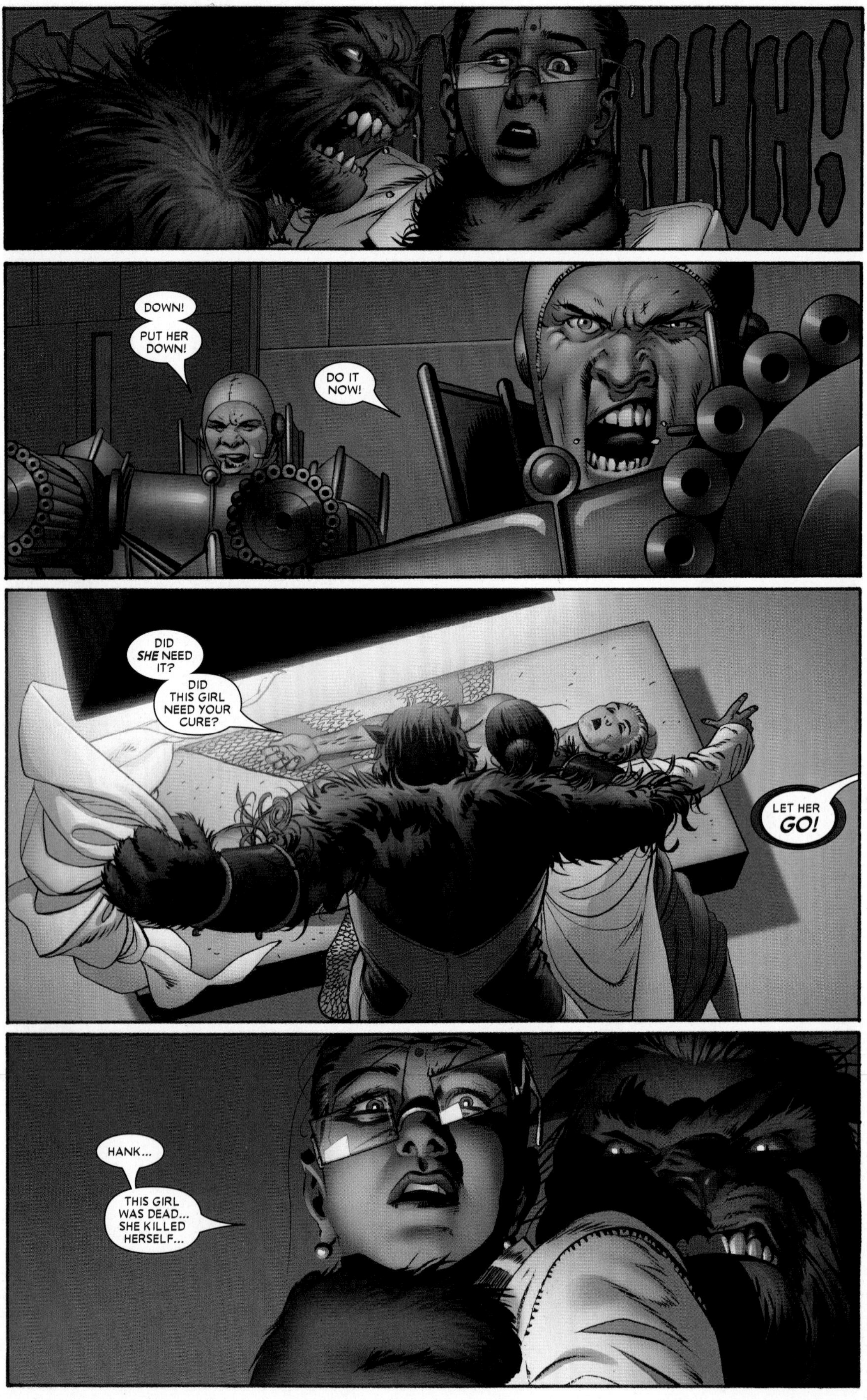
AAHHHH!
DOWN!
PUT HER DOWN!
DO IT NOW!
DID SHE NEED IT?
DID THIS GIRL NEED YOUR CURE?
LET HER GO!
HANK...
THIS GIRL WAS DEAD... SHE KILLED HERSELF...

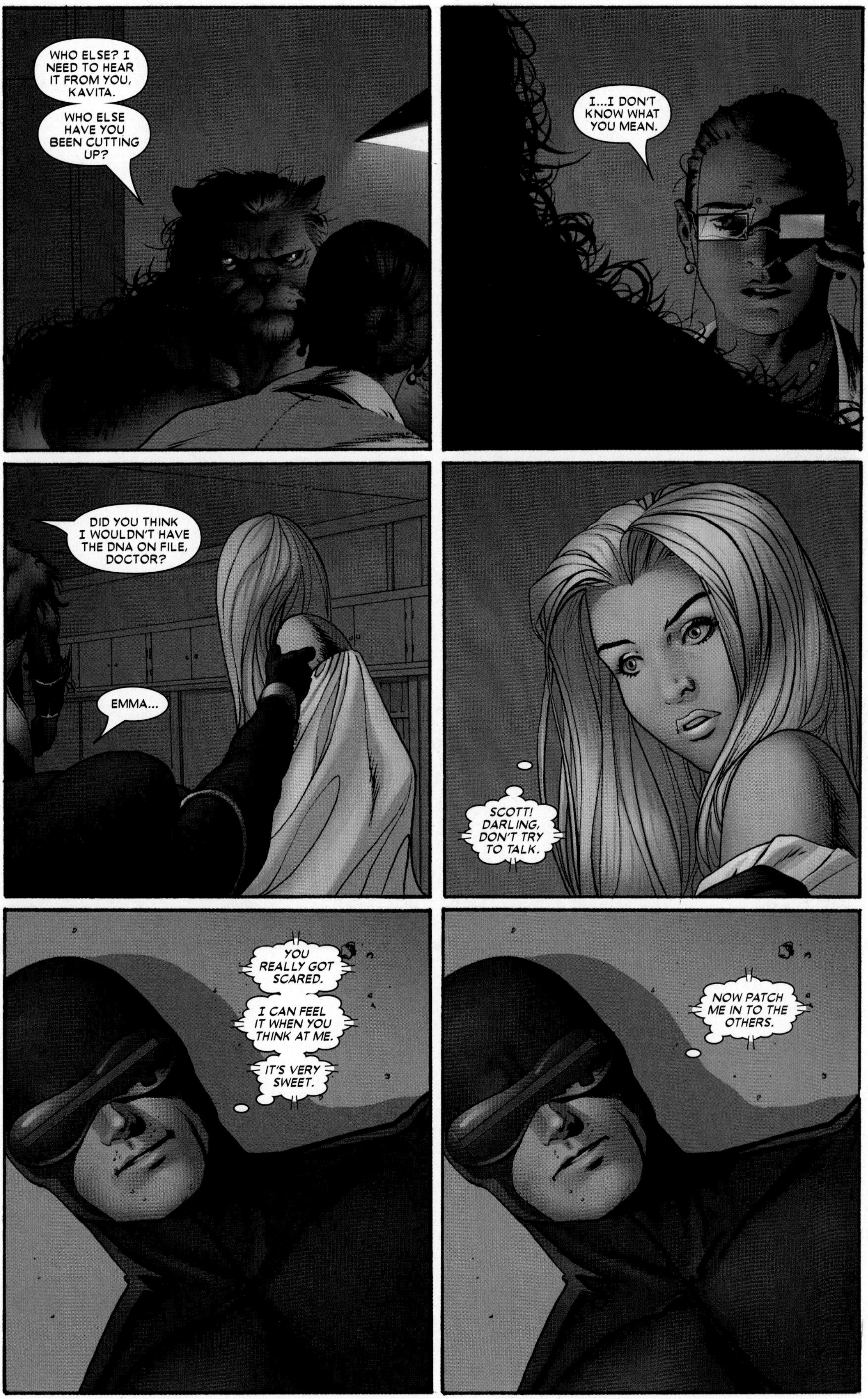
WHO ELSE? I NEED TO HEAR IT FROM YOU, KAVITA.
WHO ELSE HAVE YOU BEEN CUTTING UP?
I...I DON'T KNOW WHAT YOU MEAN.
DID YOU THINK I WOULDN'T HAVE THE DNA ON FILE, DOCTOR?
EMMA...
SCOTT! DARLING, DON'T TRY TO TALK.
YOU REALLY GOT SCARED.
I CAN FEEL IT WHEN YOU THINK AT ME.
IT'S VERY SWEET.
NOW PATCH ME IN TO THE OTHERS.

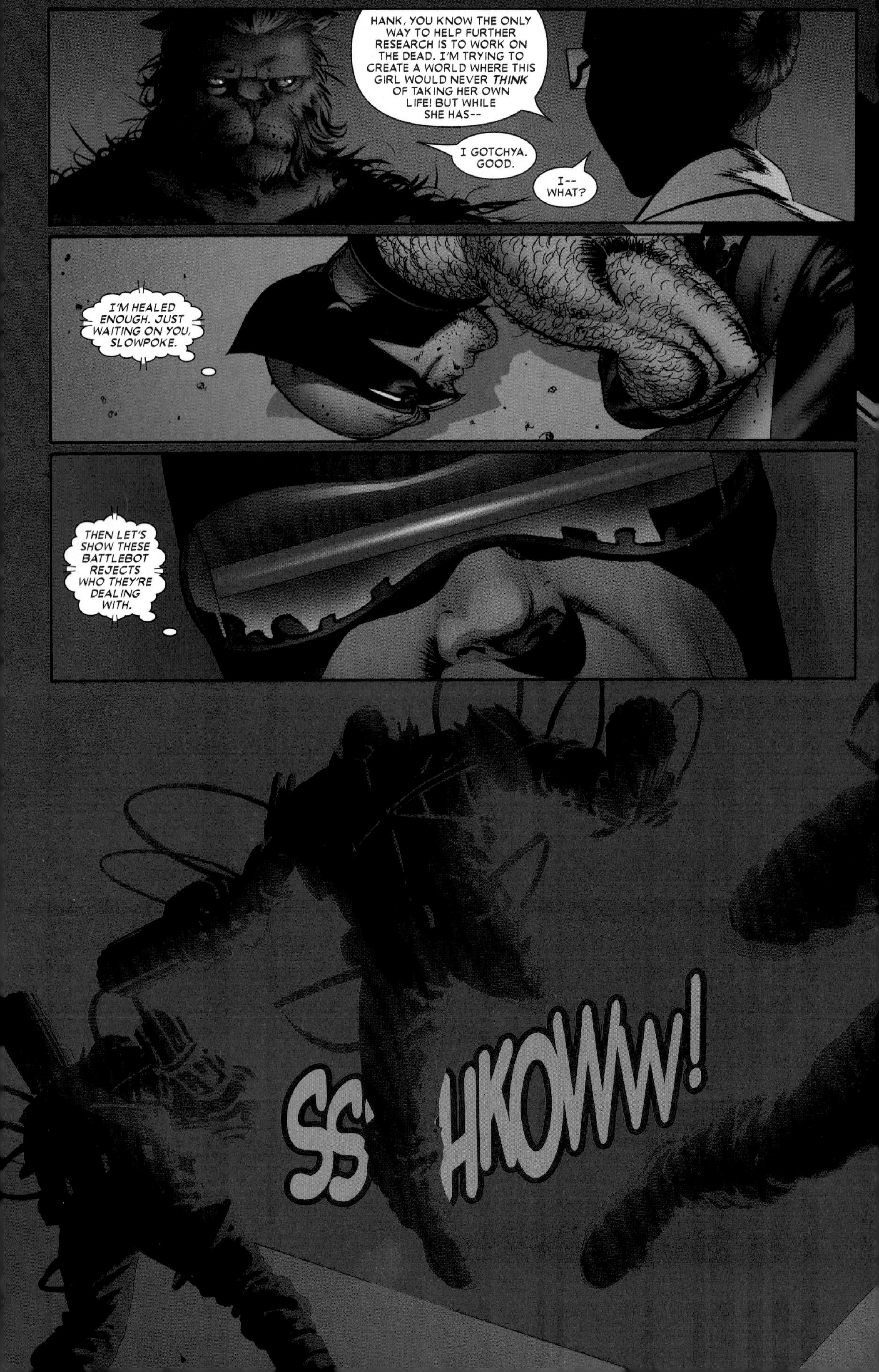
HANK, YOU KNOW THE ONLY WAY TO HELP FURTHER RESEARCH IS TO WORK ON THE DEAD. I'M TRYING TO CREATE A WORLD WHERE THIS GIRL WOULD NEVER *THINK* OF TAKING HER OWN LIFE! BUT WHILE SHE HAS--
I GOTCHYA. GOOD.
I-- WHAT?
I'M HEALED ENOUGH. JUST WAITING ON YOU, SLOWPOKE.
THEN LET'S SHOW THESE BATTLEBOT REJECTS WHO THEY'RE DEALING WITH.

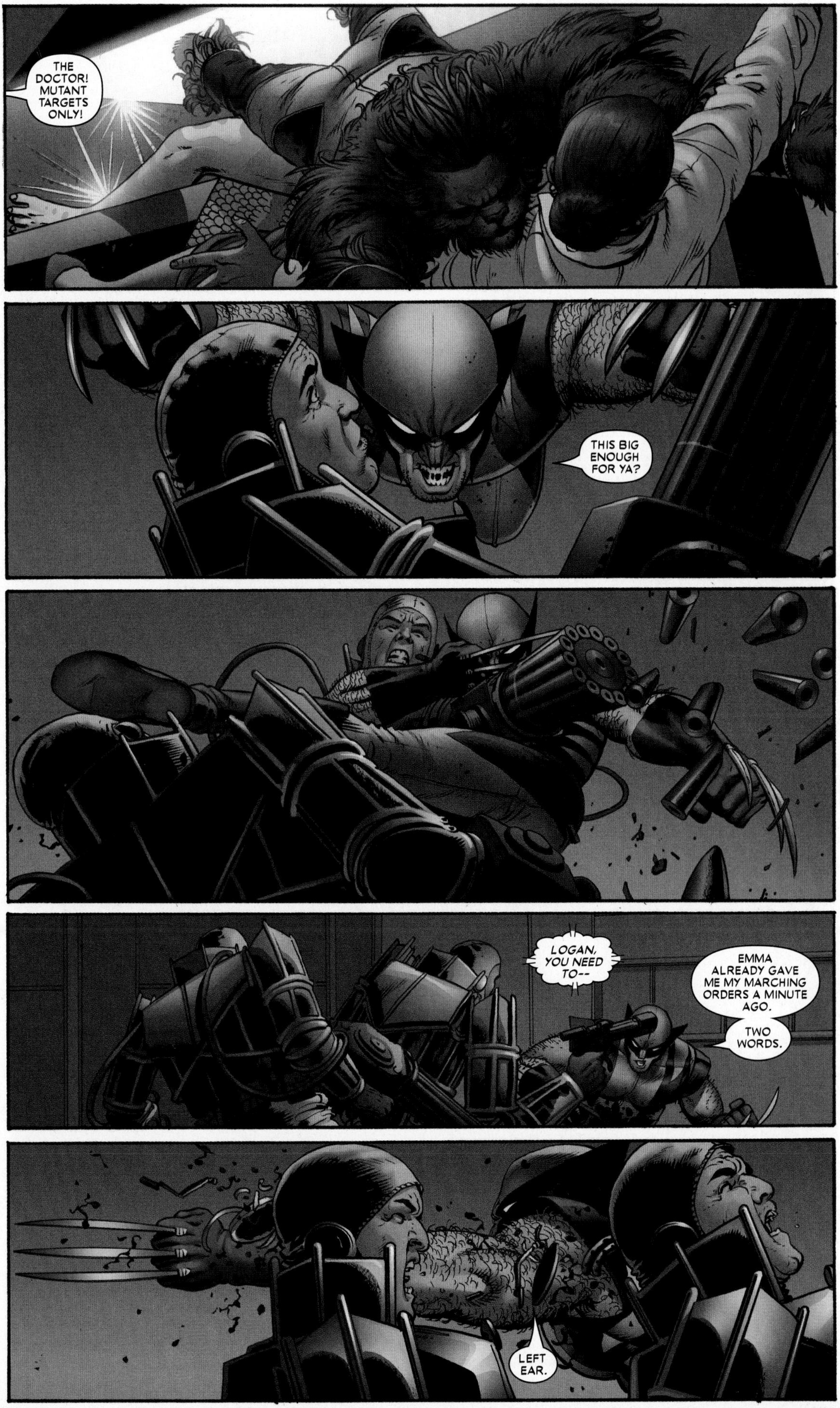
THE DOCTOR! MUTANT TARGETS ONLY!
THIS BIG ENOUGH FOR YA?
LOGAN, YOU NEED TO--
EMMA ALREADY GAVE ME MY MARCHING ORDERS A MINUTE AGO.
TWO WORDS.
LEFT EAR.

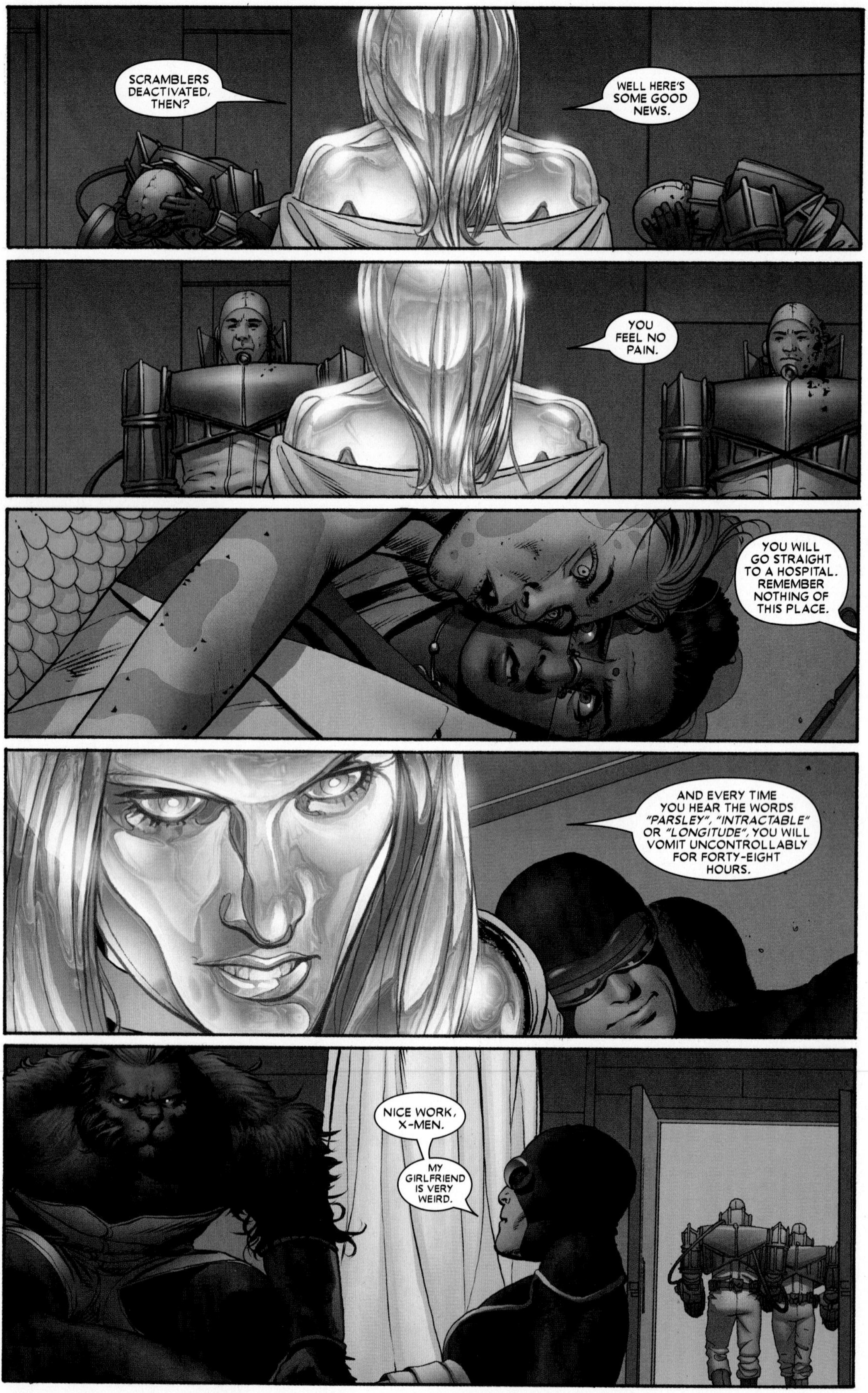
SCRAMBLERS DEACTIVATED, THEN?
WELL HERE'S SOME GOOD NEWS.
YOU FEEL NO PAIN.
YOU WILL GO STRAIGHT TO A HOSPITAL. REMEMBER NOTHING OF THIS PLACE.
AND EVERY TIME YOU HEAR THE WORDS "PARSLEY", "INTRACTABLE" OR "LONGITUDE", YOU WILL VOMIT UNCONTROLLABLY FOR FORTY-EIGHT HOURS.
NICE WORK, X-MEN.
MY GIRLFRIEND IS VERY WEIRD.

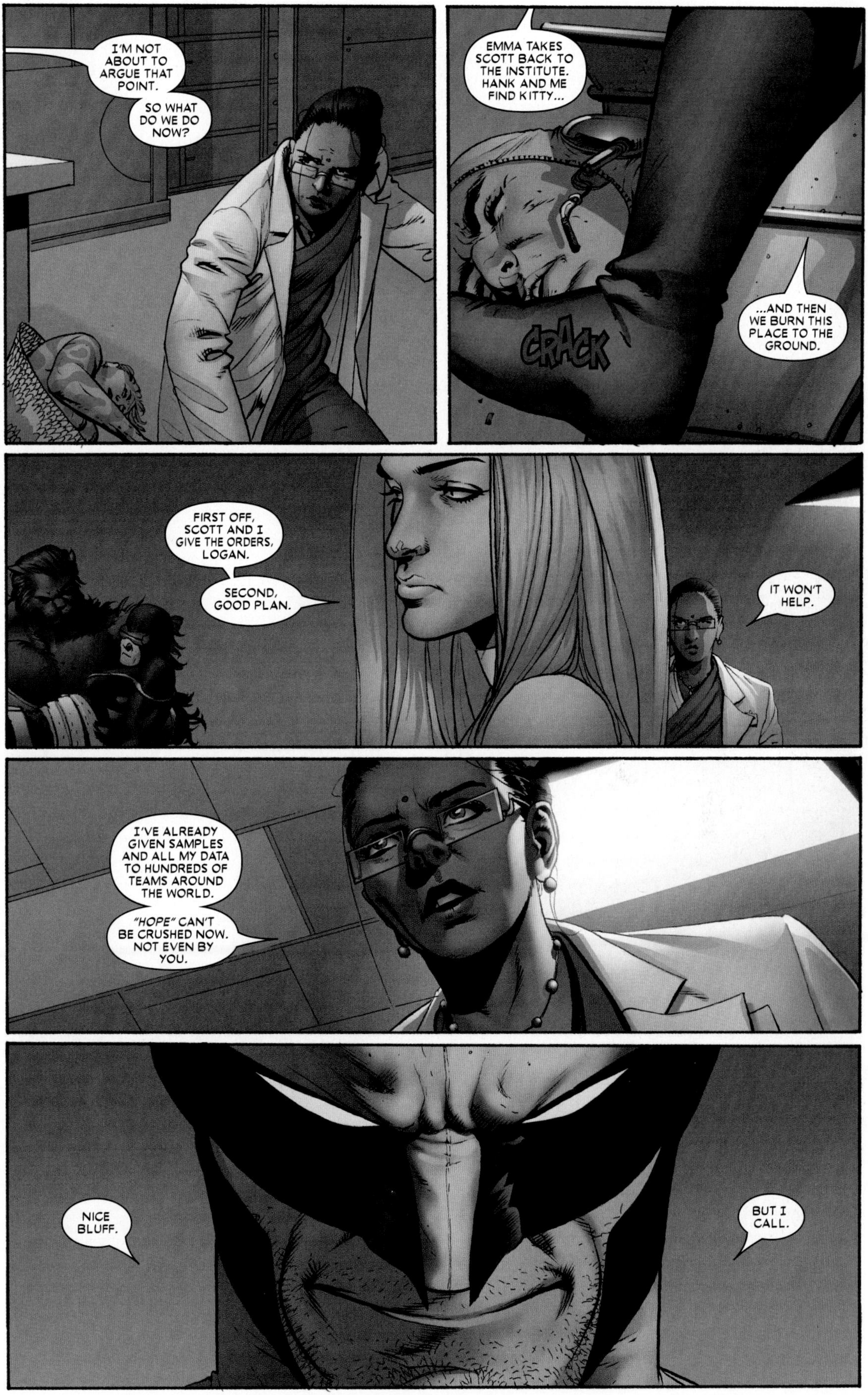
I'M NOT ABOUT TO ARGUE THAT POINT.
SO WHAT DO WE DO NOW?
EMMA TAKES SCOTT BACK TO THE INSTITUTE. HANK AND ME FIND KITTY...
CRACK
...AND THEN WE BURN THIS PLACE TO THE GROUND.
FIRST OFF, SCOTT AND I GIVE THE ORDERS, LOGAN.
SECOND, GOOD PLAN.
IT WON'T HELP.
I'VE ALREADY GIVEN SAMPLES AND ALL MY DATA TO HUNDREDS OF TEAMS AROUND THE WORLD.
"HOPE" CAN'T BE CRUSHED NOW. NOT EVEN BY YOU.
NICE BLUFF.
BUT I CALL.

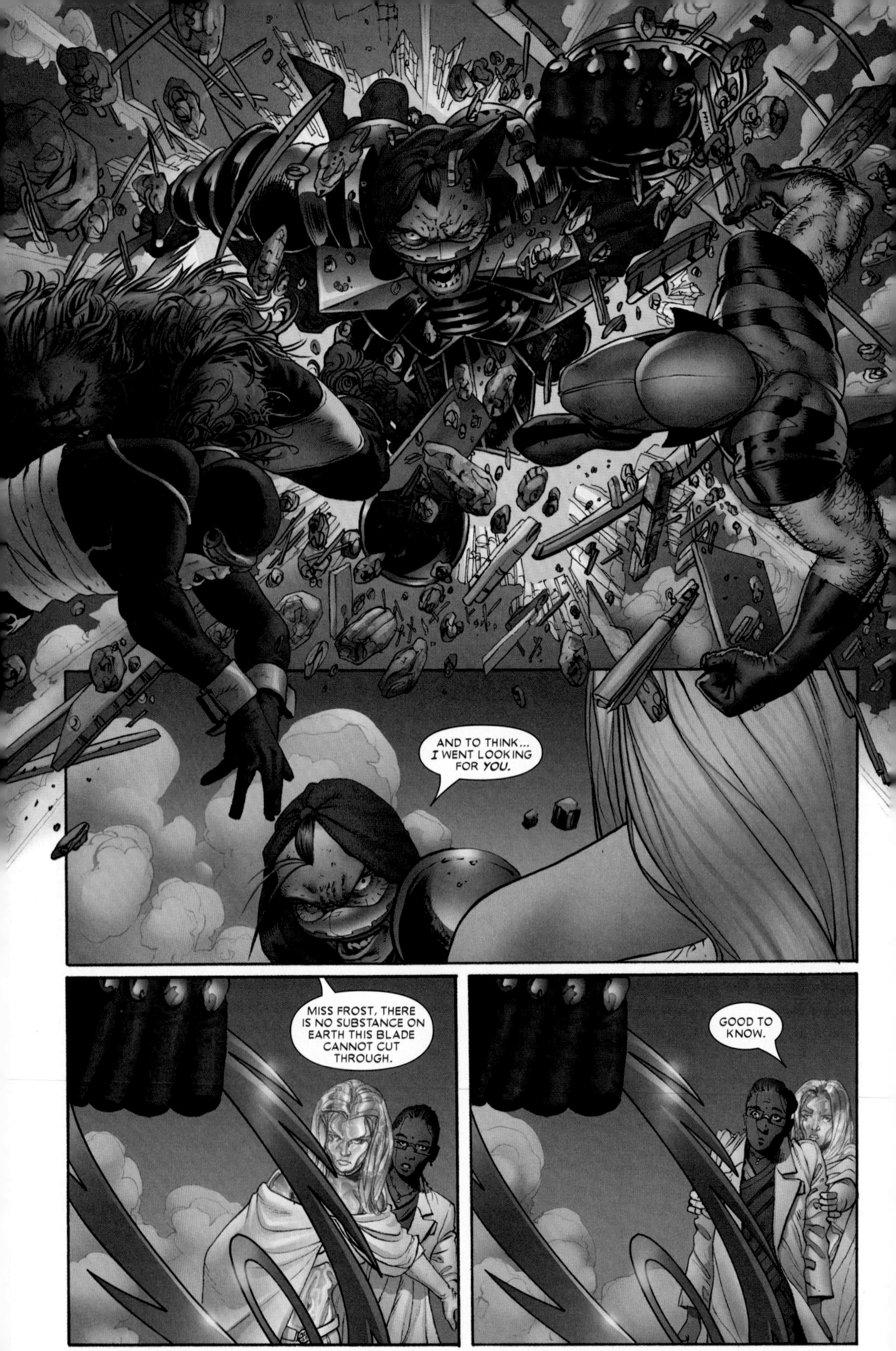
AND TO THINK... I WENT LOOKING FOR YOU.
MISS FROST, THERE IS NO SUBSTANCE ON EARTH THIS BLADE CANNOT CUT THROUGH.
GOOD TO KNOW.

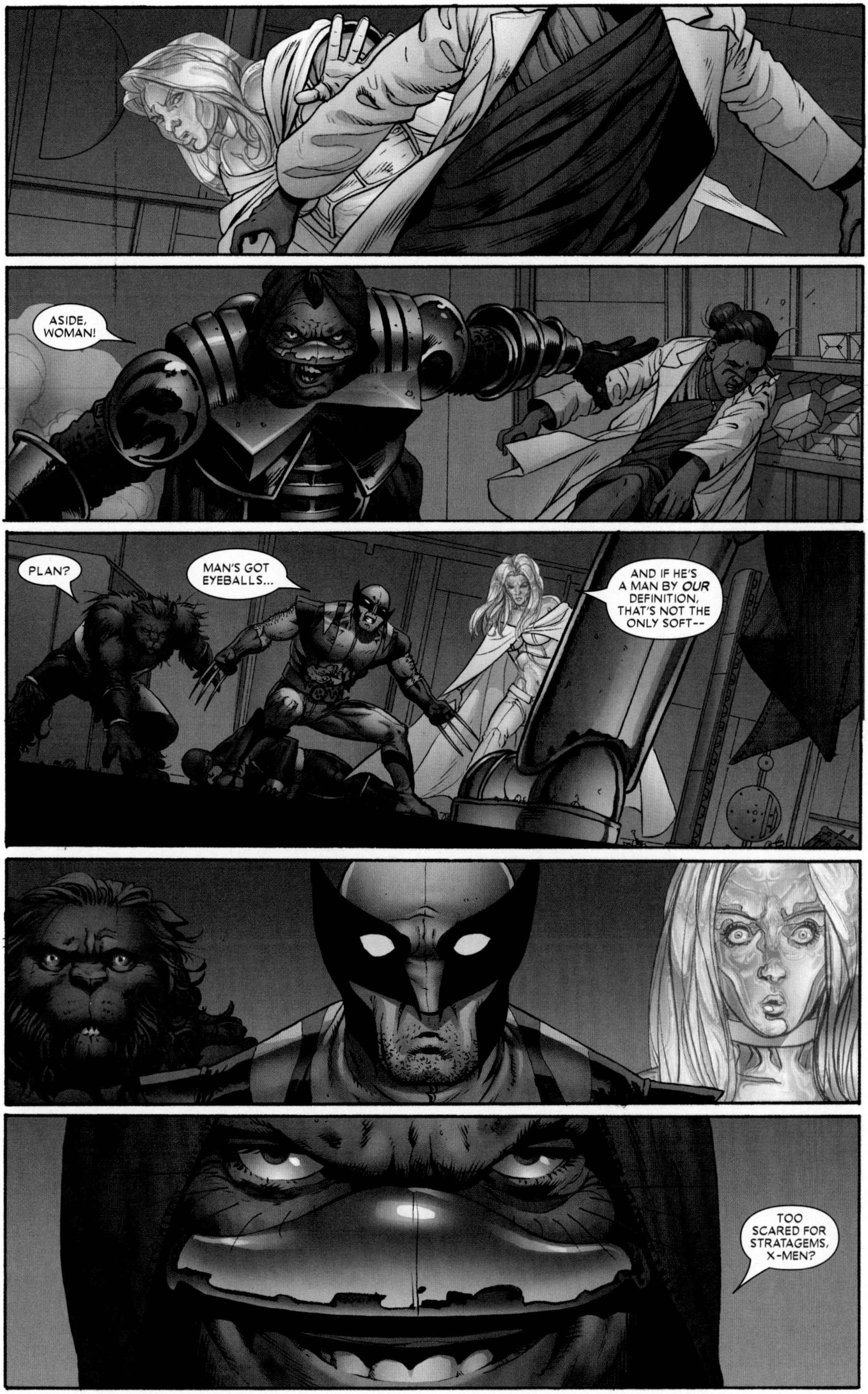
ASIDE, WOMAN!
PLAN?
MAN'S GOT EYEBALLS...
AND IF HE'S A MAN BY OUR DEFINITION, THAT'S NOT THE ONLY SOFT--
TOO SCARED FOR STRATAGEMS, X-MEN?

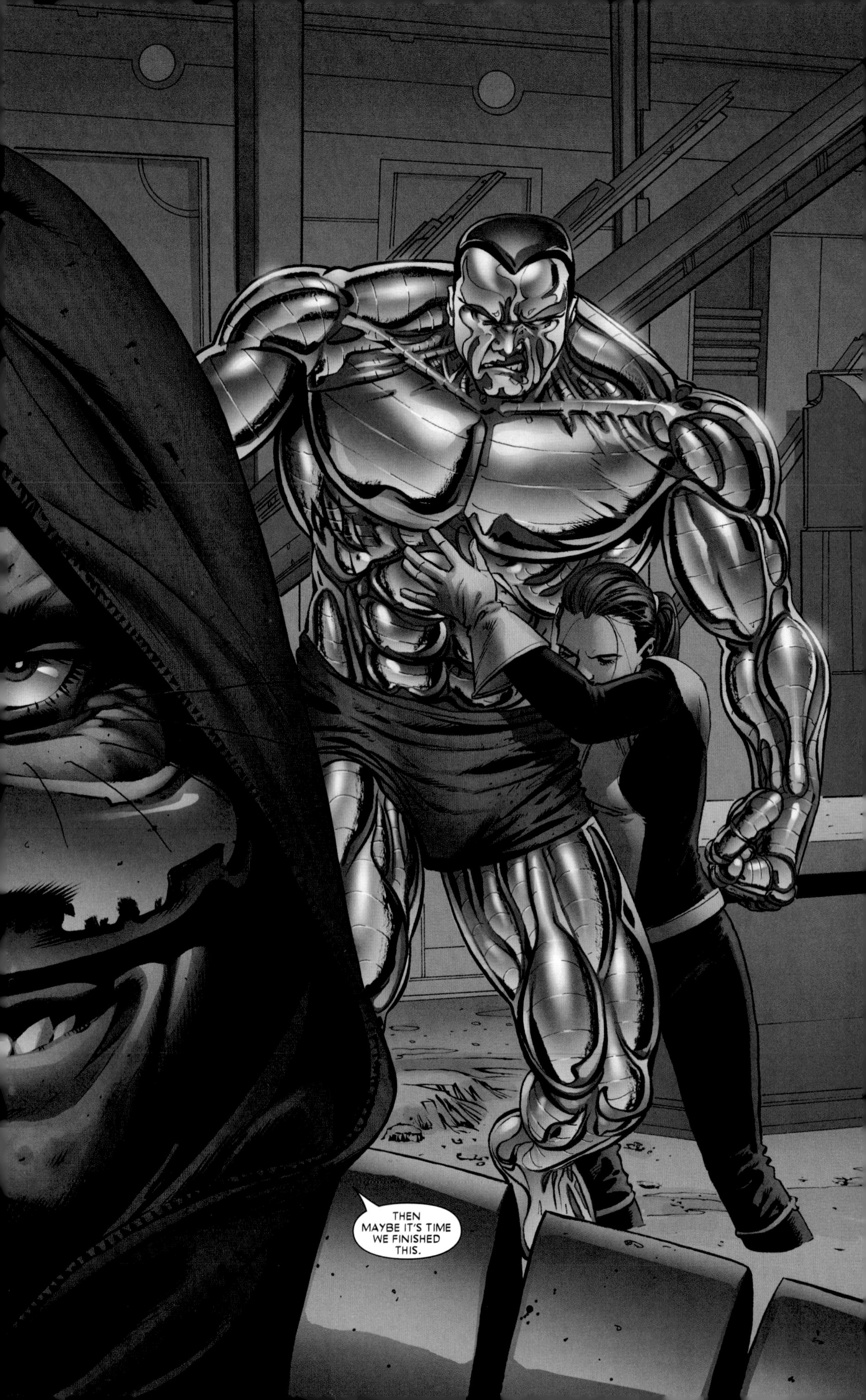
THEN MAYBE IT'S TIME WE FINISHED THIS.

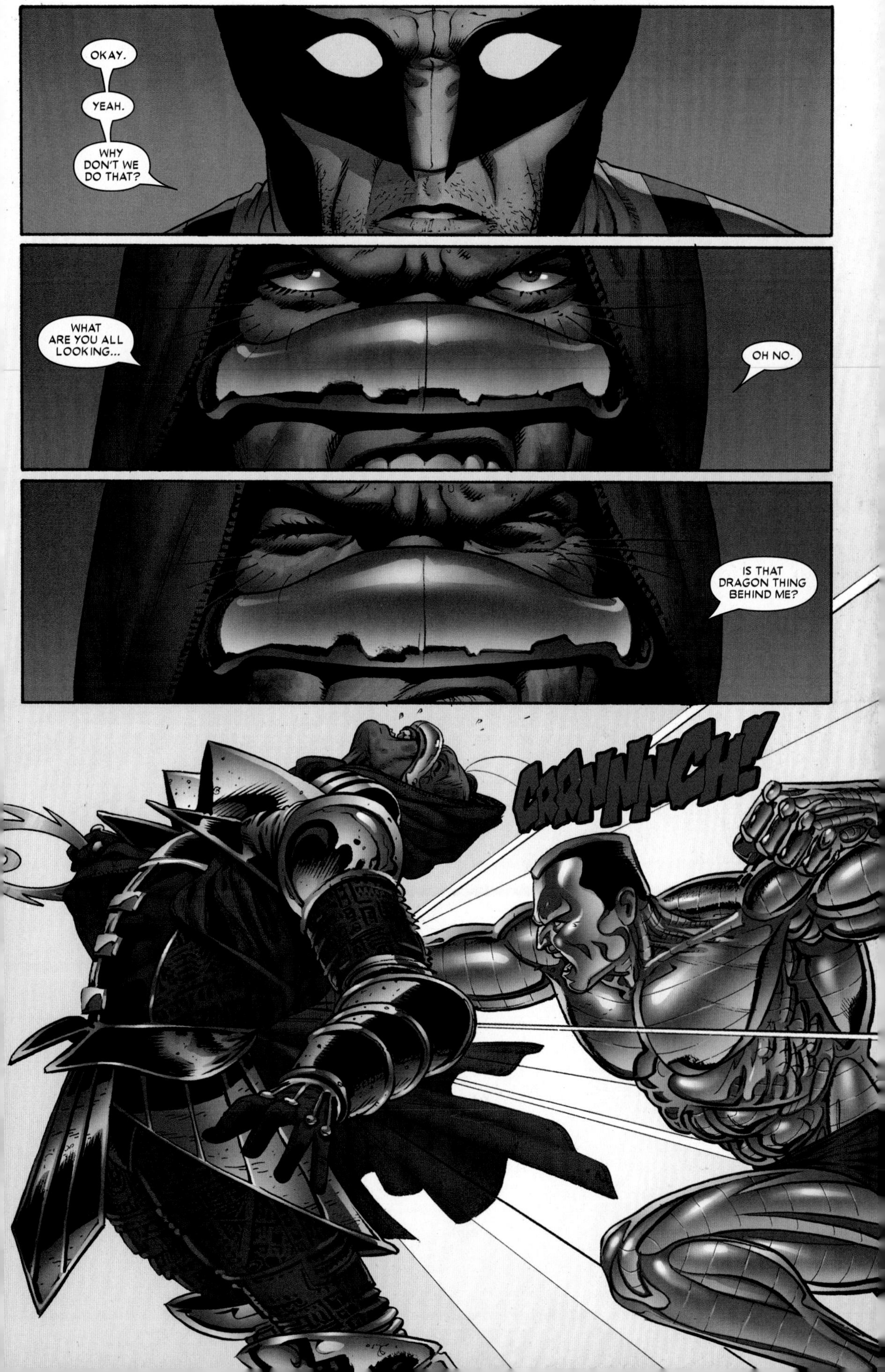
OKAY.
YEAH.
WHY DON'T WE DO THAT?
WHAT ARE YOU ALL LOOKING...
OH NO.
IS THAT DRAGON THING BEHIND ME?
CRRNNNCH!

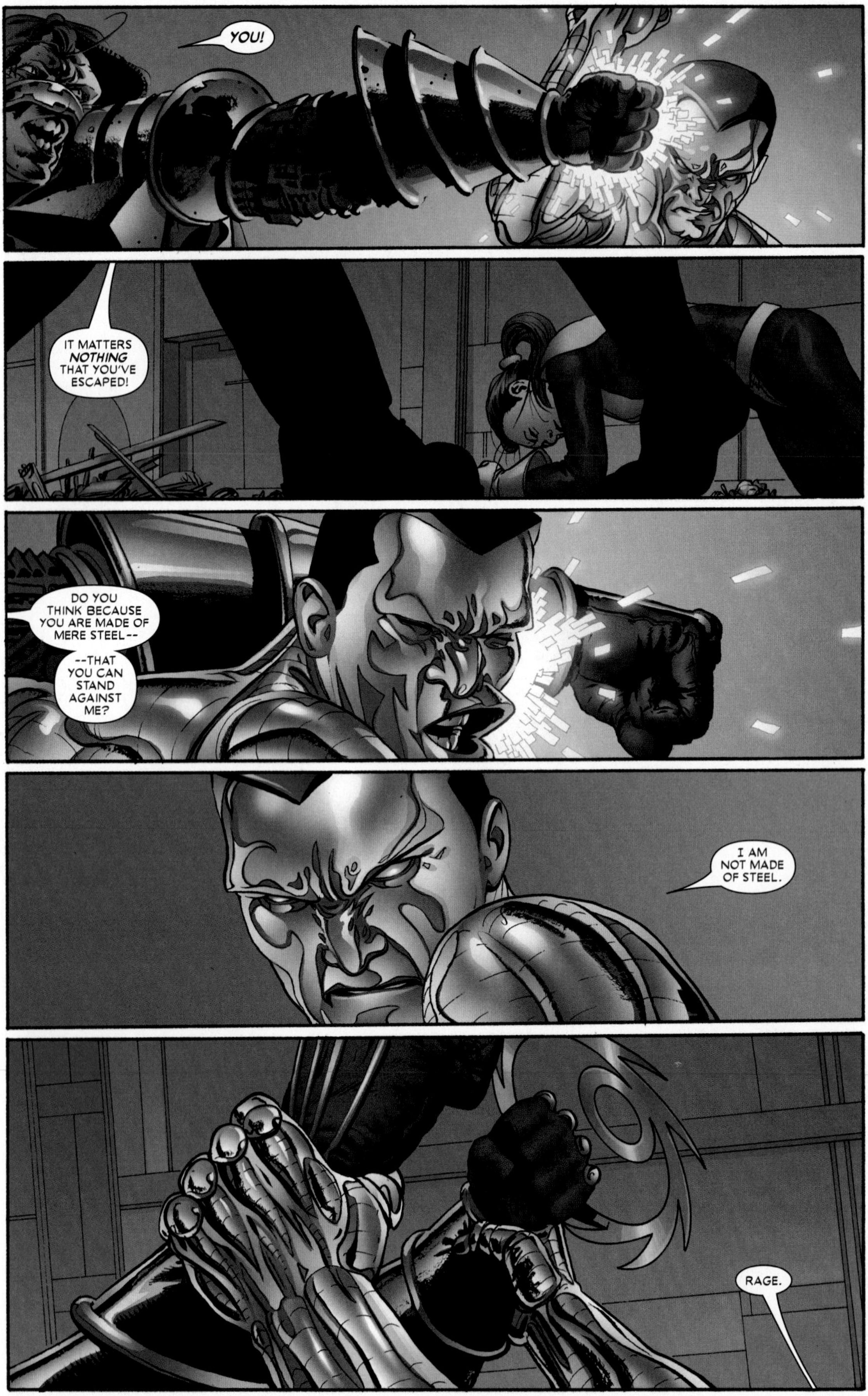
YOU!
IT MATTERS NOTHING THAT YOU'VE ESCAPED!
DO YOU THINK BECAUSE YOU ARE MADE OF MERE STEEL--
--THAT YOU CAN STAND AGAINST ME?
I AM NOT MADE OF STEEL.
RAGE.

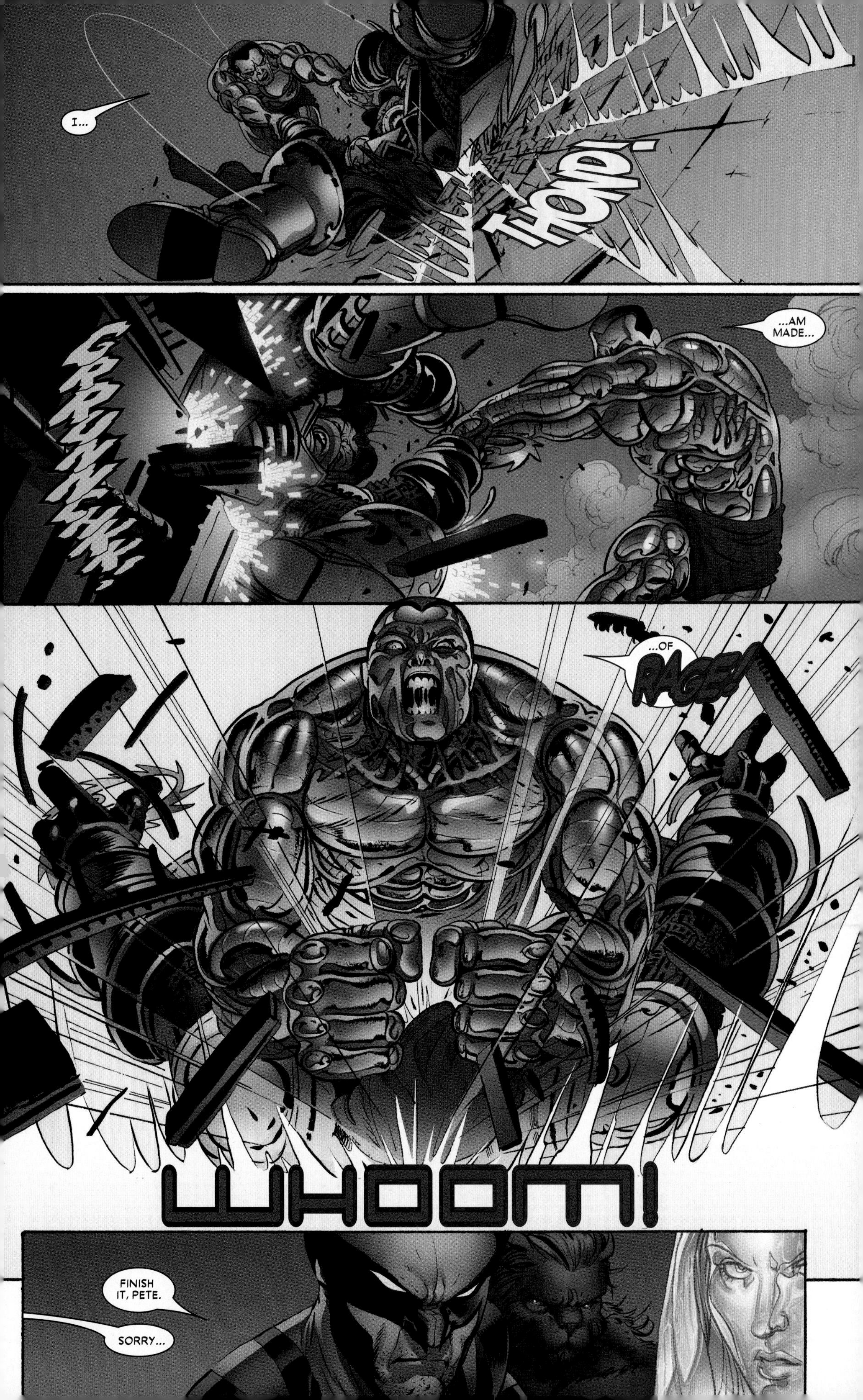
I...
THOOM!
GRRUNNCHK!
...AM MADE...
...OF RAGE!
WHOOM!
FINISH IT, PETE.
SORRY...

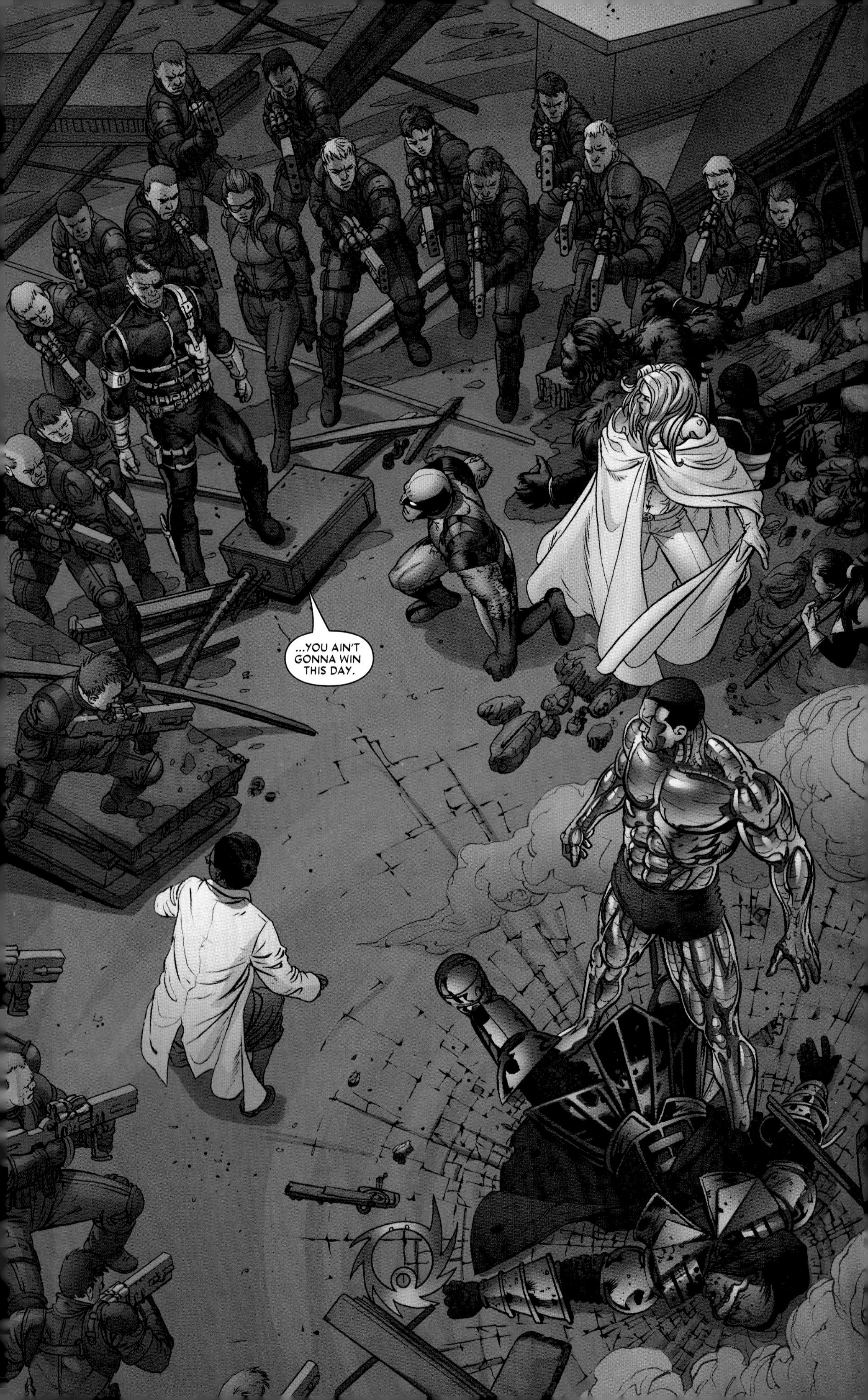
...YOU AIN'T GONNA WIN THIS DAY.

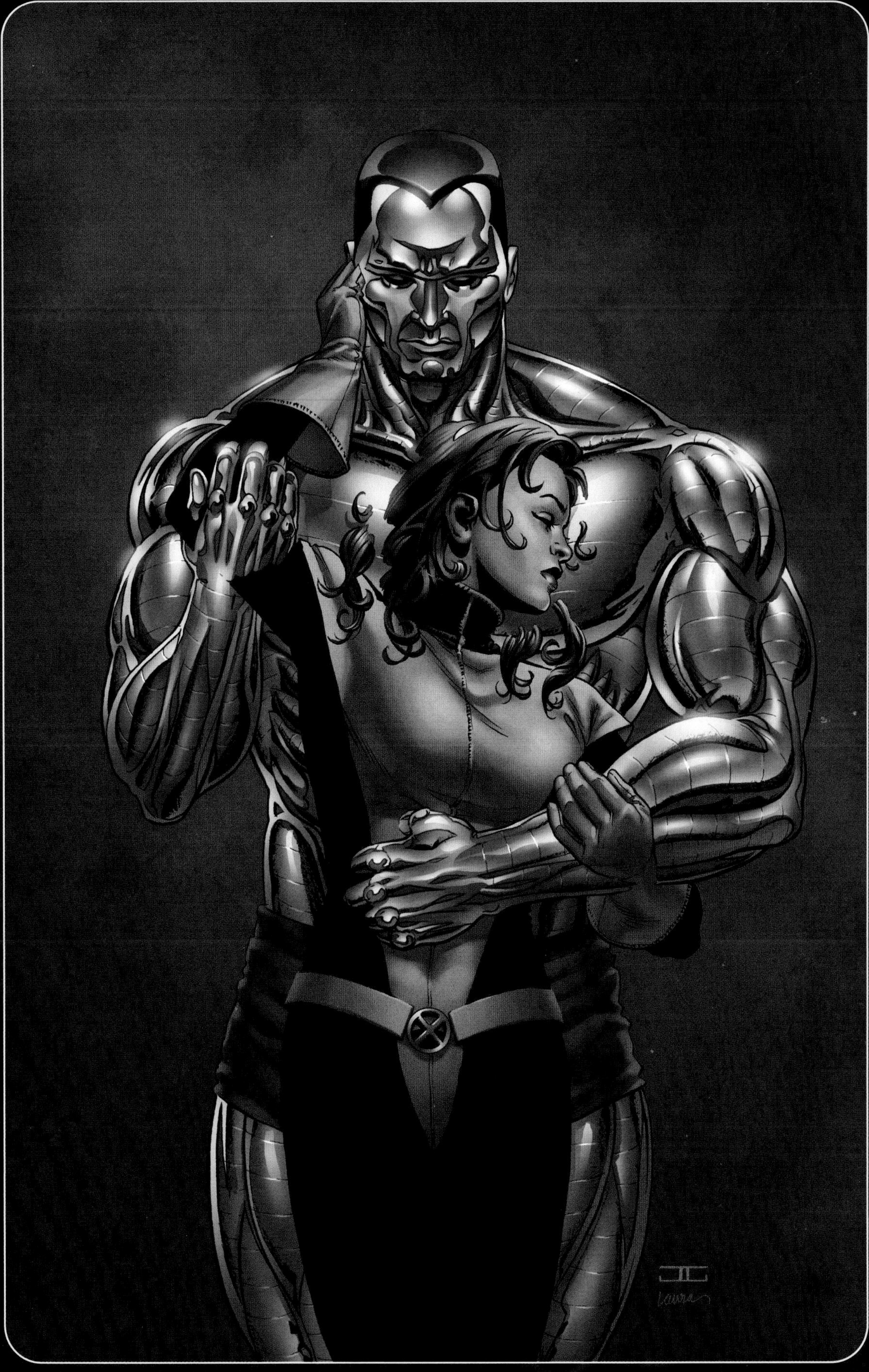

06

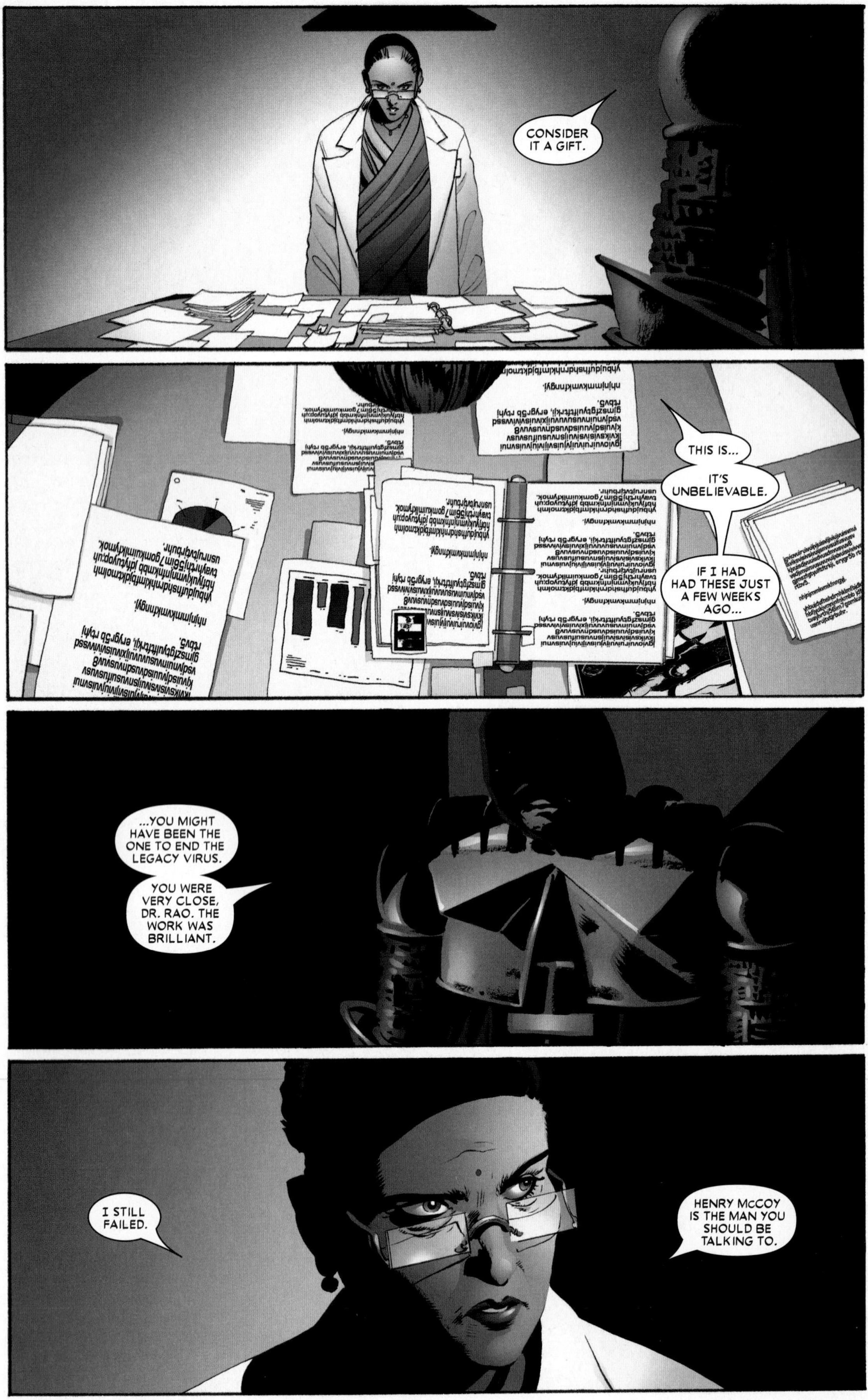
CONSIDER IT A GIFT.
THIS IS...
IT'S UNBELIEVABLE.
IF I HAD HAD THESE JUST A FEW WEEKS AGO...
...YOU MIGHT HAVE BEEN THE ONE TO END THE LEGACY VIRUS.
YOU WERE VERY CLOSE, DR. RAO. THE WORK WAS BRILLIANT.
I STILL FAILED.
HENRY McCOY IS THE MAN YOU SHOULD BE TALKING TO.

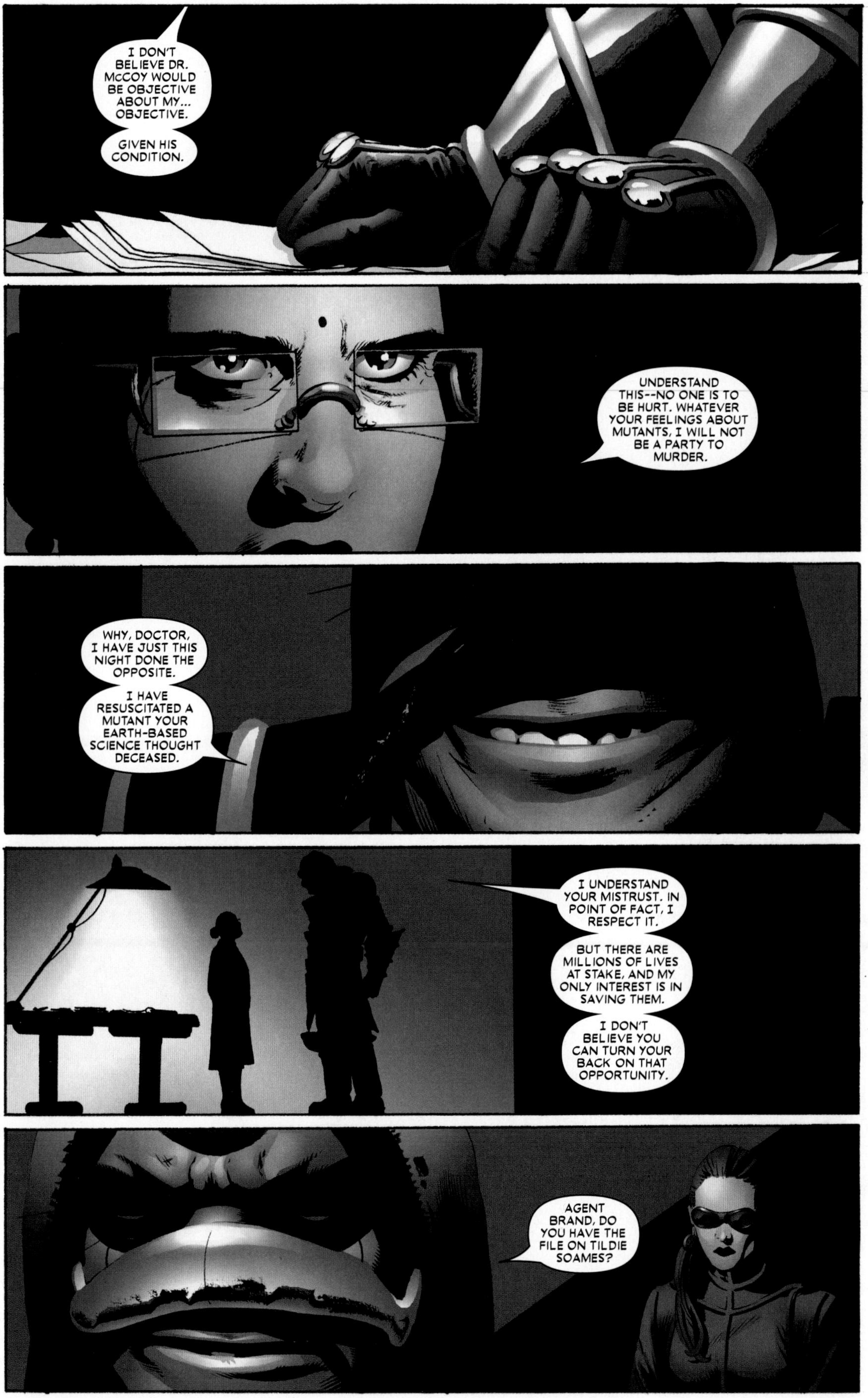
I DON'T BELIEVE DR. McCOY WOULD BE OBJECTIVE ABOUT MY... OBJECTIVE.
GIVEN HIS CONDITION.
UNDERSTAND THIS--NO ONE IS TO BE HURT. WHATEVER YOUR FEELINGS ABOUT MUTANTS, I WILL NOT BE A PARTY TO MURDER.
WHY, DOCTOR, I HAVE JUST THIS NIGHT DONE THE OPPOSITE.
I HAVE RESUSCITATED A MUTANT YOUR EARTH-BASED SCIENCE THOUGHT DECEASED.
I UNDERSTAND YOUR MISTRUST. IN POINT OF FACT, I RESPECT IT.
BUT THERE ARE MILLIONS OF LIVES AT STAKE, AND MY ONLY INTEREST IS IN SAVING THEM.
I DON'T BELIEVE YOU CAN TURN YOUR BACK ON THAT OPPORTUNITY.
AGENT BRAND, DO YOU HAVE THE FILE ON TILDIE SOAMES?

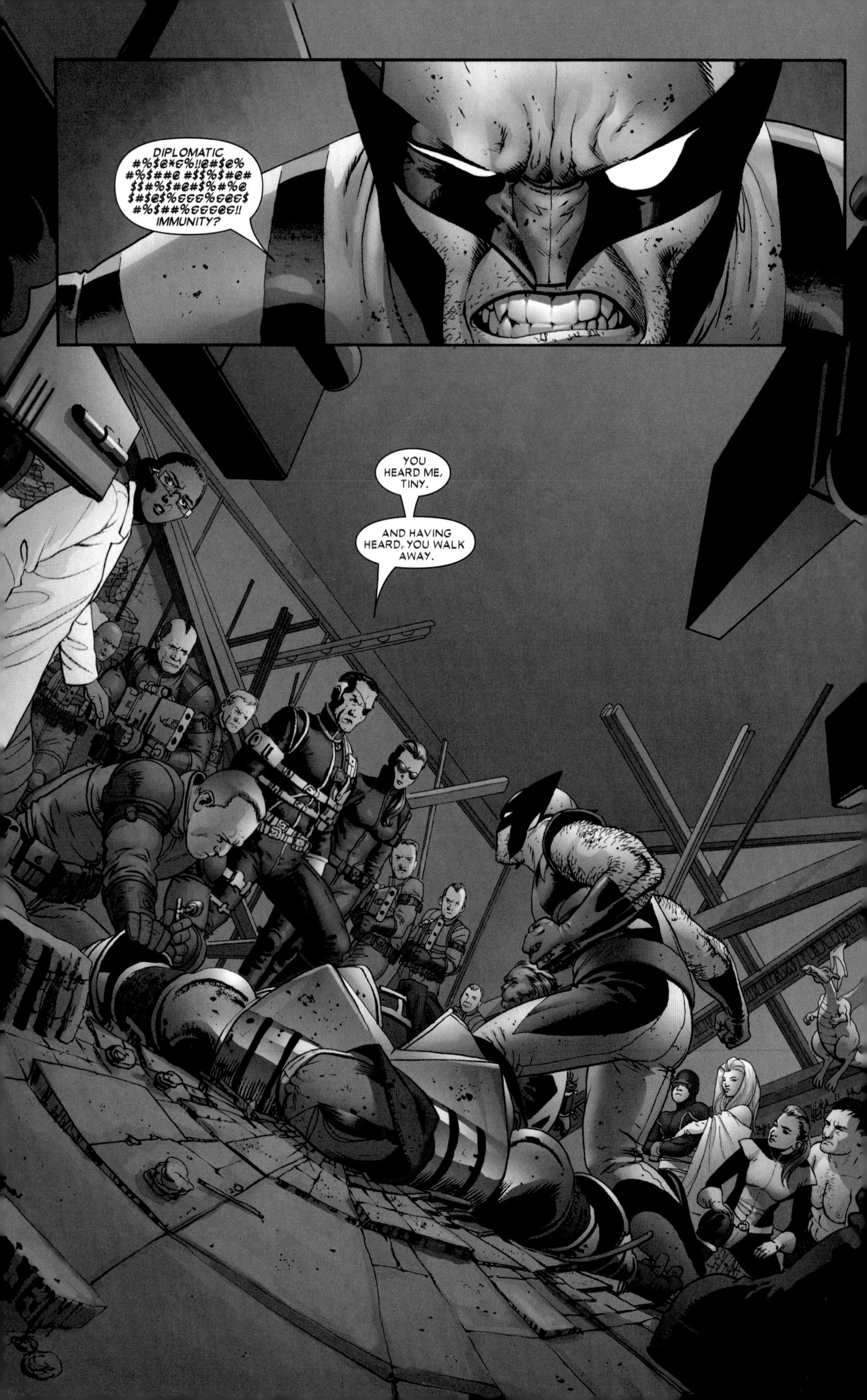
DIPLOMATIC #%$@*&%!!@#$@% #%$##@ #$$%$#@# $$#%$#@#$%#%@ $#$@$%&&&%&&&$ #%$##%&&&&&!! IMMUNITY?
YOU HEARD ME, TINY.
AND HAVING HEARD, YOU WALK AWAY.

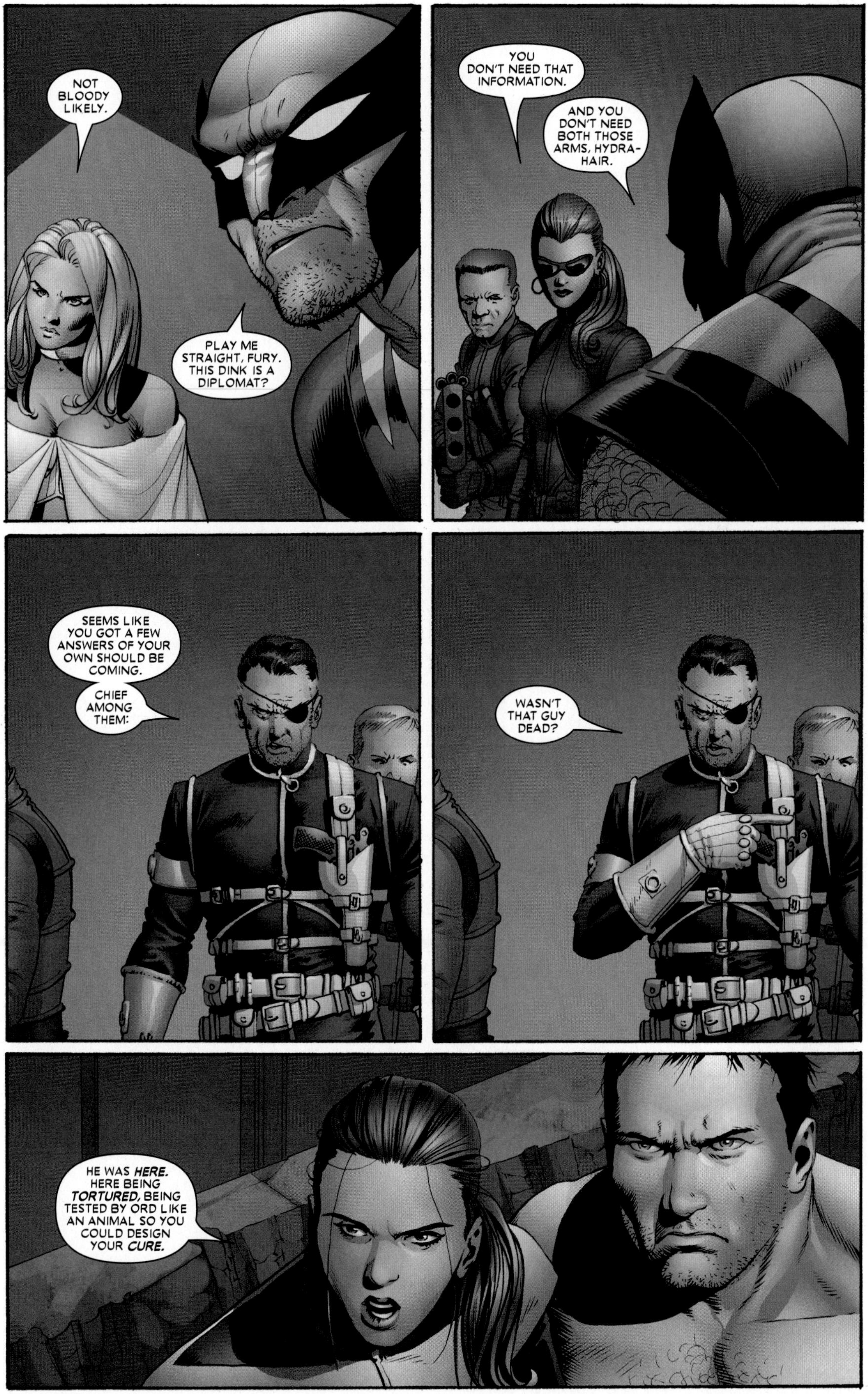
NOT BLOODY LIKELY.
PLAY ME STRAIGHT, FURY. THIS DINK IS A DIPLOMAT?
YOU DON'T NEED THAT INFORMATION.
AND YOU DON'T NEED BOTH THOSE ARMS, HYDRA-HAIR.
SEEMS LIKE YOU GOT A FEW ANSWERS OF YOUR OWN SHOULD BE COMING.
CHIEF AMONG THEM:
WASN'T THAT GUY DEAD?
HE WAS *HERE.* HERE BEING *TORTURED,* BEING TESTED BY ORD LIKE AN ANIMAL SO YOU COULD DESIGN YOUR *CURE.*

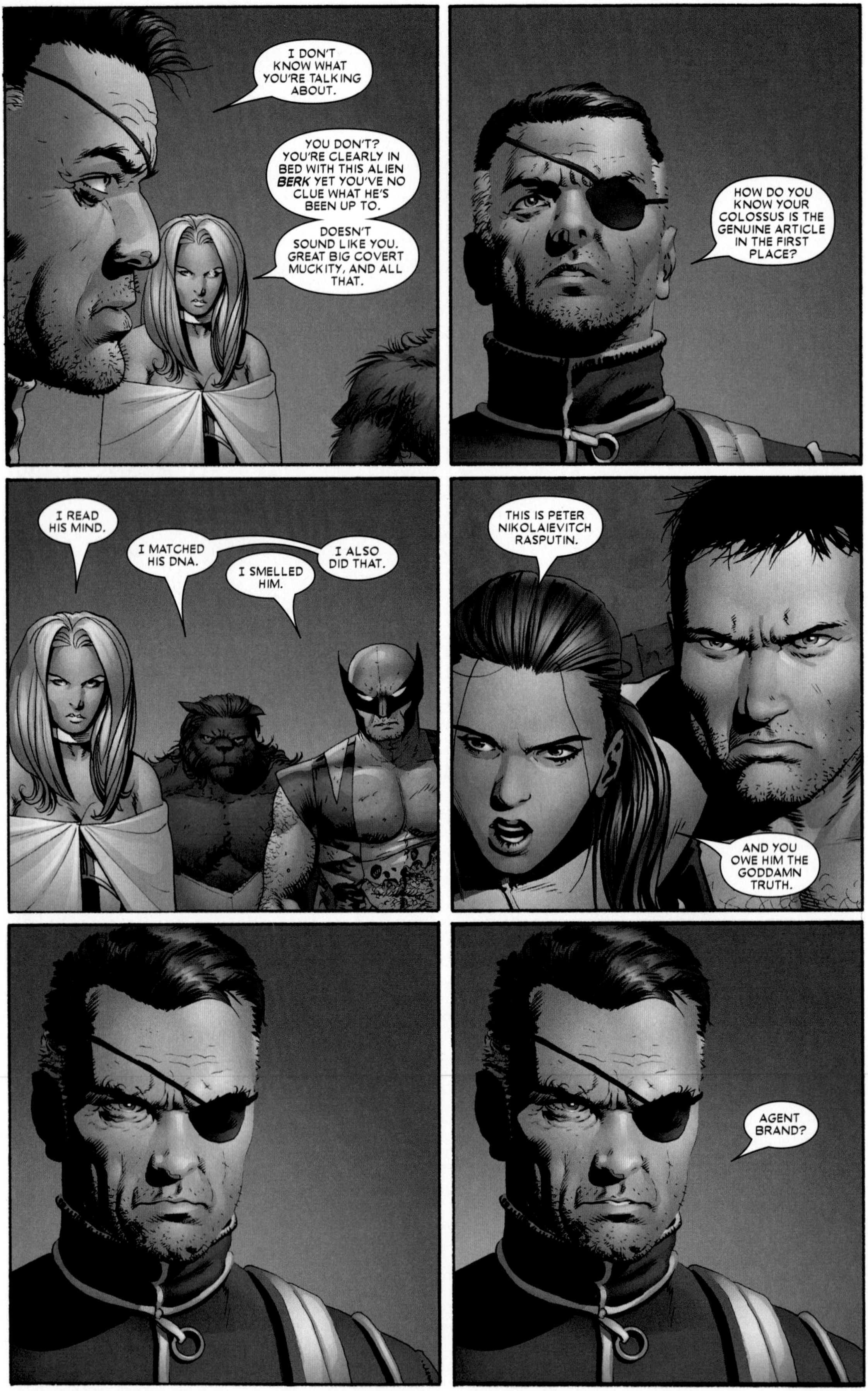
I DON'T KNOW WHAT YOU'RE TALKING ABOUT.
YOU DON'T? YOU'RE CLEARLY IN BED WITH THIS ALIEN *BERK* YET YOU'VE NO CLUE WHAT HE'S BEEN UP TO.
DOESN'T SOUND LIKE YOU. GREAT BIG COVERT MUCKITY, AND ALL THAT.
HOW DO YOU KNOW YOUR COLOSSUS IS THE GENUINE ARTICLE IN THE FIRST PLACE?
I READ HIS MIND.
I MATCHED HIS DNA.
I ALSO DID THAT.
I SMELLED HIM.
THIS IS PETER NIKOLAIEVITCH RASPUTIN.
AND YOU OWE HIM THE GODDAMN TRUTH.
AGENT BRAND?

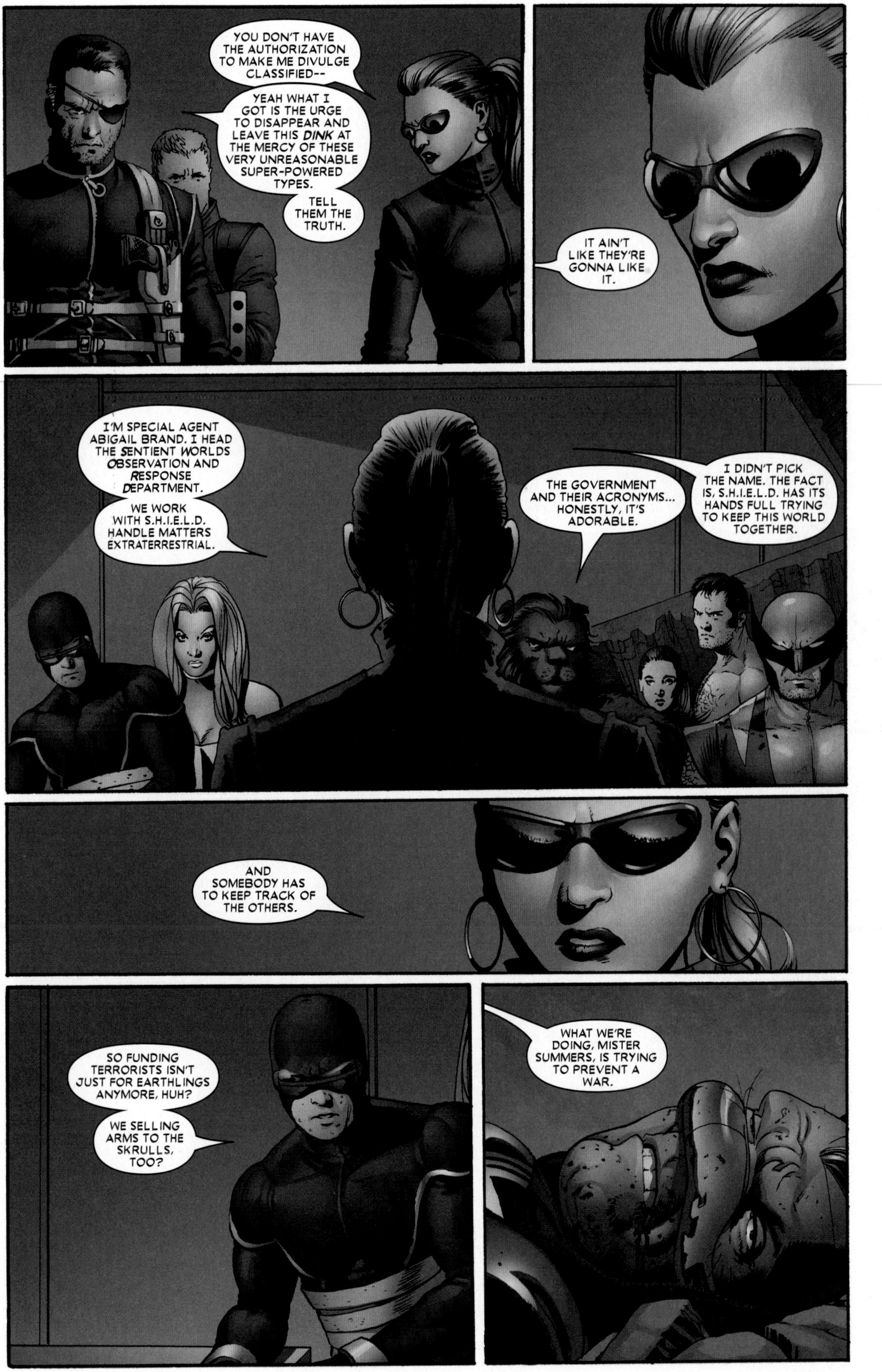
YOU DON'T HAVE THE AUTHORIZATION TO MAKE ME DIVULGE CLASSIFIED--
YEAH WHAT I GOT IS THE URGE TO DISAPPEAR AND LEAVE THIS DINK AT THE MERCY OF THESE VERY UNREASONABLE SUPER-POWERED TYPES.
TELL THEM THE TRUTH.
IT AIN'T LIKE THEY'RE GONNA LIKE IT.
I'M SPECIAL AGENT ABIGAIL BRAND. I HEAD THE SENTIENT WORLDS OBSERVATION AND RESPONSE DEPARTMENT.
WE WORK WITH S.H.I.E.L.D. HANDLE MATTERS EXTRATERRESTRIAL.
THE GOVERNMENT AND THEIR ACRONYMS... HONESTLY, IT'S ADORABLE.
I DIDN'T PICK THE NAME. THE FACT IS, S.H.I.E.L.D. HAS ITS HANDS FULL TRYING TO KEEP THIS WORLD TOGETHER.
AND SOMEBODY HAS TO KEEP TRACK OF THE OTHERS.
SO FUNDING TERRORISTS ISN'T JUST FOR EARTHLINGS ANYMORE, HUH?
WE SELLING ARMS TO THE SKRULLS, TOO?
WHAT WE'RE DOING, MISTER SUMMERS, IS TRYING TO PREVENT A WAR.

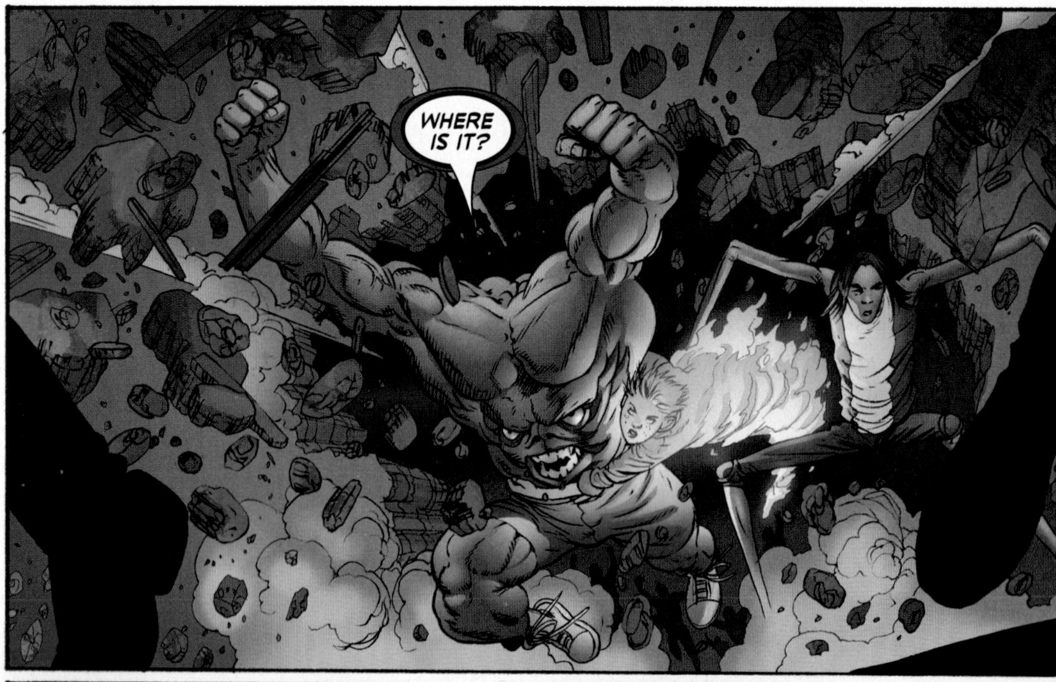
WHERE IS IT?

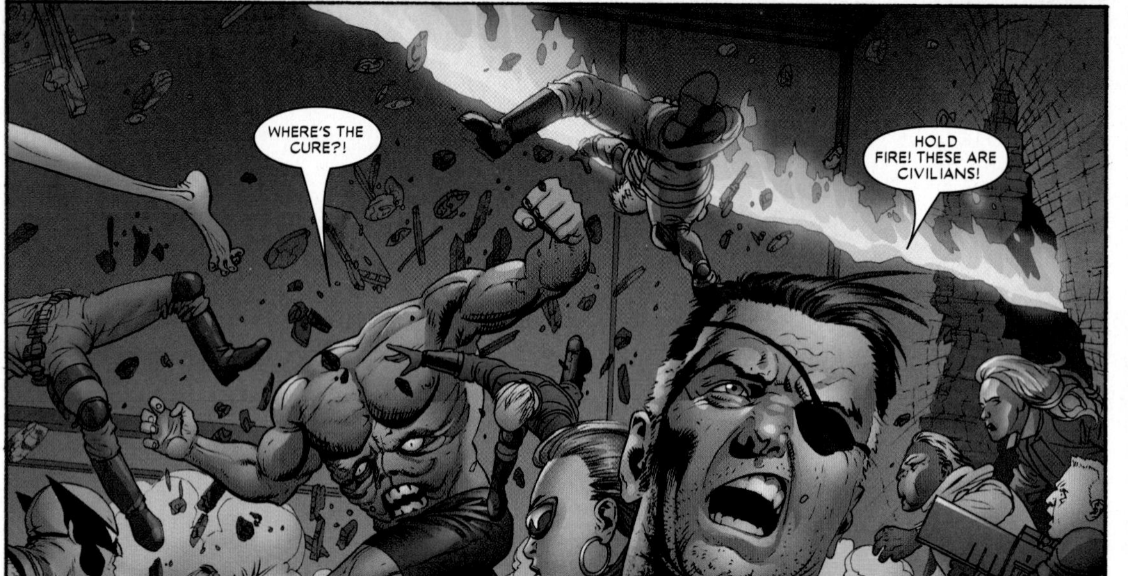
WHERE'S THE CURE?!
HOLD FIRE! THESE ARE CIVILIANS!

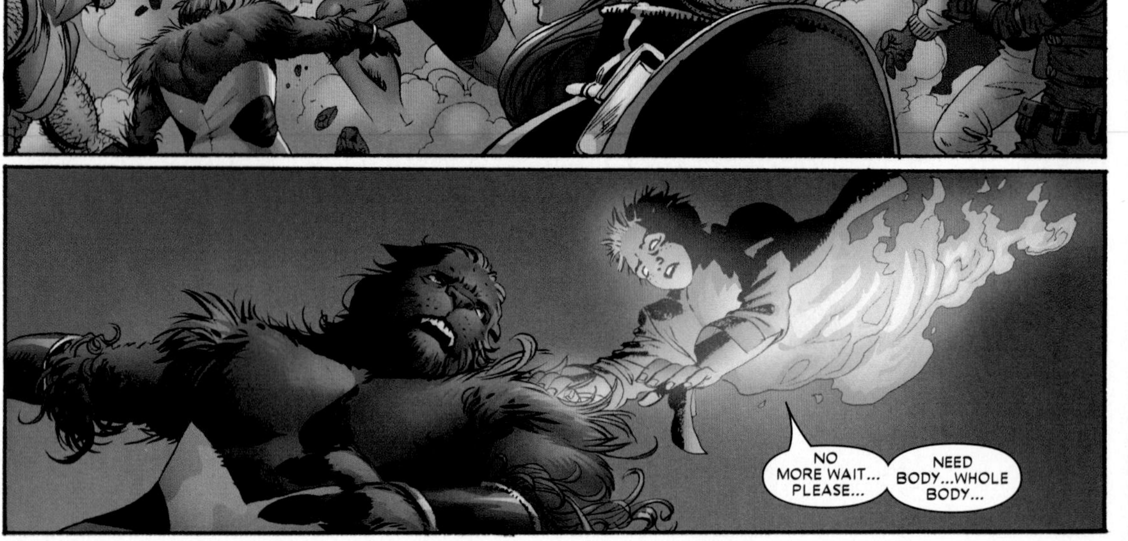
NO MORE WAIT... PLEASE...
NEED BODY...WHOLE BODY...

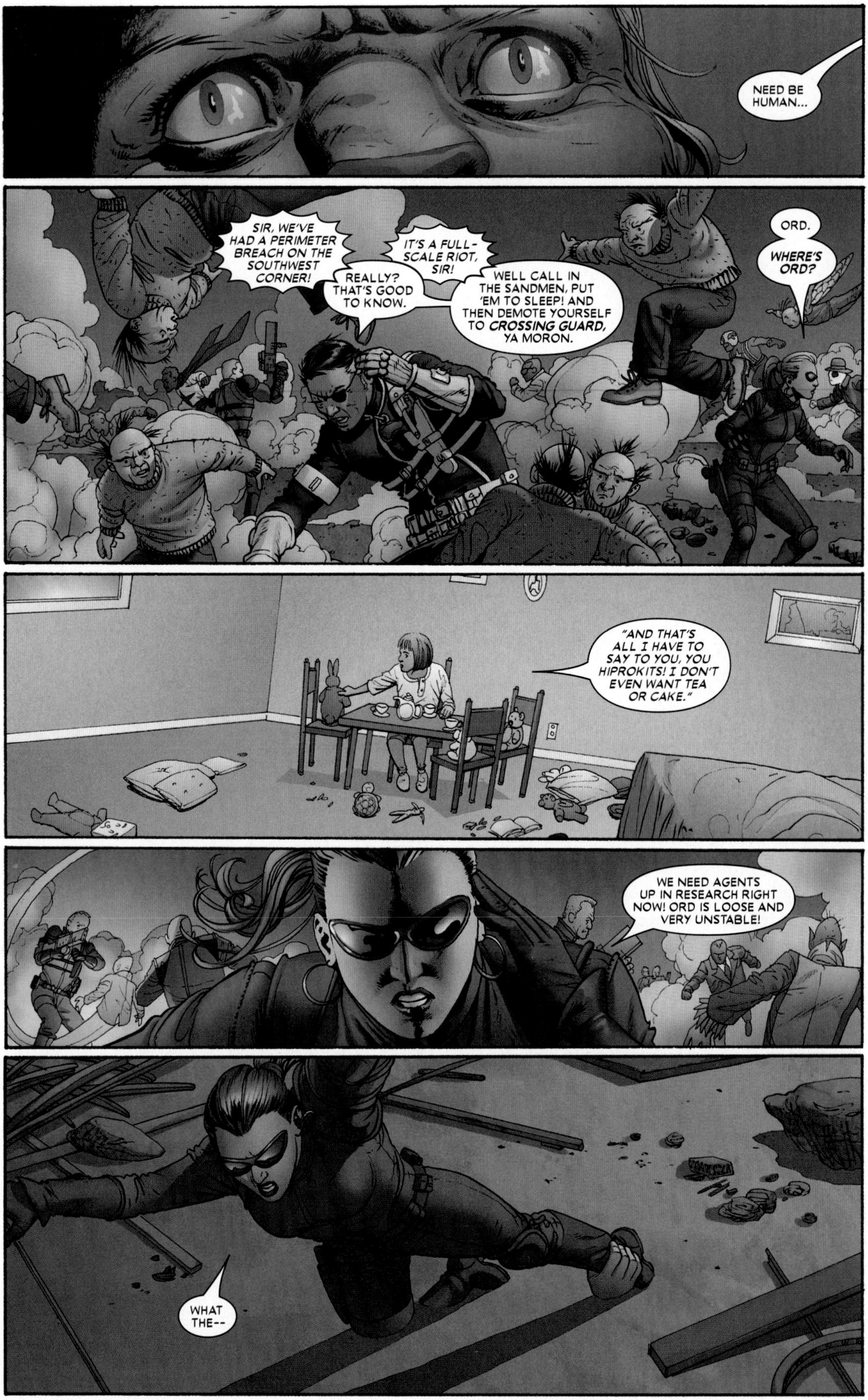
NEED BE HUMAN...
SIR, WE'VE HAD A PERIMETER BREACH ON THE SOUTHWEST CORNER!
IT'S A FULL-SCALE RIOT, SIR!
REALLY? THAT'S GOOD TO KNOW.
WELL CALL IN THE SANDMEN, PUT 'EM TO SLEEP! AND THEN DEMOTE YOURSELF TO CROSSING GUARD, YA MORON.
ORD.
WHERE'S ORD?
"AND THAT'S ALL I HAVE TO SAY TO YOU, YOU HIPROKITS! I DON'T EVEN WANT TEA OR CAKE."
WE NEED AGENTS UP IN RESEARCH RIGHT NOW! ORD IS LOOSE AND VERY UNSTABLE!
WHAT THE--

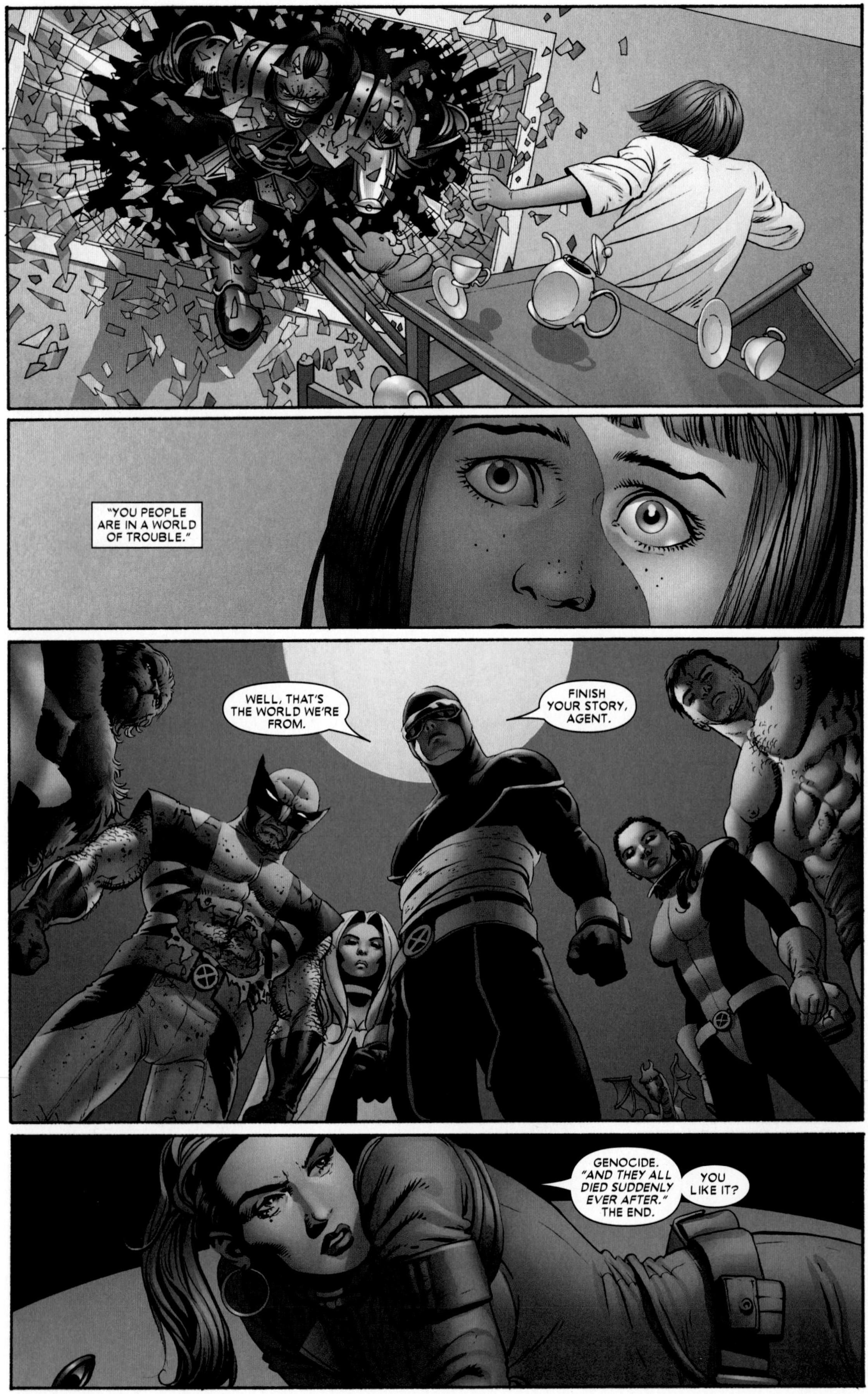
"YOU PEOPLE ARE IN A WORLD OF TROUBLE."
WELL, THAT'S THE WORLD WE'RE FROM.
FINISH YOUR STORY, AGENT.
GENOCIDE. "AND THEY ALL DIED SUDDENLY EVER AFTER." THE END.
YOU LIKE IT?

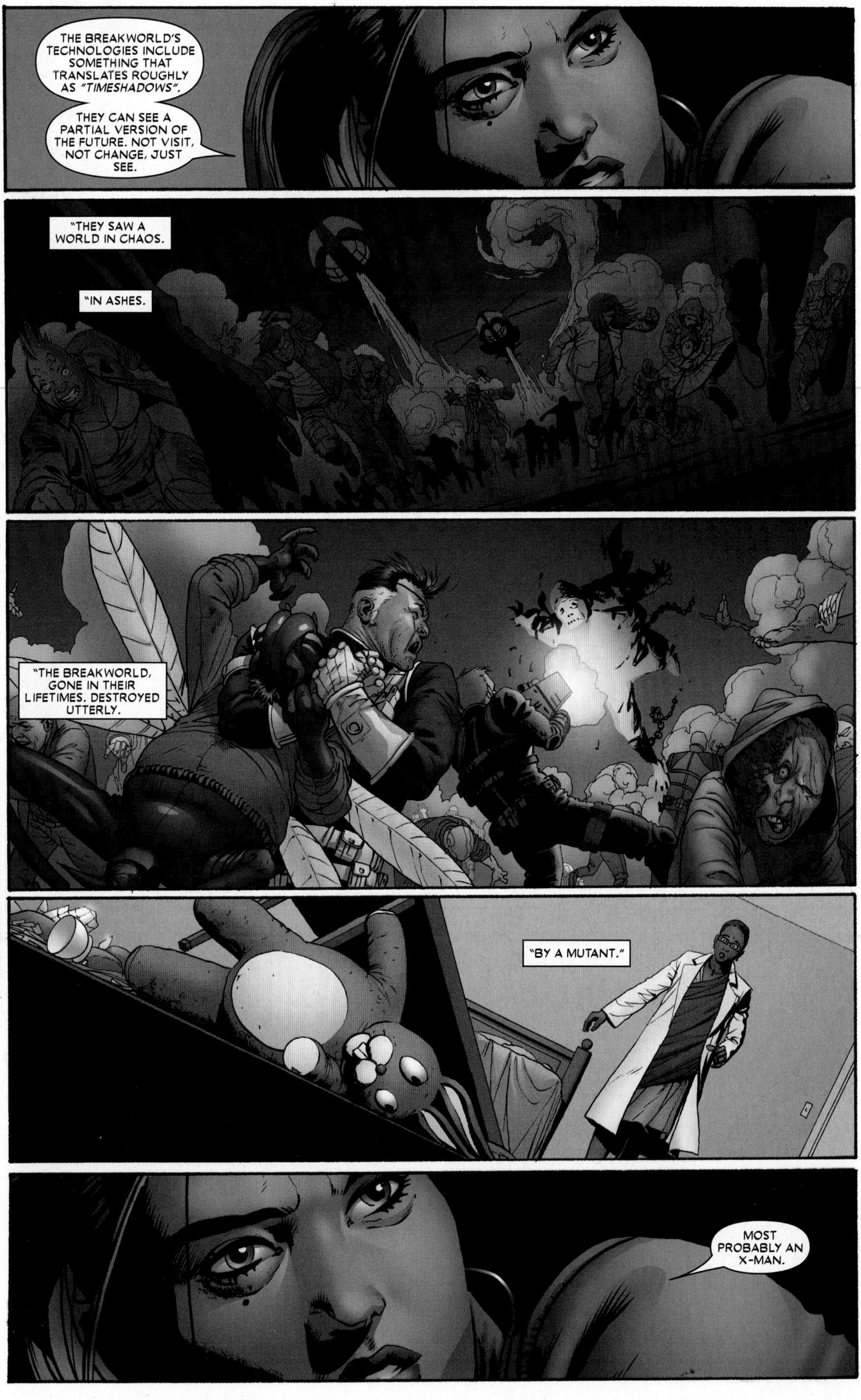
THE BREAKWORLD'S TECHNOLOGIES INCLUDE SOMETHING THAT TRANSLATES ROUGHLY AS "TIMESHADOWS".
THEY CAN SEE A PARTIAL VERSION OF THE FUTURE. NOT VISIT, NOT CHANGE, JUST SEE.
"THEY SAW A WORLD IN CHAOS.
"IN ASHES.
"THE BREAKWORLD, GONE IN THEIR LIFETIMES. DESTROYED UTTERLY.
"BY A MUTANT."
MOST PROBABLY AN X-MAN.

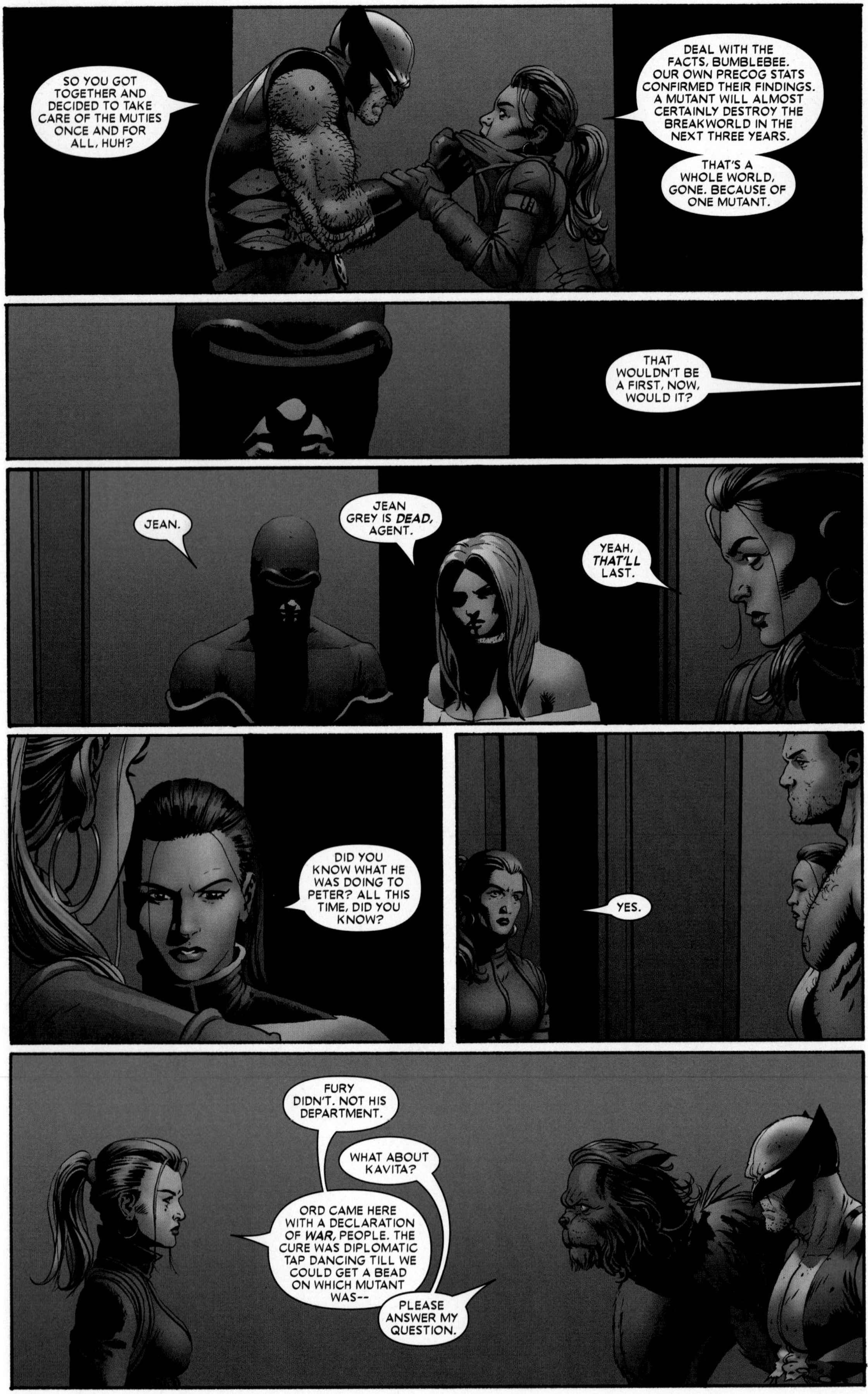
SO YOU GOT TOGETHER AND DECIDED TO TAKE CARE OF THE MUTIES ONCE AND FOR ALL, HUH?
DEAL WITH THE FACTS, BUMBLEBEE. OUR OWN PRECOG STATS CONFIRMED THEIR FINDINGS. A MUTANT WILL ALMOST CERTAINLY DESTROY THE BREAKWORLD IN THE NEXT THREE YEARS.
THAT'S A WHOLE WORLD, GONE. BECAUSE OF ONE MUTANT.
THAT WOULDN'T BE A FIRST, NOW, WOULD IT?
JEAN.
JEAN GREY IS *DEAD,* AGENT.
YEAH, *THAT'LL* LAST.
DID YOU KNOW WHAT HE WAS DOING TO PETER? ALL THIS TIME, DID YOU KNOW?
YES.
FURY DIDN'T. NOT HIS DEPARTMENT.
WHAT ABOUT KAVITA?
ORD CAME HERE WITH A DECLARATION OF *WAR,* PEOPLE. THE CURE WAS DIPLOMATIC TAP DANCING TILL WE COULD GET A BEAD ON WHICH MUTANT WAS--
PLEASE ANSWER MY QUESTION.

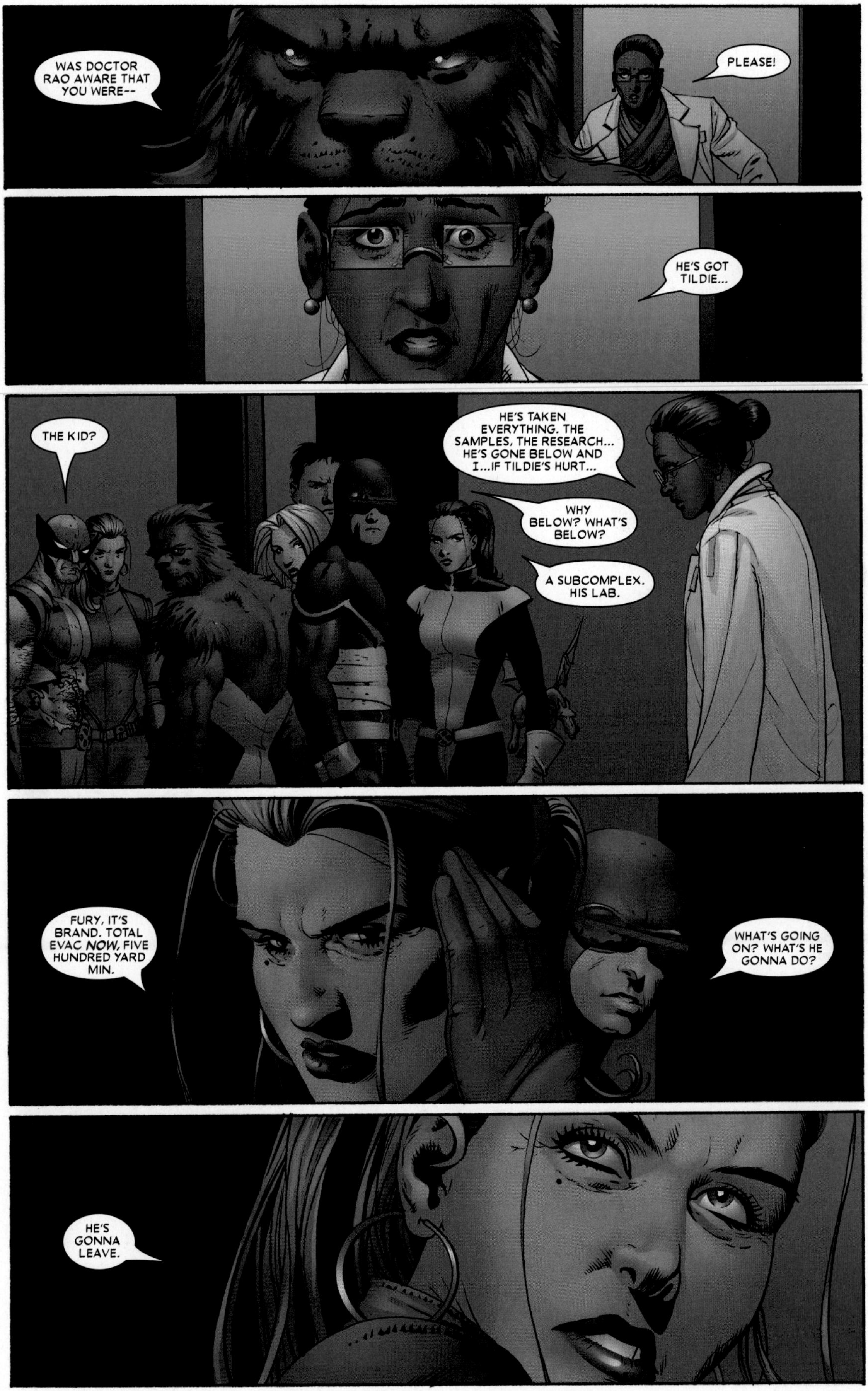
WAS DOCTOR RAO AWARE THAT YOU WERE--
PLEASE!
HE'S GOT TILDIE...
THE KID?
HE'S TAKEN EVERYTHING. THE SAMPLES, THE RESEARCH... HE'S GONE BELOW AND I...IF TILDIE'S HURT...
WHY BELOW? WHAT'S BELOW?
A SUBCOMPLEX. HIS LAB.
FURY, IT'S BRAND. TOTAL EVAC NOW, FIVE HUNDRED YARD MIN.
WHAT'S GOING ON? WHAT'S HE GONNA DO?
HE'S GONNA LEAVE.

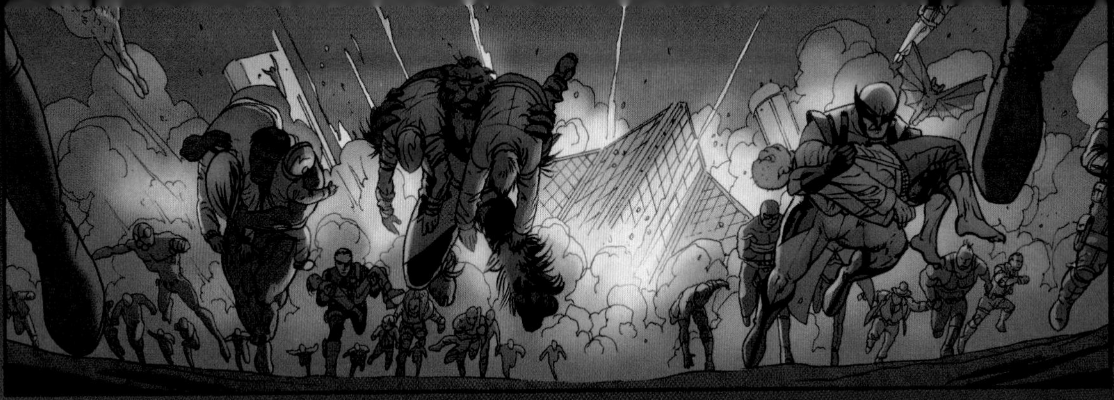

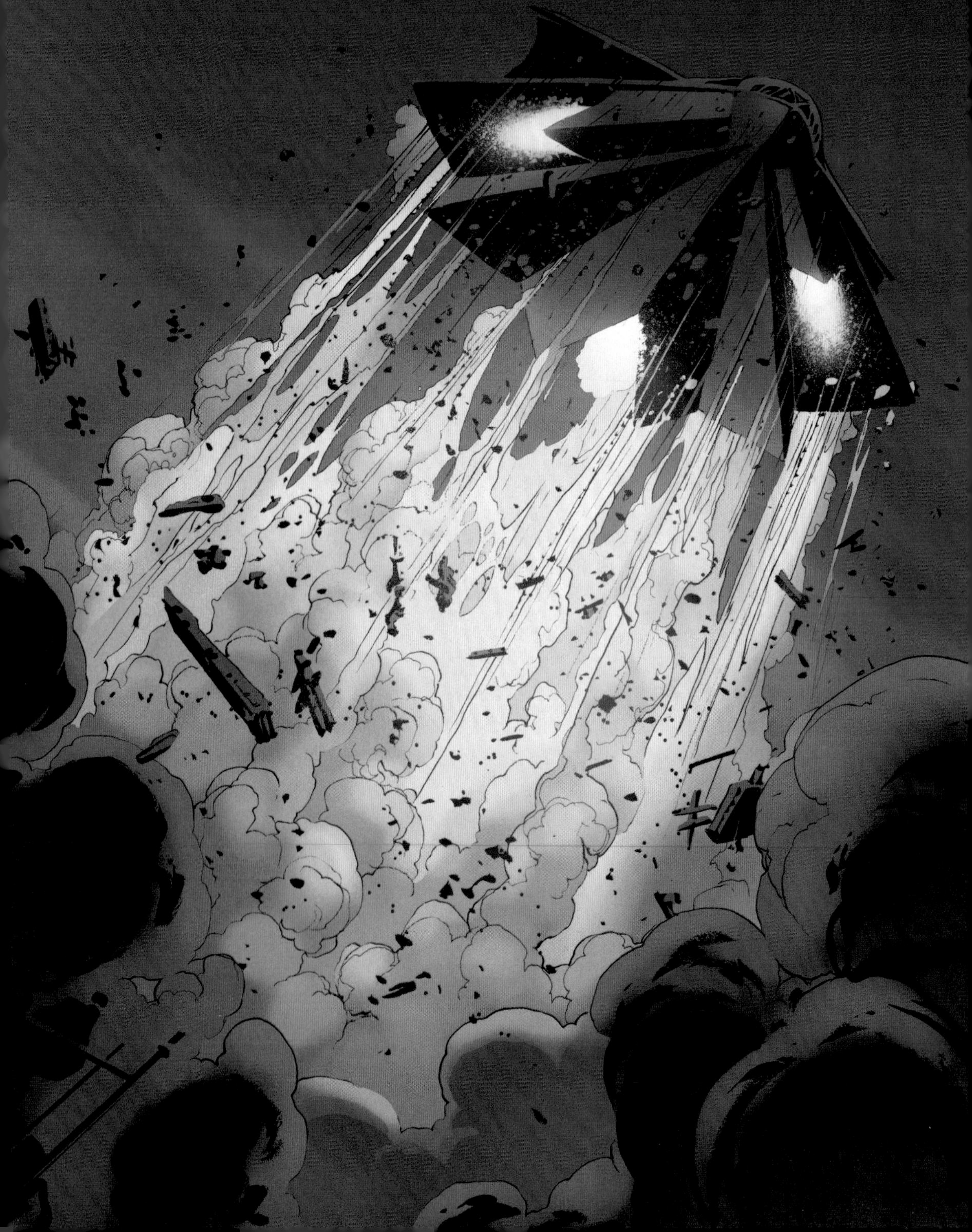

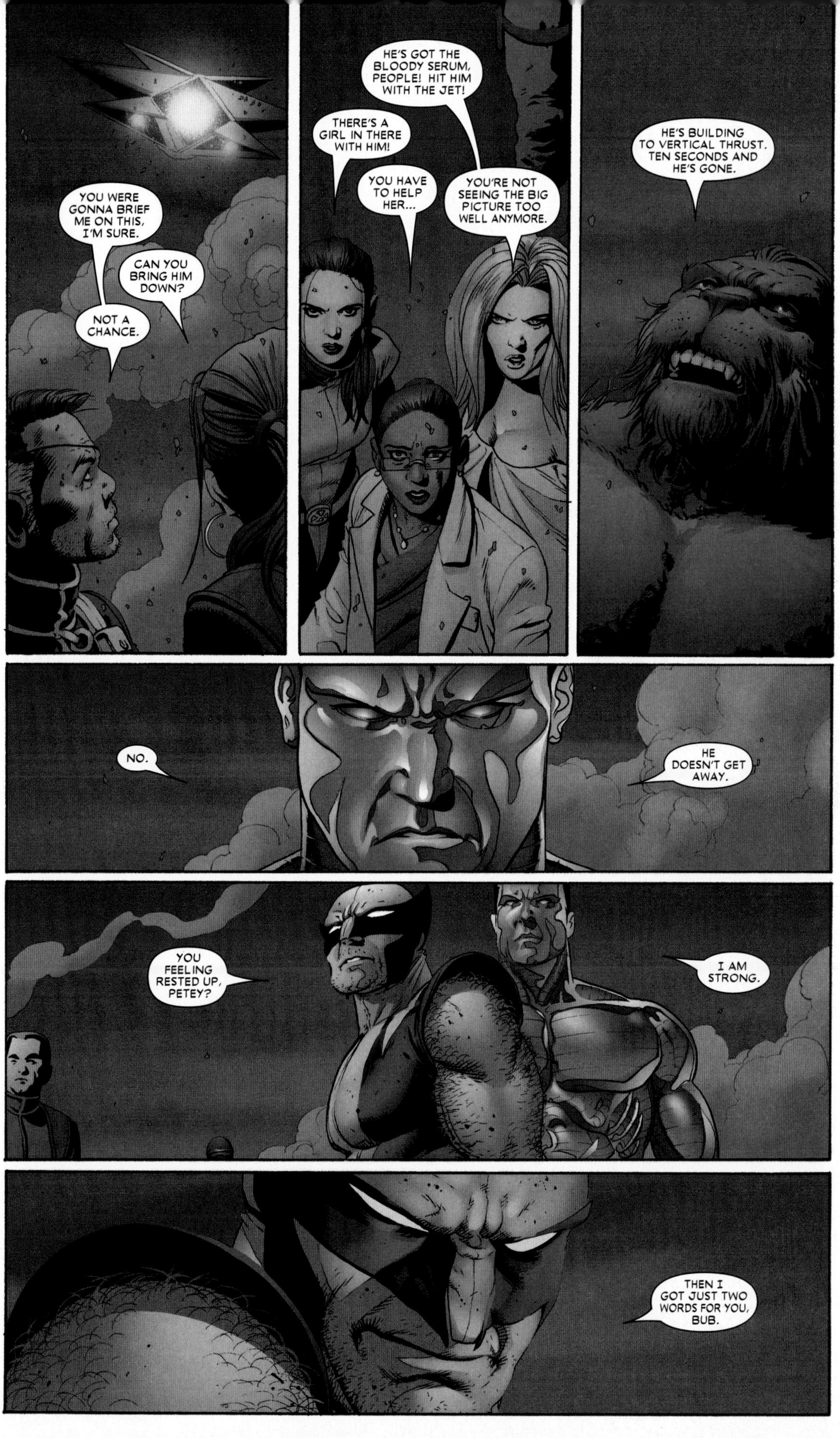
YOU WERE GONNA BRIEF ME ON THIS, I'M SURE.
CAN YOU BRING HIM DOWN?
NOT A CHANCE.
HE'S GOT THE BLOODY SERUM, PEOPLE! HIT HIM WITH THE JET!
THERE'S A GIRL IN THERE WITH HIM!
YOU HAVE TO HELP HER...
YOU'RE NOT SEEING THE BIG PICTURE TOO WELL ANYMORE.
HE'S BUILDING TO VERTICAL THRUST. TEN SECONDS AND HE'S GONE.
NO.
HE DOESN'T GET AWAY.
YOU FEELING RESTED UP, PETEY?
I AM STRONG.
THEN I GOT JUST TWO WORDS FOR YOU, BUB.

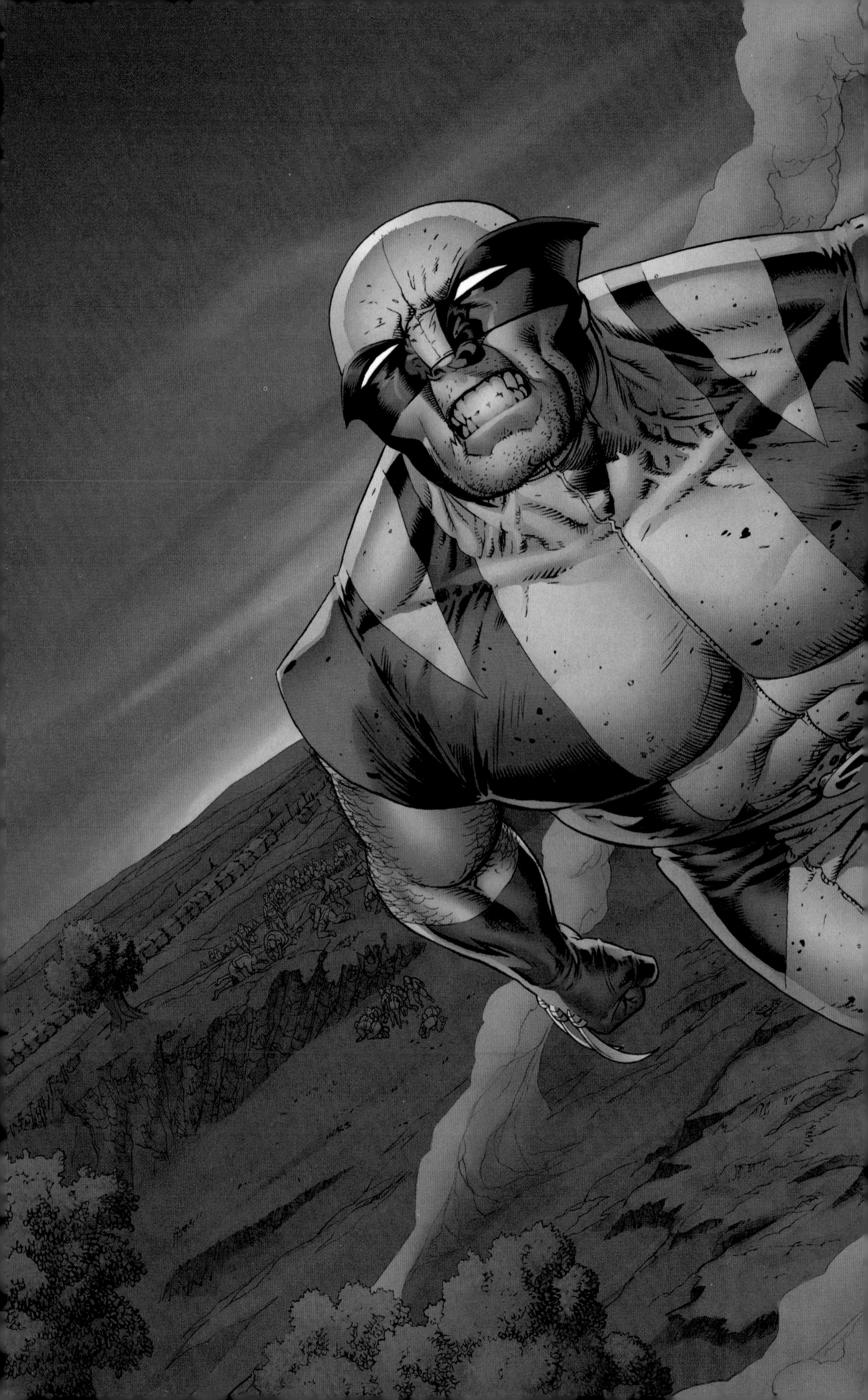

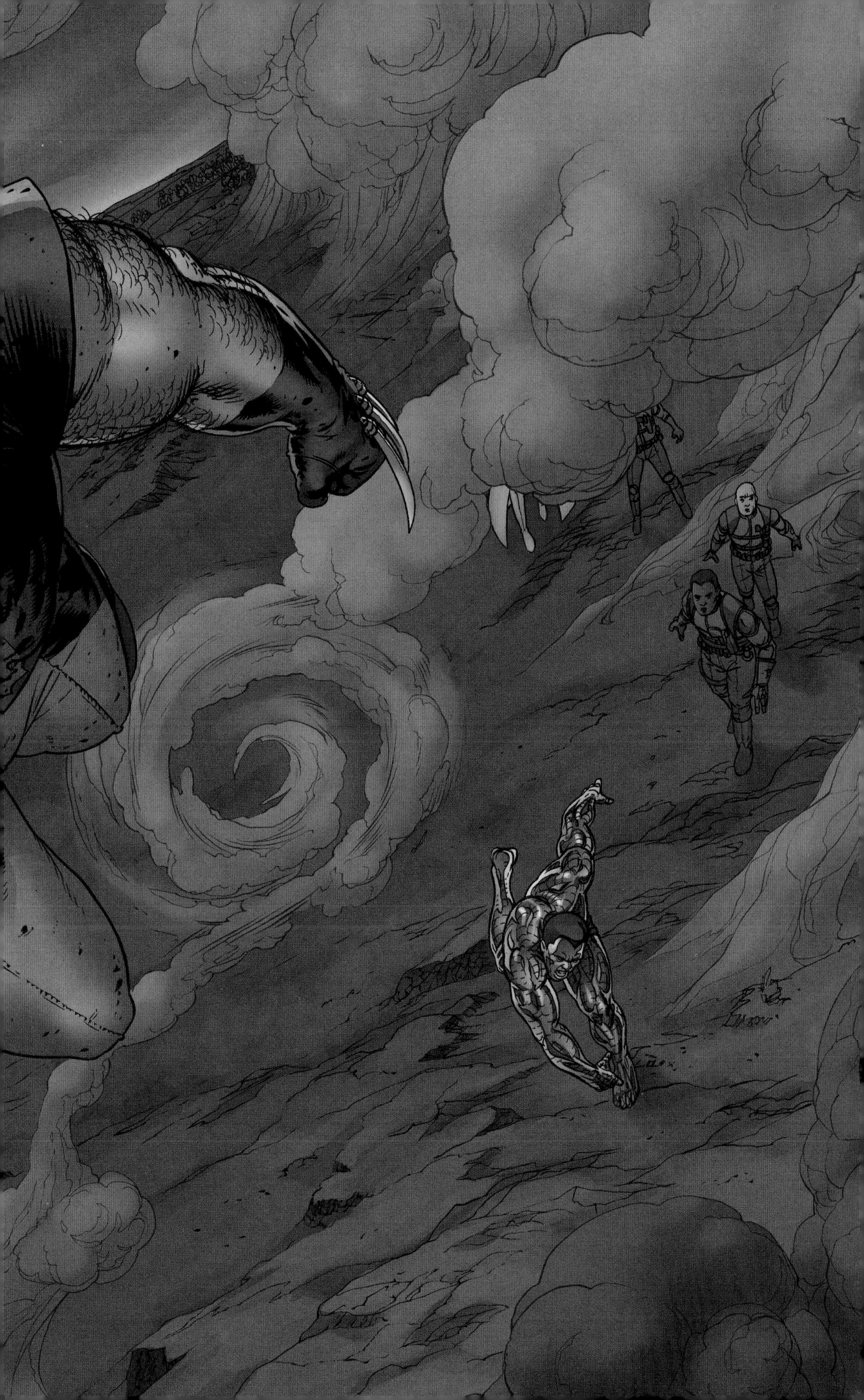

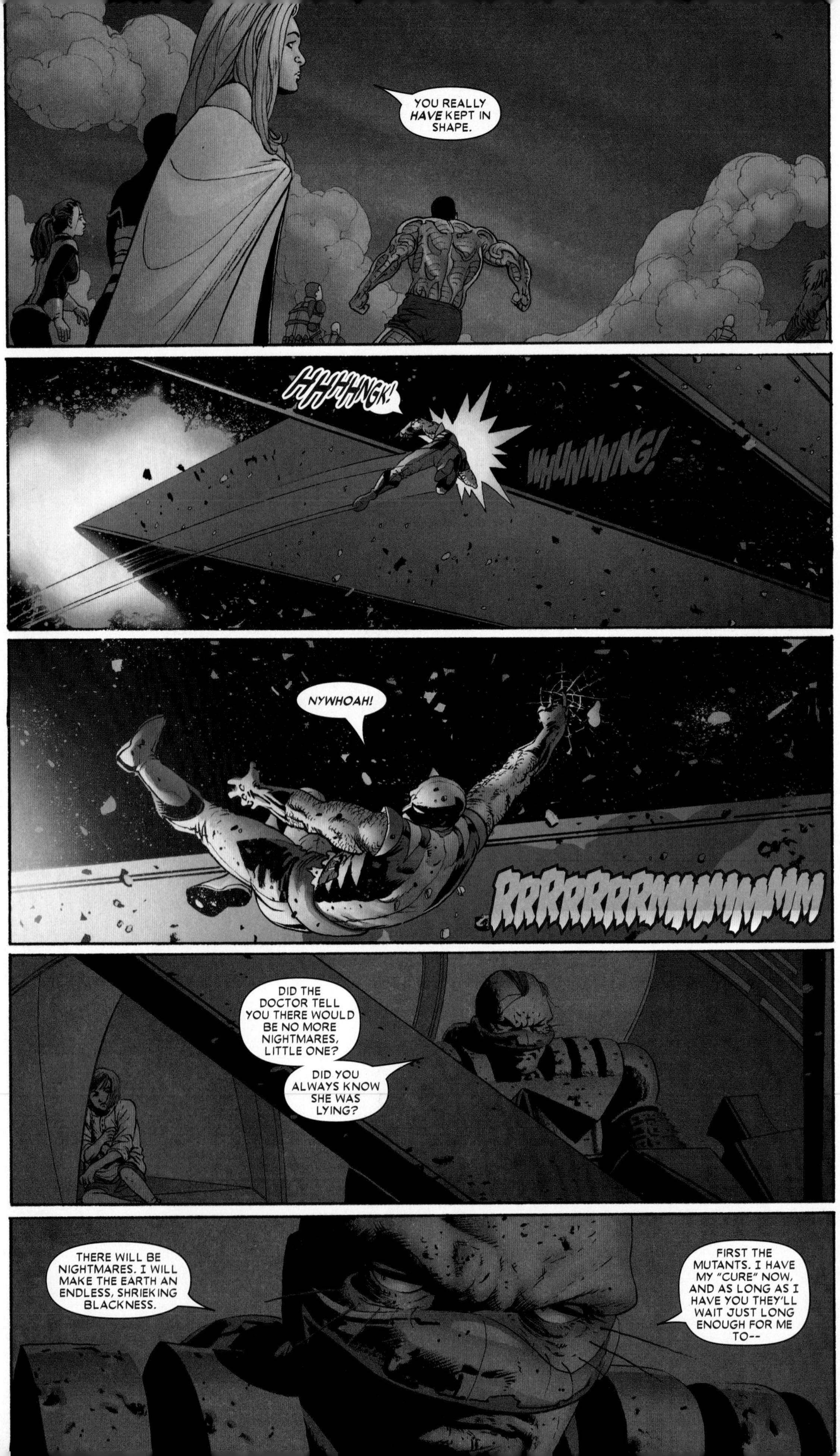

YOU REALLY *HAVE* KEPT IN SHAPE.
HHHHNGK!
WHUNNNNG!
NYWHOAH!
RRRRRRRMMMMMMMMM
DID THE DOCTOR TELL YOU THERE WOULD BE NO MORE NIGHTMARES, LITTLE ONE?
DID YOU ALWAYS KNOW SHE WAS LYING?
THERE WILL BE NIGHTMARES. I WILL MAKE THE EARTH AN ENDLESS, SHRIEKING BLACKNESS.
FIRST THE MUTANTS. I HAVE MY "CURE" NOW, AND AS LONG AS I HAVE YOU THEY'LL WAIT JUST LONG ENOUGH FOR ME TO--

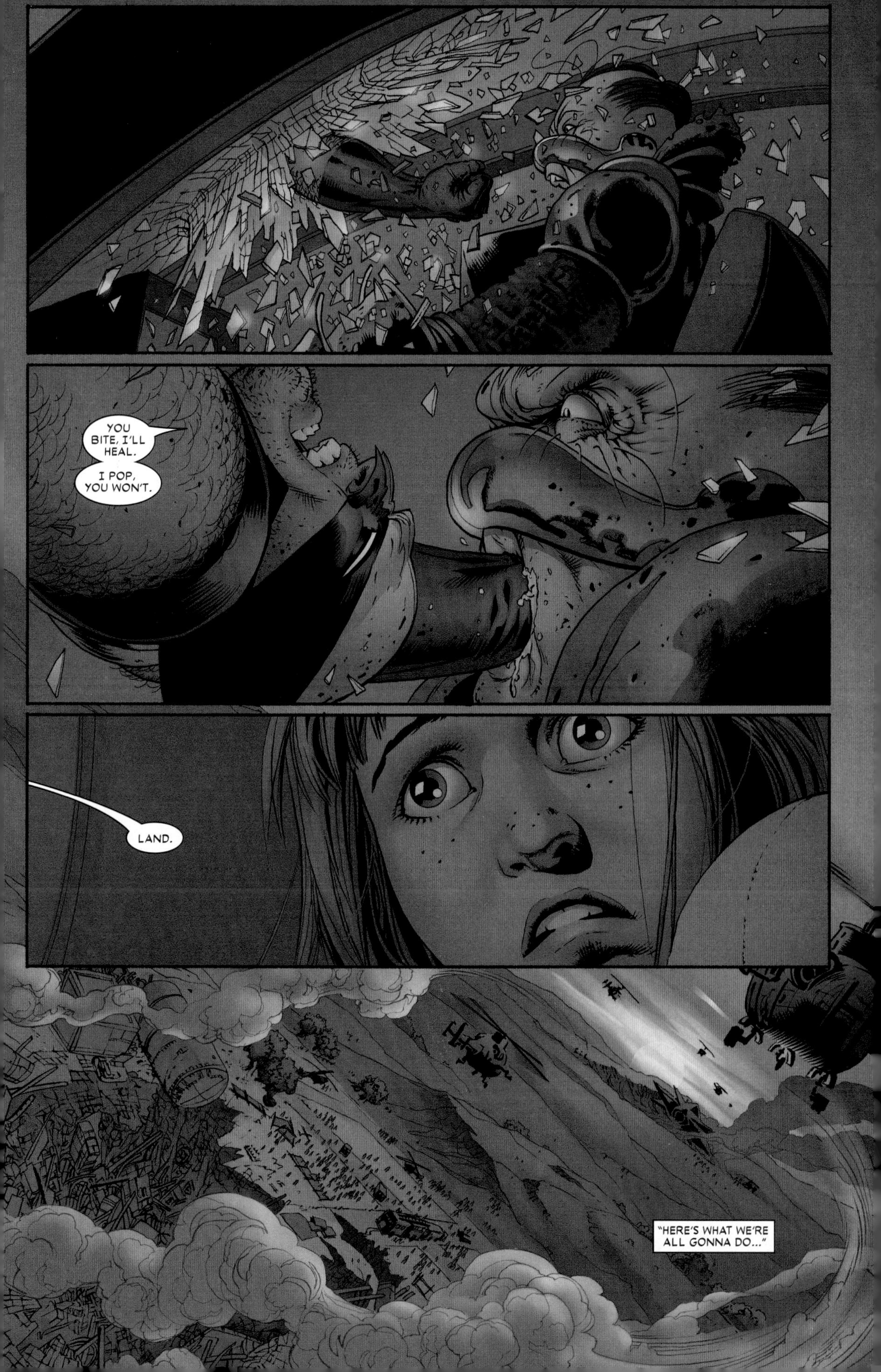

YOU BITE, I'LL HEAL.
I POP, YOU WON'T.
LAND.
"HERE'S WHAT WE'RE ALL GONNA DO..."

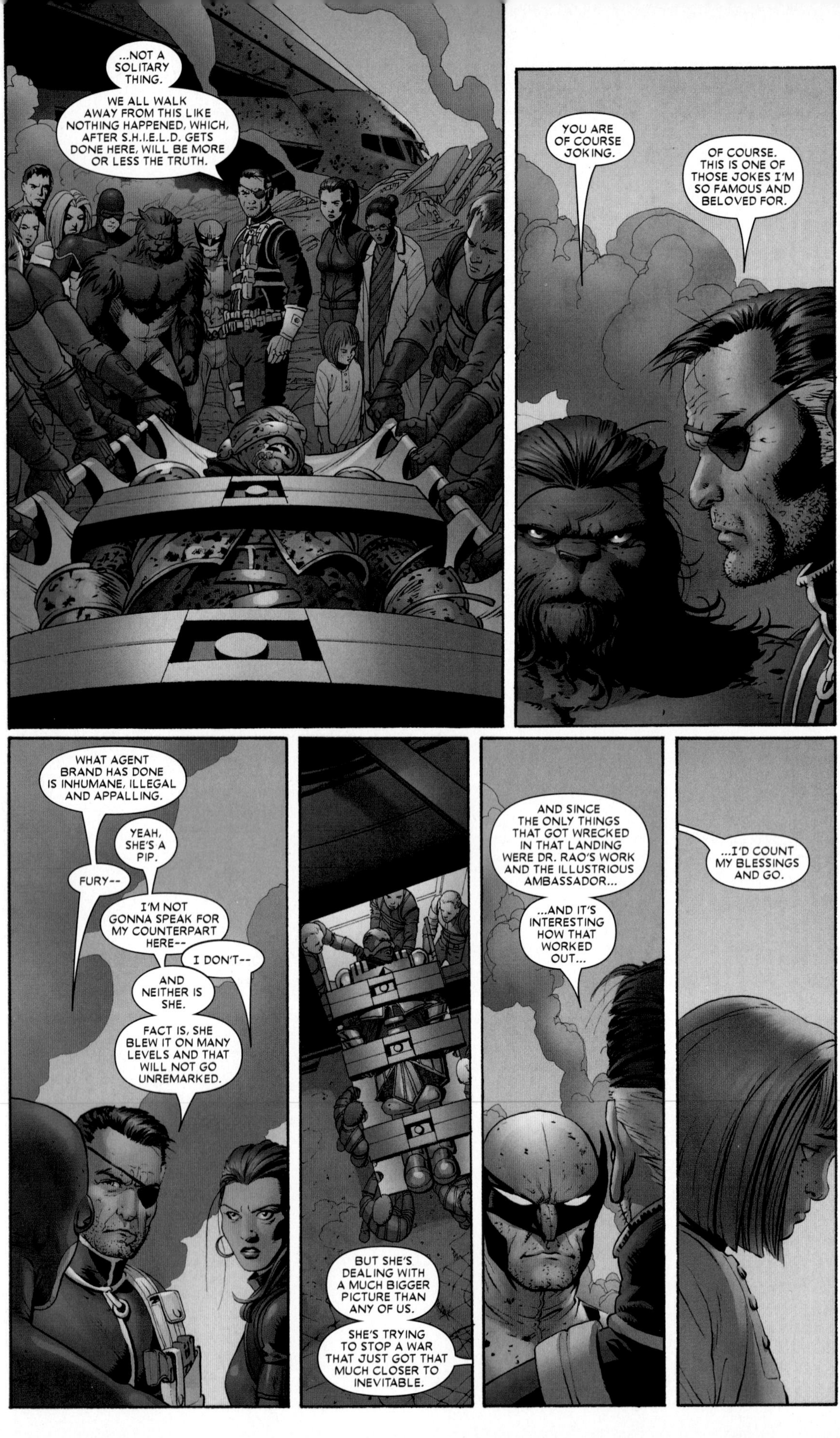
...NOT A SOLITARY THING.
WE ALL WALK AWAY FROM THIS LIKE NOTHING HAPPENED, WHICH, AFTER S.H.I.E.L.D. GETS DONE HERE, WILL BE MORE OR LESS THE TRUTH.
YOU ARE OF COURSE JOKING.
OF COURSE. THIS IS ONE OF THOSE JOKES I'M SO FAMOUS AND BELOVED FOR.
WHAT AGENT BRAND HAS DONE IS INHUMANE, ILLEGAL AND APPALLING.
YEAH, SHE'S A PIP.
FURY--
I'M NOT GONNA SPEAK FOR MY COUNTERPART HERE--
I DON'T--
AND NEITHER IS SHE.
FACT IS, SHE BLEW IT ON MANY LEVELS AND THAT WILL NOT GO UNREMARKED.
BUT SHE'S DEALING WITH A MUCH BIGGER PICTURE THAN ANY OF US.
SHE'S TRYING TO STOP A WAR THAT JUST GOT THAT MUCH CLOSER TO INEVITABLE.
AND SINCE THE ONLY THINGS THAT GOT WRECKED IN THAT LANDING WERE DR. RAO'S WORK AND THE ILLUSTRIOUS AMBASSADOR...
...AND IT'S INTERESTING HOW THAT WORKED OUT...
...I'D COUNT MY BLESSINGS AND GO.

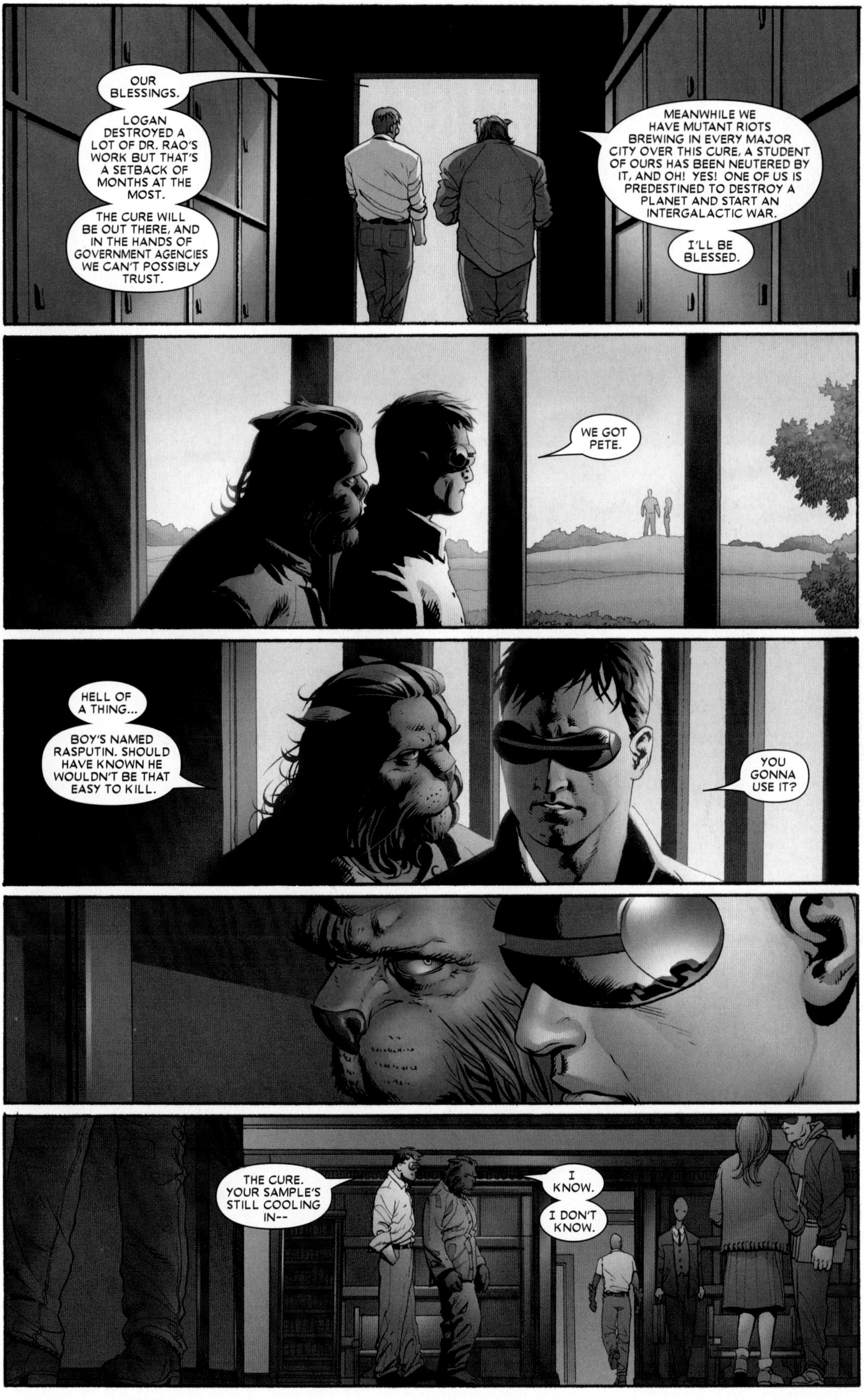
OUR BLESSINGS.
LOGAN DESTROYED A LOT OF DR. RAO'S WORK BUT THAT'S A SETBACK OF MONTHS AT THE MOST.
THE CURE WILL BE OUT THERE, AND IN THE HANDS OF GOVERNMENT AGENCIES WE CAN'T POSSIBLY TRUST.
MEANWHILE WE HAVE MUTANT RIOTS BREWING IN EVERY MAJOR CITY OVER THIS CURE, A STUDENT OF OURS HAS BEEN NEUTERED BY IT, AND OH! YES! ONE OF US IS PREDESTINED TO DESTROY A PLANET AND START AN INTERGALACTIC WAR.
I'LL BE BLESSED.
WE GOT PETE.
HELL OF A THING...
BOY'S NAMED RASPUTIN. SHOULD HAVE KNOWN HE WOULDN'T BE THAT EASY TO KILL.
YOU GONNA USE IT?
THE CURE. YOUR SAMPLE'S STILL COOLING IN--
I KNOW.
I DON'T KNOW.

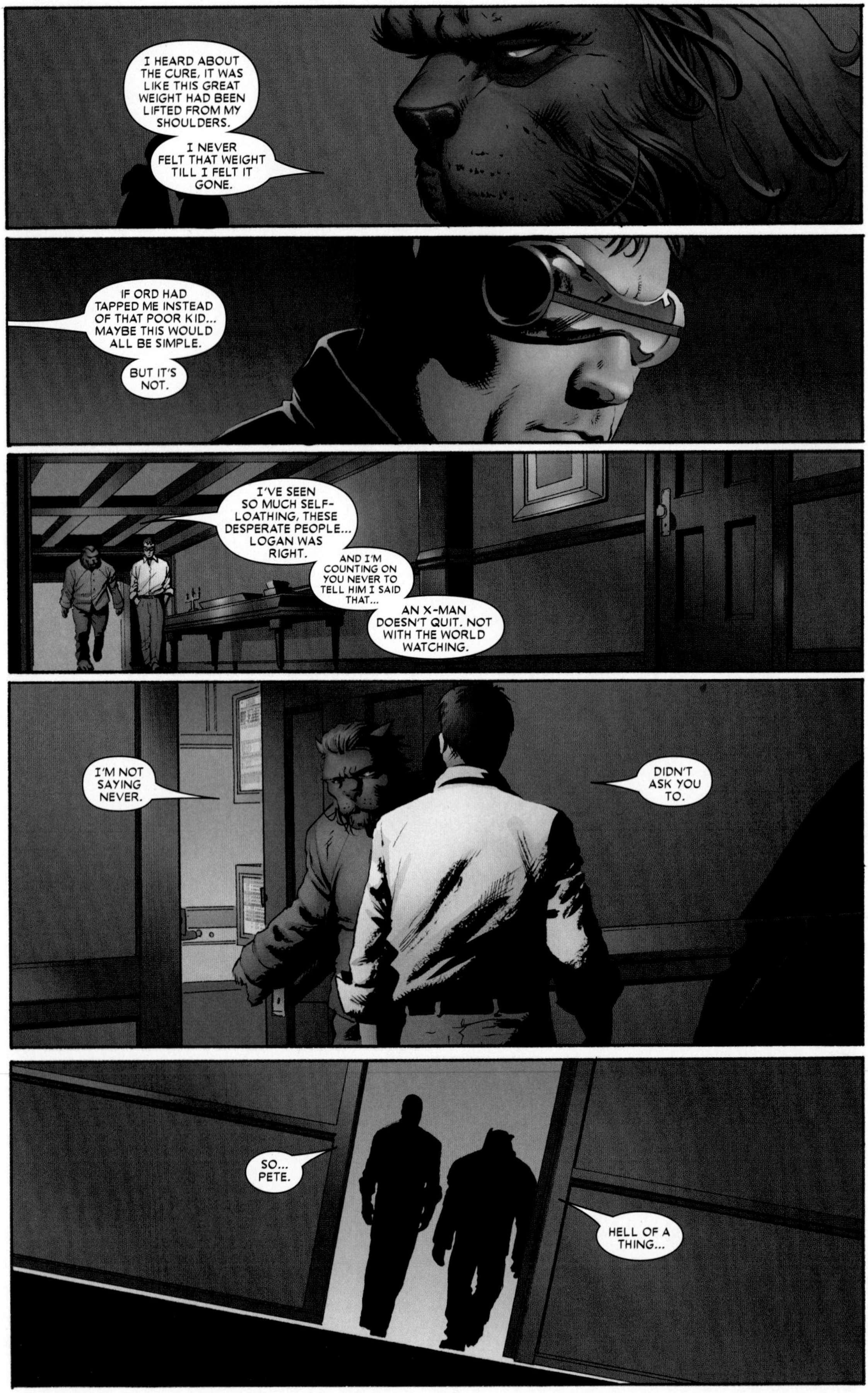

I HEARD ABOUT THE CURE, IT WAS LIKE THIS GREAT WEIGHT HAD BEEN LIFTED FROM MY SHOULDERS.
I NEVER FELT THAT WEIGHT TILL I FELT IT GONE.
IF ORD HAD TAPPED ME INSTEAD OF THAT POOR KID... MAYBE THIS WOULD ALL BE SIMPLE.
BUT IT'S NOT.
I'VE SEEN SO MUCH SELF-LOATHING, THESE DESPERATE PEOPLE... LOGAN WAS RIGHT.
AND I'M COUNTING ON YOU NEVER TO TELL HIM I SAID THAT...
AN X-MAN DOESN'T QUIT. NOT WITH THE WORLD WATCHING.
I'M NOT SAYING NEVER.
DIDN'T ASK YOU TO.
SO... PETE.
HELL OF A THING...

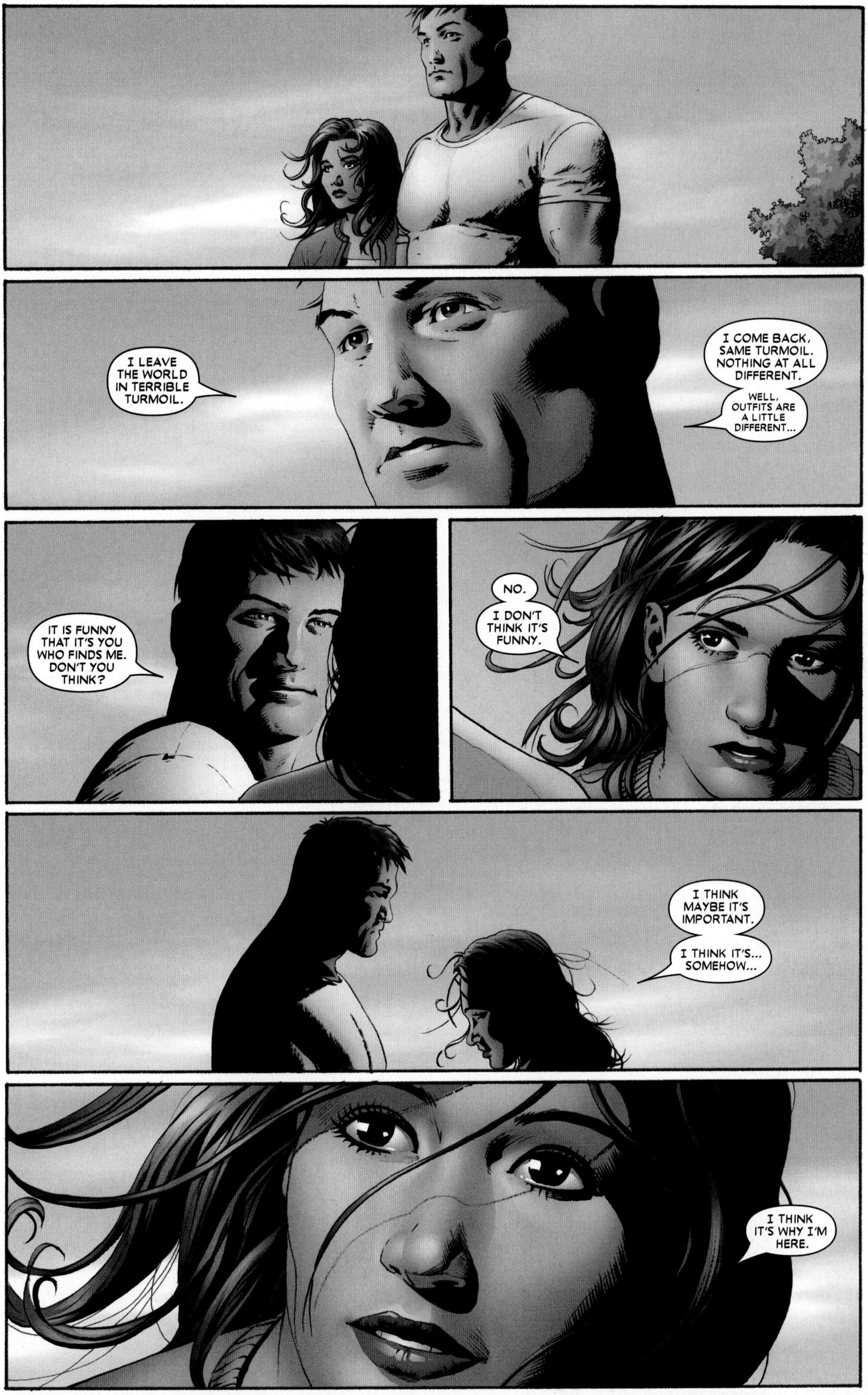
I LEAVE THE WORLD IN TERRIBLE TURMOIL.
I COME BACK, SAME TURMOIL. NOTHING AT ALL DIFFERENT.
WELL, OUTFITS ARE A LITTLE DIFFERENT...
IT IS FUNNY THAT IT'S YOU WHO FINDS ME. DON'T YOU THINK?
NO.
I DON'T THINK IT'S FUNNY.
I THINK MAYBE IT'S IMPORTANT.
I THINK IT'S... SOMEHOW...
I THINK IT'S WHY I'M HERE.

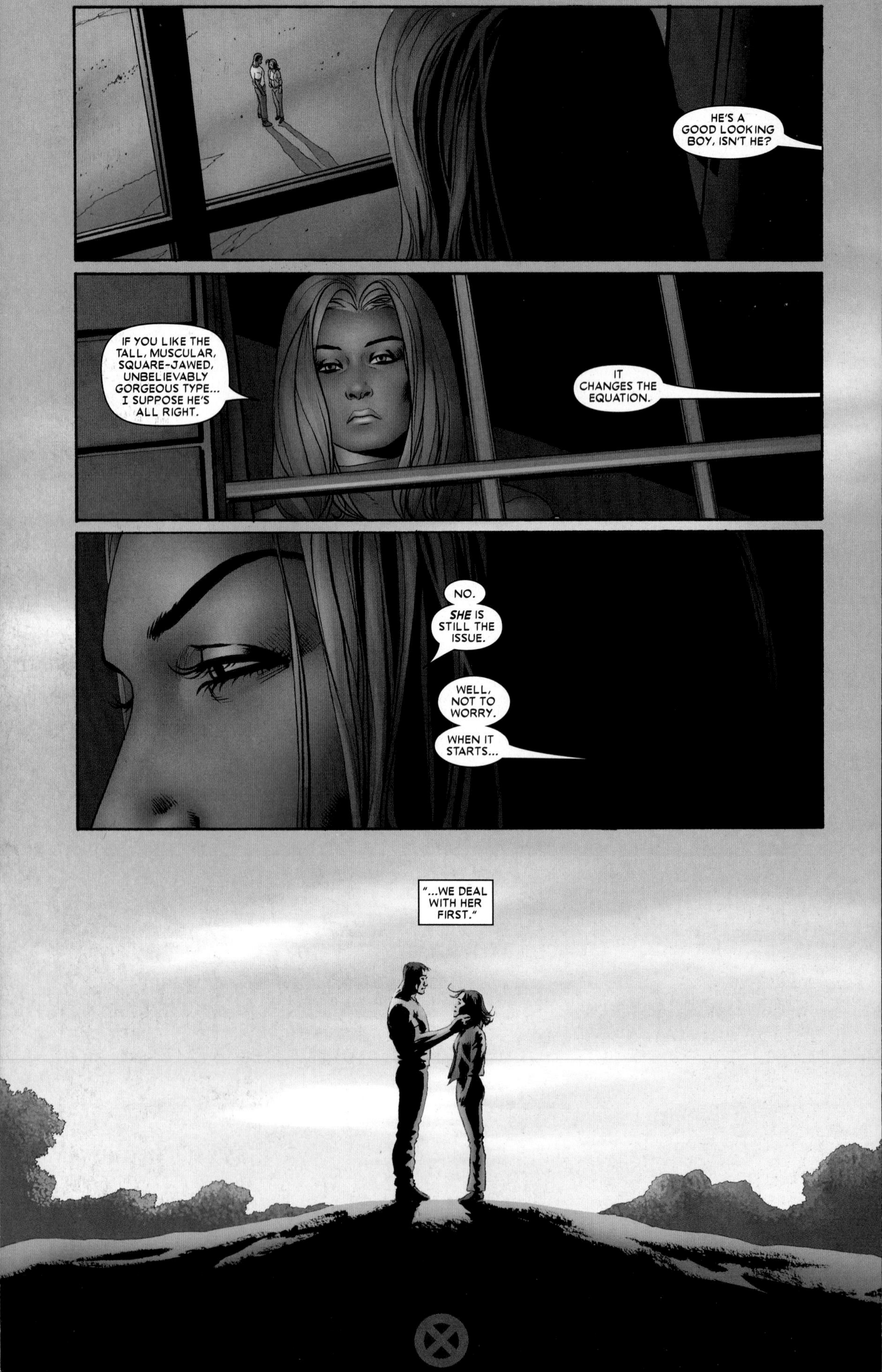
HE'S A GOOD LOOKING BOY, ISN'T HE?
IF YOU LIKE THE TALL, MUSCULAR, SQUARE-JAWED, UNBELIEVABLY GORGEOUS TYPE... I SUPPOSE HE'S ALL RIGHT.
IT CHANGES THE EQUATION.
NO.
SHE IS STILL THE ISSUE.
WELL, NOT TO WORRY.
WHEN IT STARTS...
"...WE DEAL WITH HER FIRST."

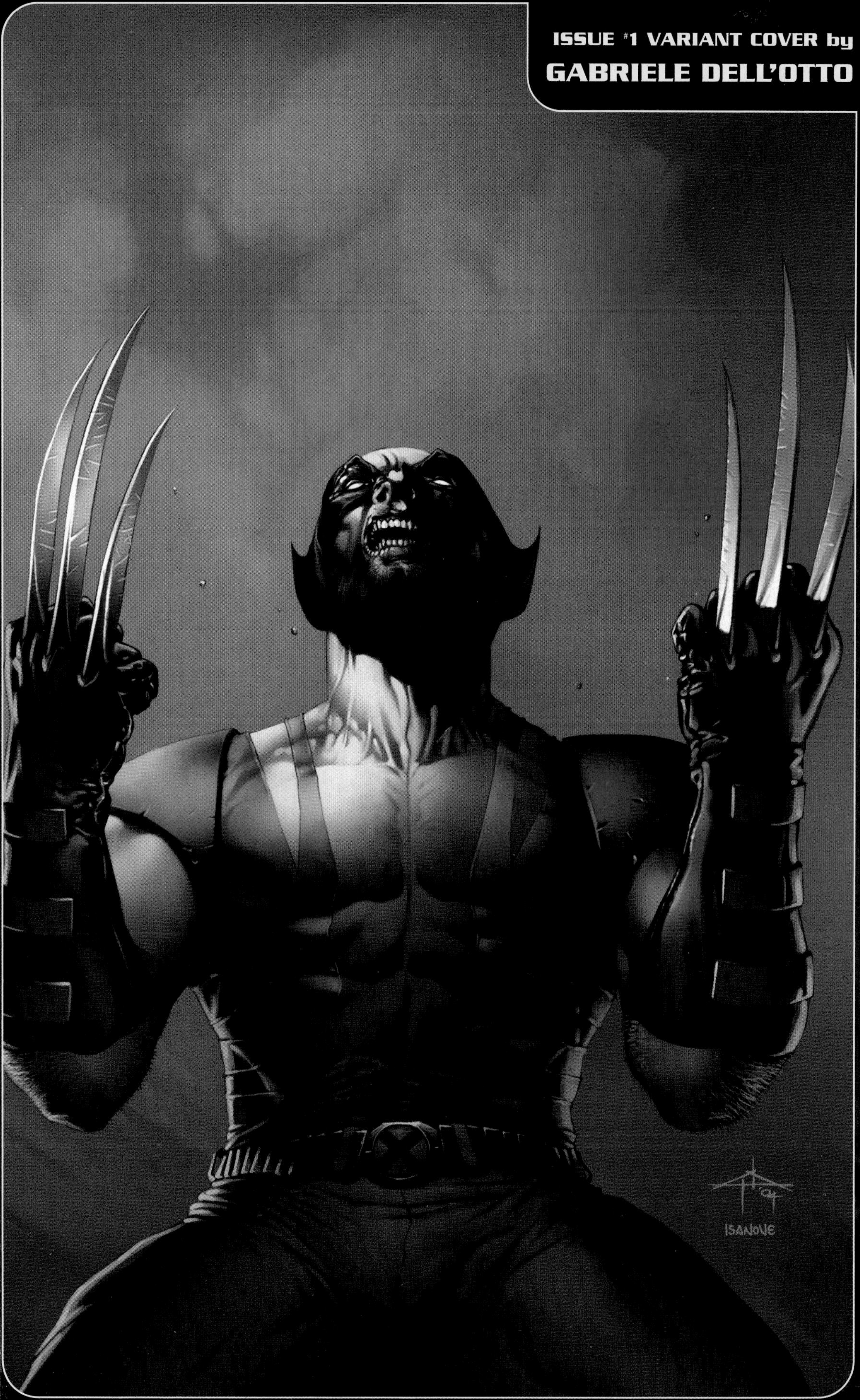
ISANOVE

ISSUE #1 VARIANT COVER by
GABRIELE DELL'OTTO

ISSUE #4 VARIANT COVER by
JOHN CASSADAY

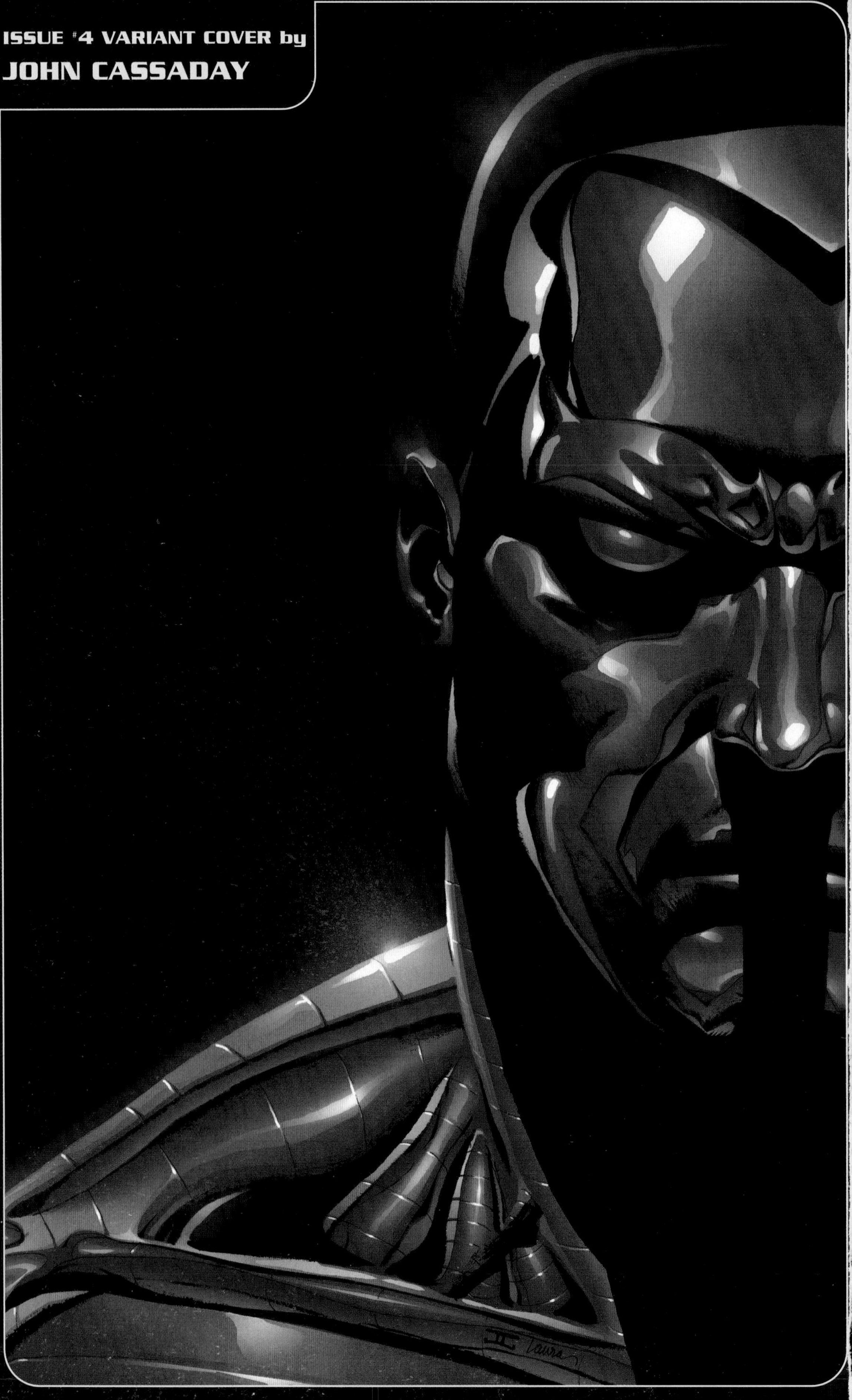